THE FAMILY IN TODAY'S MONEY WORLD

THE FAMILY in TODAY'S MONEY WORLD

FRANCES LOMAS FELDMAN

Second Edition

Family Service Association of America, New York

Copyright © 1976 by
Family Service Association of America
44 East 23rd Street, New York, N.Y. 10010

First edition, *The Family in a Money World*,
copyright © 1957 by Family Service Association of
America

All rights reserved. No part of this publication may be reprinted, reproduced, transmitted, stored in a retrieval system, or otherwise utilized, in any form or by any means, electronic or mechanical, including photocopying or recording, now existing or hereinafter invented, without the prior written permission of the publisher.

International Standard Book Number: 0-87304-131-3
(paper)
International Standard Book Number: 0-87304-130-5
(cloth)
Library of Congress Catalog Card Number: 75-27966

Printed in the United States of America
Designed by Charlotte Staub

1 2 3 4 5 6 7 8 9 10

Contents

Acknowledgments ix
Introduction xi

PART ONE: TODAY'S MONEY WORLD

1. THE ECONOMIC MILIEU OF TODAY'S FAMILY   3

    THE ECONOMIC FACTS OF LIFE: The sources of money income. Is money income growing? Whose income?

    SOCIAL IMPLICATIONS—RHETORIC AND REALITY: Sources of family income. Transfer payments. Lagging incomes.

    COSTS OF LIVING

2. ECONOMIC BEHAVIOR IN TODAY'S MONEY WORLD   21

    WHERE DOES THE MONEY GO?

    THREE SETS OF STANDARDS

    FAMILY SPENDING: For shelter. For motor vehicles. For education. For nondurables. For consumer credit. Credit cards. Consumer instalment debt. Personal loans. Debt repayment.

    THE QUALITY OF LIFE

PART TWO: THE CYCLE OF FAMILY LIFE

3. MONEY IN THE CYCLE OF FAMILY LIFE   55

    LIFESTYLES AND STAGES OF THE FAMILY CYCLE

MONEY NEEDS OF FAMILIES: Economic meanings. Social and emotional meanings.

MONEY PROBLEMS AND FAMILIES

4. BEGINNING THE CYCLE OF FAMILY LIFE   68

Income expectations. Expenditures. Money and marital conflict. Money, commitment, and nonbeginnings. Developing attitudes about money.

5. THE EXPANDING FAMILY   87

THE MONEY CLIMATE OF THE EXPANDING FAMILY

MONEY AND WORK

PARENT-CHILD RELATIONSHIPS: Money and the young child. Money and the adolescent. Money and the child in placement.

DEVELOPING CHILDREN'S ATTITUDES TOWARD MONEY: Allowances. Earnings. Preparation for the money world.

6. THE CONTRACTING FAMILY   120

THE MIDDLE YEARS

THE OLDER YEARS: Productivity and retirement. The elderly and their children. Money behavior of the elderly.

PLANNING FOR RETIREMENT YEARS

7. VARIANTS ON LIFESTYLES   140

THE SINGLE ADULT

UNMARRIED PARENTHOOD: The nonmarital child. The unmarried mother. The unmarried father.

THE BROKEN FAMILY: Death. Desertion. Divorce.

REMARRIAGE

CONTENTS

PART THREE: MONEY AND COUNSELING

8. **MONEY COUNSELING: GOALS AND TECHNIQUES**   181

    COUNSELING GOALS: Short-term and long-term goals. Income insufficiency. Personal and interpersonal problems. Young couples. Parents and children. Single parents. Elderly persons.

    THE COUNSELOR

    COLLABORATIVE SERVICES

9. **INCOME MAINTENANCE: DEPENDENCE AND INDEPENDENCE**   210

    SOCIAL POLICY AND THE QUEST FOR INCOME SECURITY: Evaluating need. Standardized budgets and grants. Unrestricted money payments. Who receives the money? Frequency of payments.

    MONEY MANAGEMENT AS A FAMILY RESPONSIBILITY

10. **PAYING ONE'S WAY**   237

    LOANS OR GRANTS?: Guidelines for decision-making. The collection of loans.

    FEES FOR SERVICES: Counseling services. Child care services. Adoption services. Health care services. The psychological value of fees.

PART FOUR: APPLICATIONS—VALUES, NEEDS, RESOURCES

11. **HUMAN NEEDS AND VALUES**   259

    NEEDS ASSESSMENT: Food. Shelter. Clothing. Taxes. Household furnishings. Household operation. Transportation. Health and dental care. Household services. Other family costs.

    SAVINGS AND INVESTMENTS

12. **FAMILY RESOURCES**   289

TANGIBLE RESOURCES: Earnings. Small businesses. Savings. Securities and investments. Commerical life insurance. Government life insurance. Annuities. Pensions. Old-age, survivors, disability, and health insurance benefits. Unemployment and temporary disability insurance. Worker's compensation. Health insurance. Veterans' benefits. Loans or mortgages. Community resources.

PERSONAL RESOURCES

13. CONSUMER CREDIT   321

THE NATURE OF CONSUMER CREDIT: Charge accounts. Instalment credit. Borrowing.

CONSUMER PROTECTION

DEBT CONSULTATION: Debt counseling programs. The wage earner plan. Bankruptcy.

14. DESIGN FOR LIVING IN TODAY'S MONEY WORLD   352

FREEDOMS AND FRUSTRATIONS

SELECTED PRINCIPLES: Immediate and long-term goals. Planning family participation and sharing responsibilities.

BUDGET STANDARDS AND GUIDES

BUILDING THE FINANCIAL DESIGN: The preliminaries. Determining income. Fixed obligations. Day-to-day needs. Balancing present and future needs. Assets and debts. Anticipating changes in the financial design.

FOLLOWING THE FINANCIAL DESIGN

Bibliography   385

Index   395

Acknowledgments

Some debts cannot be repaid in coin or currency, and it is with warm appreciation that I acknowledge here certain such debts. Dr. Spencer Pollard, outstanding scholar and Professor Emeritus of Economics, University of Southern California, critically reviewed the manuscript. George D. Nickel, Director of Consumer Education for Beneficial Management Corporation and immediate past president of Family Service Association of America, also painstakingly reviewed the manuscript. He was instrumental too in Beneficial Management Corporation's providing a small grant to the School of Social Work, University of Southern California, which could be used by doctoral students in relation to some of the data collection pertinent to the research underpinning this book. In this connection, thanks are due particularly to Dr. David Freeman and Dr. Anthony Winckowski. Of inestimable help in tracking down elusive statistical and bibliographical items and typing the final manuscript was Robert L. Webb. My gratitude goes also to John Griffith and Barbara Grow for the many services that freed some of the time I could devote to this writing project. And, of my late husband, whose own work as a mental health professional and social educator rested on his firm belief in the viability and validity of the principles set forth in the Introduction, a special acknowledgment is in order: for his unfailing wit and good humor, patience, and encouragement during this writing project, and for modeling the kind of father and husband I hope all thoughtful male readers of this book can be or become.

FLF

University of Southern California
Los Angeles, California

Introduction

In our American culture, the significance of money—its presence or its absence—takes many forms. These forms are personal and interpersonal, social, emotional, and economic. Human worth often is equated with financial achievement; success is measured in terms of material possessions and how they are managed. Both the "self-made man" who has "pulled himself up by the bootstraps" from poverty to riches, and today's woman who has overcome a variety of social and economic obstacles to attain high stature in business or a profession, her position and income attesting to her achievement, are objects of admiration. Horatio Alger lives on in the twentieth century—and Fannie Farmer occupies a place at his side!

Conversely, the man who is a poor provider, or is unable to hold a job, or for other reasons needs economic assistance, is considered "inadequate." And the woman whose economic dependence is evidenced by her need for public assistance, who may have few marketable actual or potential skills with which to support her family, and whose physical appearance may imply incapacity, frequently is viewed not only as "inadequate" but, at the very least, slightly less than moral besides. Their financial failure may be the result of personal shortcomings or due to circumstances beyond their control. Yet such a man and woman tend to appraise the lack of economic achievement (in the instance of the man) or the lack of either economic resources, or a man to provide them (in the instance of the woman) as the community does: in terms of personal depreciation and low self-esteem. Their sense of worthlessness is likely to be especially severe at times when jobs are relatively plentiful and wages are at a comparatively high level. This sense of worthlessness is exacerbated when it is accompanied by a feeling of helplessness that deepens in apposition to ascending living costs, as a result of inflation, with which adjustments in their limited incomes do not keep pace.

In western societies there have always been some people who, because of illness, mental or physical disability, or other circumstances, have been unable to support themselves. The civilized world has endeavored for many centuries to find ways to maintain those who are not provided for by the usual economic arrangements of society, in order that their well-being may be assured and their capacity for future participation in the organized system may be preserved—or to protect the society of which they are a part from the concomitants and consequences of their financial need. Their loss of income or its reduction below an acceptable level may be rooted in personal inadequacies or in the malfunctioning of the economic system.

Western society has established institutions—social agencies—whose specific function is to alleviate human distress. Whether these institutional arrangements are placed largely under governmental, voluntary, or combined auspices is determined by political, economic, and cultural factors that may be peculiar to time and geography. In consequence, the roles of the two types of agencies shift from time to time.

In the United States, some provision has always been made by units of government for people in need. Historically, these public provisions were meager and, after the Industrial Revolution of the nineteenth century, were woefully inadequate to meet the widespread problems of poverty and family disruption. As a result, many volunteer relief agencies came into being to help relieve the distress. The combined resources of public and private agencies, however, were far from adequate. The problem of meeting the needs of people was further complicated by poor administration; by exploitation of the funds by both unscrupulous applicants and unscrupulous politicians; and by a social and economic philosophy that supported Social Darwinism, advocated the principle of less eligibility, clung tenaciously to Puritan virtues of thrift, and to the Calvinistic work ethic that held that success (proved by profit) was the certain indication that the chosen vocation was pleasing to God, reconciled wealth with good conscience, and distinguished the deserving from the undeserving.

With the aim of reducing the problem of poverty, Charity Organization Societies were established in a number of cities in the latter part of the nineteenth century. The purpose of these societies was to coordinate the public and private relief resources of the community and to help in the rehabilitation of families. The latter service was undertaken by a corps of volunteer "friendly visitors." In the beginning, most of these societies did not give financial aid; later, however, they solicited and dispensed funds as part of their individualized service to families.[1] In some cities, particularly the larger ones, these societies extended their relief functions and came to be the favored agencies for meeting the economic needs of families.

The original Charity Organization Societies gradually increased in number and in prestige. From their earliest days, social welfare agencies had been forced to come to grips with the impact of money on the lives of persons they served. So, too, the meaning of money to, and its management by, individuals in economic trouble were matters of major concern to the early Charity Organization Societies. Haphazard, unstandardized, and unscientific as their methods were, the friendly visitors soon adopted budget counseling as an important function. Later, fuller knowledge about such factors as nutrition led to more scientific and standardized practices in budget construction and counseling. The Charity Organization Societies developed new techniques for helping persons with various kinds of social problems and formulated the method that came to be known as social casework. They inaugurated training classes, first for the volunteer visitors and later for the paid staff by whom the former were gradually replaced. The Charity Organization Society in New York established the first school of social work. Through the participation of many lay persons, the Charity Organization Societies, like their contemporaries in the settlement house movement, had gained much wider public understanding and acceptance than most public agencies.

During the first two decades of this century, public resources also expanded and many states began to provide pensions for widows and for the aged. Nevertheless, great variations in the standards and availability of public relief programs continued to exist throughout the country. Despite the general expansion of these programs, considerable negative feeling about public relief prevailed in the community. These negative attitudes derived from many sources: the punitive spirit of the early "poor laws" enacted both in England and in this country; abuse by public officials in dispensing relief; and the cultural concept that laid stress on an individual's ability to be economically independent and stigmatized adult financial dependence.

Negative attitudes were particularly marked in relation to the federal government's participation in relief programs. Not until the 1930s, when the mass need created by widespread and unprecedented unemployment could not be met by available public and private resources, were federal funds appropriated to provide relief for families and individuals. The federal government's entrance into the nation's relief program, motivated by the Great Depression, culminated in the passage of the Social Security Act of 1935 and its several discrete social insurance and public assistance programs, designed to meet the economic needs of specified target groups. During the early depression years, as well as during the years immediately following the passage of the Social Security Act, the widely expanded public relief agencies operated on an "emergency" basis. Since then, conditions for extending economic assistance, forms of aid, administrative auspices, eligibility factors, and the qualifications of those giving financial help have undergone many changes. But public agencies are now the major community resource for families with financial difficulties.

Following the expansion of public welfare programs, the voluntary family agency undertook to provide professional guidance to individuals and families with problems of social adjustment and interpersonal relationships. It drew heavily on the new knowledge made available by dynamic psychiatry, and developed increased skill in the counseling process. For a time there was, perhaps, an overemphasis on psychological factors in dysfunctioning but, more recently, increased attention has been given to social factors. Prominent among these social factors are the meanings and uses of money. Indeed, advancing knowledge about psychological and cultural influences on behavior has made it increasingly apparent that money is an important—often vital—factor in the social adjustment and functioning of individuals and families, irrespective of their economic status. It also has become clear that an individual cannot operate totally independently in our society, as an entity isolated from the stream of social and economic life. Nor does the individual have complete control over life-influencing conditions and circumstances; in large measure, a person's decisions are geared to the demands and expectations of the surrounding community. The individual is a part of a larger world—a money world.

Sensitivity to the importance of counselors' having the knowledge that can maximize the effectiveness of counseling families in a money world, led to an exploratory study on "The Problem of Money Management in Education and Family Counseling" some twenty years ago. Conducted under the auspices of the Welfare Planning Council, Los Angeles Region, with the aid of a grant from Beneficial Management Corporation, that study drew together the relevant knowledge that had been accumulated in social work and the allied fields of sociology, anthropology, psychology, psychiatry, law, business, marketing, economics, and home economics. The findings from that study were incorporated in *The Family in a Money World*, published by Family Service Association of America as a handbook for professionals and nonprofessionals engaged in counseling people about money matters. It sought to present in concise form some major trends in what appeared to be a rapidly expanding body of knowledge about the place of money in our culture.

But what do counselors need to know about the family in *today's* money world? Important changes in lifestyles have emerged during the last two decades. Significant modifications are evident in societal attitudes toward and about money's uses. The role of money and how it is obtained and managed in disadvantaged population groups with special needs have been highlighted as part of the civil rights and women's movements. Newer, more rapid means for creating images of desirable and desired modes of living have stimulated aspirations for homeownership, education, travel, and other amenities among wider segments of the American population—or turned some away from such "materialism." A growing number of social policy issues and concerns have accorded recognition to the centrality of the family's socioeconomic situation. We have experienced major and sometimes unprecedented shifts in our economic system that have implications for individuals as well as family life in general.

Twenty years ago, executives and practitioners in many voluntary and some public mental health outpatient services agencies could (and did) claim that they could not render social services effectively unless the client were free to "use" counseling or therapy without the more or less subtle "coercive" presence of financial assistance. Today, they are more likely to accept the relevance of client attitudes about money and the client's ways of using money as important dynamics in the individual's functioning, and as vital clues to productive coping mechanisms.

Moreover, within the last ten years especially, there have been important trends and changes in our human services delivery systems. These make it even more compelling for counselors to be aware of not only the purposes for which people need money, but also the ways in which societal attitudes regarding money are translated into social policies that are implemented in diverse ways by both public and voluntary social agencies.

Over the past three decades the trend to encourage the wider use of agency services by the nonpoor in the community has been more and more in evidence. Persons who are economically independent increasingly have sought counseling help from voluntary family and children's agencies, health and mental health clinics, and so forth. At first a fairly rare and uncertain occurrence, the practice of charging fees for such services, usually on a sliding-scale basis, has become commonplace. Fee-charging has spread to public mental health facilities, public adoption agencies, and to other tax-supported organizations. The practice of setting a fee already had seemed to sharpen the social worker's awareness of money as an emotional and functional factor in the lives of people. Yet, the discomfort felt by many about the fee-charging process has persisted, as has lack of understanding about it as a tool with useful diagnostic or treatment value.

The 1975 enactment of the Social Services Amendments (Title XX) to the Social Security Act places the spotlight on the practice and implications of fee-charging. The broadening of eligibility for social services —whether provided directly by the public welfare agency or by a voluntary or other public agency under contract with the administering public welfare agency—for the first time in some instances, officially opens public agency services to families whose income is linked not to the poverty or public assistance levels (often indistinguishable), but to the median family income in a given state. Such families are to be charged fees, and the states have statutory authority to impose fees for services on economically dependent families as well. This single social policy measure does not merely underscore the fundamental necessity for social workers, in particular, to comprehend the nature of stress on families whose income is low or uncertain or inadequately managed, and how to help them to cope effectively with such stress. It adds significantly to the dimensions of understanding about human behavior and money—about how people do and can function in a money world—that the competent social work practitioner or administrator must bring to the planning and delivery of social services to such a sizable proportion of the American population.

What, then, do counselors need to know about families in today's money world?

The "need to know" was seminal to a series of undertakings: a survey of the wide range of literature in relevant—even irrelevant—fields; individual and group interviews with persons drawn from various ethnic-minority groups and income levels, with personnel in a range of social agencies, and with others performing counseling functions; analysis of data recorded by staff of the Consumer Credit Counselors of Los Angeles regarding applicants for services in a single month; and review of a broad spectrum of popular or "slick" magazines. The purpose of the latter was primarily to gauge general interest in the problems of money and families; and to identify the trends discernible since 1970 in the perceptions of the importance, nature, and impact of financial matters troubling families, as well as the answers offered, especially in the instances of marital problems or single-parent families. The material from the original money management project was reexamined in the light of the knowledge and insights produced by these research activities. The present book, *The Family in Today's Money World,* is the result: it combines newer knowledge and insights about the place of the family and money in today's culture with those from the earlier volume that are pertinent today.

The Family in Today's Money World endeavors to add two reciprocal orders of understanding to the armamentarium of the counselor, regardless of the setting in which the counseling is conducted or the special qualifications the counselor may bring to the counseling role. One centers on understanding the meanings that money holds for individuals and families, and the uses to which they put it in seeking to fulfill a wide range of economic, social, and psychological needs. The other focuses on the economic climate in which the family lives—a climate that interacts intimately with individuals and families and bears heavily on the quality of their life and, consequently, that of the nation.

The Family in Today's Money World addresses the needs of individuals, singly or in some combination. But the chief focus on the family and segments of families is predicated on the assumption, expressed by Ralph Linton, that "There is every reason to believe that the family is the oldest of human social institutions and that it will survive, in one form or another, as long as our species exists. . . ."[2] This focus acknowledges an interaction between the family and the community that affects both, the impact of the socioeconomic milieu and the stresses and tensions it creates in the economic and social functioning of the family, and the influence of the resultant functioning on the development of the individual members and their coping abilities. As used here, "functioning" encompasses economic, social, and psychological interactions of individuals and families.

Within this framework, cognizance is taken of the fact that there are differences in familial and individual coping capabilities and opportunities; that these may vary in degree at different times and in different stages of the cycle of family life, in different places, under different circumstances; and that factors affecting the adequacy or inadequacy of the coping level may be within or beyond the control of the individual or family.

Several principles fundamental to the approach used throughout this book[3] are these:

Behavior is purposeful, whether or not the purpose is overt.

Improvement in the level of functioning can be effectively accomplished only if the family or individual has some degree of awareness of and interest in attaining the goals.

Involvement and participation of individuals and family members in the goal-achievement process require that the client have opportunity to express his or her own wishes and expectations, regardless of the extent to which they are or are not realistic.

The counselor must be sensitive to the reality needs and pressures of the money world in which the client lives, and the kinds of adaptations the client must make to function in it with a reasonable degree of personal satisfaction as well as effectiveness from the perspective of the community.

The counselor must be interested in being a helping person, listening to and hearing what the client is saying in words and feelings.

It is through the individual's or family's strengths, sparse or delicate as these may be, that movement can proceed towards the goals.

Problems centering around money may be symptomatic or causative of other problems.

Small successes, and achievement of even minor intermediate objectives, generally are essential stepping stones to reach resolution of larger money-centered problems.

It is not the intent of this book to deal with economics per se or with problems or social policy in the arena of income equality or inequality or redistribution. Rather, it is addressed to the way a family in today's money world—affected by inflation, recession (or both simultaneously), and influenced by personal and social attitudes about the meanings of money—can deal with the tasks not only of surviving in a money world, but also of improving the quality of life insofar as this can be influenced by appropriate economic behavior. While some attention is directed to differences in class, ethnicity, income levels, and other relevant variables, the focus of the book is clearly on the economic, emotional, and social meanings of money to individuals and families, and how, in the context of these meanings, they do and can cope with their financial needs.

Accordingly, the book is divided into four parts. Part One describes, albeit briefly, the economic world in which families live and work, in which they derive income and spend it. It looks at some of the social implications of the way income is obtained and the amounts families have. Against this backdrop, the spotlight turns to economic behavior of families in our society, and what their expenditure needs are in the effort to attain or maintain certain standards of living. The purpose of this section is to bring together for the counselor not familiar with the workings of our economic system (except for its personal impact!) some thoughts and facts that might broaden comprehension of where individual clients and families fit into the "normal" scheme of things, and facilitate helping them to define and work toward realistic goals in mastering the financial aspects of their lives. This part was developed with particular awareness of the fact that very little is written on the dynamics of income: more has appeared in the last several years on the role of income as an independent variable—especially as related to equality and inequality. But there remains a paucity of economics literature that touches on the human and humanitarian aspects of economics, and even that which is available does not tend to deal with the dynamics of behavior in relation to money. Notable among the few writers who approach economics humanistically are George Katona and his colleagues. For specific references, see those at the close of pertinent chapters.

Part Two considers the changing lifestyles and goals in today's money world and their effect on the stages of the family life cycle. It considers the meanings and uses of money in those successive stages: the beginning stage—and the non-beginning reflected in social rather than legal unions; the expanding family and the development of money attitudes and relationships among children and in parent-child relationships; the changes in family composition and relationships as children leave the home, couples grow older, and aging or other factors further contribute to the contraction of the family; and some of the many variations in living patterns—single adults, unmarried parenthood, dissolution of the marriage, remarriage, group and communal marriages, and others.

Counseling goals, and some guidelines and techniques for achieving them constitute Part Three. Drawing on understandings about behavior and money elements in the various stages of the family life cycle, this section considers interventive measures that can help families and individuals whose problems are expressed in money terms, or whose problems are exacerbated by or emerge from money difficulties. The intent is not to counsel families specifically about ways to obtain income or to increase the level of the recurring income or material resources. Rather, it aims to give the counselor some assistance about elements to consider in counseling families and about options that might be suggested as examination proceeds with the family. It is in this context that some income maintenance programs and principles are discussed, and that factors regarding loans versus grants, and the imposition of fees are given attention. This part then details the client needs and values that must be assessed in the course of counseling the individual and family, and the range of resources that might be called upon in the interest of the given family—with some cautions offered in examining the validity of a specific resource for resolving a specific client problem.

The final section, Part Four, is devoted to the elements necessary for tailoring collaboratively, with the client, a practicable budget plan. This section emphasizes that to optimize one's wellbeing in today's money world requires planning that is consistent with the client's interests and capacity for translating the design into the verities of daily living, and that gives due regard to the client's unique vulnerabilities and strengths.

Unless otherwise stipulated, the case material used illustratively throughout this book has been condensed and disguised from the original materials supplied by various social agencies or obtained in the course of the previously mentioned research activities. In all instances, permission to employ the material was obtained. The readings that are included in the respective "Notes" sections were compiled with the aim of enhancing the reader's knowledge about the materials to which the readings are appended. Some elaborate upon or explain relevant theory. Some offer additional insights into certain behaviors and situations. And some are included because they contain useful "dos" and "don'ts" for the counselor and family being counseled.

It is this author's strong conviction that to function effectively in our society, the individual must have a vital sense of being able to exercise a reasonable degree of control over his or her own affairs, and that having and appropriately managing money is an important ingredient in the mastery of one's own destiny. Horace succinctly stated that "Money is to each man either a master or a slave."[4] The pages that follow seek to make it possible for the individual or family to attain and retain mastery in coping with financial aspects of living in today's money world.

NOTES

1. Margaret E. Rich, *A Belief in People: A History of Family Social Work* (New York: Family Service Association of America, 1956).
2. "The Natural History of the Family," in Ruth N. Anshen, ed., *The Family: Its Function and Destiny* (New York: Harper & Brothers, 1949), p. 18.
3. The framework is essentially the same as described in the introduction to Frances Lomas Feldman and Frances H. Scherz, *Family Social Welfare: Helping Troubled Families* (New York: Atherton Press, 1967) and developed in greater detail in that work.
4. Horace. *Horace for English Readers: Being a Translation of the Poems of Quintus Horatius Flaccus,* trans. E. C. Wickham (Oxford: The Clarendon Press, 1903), p. 287.

PART 1
TODAY'S MONEY WORLD

1
The Economic Milieu of Today's Family

In this age of nuclear energy, space travel, computerization and automation, men and women are economic beings who live in a money world. Money, the medium of exchange, provides the means for distributing the vast outpouring of the goods and services of our economic system. Money also is an instrument used in our society to calibrate the individual's character and functioning while at the same time shaping the person's self-perceptions of adequacy and worthwhileness. These perceptions in turn have an impact on the effectiveness of the individual's social and economic functioning and on the quality of family life.

Economists naturally tend to view money in objective terms: as a rational tool used by rational beings. They have developed complicated mechanistic concepts, often expressed in elaborate mathematical formulas, to describe the flow and use of money. Emphasis on the objective aspects of money has been reinforced by the fact that the modern industrial and economic world has been in perpetual change. This change has been marked by technological advances, pressures for population decrease, shifts in urban centers, suburbanization and ghettoization, economic recessions in the presence of inflation, wars, and altered modes and standards of living.

Recent years have witnessed a mounting awareness of and emphasis on the so-called subjective aspects of money, with more and more attention centering on its psychological and sociological significance. To be sure, some of the basic assumptions of orthodox economic theory continue to be readily discernible: that as a rational animal, man (and the term was ascribed to the male of the species, not used generically) is concerned with maximizing his economic gains; that each individual responds to economic incentives as an isolated unit; and that human beings, like machines, can be treated in a standardized fashion. These assumptions, however, are now subject to valid challenge in the face of a growing body of evidence that there are things more important to the individual than maximizing economic gains[1] and that each person responds to economic incentives not as an isolated individual, but as one who possesses unique qualities even though influenced by and influencing others.

Increasingly, questions are being raised about attitudes, whether individual or collective, pertaining to money and to the interrelationship between these subjective elements and the workings of our economic system. To provide skilful counseling on money matters requires that the counselor have an understanding of the objective and subjective influences that affect and are the effect of money. Furthermore, the counselor who is working with an individual client or a client group (family, peer, or other) toward achieving a more satisfactory and satisfying balance in functioning in the real world, must be sensitive to the ways that the intrapersonal and environmental aspects of the client's life affect each other. Cognizance must be taken of the interaction between the client and the economic system even when the focus of the counseling is not on money matters per se.

Such understanding cannot be achieved solely through observation of the overt behavior of human beings: they are not puppets controlled by strings labelled "money," "prices," "income," or "supply and demand." It must be based on awareness of the influences of the socioeconomic and cultural climate in which the individual grows and develops.

THE ECONOMIC FACTS OF LIFE

To the economist, money is a measuring rod. It is a means of equating heterogeneous values without resorting to cumbersome and restrictive barter transactions. Barter is dependent on a mutual coincidence of wants; each party in an exchange must want the particular commodity or service of the other. Commodities, however, have different values to different people; some will pay a greater price than others for the same commodity. Thus money, as the medium of exchange, facilitates the movement of goods and services from producer to consumer.

Money is also a way of storing value. The value of money may change over a period of time, but it is much more practical to store money-values than to store a commodity itself. Although under some circumstances grain, jewels, furs, or other items may be held as a safeguard against future want, in our civilization money is the usual way to store value. It may be accumulated temporarily for the purpose of covering future uneven expenditures. Instead of being spent on consumer goods, or being invested in producer goods, it may be saved in cash, bank deposits, or stocks and other forms of investment in anticipation of a decrease in prices or future decline in income.

The universality of money as a means of exchange and of storing value is manifest in the fact that in all civilized nations it constitutes legal tender for the payment of debt and for the procuring of things that are not "free" but are "economic" goods since they are limited in supply. The very universality of money means that people like to have it. It has come to have value not only for what it will buy, but for itself—for it represents the power to buy or possess. Money simultaneously represents "dependence" and "independence": dependence to the extent that one can rely on it for obtaining the commodities one needs, and independence because its ownership implies competence and self-reliance. To many individuals, the possession of money connotes more than the realistic, practical use that the rational man or woman ascribes to it; it symbolizes economic security and social and emotional security as well.

In our broad society, social status often is in direct ratio to the place of a family unit on the income-receiving scale: the higher the income, the higher the family's social status. This cultural attitude derives from the economic thinking that income is received for producing "economic" goods—commodities or services—that are in demand because they have value. Therefore, the producer with material possessions that represent the fruit of personal production is an individual of stature in our society. The earning and spending of money are symbols of success and have come to represent status aspirations. Among ethnic-minority groups who have experienced ethnic discrimination within our society, success within or outside the minority group likewise has frequently been associated with the earning and spending of money.

In contrast, European countries have been more likely to assign social status to the person with property holdings than to the producer of income. They have long placed a premium on acquisition of land, largely by inheritance, and have minimized the importance of the "self-made man," held in such high esteem in our country. The conflict between these two standards created considerable confusion among American soldiers who encountered this "alien" concept in Western Europe. In the same way, Europeans coming to the United States not infrequently were troubled by the idealization of persons earning large incomes, and they were uneasy about spending total income instead of providing security through savings accounts or other forms of tangible assets. Their attitude was comparable to that of the earlier middle-class New Englander: one should not gratify current desires at the cost of future security.

Changing political and economic conditions in Europe, however, have been accompanied by some changes in the perception of the social status and value of the individual whose own efforts have resulted in financial success—a perception that is becoming increasingly apparent among people in highly industrialized countries around the world and reinforces the view in our own society. Nevertheless, these altering views and the contemporary trend toward higher standards of living, as reflected in the purchase of goods and services, appear not to have extinguished the attitude that thrift and saving for the future are desirable virtues, and that personal worth, adequacy, and morality are measured not only by how one acquires income—and how much—but also by how it is managed.

THE SOURCES OF MONEY INCOME

How the individual earns income and how he spends it are determined by a combination of external and internal circumstances. Although the sources of income have remained essentially the same in our country since its founding, the development of important additional sources has been stimulated by several national cataclysms that have occurred since the 1920s, and by modifications in certain societal attitudes resulting from these significant events. Until the economic depression of the thirties, the income of families in the United States was obtained primarily from four sources. By far the largest was wages, including commissions, fees, and payments for farm and other labor or services rendered. A substantial though considerably smaller source was rents. This term ordinarily includes all payments that owners of fixed resources, such as land and buildings, receive for their use. A third source of income was interest, ordinarily representing payments that owners of money receive for the use of their money. The fourth source constituted profits (from farm and nonfarm businesses) or dividends, often the payment to entrepreneurs over and above the wages of management for having assumed the risk of going into the business, investing money in it, and operating the enterprise.

Unique social problems or variants of existing problems have arisen in each stage through which the country moved from the depression of the 1930s: World War II, the postwar period, the War on Poverty and the following period characterized by simultaneously waxing inflation and deepening recession. In each stage the government has responded to new minimum standards of health, nutrition, and financial security by assuming certain economic responsibilities in the interests of individuals and groups. Thus, a fifth source of income to families has assumed growing importance—transfer payments, or income for which no service is currently rendered. Included in transfer payments are such forms of income as unemployment and old-age insurance benefits, military pensions, survivors' and disability benefits, public assistance, and other income maintenance payments. Farm subsidies to maintain price levels and to keep agricultural land out of production are also transfer payments.

Since 1973, wages and salaries or other payments for labor have accounted for more than 71 percent of our national family income, rising steadily over the last five decades. Simultaneously, the national income received by families from businesses, farms, professional practices, and rents has declined. The proportion of national income obtained by families as personal interest and dividends, although somewhat less than it was in 1929, has appreciated steadily; by 1973 it was more than 11 percent of the total national income. But undoubtedly the most dramatic shift is that transfer payments, only 1.6 percent of national income received by families in 1929, also exceeded 11 percent by 1973.[2] Indeed, as 1975 began, transfer payments constituted more than 12 percent of personal income.[3]

The significance of the vacillations in the sources of personal income of families and individuals is underscored by a number of factors. The incomes of young people are derived almost entirely from wage and salary sources. The largest proportion of those receiving transfer payments have been elderly persons, but the recent sharp increase in transfer payments also contains the increase in unemployment insurance benefits that reflects the widening picture of unemployment. All income basically derives from production. The interaction in the market place of supply and demand at any given time is markedly influenced by national and international events and, in turn, influences the income available from interests, dividends, rents, labor, and other sources. And the need for and uses of income of families and individuals are determined not only by such external factors as the aforementioned sources of personal income, but also by personal or subjective qualities that may operate consciously or unconsciously to govern how the individual's or family's income is obtained and utilized in our modern money world.

IS MONEY INCOME GROWING?
In the past two decades the steady and steep climb in amounts of personal income has paralleled that of the preceding two-decade period. For example, as recently as 1947, the median family income was well under $6,000 in current dollar values, and more than 20 percent of United

States families had incomes under $3,000. Yet, a quarter century later, the median family income, after taxes, had more than doubled, and slightly more than 5 percent of all families had incomes under $3,000.

The discriminating reader may wonder about the reality of this increase in income, pointing to the concurrent seemingly implacable rise in prices for goods and services; to the popularly expounded idea that the dollar has less purchasing power than was true a decade ago and that the lower incomes of that period were more apparent than real; to the variations in median income data for nonwhite or single-parent families; and to the continued presence of a substantial portion of the American population regarded as being "in poverty." Certainly, consumer prices climbed rapidly during the last decade: 56.3 percent from 1965 through 1974. But whether the yardstick applied is median family income or per capita disposable (after taxes) personal income, income has surged ahead of prices. By the end of 1974 median family income and disposable personal income had still outpaced the rise in prices by more than 25 percent,[4] even taking into account the first annual decline (2.5 percent)[5] in real disposable income in more than twenty-five years.

Not all families have benefited equally from the rising incomes and presumed buying power. The working man or working woman who is the sole family breadwinner has been less advantaged in feeding the family than the working man or woman whose spouse also is employed. For in families where the father was the sole provider, the median income was $12,082. If the income was provided by the woman as family head, the median was nearly halved. But the median income of families with both husband and wife working was $16,461; for families with three wage earners, $20,328. Retired persons on fixed incomes experienced an effective reduction in income because of rising prices. And the median incomes of nonwhite families and individuals in 1974 continued to lag behind median incomes of white families and individuals: 62 percent and 68 percent, respectively, of their white counterparts' median incomes.

In viewing the rise in family income and the real increase in the family's purchasing power, cognizance should be taken of how much of the income is related to higher base pay, how much to overtime earnings, and how much to "moonlighting" on a second and sometimes even a third job. Overtime earnings and other-job earnings during the first part of the 1970s represented a sizable part of current income. This fact is especially significant to counselors because changes in production schedules and other economic factors, such as those clearly evident in the 1974–76 downward turn of the national economy, quickly alter

The Economic Milieu of Today's Family

overtime or extra-work programs and culminate in a substantial reduction of family income.

The J family experienced such a reduction.

> They had been able to move into and support the mortgage on their modest "dream" house because Mr. J, an established employee in a Connecticut furniture factory, worked there sixty hours each week, and also worked at a local gasoline service station on weekends. A cutback to forty hours per week in the factory, and the loss of the weekend work because of the impact of the 1973 gasoline curtailment, required this family of five to dip into carefully nurtured savings, first to meet the payments on the house and then to keep abreast of the upward spiraling of costs of living. Long before 1974 had ended, the mortgage had been foreclosed, the family was fruitlessly seeking a loan in order to move into a crowded shabby apartment in a blighted neighborhood, and Mrs. J was attending a community mental health center three times a week in efforts to cope with her depression and her family responsibilities.

As the J family situation illustrates, overtime and other extra earnings obviously are not less committed to meet current expenditures than are earnings from base pay. Reflected also in this example is the impact on at least one family of the paradox of simultaneous inflation and recession.

WHOSE INCOME?

It should be noted that the stated increases refer to median rather than arithmetic average incomes, and to family income, not individual income. Family income represents the income of all the people living in one household, related by blood, marriage, or adoption, and spending their income together as a unit. (Also rising steadily is the number of units spending income as a family group even though no legal marriage has bound the adults to each other. Such arrangements, although taken into account in later chapters, are not officially recognized in governmental statistical presentations of income and expenditure data.) The median, or middle, income is the point at which the upper half of the people with income are divided from the lower half, and falls short of the arithmetic average, primarily because the distribution of incomes is skewed, with a long tail of incomes stretching out above the average. For instance, in 1974 the lowest fifth of American families received 5.4 percent of the aggregate income, whereas the highest fifth received 41 percent.[6]

By the end of 1974, incomes of families in the United States were distributed as shown in table 1.

TABLE 1. DISTRIBUTION OF U.S. ANNUAL FAMILY INCOME, 1974

Annual family income	Percent of all families	Percent of all white families	Percent of all black & others
Under $3,000	5.3	4.3	13.6
3,000–4,999	7.7	6.8	16.0
5,000–6,999	8.8	8.4	13.0
7,000–9,999	13.8	13.5	16.2
10,000–14,999	24.3	25.1	19.0
15,000–24,999	28.3	29.7	17.9
25,000 & over	11.5	12.4	4.5

This table shows that while nearly 30 out of every 100 white families had incomes above $15,000, and more than 12 out of every 100 white families had incomes above $25,000, fewer than 18 out of every 100 nonwhite families had incomes between $15,000 and $25,000—and only about one-third as many nonwhite as white families exceeded $25,000 incomes. Moreover, the converse is true at the lower end of the income scale. Whereas nearly 13 of every 100 families had income under $5,000, the ratio increased to almost 30 out of every 100 ethnic-minority families.

Undoubtedly, the position of a family on the income scale is related not just to ethnicity per se but also to the composition of the family in terms of the number of working adults it contains: Are both parents present and employed? Is the mother the sole worker? the father? Are children in the home also employed—indeed, is this one of the households represented by the 75 percent increase in 1973 among working teenagers of both sexes? What if the family contains no working members?

The role of the gainfully employed wife or mother as a contributor to family income has drawn increased attention from various quarters in recent years, many regarding it as a relatively new phenomenon. Although married women have been a part of the labor force for centuries, especially women in low-income families, they now permeate the work force. Given impetus by demands for increased manpower resources necessitated by World War II, an unprecedented number of married women moved into the labor market. By 1955, working wives were contributing to the income of one-fourth of the consumer units. ("Consumer unit" is a more precise measure of spending than the individual consumer. Such units are of two kinds: household units and spending units. If two families share the same house, they form a household unit in such purchases as rent and utilities. They form two spending units in purchases of clothing and food. If one family moves to its own home, the number of household units increases; spending units do not.) The wage or salary receipts in about half of these instances amounted to less than $1,000, suggesting occasional or part-time work. Few of the working wives earned as much as $5,000. Among young married couples without children, approximately three-fifths of the wives worked at least part time. The proportion of working wives was then lowest among families with young children—one-fifth. But it reached twice this proportion among young couples with children over five years of age. Among couples where the marital partners were forty-five years or older, the proportion of working wives was one-fourth.

This trend of more married women entering the labor market not infrequently provoked expressions of community concern regarding women's motivations for working and the effect of their employment on family life. More often the concern was related to the "danger" of flooding a labor market already containing increasing numbers of workers whose services were being made superfluous by technological advances. Yet by 1975 this picture had altered substantially, impelled by a cluster of circumstances, not the least of which were the women's movement, technological progress accompanied by greater demands for workers with certain skills associated with women, and social policies that underscore remunerative work as more desirable than public assistance for economically dependent heads of households.

Between 1960 and the end of 1973, while adult male employment rose about 15 percent, adult female employment expanded by nearly 50 percent to nearly 10 million women. The contributions to family income also had spurted upward, white women contributing on the average from $4,000 to $5,000 to the annual income, and black women from $3,200 to $6,000. Again, these figures suggest variations in the amount of work undertaken, with the white working wife supplying between 25 and 30 percent of family income, and the black working wife between 31 and 39 percent of the family income. The figures also reflect regional as well as occupational differences in earnings: for both groups higher earnings were reported in the North and West and for white-collar workers.[7]

The general increases in the number of wives in the labor force and in the amount of their contributions to family income has been accompanied by changes in when they enter the labor market and how long they remain there. For example, approximately a third of the wives who have young children now work outside the home, and about half of those with children over five years of age now do so. The proportion of working wives over forty-five years of age now is close to half, compared to the fourth who were in the work force twenty years ago. This suggests that many of those who entered when their children started school, continued to work, and many entered when their children had grown. The proportion of working wives drops to 7 percent after age 65—more than a third the percentage of over-65 married men remaining active in the labor force. At the time this was written data were not available regarding the impact on continued work and earnings of wives and mothers as the recession of 1974–76 became more pronounced.

Examination of peak income periods in the white family's life cycle discloses a consistent pattern for at least those years in which the growing labor force participation of wives has been so apparent. When the husband is the only earner, the high point has been reached when the family head is 35–44 years old. If both husband and wife are earners, the income has peaked when the family head is 45–54.[8] In black families, the pattern had shifted by 1972. Previously, regardless of who the earners in the family were, the income peak was reached in the 35–44 age period; now, regardless of whether one or both spouses work, earnings reach their highest level when the head is 45–54 years old.

Of special importance to those who counsel families with problems that relate directly or indirectly to money is the income situation of the family head without a spouse in the home. The median income for such male-headed households was $11,737 in 1974; for female-headed households, $6,413.[9] Without considering either the source of the latter income—whether direct earnings, transfer payments, child support, or other—or the extra demands that may be imposed on it by the presence of only one parent, this income level is very close to the magic line that purports to divide those who are in poverty from those who are not. Under the definition used by federal agencies, poverty thresholds vary according to differing consumption requirements of families based on their size and composition, sex and age of the family head, and farm or nonfarm residence. The low-income cutoffs for farm families have been set at 85 percent of the nonfarm levels, and the cutoffs are updated every year to reflect the changes in the Consumer Price Index (CPI). At the beginning of this decade, a family of four was considered to be living in poverty if its disposable income (income less taxes) was under $3,968 for the year. At that time about 5 million families and 5 million unrelated individuals (one out of ten families and one out of three unrelated individuals in the United States) had incomes below the poverty level. In

1975, the official designation of poverty was income under $5,050.

Viewed against this changing perception of poverty thresholds, what are the social implications of the level of median income of the female-headed household? Of the under-$5,000 income of 60 percent of the black and other ethnic-minority families? Of the inability of men *and* women to retain or obtain employment that will provide them with income that at least exceeds the level of unemployment insurance benefits—if, indeed, these are available to them? Of record increases in prices in tandem with a changing employment picture? Of an expanding middle-income and middle-rich class in company with un- or underemployment and thresholds of poverty?

SOCIAL IMPLICATIONS—RHETORIC AND REALITY

"Unemployment," "recession," and "inflation," singly or in combination, are chilling words. To the person struggling to support a family the prospect or even the possibility of losing a job and being unable to pay for food, shelter, and other necessities of life presents a grim specter. When "recession" is in the daily headlines, on the tongue of every news analyst, and in official government reports, the anxiety about the likelihood of job loss is exacerbated. When costs of survival items—food, shelter, clothing, and medical care—move inexorably upward, absorbing a higher and higher proportion of income and not infrequently requiring dissaving, the emotional and often the physical distress is compounded. ("Dissaving" represents decreasing assets, that is, drawing on accumulated savings or other assets.)

These harsh economic realities increase the vulnerabilities of many individuals and families: the person whose earnings are marginal; the unskilled person, especially the one with limited intellectual endowment or education, or both; the skilled worker who requires hard-to-get retraining to meet changing industrial or technological demands; the person whose age or health precludes work or salary change; the family whose composition or circumstances foreclose the prospect of a second working member or a second job to augment dwindling purchasing power. And it is these heightened vulnerabilities to which the counselor must remain sensitive.

Those who recall their own or their relatives' personal experiences with the struggles of the depression of the 1930s undoubtedly react more quickly and anxiously to the threat of reduced income than do younger persons who have had to cope with uncertainties of priorities different from income sufficiency or job stability. In succeeding generations, many have disdained materialism (most pointedly that of their parents), seeking to live "simply," either by their own efforts or the contributions of more or less affluent parents. The shifting economic conditions that have affected both the parental means and their own ability to produce income for maintenance purposes have engendered in some of these younger adults a growing cynicism toward traditional economic values, often accompanied by a new examination of their place in this modern money world, especially in the arena of work.

The economic experiences of the recent past as well as the prognostications for the foreseeable future have particular significance for social workers, regardless of whether they are in voluntary or public agency settings or whether their clientele comprises young or old, financially comfortable or deprived, or those with adequate or inadequate ability to function reasonably satisfactorily in our socioeconomic climate.

Sources of Family Income

The job market, long the major source of income for Americans, has experienced considerable change since the industrial revolution began, and promises even more. The steady increase in demand for workers with new skills to keep pace with advancing technology has been accompanied not only by obsolescence of certain skills, but by a steady reduction in the need for untrained, undereducated workers. To compete successfully in the changing labor market, individuals now need greater technological knowledge and generally, therefore, more schooling. Education may range along a continuum from limited mastery of the three Rs to an advanced degree certifying the acquisition of specific knowledge and skill in highly technical areas. The day has long passed when an illiterate person could successfully obtain at least a low-paying job if he were both able and ready to wield a mop and broom; now such a person must be able to read directions in order to mix the cleaning chemicals properly in which the mop will be dipped: an error can result in damage to an expensive floor and dismissal of the erring employee. The employee must be able to interpret signs and instructions relating to his own and his coworkers' safety, or to the proper handling of company property; failure to do so is to risk serious injury.

The period of the 1960s, stimulated by the War on Poverty and expanding welfare rolls, saw many efforts in many quarters to provide literacy training as well as to train unskilled and retrain skilled workers.

The Economic Milieu of Today's Family

Propelled further by the civil rights movement and the force of Affirmative Action, work opportunities were enhanced for members of minority groups, some handicapped persons and, more recently for women and the elderly. (Derived from federal mandates, "Affirmative Action" refers to conscious, deliberate effort to seek out, recruit, and employ members of ethnic-minorities, women, and others designated as "minorities.") Dire predictions in the 1950s that there would be fewer and fewer jobs because of accelerated industrialization and automation did not materialize; the overall number of jobs continued to increase, reaching a new high by the fall of 1974 despite concurrent growing numbers of unemployed throughout the nation. Then the number of jobs began to drop in some manufacturing areas while still rising in some nonmanufacturing areas. Through 1975, the numbers of employed stood at a new high, yet the unemployment rate had moved to at least 8.2 percent nationwide, as high as 30 percent in some communities or among some ethnic-minority or unskilled groups, and 45 percent in some regions among building-trade workers.

What are the implications as to ways in which families and individuals can derive enough income from employment in this kind of a labor market to retain the economic independence so prized in our society— and so essential to their emotional and economic well-being and functioning? What are the implications of a tightening labor market, with long-accepted hard-won seniority principles, for women workers and members of ethnic-minority groups whose entry into specific jobs is relatively recent, and often facilitated by social policies or Affirmative Action? And what are the implications for working women heads of households, or women seeking to help in the family's struggle to combat inflation through part-time or full-time work if the growing rate of unemployment leads employers to give preference to male "breadwinners" as was the case when men returned to civilian life following World War II?

Transfer Payments

What are the implications of the current employment situation for the network of social insurances and other programs of transfer payments that constitute the source of income for substantial numbers of individuals and families no longer attached directly to the work force—a work force that becomes proportionately smaller while the population receiving transfer payments from these programs grows larger?

The source of one's income affects the satisfactions derived from that income. It also affects in various ways not only one's self-esteem and sense of well-being, but also a wide spectrum of relationships with others. In American society, income not obtained directly or indirectly from work (or from an education scholarship, for example) is likely to be depreciated, as are the recipients of such income. Thus public assistance and food stamps—the major types of transfer payments received by low-income families—rely on means tests and other measures for assuring that those able to work will take prescribed steps toward at least partly replacing transfer payments with earned income

Transfer payments to higher-income groups, on the other hand, generally have the imprimatur of social acceptance. Social Security benefits (to retired or disabled persons or survivors of an individual who was previously attached to the work force), government subsidies to farmers, or benefits to veterans are usually regarded as acceptable forms of transfer payment. They are directly related to work of some kind, thereby giving credence to the idea that one can be "poor but honest" and therefore "deserving."

Accordingly, the social worker who seeks to help a family or individual cope realistically with troubling inter- or intrapersonal problems is well advised to consider the dynamic relationship between the individual's or family's functioning in the real world of work, and the income derived from that or other sources. The productive attachment of an individual to the work force is essential not only for income development but also, in Sigmund Freud's concept, "to bind [the individual] to reality," as he deals with it in *The Question of Lay Analysis*. Examination of reasons for marital discord, of precipitating factors culminating in emotional breakdown, of the acceleration in the number of suicides, and of other manifestations of personal or interpersonal distress, discloses that job loss (actual or threatened) is frequently a factor.

LAGGING INCOMES

The social implications of the nation's changing income patterns have received renewed and serious attention with the "rediscovery" of poverty during recent years. This rediscovery did not occur because part of the population lived in circumstances that were worse than in previous generations, although certainly some of those described today as poor do live under as difficult conditions as the poor of previous generations or the poor in other countries. But such poverty is not characteristic of high-income industrial nations today. Some contemporary "poor," as was particularly emphasized in the middle and late 1950s, are hungry or dwell in shelters that are inadequate for physical survival. This is not typical, however. Nor are most of those who are classified as being "in poverty" actually paupers or dependents whose only financial support comes from government assistance.

Nevertheless, there is a recrudescent concern about worsened conditions, threatened physical survival and pauperism. In nineteenth century England the focus was on pauperism. A decline of living standards was the issue in the United States in the desperate depression of the 1930s. In such low-income societies as Bangladesh and Ethiopia, sheer physical survival often is in jeopardy.

Within the more highly industrialized societies today, these do not appear to be the main difficulties—even though a growing number of voices complain that the accelerated inflation in the first part of this decade has led American families "to back-track on their living standards as prices continue to skyrocket . . . forcing cutbacks in consumption even on such basic necessities as food."[10] S.M. Miller and Pamela Roby maintain that "poverty has become the acceptable way of discussing the more disturbing issue of inequality,"[11] and that poverty has not been recognized fully as the "shorthand" it is for the much broader social problem because the historic subsistence connotations attached to the term persist.

It can be expected that there always will be low-income levels: it is customary to define poverty by some absolute income or income-needs level; thus those in the lowest-income level are "poor" and those above it are not regarded as "poor." If a distribution has a middle and a top, there also must be a bottom, and somebody is there. It is this bottom—the lowest fifth of the population—that falls below the "poverty" line. This group, regardless of the amounts of money, the sizes or conditions of the families, or other factors, is incontestably "in poverty." Conceivably, in any one year, many families who fall below the line will be there only temporarily: some will move back and forth across the line; others will be below it over a period of a few or many years. A recently completed longitudinal study of 5,000 families[12] concluded that the chances of a family in the lowest fifth of the population being persistently poor, that is, remaining below the line for a long time, are about one in four. However, given the total population, that represents a sizable number of individuals—nearly 11 million.

Who are the persistently poor? Scrutiny of Bureau of Census data suggests that the poor are more likely to be among those with less than sixth-grade education. Households headed by a woman have a considerably higher chance of being poor than families with male heads. The presence of children increases the family's chances of being among the persistently poor; this is hardly surprising, for family needs increase with additional children and are not often matched by increases in family income. That the effect of children differs between households headed by males and those headed by females undoubtedly can be explained by the greater probability that children affect differently the labor force participation of mothers than they do the participation of fathers.

Race also is an important consideration in determining that lagging income will increase the prospect that a family will be in the lowest percentile of incomes, temporarily as well as persistently. Thus a black or Chicano family is more likely to be in this income population than a white family. Influencing factors are those that bear directly on employability and earning power: age, education, intellectual capacity, race, motivation, family size and composition, the sex-marital-child status of the head of household, the size of the city of residence or distance to a city with work opportunities, the unemployment rate in the area in which the individual resides, and the financial and transportation resources available to reach a place of employment. For example, a study conducted under the auspices of the Commission to Study the Los Angeles Riots of 1965 (the Watts Riots) disclosed that to maintain a domestic job, for which the then-prevailing daily wage was about $13, many women had to pay as much as $3 per day just for infrequent public transportation that consumed three to five travel hours daily, and in effect extended the working day for which child care had to be arranged.[13]

It is apparent that the establishment of a dollar figure as the symbol of poverty or nonpoverty status clearly does not signify that those whose incomes fall below it, either temporarily or (more often) persistently, are therefore starving. The issue is one of lagging incomes rather than low incomes. An important consideration in assessing poverty also might well be that the absence or the unavailability of resources and amenities, irrespective of income, may contribute to an impression of poverty. For example, a sizable segment of Eskimo villagers in Southwest Alaska live in shelters without running water, electricity, and inside plumbing; their irregularly received annual income may not deviate greatly from the national median income figures, but the quality of many of the dwellings is below that of most American families with less income.[14]

COSTS OF LIVING

In recent years the Consumer Price Index (CPI), reported regularly by the Bureau of Labor Statistics, has almost taken on a life of its own as it increasingly mirrors the ability of a family to meet its economic needs with current income. The CPI has become a common measuring rod for determining whether wages or transfer payments should be increased. Accordingly, some union contracts call for an automatic adjustment (usually upward) in wage rates when specified changes occur in the CPI; and the 1972 Amendments to the Social Security Act instituted an escalator provision for adjusting benefits to retired and disabled persons that parallel changes in the CPI. Upward and downward movements in the CPI generally are presented in bold headlines by the news media. In the next chapter, we discuss Bureau of Labor Statistics budget standards. These budget standards are periodically adjusted, taking into account repricing of items included or applying changes in the CPI. Thus, the most recent family budget data available are those covering the time period from autumn 1971 to autumn 1972 and updated to 1974 by applying the CPI to budget costs for each major class of goods and services, and estimating 1974 income and Social Security taxes.

The public thinks of the CPI as a cost of living index. Yet in several ways it falls short of being a true index to costs of living. For one thing, it includes neither the cost of obtaining the income nor Social Security taxes. For another, it assumes that the "market basket" mix of goods purchased remains constant; but, in fact, consumers shift the composition of their market basket purchases in response to relative price changes and to changing tastes and styles. Thus the CPI does not indicate precisely the final price changes in the consumer's overall budget. How many extra dollars did the J or M family (the latter, Chicano) have to spend in 1974 or 1975 to maintain previously established living standards? How did inflation influence the allocation of their budget dollar? How much of the budget dollar went for increased tax payments? How much for items now regarded as necessities but in prior years either not contemplated by the family or not even in existence? For example, Mr. J now pays for health insurance to help defray possible family medical costs. The M's son now has tuition assistance so that he can acquire the modest education essential to provide him with the vocational opportunities that were not accessible to his father.

In spite of the limitations and fluctuations in the CPI, it can serve the counselor as a valuable tool in distinguishing reality money pressures from neurotic responses that focus directly or indirectly on money matters. And there are special reality implications to be taken into account in working toward resolution of various social or emotional problems of families or individuals whose income does not keep pace with the rising costs of daily living, or whose Social Security tax increases sharply erode current income, or whose other problems are painfully compounded by conditions of inflation or recession or both.

NOTES

1. See, for example, George Katona, *The Powerful Consumer: Psychological Studies of the American Economy* (New York: McGraw-Hill, 1960).
2. U.S., Department of Commerce Conference Board, *Guide to Consumer Marketing 1974–1975. The Wall Street Journal* reported that transfer payments rose from $103 billion in 1972 to just under $159 billion in 1975 at the January annual rate. February 24, 1975, p. 1.
3. *Economic Report of the President, 1975* (Washington, D.C.: U.S. Government Printing Office, February 1975), p. 54.
4. *The Wall Street Journal,* September 23, 1974, p. 1 and February 24, 1975, p. 1.
5. *Economic Report of the President,* pp. 41–42.
6. U.S., Department of Commerce, Bureau of the Census, *Statistical Abstract of the United States 1975: National Data Book and Guide to Sources,* 96th ed. (Washington, D.C.: U.S. Government Printing Office, 1975), p. 392.
7. Ibid., table 648, p. 397.
8. Ibid., table 647, p. 397. It is noteworthy that "head" is not defined, clearly leaving to the reader's subjective interpretation—or preference—whether the husband or the wife is so designated.
9. Ibid., table 635, p. 391.
10. Frances Lomas Feldman, "Public Welfare: Despondency, Despair—and Opportunity," in *Riots in the City: An Addendum to the McCone Commission Report* (Los Angeles: National Association of Social Workers, 1967).
11. Quoted by Anne Draper in "The Price Squeeze on Living Standards," *The American Federalist,* 81 (July 1974):1.
12. James N. Morgan et al., *Five Thousand Families: Patterns of Economic Progress,* 2 vols. (Ann Arbor: Survey Research Center, Institute for Social Research, University of Michigan, 1974).
13. Ibid., p. 3.
14. Frances Lomas Feldman, *Human Services in Rural Alaska: Highlights from the Evaluation of the Rural Areas Service Project* (Los Angeles: University of Southern California, 1972).

2
Economic Behavior in Today's Money World

Some nostalgia persists for the simplicity of life in previous years; indeed some people make a strong effort to recapture "the good old days." But by and large there is general concurrence that the intervening years have brought a marked improvement in the level of living of a large proportion of American families and thereby, in the American standard and quality of life.

Not only has the average family income moved upward, especially over the past quarter century, but output and pay for each hour worked have increased. In consequence, goods and services available per worker and per family also have increased. The rise in general levels of family living is evident in the fact that fewer working hours are required to satisfy basic needs and to provide an increasing number of items that either add to the comfort of living or are regarded as luxuries. It is mirrored in the increased amount of goods consumed and in the changes in the buying habits of the American people. It is seen in the greater volume of sale of goods and services designed for leisure-time activities.

Certain more or less subtle pressures have accompanied the rise in level of living achieved by so many families during the past several decades. The pressures appear in sharper relief as the cost of living has moved steadily upward and the job market has become tighter. Goods and services once thought to be luxuries, within reach only of the very rich, have come to be commonplace. The model of the American family, so widely publicized by the communication media is hardly separable from the "good things in life" and appears accessible to any individual with commonly held aspirations and reasonably good credit standing.

Yet inflation has spelled difficulty for many in acquiring or maintaining goods and services they have come to view as basic to their lifestyle. Some individuals have found it necessary to return to longer hours of work, or to take additional "moonlighting" jobs. Family members who had not previously been employed now seek work to augment family income. In other families, the level of living has been affected by the loss or lessening of earnings of one or more members.

Whether the economic milieu is one of inflation or recession, or both simultaneously, the shift in spending and saving patterns has created for many people a major personal problem—how to balance income with outgo. The problem may be magnified if income has declined for some reason. In fact, the problem may even reach crisis proportions if income has remained essentially the same and family purchases have declined. Irrespective of the level of actual or seeming sufficiency or insufficiency of income, there are three possible spending patterns. One is to spend the total income. Another is to spend part and to save part. The third is to spend more than comes in. Conformity to one of these patterns does not assure that the spending unit is managing either well or poorly, or without some essentials. But the patterns do seem to have strong cultural and social determinants. Thus we must ask: What is purchased with the family money, and what are some of the factors that influence expenditure patterns?

WHERE DOES THE MONEY GO?

In good times and bad it is not uncommon to hear "Where does the money go?" uttered with surprise or anxiety or resentment. This refrain has frequently accompanied the chaotic upward movement of prices during the past several years. As inflation mounts, so does the strain on family financial planning and management. People with low incomes and many families with children are especially affected, but not only they. Regardless of the amount of its income, each family or consumer unit must expend some portions on such fixed items as shelter and food. The proportions differ by size of family, neighborhood in which the family lives (rural, suburban, or urban), food costs (which may be less in rural sections, as income tends to be; or more in certain central city ghettos, where income also tends to be less), and a variety of other factors.

On a national basis, consumption expenditures reveal a striking pattern in the 1960s and well into the 1970s. Expenditures for food, tobacco, and alcoholic beverages, which accounted for 30 percent of national spending in 1960, declined to less than 22 percent in 1972. National expenditures for housing changed very little in proportion to total spending, remaining in the vicinity of 14 percent. This low figure is partially due to the fact that homes that are part of farms were excluded; also, many people occupied mortgage-free homes. The ratio for expenditures for other items—clothing, personal care, household operation, personal business—likewise stayed fairly constant. Transportation costs rose slightly, from 13.3 to 13.8 percent. Medical care expenses and recreation costs, however, showed a larger proportionate increase, the former moving two percentage points to 7.9 percent, and the latter one percentage point to 6.6 percent. Expressed in percentage points, the changes seem small; in dollar terms, they are substantial. And for individual families, the increases were dramatic.

National consumer spending reached record levels in 1973—$804 billion on "personal consumption expenditures" for everything from automobiles, furniture, and stereo equipment to food, clothing, and toothpaste. But, increasingly, consumers purchased less for their money. During 1974 the rate of inflation accelerated to 12 percent and, concurrently, a rapidly spiraling downturn of the economy led to sharp increases in unemployment. Therefore, while for many the growing problem as we moved through 1975 was how to balance income with outgo when income was rising by less than the rate of inflation, for many others the problem centered on managing with sharply curtailed incomes. During 1973 food prices soared 20.1 percent, the price of gasoline 19.7 percent, and home heating fuel 46.8 percent. Contrary to the 1973 experience, the 1974 inflation was more broadly based: prices of all major components of consumption (food, housing, utilities, clothing, transportation, and medical care) rose by more than 10 percent.[1] Spending for automobiles trended steeply downward as a result of the decline in workers' real earnings, and the Arab oil embargo and increased petroleum prices.

THREE SETS OF STANDARDS

There is no existing government index or set of statistics that report how families actually spend their money as they attempt to grapple with fluctuating costs of living. Periodically, the United States Department of Labor's Bureau of Labor Statistics (BLS) publishes a set of "Urban Family Budgets" which helps to answer the question about where the money has gone—but not where a particular family's money has gone or should go. The budgets were developed in response to a Congressional request in the mid-1940s "to find out what it costs a worker's family to live in the large cities of the United States,"[2] and to calculate both the total dollars required and the relative differences in costs among the cities. The three family budgets show how much it costs a family of four persons to maintain certain hypothetical living standards: lower, intermediate, and higher. Similarly, three budgets have been constructed for retired and other selected persons.

In the family budgets, the costs are calculated specifically for the hypothetical family of four that for a century and a half has been used as the baseline for determining family needs and expenditures—perhaps because, at least from the time of Mathew Carey's 1833 essays on wages and family expenditures,[3] there has been family sensitivity to the food requirements of adolescent sons. Hence, the BLS four-person urban family comprises an employed thirty-five- to forty-four-year-old husband, a wife who does not work outside the home, a boy of thirteen, and a girl of eight. The budgets cover necessary current outlays for living expenses, including certain costs connected with holding a job, and Social Security and income taxes withheld from gross earnings. The cost of living estimates are formulated by translating three general living standards (the lower, intermediate, or higher budget) into a list of the commodities, services, and taxes necessary to reach those standards.

The three sets of budgets developed by BLS have become benchmark estimates for budgeting costs for different standards of living. They are widely used by government agencies and private organizations for a variety of purposes, including collective bargaining and determining the costs of welfare services. They are reference points in certain types of legislation dealing with income cutoffs or eligibility for benefits. In point of fact, though, the budget costs at each level are designed to be compared directly with the total annual income (before taxes) of families of the type for which they were prepared: four-person husband-wife families living in urban areas, with a steadily employed head thirty-five- to forty-four years old, a wife who is not in the labor force, a thirteen-year-old son, and an eight-year-old daughter. The family that has been selected, however, does not represent a stage through which most families pass, for the average family size today is less than 3.5 persons. (For application to smaller or larger families, see table of "Annual Consumption Budgets" later in this chapter.)

The budgets are described officially as assuming "that maintenance of health and social well-being, the nurture of children, and participation in community activities are both desirable and necessary social goals for all families of the type for which the budgets were constructed. Within this broad framework the procedures were designed to distinguish different levels of living by varying the assumptions concerning the manner of living, and by providing different quantities and qualities of the necessary goods and services."[4] Accordingly, the manner of living represented by the lower budget differs from that in the intermediate (or moderate) and higher budgets primarily in these specifications: the family lives in rental housing without air conditioning; performs more services for itself; and utilizes free recreation facilities in the community. The lifestyle reflected in the higher budget, on the other hand, specifies a higher level of homeownership, more complete inventories of household appliances and equipment, and more extensive use of purchased services. For a majority of the items in the list of goods and services that are common to the three budgets, both the quantity and quality levels in the lower budget are below, while those in the higher are above the levels designated for the intermediate budget.[5]

All three budgets were priced in various cities, thereby allowing for regional differences. Since their original pricing (spring 1967 and spring 1969), they have been updated from components of the Consumer Price Index (CPI) rather than by direct pricing. Consequently, the budgets have some special value for the counselor who wishes to compare living costs in one city with those in another, or who wants some clues to changing costs that are likely to affect a given family's allocation of income for personal consumption items.

The intermediate standard budget undoubtedly may be regarded as the key one, especially for wage earners whose income falls at or near the median. This budget includes essentials, and some of the amenities American families take for granted as necessities. This standard of living cost $12,626 in the autumn of 1973 according to BLS, or about $243 a week for the 52-week year. Median family income in all households where only the father worked was then $11,418, regardless of family size: about 36 percent of all family incomes fell between $8,000 and $15,000. By autumn 1974 the cost of this budget standard was calculated at $276 per week, or $14,333 for the year.[6] This standard was regarded as neither a subsistence budget nor a luxury budget. Rather, it was an attempt to describe and measure a modest but adequate standard of living.

Family lifestyle is suggested by the budget items listed for the intermediate standard. The family lives in a home bought six years earlier, on which it is making mortgage payments. (In calculating composite budget costs, 75 percent of the families are considered to be homeowners, while 25 percent are renters.) Almost all the families own a car, which is two years old when purchased and is kept for four years. In some cities with extensive public transportation facilities, the car ownership rate is considerably lower. The family eats on the "Moderate Cost Family Food Plan" worked out by the United States Department of Agriculture, which allows for some variety in nutritionally adequate meals. The family can buy some of the higher-priced cuts of meat, a few out-of-season foods, and some convenience foods. The home is equipped with a refrigerator, stove, washing machine, vacuum cleaner, iron, and sewing machine, but the family sometimes uses a laundromat. There is a telephone, television set, radio, and record player. The family subscribes to a newspaper, but little money is allowed for magazines and books. The children go to the movies once a month, the parents go every three months. The family has a hospital-surgical insurance contract for medical care, partly financed by the husband's employer; other medical expenses are paid by the family. There is provision for only $160 a year for life insurance premiums.

The lower and higher budgets in many respects resemble the intermediate. Where it is possible, the lower budget family buys cheaper alternatives or purchases items at below-average prices, thus generally of poorer quality. Smaller quantities are specified for some items, whether or not they are cheaper, and some items are omitted. The higher standard budget, on the other hand, generally provides for more expensive selections where alternatives are available, or for payment of above-average prices that reflect better quality. Several items are added at the higher standard, and quantities frequently are more generous.

Housing costs are the most important difference between the lower budget and the intermediate budget. It is assumed that all of the lower-budget families live in rental housing, with lower rents reflecting less desirable quarters. Fewer families own a car—about two-thirds; the car is six years old when purchased and is driven fewer miles. The food component in the lower budget is based on the Department of Agriculture's "Low-Cost Family Food Plan," which specifies cheaper foods and less variety. Although this plan is nutritionally adequate if it is carefully followed, it has been found that less than one-fourth of the families spending the amount of money budgeted actually do achieve nutritional adequacy. The family buys cheaper clothes and has smaller allowances for recreation and leisure, but the allowance for medical care is the same as in the intermediate budget. At autumn 1973 prices, the overall cost of the lower budget, excluding taxes, was one-third lower than the intermediate budget standard, mainly because of the difference in housing and the lower-cost food plan. The total cost was $8,181, a figure exceeding the income of the 29 percent of all families with the husband as the sole worker and the income at or below $8,000. It also exceeds the median income of female-headed households by more than 30 percent. Although more than a bare subsistence standard, the lower budget does not even approach the minimum satisfaction point represented in the intermediate standard budget; and by autumn 1974, the cost of the lower-standard budget had jumped more than $1,000, to $9,198.

The higher-standard budget (with a more comfortable level and manner of living, sometimes known as the "American Standard of Living") exclusive of taxes is nearly 40 percent higher than that of the intermediate: $18,201 in autumn 1973. It had reached $20,777 a year later—a figure exceeding the incomes of all but approximately 20 percent of American families, and exceeding the median family income of $18,500 comprising earnings of three of its members. Housing is the largest cost component: all but 15 percent of the families are considered to be homeowners, and the cost of housing, whether rented or owned, is higher. Excluding income taxes and Social Security payments, almost 33 percent of this budget is allocated to housing. Food costs account for nearly 30 percent despite the higher costs of food stemming from the utilization of the Department of Agriculture's "Liberal Family Food Plan," which allows for a greater variety of foods and more expensive selections, and from the fact that the family eats out more frequently and at higher-priced restaurants.

Food is the largest component in the net (after taxes) intermediate budget—nearly 33 percent—and housing expenses are just under 30 percent. In the lower-level budget, food is an even more important component of the after-taxes living expenses, even though, in both quantity and price, less money is allocated for food costs—37.8 percent. Housing costs are markedly lower than the intermediate-standard's, and consume about 24 percent of the total living expenses.

All the families in the higher-level budget are presumed to own a car, with 60 percent buying a new one and 40 percent buying a two-year-old car. There is more expensive insurance, and a larger allowance is made for out-of-city travel by public transport. Accordingly, 10.2 percent of the net budget is used to meet transportation costs. Among families in the intermediate-level model, close to 11 percent of the budget is absorbed for transportation. It is expected that 94 percent of the hypothetical families in the intermediate-budget group own cars, except in central cities of large metropolitan areas. The auto-owning family buys a two-year-old used car every four years, trading in a six-year-old car. An allowance is included for a short trip out of the city once a year.

The transportation allowance is lowest in the lower budget—9 percent. It derives from the expectation that two-thirds of the families are automobile owners, the car is six years old when bought, insurance covers liability only, and fewer repairs can be accommodated in the budget. There is no provision for travel out of the city.

Clothing and personal care costs range from 13 percent in the lower to 13.6 percent in the higher budget. Medical care is nearly the same dollar amount in the three budgets except for an additional premium for major medical insurance coverage in the higher budget; however, this cost accounts for a higher proportion of the lower budget (10 percent) than of either of the others (6.8 percent of the intermediate, and 5.2 percent of the higher). Recreation, on the other hand, both in dollars and percentages, is a larger item (8.8 percent) in the higher budget.

Total budget costs included the income and Social Security taxes the family would have to pay on income received from earnings. Sales and property taxes are not included because the former are incorporated in the prices of purchased items and property taxes are included as part of the costs of homeownership. Accordingly, for the hypothetical families at the lower-budget level, the taxes amount to 16 percent, leaving a "spendable" income of $7,318. The intermediate budget provides for taxes that are 19.5 percent of the total income, leaving a spendable income of $10,880. At the higher-budget level 22.6 percent is allocated for taxes, leaving a net budget figure of $14,976.

The budget costs vary substantially between cities because of the differences in price levels and other conditions. Climate, for example, affects clothing and home heating requirements. Types of food bought vary in different regions; budgets for southern cities reflect lower cost foods. Transportation costs vary depending upon automobile usage. State and local taxes may differ significantly. Generally, however, the largest cost differential from city to city occurs in housing.

Price trends for older and elderly couples follow roughly the same pattern as for families in all three budget standards. At all three levels prices rose more than 20 percent in 1973, with the greatest increases experienced by the intermediate-budget level couples. The following year saw price increases moderate somewhat at all levels, but expenditures for a low-cost food plan increased 11.5 percent for the older couple (aged 55–75) while the liberal food plan cost rose only 9.2 percent.[7] For an elderly couple over 75 years of age, the disparity between the low-cost and liberal food plans was even greater—2.5 percentage points.

In addition to the broader community purposes attributed to them earlier, the three sets of standards for the retired couples and for families as shown in Tables 2 and 3 offer a point of reference for understanding how much income families need to cover necessary outlays to maintain a given standard of living. As working tools for the social worker, the three standards for the stipulated hypothetical families and retired per-

TABLE 2. ANNUAL CONSUMPTION BUDGETS FOR A FOUR-PERSON FAMILY AT THREE LEVELS OF LIVING, URBAN UNITED STATES, AUTUMN 1974

Budget comparison	Lower level $	%	Intermediate level $	%	Higher level $	%
Total budget, 1974	$9,198		$14,333		$20,777	
Increase over 1973	1,017	12.4	1,707	13.5	2,576	14.2
Total family consumption	*$7,318*	*79.6*	*$10,880*	*76.0*	*$14,976*	*72.0*
food	2,763	37.8	3,548	32.6	4,453	29.7
housing[a]	1,758	24.0	3,236	29.7	4,900	32.7
transportation[b]	643	9.0	1,171	10.8	1,521	10.2[b]
clothing	759	10.0	1,085	10.0	1,589	10.6
personal care	231	3.0	310	2.8	439	3.0
medical care	738	10.0	742	6.8	774	5.2
other family consumption[c]	423	6.0	786	7.2	1,297	8.7
Other items	*$415*	*4.5*	*$662*	*4.6*	*$1,113*	*3.4*
Taxes and deductions	*$1,463*	*16.0*	*$2,790*	*19.5*	*4,686*	*22.6*
Social Security & Disability	553	6.0	780	5.4	787	3.8
Personal income taxes	910	10.0	2,010	14.0	3,899	18.8
Totals	*$9,198*	*100.0*	*$14,333*[d]	*100.0*	*$20,777*[d]	*100.0*[d]

SOURCE: U.S., Dept. of Labor, *Autumn 1974 Urban Family Budgets & Comparative Indexes for Selected Urban Areas,* 4/9/75, p. 2.
[a]Housing includes shelter, household operations, house furnishings and lodgings out of the home city.
[b]All families are considered to be automobile owners.
[c]Insurance (life), contributions, occupational expenses.
[d]Rounded off.

sons are of great value. At the same time, their implied prescription for expenditure oversimplifies the relationship of a family of given size and income to its anticipated and actual expenditures. A family's well-being is dependent upon many complex factors, among which are such common measures as the source and amount of family money income or the earnings of the family head, the quantities and types of food required for adequate nutrition, the cost of rent or homeownership in a particular community, and so forth. But also of importance are the instability of family economic status (as well as of economic milieu), the aspirations of individual members in the family and their potential for realizing these

TABLE 3. ANNUAL CONSUMPTION BUDGETS FOR SELECTED FAMILY TYPES URBAN UNITED STATES, AUTUMN 1974

Family size; type; and age	Lower level	Intermediate level	Higer level
Single person, under 35	$2,560	$3,810	$5,240
Husband and wife under 35			
0 children	3,590	5,330	7,340
1 child under 6	4,590	6,750	9,290
2 children; older, under 6	5,270	7,830	10,780
Husband and wife, 35–54			
1 child, 6–15 years	6,000	8,920	12,280
2 children; older, 6–15[a]	7,318	10,880	14,976
3 children; oldest, 6–15	8,490	12,620	17,370
Husband and wife, 65 and over[b]	3,730	5,550	7,640
Single person, 65 and over[c]	2,050	3,050	4,190

SOURCE: U.S., Dept. Labor, *Autumn 1974 Urban Family Budgets & Comparative Indexes for Selected Urban Areas*, 4/9/75, p. 7. For details on estimating procedures, see "Revised Equivalence Scale," *BLS Bulletin 1570-2*.

[a] Costs for the BLS budgets for a 4-person family from which estimates for other family types are derived.
[b] Estimated from the equivalence scale value of 51 percent of the base (4-person) family.
[c] Estimated from the equivalence scale value of 28 percent of the base (4-person) family. May differ slightly from estimates obtained by applying a ratio of 55 percent to the BLS Budget for a retired couple.

aspirations, the perceptions of family members and groups about the lifestyles of peers or other models, and other attitudes and feelings that are shared or unique.

FAMILY SPENDING

Although family income and standards of living largely determine the proportion of after-taxes income that can be utilized for food and shelter, the consumer generally has considerable discretion as to what will be purchased with the balance of the income. Relatively heavy fixed payments occur at the lower-income level: rent; property taxes; payments on mortgages, instalment debts, life insurance, Social Security, retirement and pension funds; and payments mandated by law or by prearranged contractual or quasi-contractual commitment. Such payments tend to account for more than 40 percent of the family's income. As income rises, the proportion obligated to fixed payments tends to become smaller, dropping to the lowest level when income exceeds $20,000. But at what point does a family live within its means—that is, meet its needs out of recurring income?

A Gallup opinion poll taken in August 1974 sought to learn the answer by asking its respondents whether the family currently lived within, somewhat beyond, or far beyond its means.[8] The composite national response disclosed that while 80 percent did live within their means, only 67 percent of the families in the $5,000 to $7,000 income group and 71 percent of those with annual incomes under $3,000 did so. These latter two income groups also contributed the largest number reporting that they live far beyond their means. (Here, too, were the largest fractions of those classified as expressing "no opinion.") Respondents under thirty years of age were noted as more inclined to be living beyond their means—more than a fourth—with a substantial portion classified as living far beyond. The proportion of nonwhite respondents living within their means was substantially smaller than the proportion of white respondents, 62 percent compared with 83 percent. How many of these nonwhite respondents were also in younger-age or lower-income groups was not shown. The poll did not suggest (other than "somewhat" or "far") how far beyond their means any of the respondents were living. Nor did it indicate how the deficiency was being met, if it was. As in other instances, however, the likelihood is that the deficiency is met either by dissaving—that is, drawing on accumulated savings or other assets—or, especially in the higher-income groups, by borrowing and otherwise increasing liabilities.

For shelter

Despite the fact that the proportion of income paid for shelter has been markedly consistent over a number of years, the housing situation itself has changed dramatically. Homeownership has long been an acknowledged part of the American dream; it represents a measure of economic or emotional security, independence, privacy, income, achievement, social status, or some combination of these. Both numerically and in proportion to total population, homeownership has increased steadily.

The 1970 Census disclosed that nearly 63 percent of all families lived in houses they owned, with another 4 percent in trailers or mobile homes. Lower-income families were more likely to rent, and families with higher incomes were more likely to own. For example, barely half of those with incomes below $5,000 a year owned their homes; nearly 85 percent of those with incomes above $15,000 owned their homes. Furthermore, the proportion of homeowners among families living in suburbs rose to nearly 96 percent, regardless of income. Whether a family owns or rents is highly dependent on the age of the family head. While the median age of the homeowner was fifty, nearly 16 percent were under thirty-four.

In most parts of the United States, improved incomes and the availability of mortgage arrangements have made possible more privacy and better space per person. Veterans' loans for mortgages and other government-insured mortgage plans have contributed significantly to the improvement of housing conditions. At the same time, they also have contributed significantly to an increase in the number of persons who incur relatively large debts early in the family life cycle. Thus, in reporting on mortgage, construction, and real estate markets for the first three years of the 1970s, the *Federal Reserve Bulletin* pointed to an increased demand for homeownership by individuals and family heads entering the twenty-five to thirty-five-year-old age group, a group "with the highest potential for a first-home purchase,"[9] a group containing many veterans recently eligible to use federal or state mortgage programs as a mortgage resource.

The trend toward homeownership continued steadily well into 1974 despite the equally steady rise in mortgage-interest rates so intimately a part of the inflationary cycle. The elevated median costs of new homes ($32,200—$5,000 above 1972) and existing homes (nearly $30,000)[10] represented an increase in building costs, expansion in size of quarters, and greater availability of modern plumbing and labor-saving devices.

There has been a marked change, however, in the kinds of homes being purchased, a change indicating both differences in lifestyles and costs attendant on homeownership. More families have been buying apartments, through either condominium or cooperative arrangements. (The buyer owns the apartment in the condominium; in the cooperative, the buyer owns shares in a group which owns the property.) But undoubtedly, the fastest-growing type of housing is the mobile home. In 1971, trailer owners were largely in the lower middle-income group, earning between $3,000 and $10,000 annually, and often were either very young or early retirees on fixed incomes. The former were more likely to be families without children or with only one child, and non-white families were only a small fraction of the trailer owners. A large part of the growth in mobile home sales during the 1971–73 period probably can be attributed to the limited number of conventional low-priced single-family dwellings constructed in recent years. Moreover, mobile home construction standards and parks have been upgraded to make mobile homes a more acceptable type of shelter. Most of these homes have been relatively inexpensive, costing under $10,000. During 1973, however, the average new contract including finance charges came to $12,250 and these purchases—ebbing in 1974 for lack of financing—accounted for a substantial portion of homes under $20,000 purchased in that period.

During the past two decades, paralleling somewhat the rise in homeownership and undoubtedly closely related to it, there has been a steady overall decrease in the doubling of families in housing accommodations; and the number of married couples with no home of their own has declined. Families broken by death or other causes have not given up their homes as readily as in the past. It has not yet been documented whether these trends have been halted or even reversed in the recent climate of economic inflation. However, there are increasing signs that unemployed young families join forces with families of older relatives; that divorced family units are often unable to continue to meet the costs of homeownership on incomes that must support two separate households; and that retired couples move into their adult children's households to stretch inflexible incomes.

The steady movement of households from rural-farm to nonfarm areas has been continuing, as has the trend to suburban living. The latter trend has brought about many changes in living patterns and, therefore, in expenditure patterns. Recently, black families and families of other ethnic-minority groups also have followed this pattern as conditions of discrimination in housing and jobs have been altered. At the same time, the flow of white middle-income families from the central cities—and especially the inner core of the urban center—to the outlying residential areas has accelerated, leaving behind relatively dense populations of families and elderly persons with lagging incomes, regardless of ethnicity. A counter trend also appears: families moving back to restored central-city areas, like Georgetown near the nation's capital.

Whether one owns or rents a home—conventional, mobile, or apartment—or whether the family lives in or out of a metropolitan area often may be explained by clusters of demographic variables. Income, age, family size, and family composition are interrelated throughout the life cycle. Income alone does not appear to determine the facts of home ownership or where the home is located. The decision to buy or rent seems to be less related to the availability of rental units than to job-related stability or mobility. Female-headed families have lower homeownership rates than do male-headed families. This is explained not only by the lower income generally available to the female-headed family, but also by the fact that women have faced discrimination in mortgage markets and this fact has reduced the probability of their becoming homeowners. Public Law 93–495, which became effective in late 1975, amends the Truth-in-Lending Act by prohibiting discrimination in granting credit because of sex or marital status. The impact of this legislation on property ownership by women seeking mortgages is yet to be seen.

Of interest is the growing number of families who own a second home which may be rented seasonally or continuously, or serve as a vacation cottage for the family. In 1967, 2.9 percent of American households owned a second home; by 1970, the percentage had increased to 4.6.

FOR MOTOR VEHICLES

The proportion of American families not owning a car has been steadily contracting during the past several decades. By early 1971 only 17 percent of American families owned no motor vehicle.[11] More than 30 percent of American families, however, owned two cars. In that year and until late 1973, a boom in new-car sales was fostered by anticipation of future price increases and the availability of new models on which prices were held to prior levels by the wage-and-price-freeze authority granted under the Economic Stabilization Act. Before the freeze, as in previous periods of rapidly rising prices, consumers had been allocating an unusually large share of their disposable income to saving. Indeed, 1970 had witnessed a sharp decline in the purchases of new automobiles, with only 9 percent of American families buying new cars as contrasted to the preceding year with 13 percent who purchased new cars. But purchases of used cars had increased slightly, many families buying late model used cars instead of new ones or also, used cars two to four years old.

TABLE 4. OWNERSHIP OF TWO OR MORE CARS, BY ANNUAL FAMILY INCOME, 1973

Annual family income	Percent of all households
Under $3,000	8.3
3,000–4,999	12.5
5,000–7,499	18.4
7,500–9,999	28.4
10,000–14,999	41.2
15,000–24,999	59.4
25,000 & over	69.0

Ownership of two or more cars was to be found at every income level during 1973 as table 4 shows.[12] These figures do not, of course, suggest the vintage of the cars. Nor do they indicate the changes that might have occurred in either ownership or usage of the cars when the gasoline costs rose precipitously in the subsequent years. But they do underscore the reliance of Americans on automobiles for transportation, especially in relation to the movement to suburbia. And they point to the associated expenditures for maintenance: insurance, repairs and replacement of parts, fuel, and instalment payments. Even with the rate of expansion in automobile purchases diminishing in 1973–75, automobile credit continued to be the largest single component of total outstanding consumer credit. Approximately 17 percent of car purchasers pay cash.[13] In December 1974 alone, the other 83 percent owed $51.6 millions in instalment payments for automobiles.[14]

A sizable proportion of American families own trucks of some sort, sometimes in addition to a passenger car, and sometimes more than one truck. In 1971, for example, 17 percent of all families owned a truck, pick-up, van, or jeep-type vehicle; indeed, one percent of all families owned more than one, with the largest proportions among families with incomes of $5,000 to $7,499 (2 percent) and $15,000 or more (4 percent).[15] When ownership of trucks was added to the ownership of passenger automobiles, the proportion of families without a vehicle dropped to only 15 percent.

The motorcycle has gained growing ownership in the past several years. Featured increasingly in television and magazine advertisements, motorcycles appear to find special favor in periods marked by gasoline shortages and higher gasoline prices.

FOR EDUCATION

The role of the automobile in the current economic scene, stellar though it is, is not as dramatic as that of education. It has had a marked impact on the economic situation of individuals and families and, indeed, on the economic system itself. Probably the single most important factor in reducing social and economic inequality in the past several centuries has been the increasing accessibility of education, particularly public education. A sharp upward trend in high school enrolment followed World War I. The years immediately after World War II saw a tremendous increase in college enrolment, probably because of the availability of veterans' benefits and also because the provision of a wide spectrum of public and private scholarship aid plans was stimulated by the increasingly accepted concept that every young American with the capacity for college education should be able to have it. In 1950, for example, nearly 70 percent of American adults had not completed high school. By 1975 the figure had dropped below 20 percent. In 1950 the median number of years of schooling completed was 9.3; in 1975 it reached 12.7, with more than 20 percent of the adult population having completed four or more years of college.

Why is there so much emphasis on the economics of education? A necessary correlation between education and mental ability is often assumed—that higher achievement in the former is dependent on higher capacity in the latter. Human capital theory states that there must be an interaction between them; that if ability and education simply had added ill effects on wages, then those with lower ability would have had the greatest incentive to acquire more education because the pay-off to education would be the same for all. However, the foregone earnings of those with higher ability would be greater. Thus, while it would appear to be true that the greatest return from education is to those with greatest ability, persons with lower ability nevertheless benefit from increased education.[16] Certainly, this is evidenced negatively in the high rate of unemployment and underemployment among those with limited education and among the one percent of the population (over 3 percent of the black population) deemed to be illiterate.[17]

According to the Bureau of Labor Statistics, in 1972 men with college degrees could expect to have lifetime earnings more than two-and-one-half times those of the man with less than eight years of schooling.[18] Comparable data were not available for women. However, while earning potential is frequently cited as a primary reason for obtaining more education, there is also sensitivity to the importance of education as a component in individual well-being and in the attainment of life satisfactions in general. The status- and satisfactions-importance of achieving educational aspirations is evident in the pervasiveness and continued appearance of "slick" advertisements that directly or inferentially paint the image of the thoughtful and provident father as one who safeguards the future college education of his young children by purchasing and maintaining the "right" kind of insurance. The growing regard for more education as an essential ingredient for economic security and assurance of a good quality-of-life standard is manifest in the 7.4 percent of the 1974 gross national product that represented public and private school expenditures. In 1960 such expenditures accounted for only 5.1 percent. Whereas approximately 5 percent of the latter centered on higher education in 1960, more than 25 percent of the 1974 education expenditure went for higher education, chiefly in the public sector.[19]

More people appear to want more education and to be willing to make the financial and other investments necessary to acquire it. Although a usual concomitant of prolonged education is a delayed earning period—characterized by greater earning capacity and a higher potential earning peak—a substantial proportion of college students earn part or all of their expenses throughout the educational experience. The increased availability of work-study arrangements sponsored by government and by educational and other institutions has brought higher education (even the likelihood of completing high school) within the reach of many who in other times would have been unable to maintain themselves as students. This has been a particularly noteworthy trend among poor and marginal-income Caucasian and non-Caucasian families.

Rising costs of education, coupled with generally greater inflationary and other demands on family income, have begun to have a negative impact on the educational prospects of young people in middle-income families, especially those with several school-age children. Some state and federal government programs have endeavored to be responsive to the particular plight of the middle-income family unable to divert enough of its recurring income to meet steadily growing educational costs. The form and extent of this responsiveness, however, are subject to modification because of such factors as the nation's economic health at any given time, and governmental program and expenditure priorities.

FOR NONDURABLES

The ownership of homes, of college degrees, of cars, and of other durables has long been regarded as an indicator of the general standard of living and the economic position of Americans. These, of course, are visible clues. Other dimensions of family spending mandate consideration of the quality of individual and family life: expenditures for food, health care, fuel, recreation, clothing, telephone, and others.

Over the past several decades, increasing and well publicized knowledge about food and health care has influenced markedly the amount families spend for food. Although changing food patterns and generally improved nutrition have not been an inevitable consequence of mounting incomes, the sums families spend on groceries and on dining out have risen dramatically. A recently released government survey reported that the amount spent for restaurant meals rose steeply as income increased, exceeding one-third of the total spent for food by families earning more than $10,000 a year.[20]

The growing utilization of health and mental health services often has stemmed from or led to substantial nongovernmental expenditures for health insurance and other arrangements for meeting health costs. These may be group hospital and medical plans, with the costs met fully or partially by employers or unions, or met entirely by the employee individually or as a member of a professional or other organization. In 1973 more than 74 million persons under age 65 had some form of group health insurance coverage; another nearly 8.5 million carried individual and family policies.[21] Just what the actual cost of health care is to the average family is uncertain. What is paid for by insurance plans and what is supplemented by family payments under given circumstances varies tremendously because of a wide range of factors including age, geographic location, nature and duration of medical treatment, availability of specialist and laboratory resources, and even because of the breadwinner's denying illness to avoid absence from work and possibly reduced earnings. The accelerated pressure to develop a national health care plan is evidence of our sensitivity to the importance of assuring that all Americans have access to reasonable health care at a price they can afford. This sensitivity has been heightened by recent awareness that thousands of families overtaken by unemployment have also lost their employment-related group health insurance protection, which they are unable to maintain independently at the same level. Health care thus has become a "nondurable" with several meanings! The absence of adequate health insurance or other resources for meeting health costs is now an increasingly compelling reason for dissaving, for borrowing, and for shifting to instalment-buying arrangements the purchase of certain durables that under other circumstances the family would have purchased on a cash or thirty-day-pay plan.

Industrialization and advances in modern technology have contributed to changes in our perception of and investment in health care needs; they have also made available and created an ever more avid demand for telephones, and for electricity, natural gas, and other forms of energy. What not long ago were regarded as luxuries have become essentials—long-distance telephoning for closer contact with absent relatives, for example. Moreover, the dependency of so many households on such durables as automobiles, freezers, and air conditioners has led to a concomitant dependency on certain nondurables: unprecedented fuel and energy requirements, and the convenience of purchasing frozen foods or freezing home-prepared foods.

Since 1973, spending for nondurables has risen with relative rapidity, especially for food, beverages, clothing, shoes, and gasoline—reaching an increase rate of 15 percent per year.[22] The outlays for all these items did not reflect much change in the actual amount purchased; the upsurge in spending was attributable mainly to very large price increases for food, fuel, gasoline, and oil. For some key items (food primarily) spending rose less than prices, thus confirming what various public opinion polls had indicated; decreased consumption of food or the purchase of cheaper foods was significant among the measures families took to keep the outgo of their financial resources in better balance with their income. Real consumption of gasoline and real outlays for household consumption of electricity, gas, and other forms of energy dropped appreciably, despite the substantial increase in the number of dollars being spent for these nondurables.

Consumer spending for services also was trending downward in 1974 and early 1975. A new pattern had emerged: a larger share of the buying dollar was going into nondurable goods and a smaller share into durable goods.[23] What does this shift signify with respect to the longtime steady rise in the living standards of American families and the overt manifestations of this rise?

FOR CONSUMER CREDIT

A high and rising living standard has been especially prized in the United States. For two centuries, rostrums around the world resounded with admiration for this nation's vast natural resources and the unlimited opportunities available for those ready to struggle to improve their lot. Indeed, the elevation of median family income figures and the data on expansion of home and auto ownership as well as rising educational levels in the years following World War II are indicators that the American middle-class standard came within reach of a substantial proportion of the total population. And despite their low annual incomes, even the rural and urban poor have had access to middle-class amenities and accouterments. By 1974 half of all American families had moved into newly built houses. The number of privately owned automobiles had increased three times as fast as the population. Four-fifths of the population owned at least black and white television, and close to half owned color television. More than three-fourths had automatic washing machines and refrigerators. Substantial numbers at all income levels had automatic clothes dryers, dishwashers, and air conditioners.

Is the larger volume of owners of homes or durables possible simply because disposable income has advanced faster than costs in the past few decades? Is it the consequence of the entrance into the labor force of more family members—millions of wives and teenagers—that resulted in families having more spendable income? The likelihood exists that increased family income has merely accelerated the ease with which families can purchase their advancing standard of living on the instalment plan. For the use of credit as a device to cope with the difference between family income and outgo has long been with us, perhaps changed largely in form and scale rather than in purpose or outcome. Furthermore, the growing use of credit and the newer forms in which it is available have contributed to changing attitudes about consumer credit, and led to myriad legislative measures to clarify and even control the increasingly prevalent and complex creditor-consumer relationships.

The expanding use of credit has been simultaneously a contributor to and a consequence of changes in societal attitudes that once openly despaired about the morality of people "living on credit" but now complacently accept consumer credit as a "way of life." Certainly the early generations in this country considered the maxim "neither a borrower nor a lender be" good advice, and they admired Poor Richard's advice to earn a penny by saving it. This bent toward living well within one's means, saving for the future, postponing gratification until its costs could be met with cash, had at least some of its roots in two facts laced together with necessity. One was Benjamin Franklin's personal predicament, about which he said: "It is necessary for me to be extremely frugal for some time, til I have paid what I owe."[24] The other was the reinforcement of the Pilgrims' adherence to the Puritan ethic of thrift through devotion of effort to repaying the loan that had enabled them to sail to the New World, a debt negotiated and renegotiated and finally discharged after a quarter of a century. The mortgage was perhaps the primary exception to censure, for payments toward purchase of a modest home, and particularly land, connoted stability and worth in contrast to the self-gratification or improvidence to be inferred from the presence of other debts.

However, debt is no longer frowned upon or viewed as disgraceful. It is an integral part of the pattern of living for most American families. Banks, consumer finance companies, manufacturers, and retailers encourage families to mortgage the future in order to enjoy today. Even the credit union urges its members not just to use its services to meet financial emergencies but to finance a new car and other durables as well. New cars, television sets, automatic dishwashers, electric refuse compactors, or travel in or out of the country can be bought on credit. The fact that neighbors and friends have adopted this pattern provides incentive to yearning young couples to do the same. Inflationary changes or other economic trends may affect both prices and accessibility of certain commodities or services. Wars, sickness, or sensitivity to other circumstances beyond the control of the individual may encourage older families to decide to "live it up," for "you can't take it with you." More than 82 percent of the money on loan to family units in December 1974 was in the form of instalment credit: more than $156 billion in that single month was for loans to purchase automobiles or other durables, for home improvement loans, and personal loans. In that single month an additional $34 billion was outstanding in the form of noninstallment loans: single-payment loans, charge accounts in retail outlets and credit cards, and service credit.[25]

CREDIT CARDS
Particularly significant is the growth in credit card usage, notably bank credit cards. Consumers have been increasing their use of bank credit cards not only in lieu of cash when making retail purchases of goods and services but also as a substitute for small short-term personal loans.[26] A study of bank credit-card lending, summarized in a 1973 *Federal Reserve Bulletin*,[27] shows that the average balance on active bank-card accounts at the end of the preceding year was slightly more than $250; retail purchases using bank credit cards averaged about $20 per transaction; and, although finance rates on balances carried beyond the "interest-free" period were in a range of a 15 to 18 percent annual rate, fewer than 3 out of every 10 accounts typically were paid within the interest-free period. It should be noted that some states have placed statutory ceilings on the amount of interest that may be charged after the interest-free period; these maximums may fall below the 18 percent annual rate. One might wonder whether the growing credit-card culture and mentality may yield a generation of Americans so accustomed to having their bills paid for them by credit-card purveyors that the bill-paying process, except to the bank or credit-card company, becomes increasingly remote, taking on a semblance of unreality that ultimately disenfranchises the individual from management of his or her income! And today's credit-card purchasing may soon be handled by a routine transfer of funds out of a bank account to which the employer has forwarded the individual's paycheck.

CONSUMER INSTALMENT DEBT
American families not only have gone into credit-card debt in large numbers, but one out of every two families has some form of consumer instalment debt.[29] Instalment debt ordinarily comprises all private, non-mortgage debt which is subject to three or more regular payments by the individual or family, regardless of timing. Not included are thirty-day charge accounts and transactions in which the purchaser promises to pay within that period. However, instalment indebtedness includes revolving charge accounts. Purchases of cars or other durables, such as automobiles, refrigerators, and furniture, loans for nonmortgage debt related to house additions or repair expenses, loans for other major transactions

centering on specific items, including loans to consolidate debts—all of these are categorized as instalment debt. Current bills and financial obligations related to business or other investments to make money, or to real estate not being used personally by the family are excluded from the definition.

On the average, the percentage of family net income used to pay instalment debt is now close to 20 percent nationwide, ranging from one (or a minimal percentage) to 30 or 40 percent. Studies have found that the highest average ratios of outstanding instalment debt are among middle-income families and, contrary to the fairly widely held view, low-income families are in fact less inclined to be deeply in debt: these families are voluntarily more cautious in their use of instalment debt, maintaining debt balances that are smaller proportions of their income than do middle-income families, or they are excluded from the credit market because they are not deemed to be good risks. The higher the income above the median point, the lower is the ratio of debt to income,[28] perhaps because of a greater capacity to pay cash for expensive purchases from the larger recurring income or from accumulated resources. The reluctance that was so prevalent until recently on the part of credit grantors to extend credit to single women or to women heads of households, even when their incomes were above the relatively low median income of woman family heads, undoubtedly has contributed to the fact that families with a single parent as the family head spend less of their income on durables. And these items are a major reason for instalment debt.

Senator William Proxmire also reported that the heaviest users of consumer credit are families with children, with household heads under 45 years of age, and with annual incomes ranging from $10,000 to $15,000; that two out of every three families with these characteristics are in debt; and that for those with instalment debt the average debt is over $4,000. Others also point to young middle-income families as deepest in debt.[30] They have come to be the stereotype of persons who use consumer credit.

Yet, these users of consumer credit live in different environments geographically and culturally and are motivated in their use of instalment credit by various factors. Tests for differences in expenditure patterns for durables among income and life cycle groups[31] revealed that regardless of income, families in the younger life cycle groups, childless or not, tend to spend a larger proportion of their income on durables than do older people. Older married couples in income groups under $15,000, whose children have left home, spend a substantially smaller fraction of their income on instalment payments for durables. This difference may be the result of the number of retired persons among this group. It may arise from the fact that older persons are likely to have the durable consumer goods they feel they need. It may also reflect attitudes of an older generation toward the use of consumer credit, reinforced by access to resources that permit payment in cash and saving of the costs inherent in the purchase of instalment credit. However, even among high-income families with few retired persons, families whose children have left home have fewer than average expenditure rates for credit purchases of durables. Again, this may be because they possess sufficient income and financial reserves to procure the wanted item; or it may stem from the fact that they grew up amidst attitudes toward consumer credit that were unfavorable and when thrift, rather than nonthrift, was considered a desirable attribute.

Borrowing for home improvements was bolstered during 1973 and rose to a new high by the beginning of 1975, probably because of the energy shortage. Reportedly, families took advantage of special terms offered by many lending institutions for such improvements as conversion of heating units or installation of storm windows or insulation.[32] In addition, the relatively high level of interest rates on new mortgages, as well as other factors, prompted some homeowners to add to or alter their dwellings in preference to acquiring a new residence.

PERSONAL LOANS

The overall rate of expansion in personal loan indebtedness has been substantial during the past five years, notwithstanding some lag behind that for other major types of consumer instalment credit.[33] This may be more apparent than real because cash advances on bank credit cards are not counted as personal loans. The average term for personal loans made by consumer finance companies as of the end of 1974 was 34 months, and at commercial banks, 12 months. Rates of charge for cash loans generally vary from 36 percent annually on the smallest to 12 percent on larger well-secured loans. The rates, established by statutes in the various states, take account of the fact that the consumer applies for a loan or financing without verified evidence as to assets and liabilities. This practice is in contrast to the usual basis on which business loans are negotiated, wherein the borrower is required to provide a verified statement of net worth to support the loan application. This practice suggests the likelihood that the borrower from the consumer finance company had limited resources. Indeed, the largest proportion of borrowers from these facilities appears to fall in the $3,500 to $11,999 income bracket.[34]

The national average for loans from all consumer finance companies surveyed over a two-year period and reported in the *Federal Reserve Bulletin* exceeded $1,000. The national average monthly payment per borrower was more than $21 per account.[35]

DEBT REPAYMENT

Whether borrowing is a plan of choice to facilitate meeting the costs of nondurables or to finance the purchase of durables, many families and individuals find their debts outpacing their ability to pay. During 1972 and 1973, delinquency rates at major financial institutions climbed quite steadily, to a level not seen since 1949.[36] Various reasons have been proffered for this situation but the primary ones appear to be business recession in combination with inflation, and the costs and presumed scarcity of fuel. To the latter have been attributed the delinquency rates for recreational vehicles such as campers, and for cars. Repossession of these vehicles has become more frequent. A sharp increase in the delinquency rate of mobile homes has also been observed,[37] and perhaps this is more alarming than repossession of campers and automobiles, for in a time of reduced home building, mobile homes have become a shelter mainstay of two relatively low-income age groups: very young families and retired couples.

Families and individuals have resorted to various ways to cope with the necessity for repaying debt. They have refinanced home mortgages, but the substantial rise in mortgage interest rates for more than a decade has made such long-term refinancing relatively less attractive and, for lower-income families, unfeasible. A sizable number of homeowners have borrowed on a second mortgage. In 1970 such mortgages had an outstanding balance of approximately $3,250, about a quarter the size of the average first mortgage.[38] For many consumers, the advantage of being able to borrow such a large sum on a second mortgage, which often can be repaid on an instalment basis over a medium-to-long time period, apparently outweighs the disadvantage of an additional trust on their property. For many, moreover, it is likely that this is the only borrowing resource available to them.

An increasing number of families in recent years have been turning to nonprofit consumer credit counseling agencies for help in working out ways of discharging their accumulated debts. The reason for the indebtedness that brings families to such an agency are legion and the amount of the indebtedness per family is generally substantial. An analysis, for example, of 79 families who, in January 1975, sought counseling help from the nonprofit Consumer Credit Counselors of Los Angeles revealed indebtedness ranging from approximately $600 to $21,000 (exclusive of mortgage obligations), with the average exceeding $5,700, while the average monthly take-home salary approximated $700. Two-thirds owed substantial sums on automobiles, and nearly this number were in debt to no fewer than six creditors, some having more than thirteen. By far the largest number gave "mismanagement" or "overextension" as the reason for the unmanaged debts. Health and health care bills (including dental) were second, with marital problems following close behind. Whether the marital problems were precipitants or distillates of the financial difficulties was not ascertained; nor was the extent of overlapping in categories assayed.

Especially noteworthy is that six of the couples in the 79-family sample had already experienced personal bankruptcy prior to seeking help in managing their current indebtedness. The utilization of bankruptcy as a device for "starting fresh"—often an expectation grounded in myth—has trended upward for several years and is currently accelerating. There are differences of opinion as to the significance of the numbers of personal bankruptcies that have been filed in this decade, the differences possibly occasioned at least in part by fluctuations reflecting the limitations in state laws and in the 1968 (Federal) Consumer Protection Act that exempt more of the debtor's income from wage attachments and garnishments and, hence, lessen the need for officially declaring bankruptcy.

There also are differences of opinion as to whether bankruptcy is or is not an honorable way of coping with indebtedness. That the longtime uncertainty felt by individuals in our society on this point has a basis in tradition is evident in the history of social policy development in this arena—from at least ancient Roman times when bankruptcy was intended solely to protect creditors against unscrupulous borrowers, especially those thought to merit being made miserable as punishment for either absconding or having untruthfully described themselves as insolvent and unable to meet their just obligations. Degradation—even to wearing specified types of garments—was the statutory punishment to which debtors were subjected in the Middle Ages. Not until the latter part of the sixteenth century did statutes distinguish between dishonest debtors and those truly bankrupt. However, such statutes, enacted first in Great Britain, did little to affect general attitudes about bankrupts. The indecision as to whether the debtors deserved protection was mirrored in the American legislative experience as well. From the beginning, Congress was empowered to pass "uniform laws on the subject of Bankruptcies throughout the United States" but did not do so until 1800, and then repealed the act several years later. A series of panics led to the passage of several bankruptcy laws, culminating in the Bankruptcy Act of 1898 which still constitutes the core of American bankruptcy law, although modified during and after the Depression of the 1930s.

While the primary intent of today's law is to enable the hopelessly overburdened debtor to make a fresh start, the traditional attitude persists that an insolvent bankrupt is something of a criminal. Consequently, even though persons unable otherwise to cope with their debt burdens have turned in greater numbers to existing laws for help, others have not sought such remedies and instead have contemplated or resorted to suicide. The 1929 stock market crash left a legacy of dramatic reports of debtor suicides. Today, surveys disclose an increase in the suicide rate linked to financial pressures exacerbated by indebtedness and unemployment.[39]

Many Americans have accumulated savings in various forms that they can call on not only to protect them against financial emergencies but also to soften the fall into deeper debt. Such liquid assets include checking and savings accounts, savings bonds, stocks. A currently popular television commentator on personal financial matters repeatedly admonishes his listeners to have six months' income in savings. That this admonition has not been followed by any sizable fraction of the population may be inferred from the fact that in 1971 the median liquid asset holdings, irrespective of income level, amounted to $700, down from the previous two years. Indeed, 16 percent of families were reported to own no assets, another 26 percent to have less than $500, 24 percent to possess as much as $2,000, and only 12 percent to have $10,000 or over.[40] The latest official data were reported for the year 1971, although news releases all through 1974 and 1975 implied that Americans were saving rather than spending, and dissaving to keep their outgo in balance with their income.

THE QUALITY OF LIFE

Studies made in the 1930s show that first-generation immigrants who came to the United States as adults tended to maintain a minimal level of consumption, somewhat comparable to that prevailing in the home country, and to save as much money as possible in order to acquire material security. The second generation did not place primary emphasis on saving but on maintaining a standard of living that conformed with that of the group with which they wished to identify. The first generation higher income and the higher living standards, often made possible primarily through the use of consumer credit, in recent years have come to be regarded as major measures of the quality of life. The growing use of this term can be traced to at least two sources. The statement of President Dwight Eisenhower's Commission on National Goals in 1960 developed criteria for assessing the quality of life. Later, President Lyndon Johnson, speaking at Madison Square Garden (October 31, 1964) stated: "These goals cannot be measured in the quality of the lives that our people lead." More and more that phrase, "quality of life," has been replacing "well-being," "welfare," and "happiness" in contemporary consideration of public policy, particularly with respect to economic and social problem issues. To be sure, quality of life is a very subjective expression of an individual's sense of well-being. It expresses the set of material and other "wants" that, in combination, make the individual happy or satisfied. It is also an objective expression of a pattern of life, the merits of which are assessed in terms of individual status, equality, living conditions, economic status, and other factors.[45]

Quality of life is affected by present-day personal and societal attitudes toward debt, saving, spending, and other elements in a money world. The increasingly common way of life—buying today, paying later —is predicated upon a changing use of actual and projected income. It represents a modification in attitudes toward the meanings and uses of money in family living. It reveals a movement away from certain ethics in the puritan heritage, chiefly the middle-class standard of postponing the gratification of desires. It also reflects a changing relationship between people and government: a dependence on government for the creation of programs and controls when economic or social crises indicate they are necessary.

This new way of life has many positives but it also poses many problems for individuals and families. And these must concern all who, providing families with money counseling in today's world, often see in practice the philosophy expressed by Artemus Ward: "Let us be happy and live within our means, even if we have to borrer the money to do it with."

NOTES

1. U.S. Congress, Joint Economic Committee, *"Inflation and the Consumer in 1974,"* a staff study prepared for the use of the Sub-committee on Consumer Economies of the Joint Economic Committee, Congress of the United States, February 10, 1975, mimeographed.
2. U.S., Department of Labor, Bureau of Labor Statistics, *Three Standards of Living for an Urban Family of Four Persons, Spring 1967,* Bulletin No. 1570-5, 1969, p. vi.
3. See Ralph E. Pumphrey and Muriel W. Pumphrey, eds., *The Heritage of Social Work* (New York: Columbia University Press, 1961), pp. 80ff.
4. *Three Standards,* p. 1.
5. Ibid.
6. U.S., Department of Labor, Bureau of Labor Statistics, *Urban Family Budgets and Comparative Indexes for Selected Urban Areas, Autumn 1974,* April 9, 1975, p. 2.
7. Ibid., p. 12.
8. *The Gallup Opinion Index,* Report No. 112, October 1974, pp. 9-13.
9. "Mortgage, Construction, and Real Estate Markets," *Federal Reserve Bulletin,* July 1973, p. 490.
10. Ibid., p. 491.
11. "The Pattern of Growth in Consumer Credit," *Federal Reserve Bulletin,* March 1974, p. 176.
12. U.S., Department of Commerce, Bureau of the Census, *Statistical Abstract of the United States 1974: National Data Book and Guide to Sources,* 95th ed. (Washington, D.C.: U.S. Government Printing Office, 1974), p.397.
13. Lewis Mandell et al., *Survey of Consumers 1971-72: Contributions to Behavioral Economics* (Ann Arbor: University of Michigan, 1973), pp. 30ff.
14. *Federal Reserve Bulletin,* February 1975, p. A47.
15. *Survey of Consumers,* pp. 33, 41.
16. John Hause, "Earnings Profile: Ability and Schooling," *Journal of Political Economy* 80(May-June 1972):S108-38.
17. *Statistical Abstract 1975,* p. 120.
18. Ibid., p. 123.
19. U.S., Department of Commerce, Bureau of the Census, *Statistical Abstract of the United States 1974: National Data Book and Guide to Sources,* 95th ed. (Washington, D.C.: U.S. Government Printing Office, 1974), p. 109.
20. U.S., Department of Labor, Bureau of Labor Statistics 1972-73 consumer price survey of 10,000 families, reported by *The Los Angeles Times,* April 17, 1975.
21. *Statistical Abstract 1974,* p. 71.
22. Anne Draper, "The Price Squeeze on Living Standards," *The American Federalist* 81 (July 1974):1-8.
23. Ibid.

24. Jared Sparks, ed., *Autobiography,* "The Art of Virtue," in *The Works of Benjamin Franklin* (Boston, 1844), 1:105.
25. *Federal Reserve Bulletin,* February 1975, p. A47.
26. *Federal Reserve Bulletin,* March 1974, p. 181.
27. *Federal Reserve Bulletin,* February 1973.
28. Gary Hendricks and Kenwood C. Youmans, *Consumer Durables and Installment Debt: A Study of American Households* (Ann Arbor: Survey Research Center, Institute for Social Research, University of Michigan, 1973), pp. 20–26.
29. David Caplovitz, *Consumers in Trouble* (New York: The Free Press, 1974), p. ix.
30. Hendricks and Youmans, *Consumer Durables,* pp. 20, 46–49.
31. Ibid., pp. 46–68.
32. *Federal Reserve Bulletin,* March 1974, p. 182.
33. Ibid., pp. 182–83.
34. Ibid.
35. Ibid., p. 181.
36. *Pasadena* (Calif.) *Star-News,* March 13, 1974.
37. *Federal Reserve Bulletin,* March 1974, pp. 185–87.
38. Ibid., pp. 181, 186.
39. *The Los Angeles Times,* April 20, 1975, pt. 8, pp. 2, 5.
40. *Statistical Abstract 1974,* p. 397.
41. Robert Chandler, *Public Opinion: Changing Attitudes on Contemporary Political and Social Issues* (New York: R. R. Bowker Co., 1972), pp. 56–97.
42. Ibid.
43. Thorstein Veblen, *The Theory of the Leisure Class* (New York: H. B. Huebsch, 1922).
44. "How the New Suburbia Socializes," *Fortune* 48(July 1953):84–89, 156–60.
45. Ben-Chieh Liu, "Variations in the Quality of Life in the United States by State, 1970," *Review of Social Economy* 32(October 1974):131–47.

PART 2: THE CYCLE OF FAMILY LIFE

3
Money in the Cycle of Family Life

Families, like individuals, pass through a cycle of growth, maturation, and decline. The stages of the family life cycle are marked by marriage, the birth of children, their emancipation, the return of the parents to a childless state, and the death of each spouse. At each stage money is the weft in the fabric of family life, giving it color, design, and texture, and contributing to its strength, durability, and resiliency or vulnerability. Money has special meanings and is put to various uses in different phases of the family's development. The financial situation in any given phase is influenced by what has or has not been accomplished in the earlier stages.

The presence or absence of financial resources affects not only the degree of physical well-being of family members but also the quality of their personal relationships. It influences the attitudes an individual develops about money and its management and uses, uses which in turn play a part in determining the nature of the individual's role and relationships within our society. Even if the individual's lifestyle deviates from the family model of two parents—married to each other—plus one or more children, the place and plentifulness or paucity of money bear on the quality of life that is shunned or sought.

LIFESTYLES AND STAGES OF THE FAMILY CYCLE

Two individuals enter a union with myriad attitudes, impressions, and expectations created by their particular experiences in a money world. They bring attitudes formed by their social class and ethnic background. And they bring attitudes that are responsive to those of their contemporaries. These social-cultural factors have given them various expectations and aspirations that may or may not be in harmony. Perhaps because of a trend that emphasizes value in self-realization and reflects the idea that each person should live only with those with whom life is satisfying, young people are more likely now than in the past to set up households before marriage. These social unions (in contrast with legal marriages) may culminate in legal marriage, may continue as longtime social relationships, or may simply end. Regardless of their status or durability, these unions or relationships are profoundly affected by money elements and attitudes.

The adjustment inherent in the formation of a new household becomes more complex with the arrival of children and the naturally attendant family expenses. As the family and family needs expand, the availability of income for use and how it is used take on increasing meaning.

Throughout the children's growing-up years, the family is under heavy pressure to meet the standards of peer groups, both those of the children and those of the parents. Expenses tend to increase steadily until the children have completed their education. After this, a plateau is reached that brings some respite from the cares and costs of childrearing and gives the parents an opportunity to make provision for their retirement.

During the past three decades, discernible changes have taken place in the time element of the family life cycle. There was much headshaking over the youthfulness of the 1950 bride and bridegroom, and over the more than half of the marriages that ended in divorce within the first year or two when the bride was under twenty years of age. Since then, the median age of men and women at first marriage has moved slowly upward. The median age of today's bride is twenty-one years: the median age of the bridegroom is approximately twenty-three years. These figures have remained fairly constant since 1970 but are still well below the median ages at which pre-World War II marriages took place.[1]

Many factors doubtless have contributed to this trend: the unidentified but substantial number of young couples who set up housekeeping together some time before taking the formal step to legalize the marriage; the relative difficulty experienced by men and married women, and especially by members of minority ethnic groups over much of this period in obtaining employment; the impact on youth that derived from American involvement in military operations in Southeast Asia as well as in Europe; the larger numbers of girls going to college; the willingness of middle-class parents to continue financial support of young married persons attending college; and the reduced pressure on girls to marry, many of whom try alternatives they find satisfying.

rarely acquired automobiles or used credit plans, but subsequent generations did. The differences in attitude between those immigrants and their children suggested the younger generation's wish to become acculturated and assimilated. The attitudes of the older generation in this group bore striking resemblance to those of their American contemporaries who viewed with suspicion the ready use of instalment or consumer credit by the younger generation.

In more recent years, generation-gap studies and studies seeking insights into the thinking and behavior of youth challenging orthodox and traditional American values[41] have disclosed strong distrust of parental values—the parents often being individuals who were the younger generations described above—that apparently or actually incorporate high material expectations or achievements. Although there are no reliable statistics regarding the size of this disaffected group, it is generally thought to be large, though nevertheless a minority. On the other hand, while a substantial proportion of all youth included in one study (1,340) would like to see less emphasis on money, they rejected less emphasis on working hard, and generally believed in saving as much as possible regularly in order not to lean on others when financial problems emerge. But the large number of black youth respondents in the same study did not challenge such traditional values as money and hard work, and religion to the same degree as their white counterparts.[42]

It must be recognized, of course, that many ethnic and cultural factors influence saving and expenditure behavior. The impact of the broader society upon the economic behavior of different ethnic groups has a parallel in the apparent effect on individuals of the class or group to which they belong or wish to belong, and on the quality of life they wish to attain. Thorstein Veblen has this to say about a standard of living: "It is a habitual scale and method of responding to stimuli. The difficulty in the way of receding from an accustomed standard is the difficulty of breaking a habit that has once been formed."[43] Veblen believed that the accepted standard of expenditure in the community or in the class to which a person belongs largely determines what his standard of living will be. The accepted standard influences him directly by commending itself to his common sense as right and good, by his habitual contemplation of it, and by his assimilation of the scheme of life characterizing the segment of society to which he belongs. It also influences him directly, by popular insistence under threat of disesteem or even ostracism, to conform to the accepted scale of expenditure as a matter of propriety.

Veblen relates these points to his theory of "conspicuous consumption"—the use of consumer goods as a means of demonstrating one's wealth or status. An increase in an individual's income is likely to be reflected in increasing expenditures for conspicuous consumption: a more expensive car, a more fashionable neighborhood, a trip to Europe rather than to an American resort. Conspicuous consumption has been more prevalent in the larger city than in the country. In the city, means of communication and mobility expose the individual to the observation of many persons who judge his reputability only by his display of goods. There has been a noticeable change, however, in some rural areas, undoubtedly the product of increased communication and mobility. The change led the wife of a university professor in a noted agricultural college (herself a frequent consultant on financial problems) to complain: "We can barely afford to own and run a car, but there's hardly a farmhouse in this area without the finest freezer and clothes dryer, and it seems that every farmer owns his own private plane."

The continued importance of this concept of conspicuous consumption should not be underestimated. At the same time there is another pattern, defined by William H. Whyte, Jr., as "inconspicuous consumption."[44] He suggests that spending and saving constitute a form of social as well as economic behavior which is partly controlled by the social values of one's social group or community, or by the expectation of one's friends and neighbors. In contrast to conspicuous consumption, inconspicuous consumption is an endeavor not to keep *up* with the Joneses but to keep *down* with them.

Differences of opinion also exist about optimal upper limits that consumer credit should reach. What is a reasonable limit, and by what criteria is it determined? Experts disagree about the level that will make a maximum contribution to the economic health of the individual and of the nation. This disagreement was highlighted in the course of efforts in the 1970s to bring galloping inflation under control and to avoid increasing the level of unemployment, with the issues revolving around whether Americans should spend or save, and whether their credit opportunities should be eased or tightened.

A new way of life has now emerged for the average American. Although the pace and the level achieved have varied for members of some population segments or regions, overall there has been a steady rise in income despite fluctuations in the economy, and individual living standards have moved upward proportionately. Economic goods have been plentiful. Through the use of consumer credit, durable goods have been accessible to those able to accumulate enough reserve for a down payment and able to budget their income for future spending. And the

Changes have also taken place in the average number of children per family and in the ages of parents at the births of these children. Husbands and wives, at the time their last child is born, tend to be younger than parents in earlier generations. For parents whose last child was born in 1890, the median age of the father was thirty-six years; of the mother, 31.9 years. For parents whose last child was born in 1950, the median age of the father at the birth of the child was 28.8 years; of the mother, 26.1 years. But in the 1970s, young couples who are marrying a little later and, often, delaying having children until their own schooling has been completed or the wife has satisfied an ambition to establish herself in a career, or for other reasons, will have had their last child before the mother is thirty. The parents will be in their early or mid-thirties by the time the youngest child is in school.[2] If the present trend holds, it can be expected that the parents will be relatively young when their last child marries or leaves the home for other reasons. The period between the departure of the children and the dissolution of the family through the death of the parents, therefore, has lengthened markedly. On the average, this period now exceeds twenty-five years—a few years less for black men and women.

Another change is also evident: the attitudes and expectations regarding the number of children, if any, today's young couples plan to have. Diverse reasons are offered for limiting the size of the family: children curtail freedom; economic conditions are not conducive to undertaking the financial obligations incurred in the rearing of children; world tensions; environmental and population control factors; decreasing natural resources; and others. Whatever the reason or combination of reasons, there has been a decline in the average family size. Census Bureau figures (1973) indicate that one of every twenty-five wives between eighteen and twenty-four years of age now expects to have no children; as recently as 1967, it was only one of every one hundred. The number of couples who want only one child also has grown in these years: from 6 percent to 10 percent. And the number of women planning to have one child or none has increased more than 80 percent over this time period.[3]

In the first few years of the 1970s, the average number of under-eighteen-year-olds per family dropped from 2.29 to 2.18 in husband-wife families, and by an equal degree for families headed by women.[4] On the average, as in previous years, there were fewer children in families with working mothers than in families with mothers who were not in the work force. This statistic held true whether the families were white or black, and whether they were headed by a man or a woman. The great majority of these children are in husband-wife families (86 percent). However, this proportion has been sliding downward in recent years, while the proportion of those in one-parent families has been rising: 13 percent, or nearly 8.5 million children.[5]

Why is there this increase in numbers of children in one-parent families when the number of marriages is actually growing? Despite frequent dire predictions that the American family is in jeopardy and that marriage is becoming an obsolescent institution, it is a fact that the marriage (and remarriage) rate has been maintained. Annually, there are now close to eleven weddings per thousand population, and some demographers anticipate this marriage boom will persist through the 1980s. It is noteworthy that even though one in four marriages ends in divorce (with, conversely, three out of four remaining intact), four out of five divorced persons will marry again. Only two percent of those who marry will be divorced twice and marry a third time; and those who marry a fourth time constitute only one fourth of one percent.

As has already been noted, half of the wives under twenty years of age of the couples married in 1950 terminated their marriages by divorce. But at the same time the median duration of all marriages is seventeen years: nearly 70 percent of those currently in their first marriage have been married for more than ten years, and more than 43 percent of those in a second marriage have been together for more than ten years. For black families, the figures are somewhat different: the median duration of the marriage is approximately fourteen years; 61 percent of women in their current first marriage have been married for more than ten years, as have 56 percent who are in the current second marriage. Attesting further to the general durability of current marriages is the fact that more than 46 percent of those in their first marriage entered wedlock more than twenty years ago, and nearly 25 percent of the women in their second marriage likewise have been married for more than twenty years. The percentages are slightly smaller among black women in their first marriage and a little larger among black women in a second marriage.

The rapid rise in the number of children being reared in one-parent households reflects several developments: the increasing number of marriages ending in divorce and one-parent households where remarriage may be pending; the trend toward the postponement of marriage; the continued high rate of out-of-wedlock births, and "perhaps also a tendency for mothers who have never married to report their marital status correctly."[6] Also included among the larger numbers of children in one-parent families are children adopted by a single man or woman, and the growing number of instances of children who remain with the father following maternal desertion or legal termination of the marriage.

In addition to the attention being directed to children in single-parent households, cognizance should be taken of another phenomenon of our time: the sizable ranks of children who are stepchildren—about one of every nine children. These may have several sets of parent-stepparents, and live sometimes with one own parent and subsequent spouse, sometimes with the other. They may reside in a traditional household; or they may be part of an "alternative" household arrangement—a communal family, a multiple or group marriage, a time-limited marriage contract. In all or any of these lifestyles, financial resources play an important role, whether the family has a single-parent or a multiple-parent arrangement, once-married parents, not-married parents, or other.

At different stages of the life cycle, and with different lifestyle patterns, individuals and families have different needs, wants, and values. Resources change, too, as do the relationships of family members with each other and with persons outside the family group. There is no clear line of demarcation, however, between the ending of one phase and the beginning of another. Progression from one phase to another may be interrupted by catastrophe: death of a spouse or the protracted absence of a spouse or parent from the home because of hospitalization, imprisonment, military service, or desertion. Some people may skip a stage, for not all people marry; nor do all married people have children. The chapters that follow consider the impact of money on family life in the various stages of family development, starting with the *beginning of the cycle of family life*, moving to *the expanding family, the contracting family*, and *variations in living patterns*, some of which may appear to reflect new lifestyles. Regardless of the taxonomy used, however, certain considerations about money and people are common to all lifestyles and stages of the family cycle.

MONEY NEEDS OF FAMILIES

Nineteenth century author Samuel Butler described money as "the last enemy that shall never be subdued. While there is flesh, there is money —or the *want* of money, but money is always on the brain so long as there is a brain in reasonable order." Although the sufficiency or insufficiency of money may not preoccupy everyone, there are few in our society who can totally or indefinitely disregard the part money or what it represents plays in their lives. It has economic importance to everyone. Without it, survival needs—food, shelter, clothing, and medical care—

generally cannot be met. Without it, the growing list of items essential to maintaining a minimal level of comfort in daily living cannot be procured: refrigeration for healthful food storage and preservation; "wheels" for transportation, whether an automobile, a bicycle, or a public bus; telephone, television, radio, or other rapid communication devices that contribute to socialization or link the individual or family to sources of help or warning systems against dangers from nature or other sources.

And money has emotional and social importance to individuals and families in our society either because they have it or do not have it, and because of their greater or lesser sensitivity to the perceptions both that they hold and that they attribute to others about the significance of having or not having money.

Economic meanings

In the economic meanings of money to families and individuals are likely to be found the keys to their value systems and their effective functioning. The meanings have wide variations, as these situations disclose.

> The Ms are expecting their first child in a few months. They have been living with Mrs. M's parents while Mr. M completed training for the job on which he recently started. The parental home is too small to accommodate a baby; besides, the couple believes that the elderly parents could not "handle" the presence of the baby, and already strained relationships would deteriorate further, making all the household residents uncomfortable and unhappy. The Ms have been searching for an apartment or a small house they can afford to rent, without success.
>
> Mr. R, an outside salesman whose route covers three contiguous counties, learns that the seven-year-old car which he uses to carry on his work, requires extensive and expensive repairs. Mrs. R has become increasingly restive because of what she calls "banishment to the country" since the family bought a suburban home. She wants to resume work as a secretary now that the children are in school, but without a car there is no way for her to reach prospective places of work. The Rs are considering how they can afford both to repair the one car they now own and to buy another.
>
> Jim B and Chuck J, both 18, will graduate together from high school this year. Jim wants to be an engineer and has applied to the local university for scholarship aid and work to enable him to carry out the educational plan. He knows that his parents, with three younger children and a modest income, can do little to help him. Chuck wants to postpone going to college in favor of extensive travel around Europe. His parents think this idea offers an important educational opportunity for him before he settles down to

formal education, and have offered to finance the portion of the trip that cannot be met by the savings Chuck has accumulated from work over the preceding two summers.

Lee W has been giving his mother $150 per month since she was widowed two years ago and this sum, together with income she has from her husband's estate, permits her to maintain the living style to which she has long been accustomed. Lee's wife, who has worked during all the eleven years of their marriage, has been laid off and is unable to find other work. The curtailed income and rising costs of living have been twin subjects of increasingly acrimonious discussion between them. The wife resents giving the mother money the Ws now need, and suggests it is time for the mother to "come down to earth" and adjust her level of living to the level of her income. Mr. W retorts that he cannot be expected to ask his mother, after all she has done for him and in the face of her bereavement, to forgo this "piddling" contribution from her oldest son. What would his mother *think* if he stopped the contributions? What would his *friends* think?

Families—and individuals not part of family units—must have access to money or some equivalent in kind or in credit in order to purchase goods and services for survival, for luxurious living, or for economic protection in the future. The amount of money required for physical maintenance and economic survival varies with the different stages of family life. Each phase, from infancy through old age, has economic needs specific to it; and how or if these needs are met affects the later phases of the life of the family or its individual members. For example, certain nutritional needs are common in the healthful development of all children. Failure to provide young children with adequate nutrients, especially in the first twelve to eighteen months of life, may result in impairment of spatial and time perceptions, in reduced learning capacity, and in increased vulnerability to illness. Children so deprived not infrequently grow into youngsters who just cannot manage to be at school on time, and into adults whose employability is reduced because they find it difficult to report to a job at a specified hour. These are often adults who also, whether or not they have the resources, simply cannot meet time payments and thereby jeopardize their credit standing.

Such failures may be the result of parental neglect or lack of knowledge regardless of the family's financial resources; or they may be the consequence of insufficient funds to provide children with appropriate nourishment and at the same time to meet other essential demands on the family's limited income. Such insufficiencies in income may be related to the cost of living in a particular locality, to underemployment, or to entirely different economic circumstances.

As children grow into adolescence, their needs (and demands) for money also grow and change. They matriculate from allowances for comics and candy, to educational expenses and money for clothing and other items highly regarded among their peers, for dating and for other recreational and developmental purposes.

In these same years, the parents carry special responsibilities that entail the availability and use of money not only for the previously mentioned survival and developmental needs but also for protection. A long-accepted function of the husband and father has been to provide through savings or insurance (commercial as well as social insurance) for the financial care of his dependents in the event of his serious illness or his death, or, at the very least, to pay some of the bills attendant upon severe illness or death. More recently, the wife or mother has also been expected to purchase such protection for family survivors or to insure against medical costs that would absorb the family's financial resources were illness to strike.

When the children leave home, the financial needs of the parents are altered. There may be some leveling off of the need for income. Simultaneously, there may be increased evidence of the need to prepare for a long span of life in which the family level of living will be influenced directly by the amount of money the family has required and acquired in preceding stages of the family life cycle, and the purposes for which this money has been used—or abused.

The financial needs of older persons tend to undergo further change; there is a sharp reduction in some areas, a steep rise in others. Medical care or household assistance are examples of the latter, as are gifts for grandchildren. The financial situation of the older individual or couple often is affected by the fact that limited income, though recurring, is not readily augmented and may not be adequate to correct or alleviate deficiencies and problems resulting from previous financial constraints.

The form, nature, and size of financial needs shift and change along the continuum of the life span of individuals, families, and family segments. The satisfied or unsatisfied needs of earlier stages may markedly affect later economic coping behavior as well as needs. The Ms need separate housing *now*. The Rs have to decide *now* what they should and will do about the car issue. Jim and Chuck and their respective parents are planning their future *now*. The Ws are engaged *now* in a struggle that began in the past and will continue into the future.

SOCIAL AND EMOTIONAL MEANINGS

But the current money needs of such families and young adults have social and emotional elements that influence their everyday economic and psychological functioning. These elements shape their social and emotional well-being both as individuals and in their relationships with others. How will the Ms cope with the mounting strain between themselves and on their parents? How will their frustrations affect the baby if the three generations reside together in the cramped, tension-filled dwelling? What will be the impact on the Rs and the interrelationships of family members if the obligation for paying for a new car is or is not assumed? What if Jim is not awarded the scholarship, or cannot find work that will enable him to pursue his career choice? How and when will Chuck and his parents decide that his emancipation should begin? How will the Ws deal with the reality of their economic stress, the paternal mother's real or fancied need, and the couple's respective feelings about priorities in the discharge of their filial, marital, and parental responsibilities?

The value of money lies not only in the varied purchases it represents, such as housing, cars, education, current physical care of dependents, their future protection, and financial support. It has value in itself. It represents the power to have or to buy what is needed and desired for current maintenance and for protection against the economic hazards or exigencies of the future. While everyone can readily recognize the intrinsic value or face denomination of coins or currency, concepts of money differ and variously influence the individual's conduct, aspirations, self-perceptions, and interpersonal relationships. Accordingly, some people regard money as having the power to accord social status or to reflect vocational, professional, or other achievement. These concepts are strongly molded by environmental factors and societal attitudes. The latter may be contradictory, a fact that no doubt actually makes it easier for many people to reach out, consciously or otherwise, for those attitudes that will justify or rationalize behavior taken or contemplated by them.

Thus, we say that "money isn't everything" and that "the best things in life are free" at the same time that money is needed for survival. In this connection, Ogden Nash strikes a responsive chord with his

>   Certainly there are lots of things in life
>   that money won't buy,
>   but it's very funny—
>   Have you ever tried to buy them without money?"[7]

We joke about "filthy lucre" as though money were unclean or tainted, but we still regard its possession as an admirable reflection of virtue and thrift. In these conflicting perceptions are to be found the reasons proffered by some young people in contemporary communes for embracing the "simple" and "antimaterialistic" lifestyle; and by others for surrounding themselves with possessions—procured by cash, by credit, or by gifts—that present a facade of success. It also is this extension of the Calvinistic equating of goodness with being rich and poverty with wrongdoing and shiftlessness, that continues to compel respect for adults who are economically independent and deplore the economic dependence of others. Hostility is directed especially toward those who, seemingly able-bodied, are not employed.

Just how the individual will function in meeting economic needs and will respond to societal attitudes and expectations will be shaped to a considerable extent by individual personality and behavior. These personal behaviors meld with the individual's reactions to societal attitudes reflected in the symbolism and uses of money, and produce personal meanings of money that are emotion-laden for the individual and the family. These personal meanings, in turn, affect the essential ingredients of effective individual and family functioning: a sense of identity, of self-worth, and of trust. The amount of money available, while always important, becomes secondary to what money represents to the individual. Indeed, in many significant ways, the petty economies of the rich (for example, long one of the richest women in the world, Hetty Green wore her tattered stockings until the shreds no longer held together) are as amazing as the silly or seemingly pointless extravagances of the poor (the man who buys an ostentatiously costly car to park in front of the dilapidated house from which he and his family face imminent eviction because they have been unable to muster the rent money from their below-poverty-level income and resources).

At what point will the Ms resent their continued dependence on Mrs. M's parents for housing? Under what circumstances and with what consequences will Mrs. M protest that her husband is not earning enough—is not up to earning enough—to meet his family obligations? When will Mr. M's struggle to do his "best" in a job-scarce economy be transformed into frustration, self-anger, growing doubts about his adequacy, and loss of confidence that are expressed in the lessening of his struggle? How will Lee W cope with his wife's seeming effort to "force him" to "choose" between his wife and children and his mother? How will he cope with the overflow of his wife's many years of resentment of her mother-in-law's closeness to Mr. W? These are situations in which the rational and irrational elements are closely intertwined, affecting not only the principals in each situation but those around them.

Emotions related to having or not having money, or using or not using money, may stem from financial circumstances per se, or may cause or contribute to the economic situation of an individual or family. It has already been stated that each stage in the cycle of family life has characteristic economic features. So, too, each phase in the individual and the family life cycles evokes feelings and perceptions about money that tend to be unique to that stage in life. The complexity and form of both economic and psychological monetary needs may be further complicated when the family or individuals are disadvantaged (or so regard themselves) because of poverty or lagging incomes, minority-ethnic or nationality membership, ghetto residence, or other socioeconomic factors.

MONEY PROBLEMS AND FAMILIES

Everyone is touched to some degree, directly or indirectly, by the social, economic, and emotional aspects of money. Some feel the impact more or less profoundly than others. Some cope comparatively easily with the financial problems they encounter. Some do so with considerable effort, but are able through this effort to attain a satisfactory equilibrium in dealing with the necessary tasks. Others, given some information or guidance to overcome gaps in knowledge or essential experience, are able to manage their financial affairs adequately, sometimes even superbly. Still others need more intensive or extensive help in mobilizing and utilizing their internal and external resources in order to improve their situation, to arrive at a reasonable accommodation with reality, or to prevent their monetary or family situation from deteriorating.

Not all who need help can bring themselves to request it or to use it. This is especially true of the many people who perceive the insufficiency of their financial resources, or their difficulties in managing their resources as evidence of inadequacy or immaturity, regardless of the reasons for the predicament. Unable to expose what they regard as deficiency, they either decline to seek help or independently devise a solution that fails to touch the overt or expose the covert contributing problem but only permits it to persist or even worsen.

There has been some discernible change in the readiness of such troubled families or individuals to solicit help from various kinds of sources. This increased readiness possibly is attributable to certain developments in our culture that, by their very visibility, subtly encourage troubled people to be more open about their own personal distress, to share with others their need for help. Among these developments are the growing amount of frank discussion about intimate aspects of family lifestyles ("Imagine *talking* about it"); the widespread advertising about available sources of consumer credit to improve levels of living and maintain certain lifestyles (and also to cope with overextension in the use of such credit); the trend toward enacting and implementing consumer protection legislation; the expansion of consumer credit counseling organizations that endeavor to assist the individual or family to bring their indebtedness under control; and the broadened spectrum of public and private agencies that offer counseling aimed toward assisting the family in improving the socioeconomic functioning of its individual members and of the family as a unit.

It is especially important for social workers and others who counsel in agency or proprietary settings to understand *how* to help families and individuals with their money problems, and what consideration to give to the economic, the social, and the emotional components and implications. They need to be sensitive to the elements in the Ms' situation that flared into the marital conflict that the couple now wants to resolve by separation or divorce. Because the Ms are black, have had limited educational and work opportunity, and share ghetto housing, the counselor must be alert to different or additional social pressures and problems that must be overcome if a reasonable solution to their complex of problems is to be found.

The counselor needs to be cognizant of the ramifications of the fact that the Rs' indebtedness is not being met even with the additional income from Mrs. R's full-time but low earnings on her new job; that the adolescent children are escaping the persistent and angry bickerings of the parents by disappearing from the home each evening, for which the parents loudly and bitterly blame each other. Does the social worker comprehend the impact on Mr. W and his mother from her having lapsed into deeper and deeper depression as her feeling of rejection and isolation has mounted? The counselor may have to consider the unremitting struggle of Jim's uneducated immigrant father to assure that his son obtains the high school education the father had been denied, his tremendous identification with the boy's plans to be an engineer, and his representations to the younger children that they too can expect to fulfill vocational dreams. And what does the counselor have to take into account to understand and assess the evidences and consequences of the Js' self-recriminations that they had "given Chuck too much, everything he wanted, and spoiled him," which is why "he's ended up arrested on a drug charge in a foreign country"?

What understandings should social workers and other counselors possess about troubled people and their money? How can individuals and families be helped most effectively with problems that have fiscal dimensions? The concern of counselors cannot be solely with income insufficiency for meeting daily needs. Their concern must also embrace the psychological and social implications for the family of a lagging income, and the behavior of those who are unable to manage on their incomes because of social or psychological problems or because they use their money irrationally. To counsel effectively with today's family requires sophistication about and sensitivity to the economic, social, and emotional meanings of money to the family endeavoring to function at an optimal level in today's money world.

NOTES

1. U.S., Department of Commerce, Bureau of the Census, *Statistical Abstract of the United States 1974: National Data Book and Guide to Sources*, 95th ed. (Washington, D.C.: U.S. Government Printing Office, 1974).
2. Ibid., pp. 53ff.
3. Current Population Reports, "Birth Expectations and Fertility," *Population Characteristics*, ser. P-20, no. 248 (Washington, D.C.: U.S. Department of Commerce, Bureau of the Census, 1973), p. 1.
4. Current Population Reports, ser. P-22, no. 76 (Washington, D.C.: U.S., Department of Commerce, Bureau of the Census, 1974).
5. Reports, ser. P-20, no. 248.
6. U.S. Census Bureau data quoted in *U.S. News and World Report* 77 (December 2, 1974): 85.
7. Ogden Nash, "The Terrible People," in *The Selected Verse of Ogden Nash* (New York: Modern Library, 1931), pp. 5–6.

4
Beginning the Cycle of Family Life

The system of interpersonal relationships that characterizes a family constitutes a network of forces and roles that has a telling effect on the uniqueness of each family's goals and the way it functions to achieve them. The system generally begins with marriage partners whose separate and common goals, identities, and problems are maintained, but whose interests and goals become integrated with an overriding goal.

It is in the climate created by the beginning family that an individual becomes prepared to undertake the tasks of day-to-day living. These life tasks are of four kinds: providing for security and physical survival, for emotional and social functioning, for sexual differentiation and the training of children, and for support of growth of the individual members in the family.[1] The family may perform these tasks competently or inadequately. It may perform them with a sense of satisfaction and positive achievement. It may carry them out partially, reluctantly, dismally, or not at all. But from its beginnings, every family must struggle with two separate but interrelated and interdependent tasks of particular significance in our money world: loving and working; neither can be isolated from the meanings and management of money.

In our culture love and affection form the basis for the selection of a marriage partner, but this selection is not devoid of economic considerations. The old-fashioned dowry, however, has long since faded from the American scene; it is no longer the custom for the bride to bring money, goods, or an estate to her husband as part of a marriage agreement. Nor are her growing-up years necessarily filled with purposeful learning of household arts and activities. In former years she was exposed to a rigid training designed to equip her for her future tasks as wife, mother, and manager of her household; such training was predicated on a clear though not always happily accepted understanding that she was to fill these roles. There was also an equally clear understanding that the husband was expected to be the breadwinner for the family.

Marriage today is valued not so much for its economic advantages as for the emotional security, love, companionship, and other personal satisfactions that a family setting provides. The roles of family members have changed as the family has shifted from a self-sufficient unit producing most of the needed materials to a dependent, consuming unit; from a rural to an urban unit; and from a geographically stable to a highly mobile unit. The dowry concept, therefore, is obsolete to the extent that the wife is not expected to bring to the marriage either capital assets or the ability to produce, in the home, goods that are essential for living. However, she may—and in today's culture commonly does—bring a capacity for earning in the open labor market. She also brings certain expectations to the marriage that either parallel or run counter to those brought by the husband. The expectations of either partner may be related to the achievement of a certain social status, professional attainment, or level of earnings. They may arise from each partner's self-perception and conception of an ideal mate. The rigidity or the flexibility of these expectations are apt to affect the extent to which each partner can make the kind of personal adjustment that is necessary to a successful marriage. These expectations, molded by sociocultural, psychological, and economic influences in the lives of the two partners, to a large measure are determinants of the degree of happiness or unhappiness that the total family will experience.

Intimately related to the effect of the nature and quality of these expectations are the dynamics of complementarity—the intermeshing of the couple's conscious and unconscious needs and wishes. The success with which this meshing proceeds so that conflicts either are resolved or are prevented from impinging upon the performance of tasks that are part of a healthy marriage is also an indicator of the development that can be expected on the part of the marriage partners and the children they may have.

The money world in which we live exerts an influence on the age at which people marry and on family attitudes about "dowering" a marriage. During the depression of the 1930s, for example, many young couples tended to postpone marriage because of the scarcity of jobs and because of their responsibility for contributing to the support of their own families. Many who did marry found it necessary for both husband and wife to work, provided they were successful in obtaining employment. They rarely brought to the marriage an accumulation of worldly goods, and the wedding gifts they received were usually simple and practical in nature.

Although the climate of that economic depression undoubtedly stimulated certain positive elements in the sharing relationship, it also brought numerous problems. For many couples it necessitated the prolongation of a childless state. In many marriages it provoked hostility. The husband often felt guilty about his failure to meet the expectations of his wife, his associates, or himself; and the wife as often resented having to assume an earning role.

The period of World War II and the subsequent periods of international unrest and conflict created new attitudes and expectations on the part of young couples embarking on marriage. The financial stringency of the previous years gave way to higher salaries, a freer labor market, and governmental controls on prices, rents, and other expenditures. But insecurity of another kind developed. Young men were recruited into military service; their brides went into industry or tried to manage a household on the governmental military dependent's allotment. Sometimes the bride followed her husband from post to post; sometimes she remained with her parents, in the anomalous state of being a married woman and yet a child in the parental home. Patriotic fervor stimulated marriage among couples who hardly knew each other and whose only link with each other became the dependent's allotment. Obviously, not all of these marriages were doomed to failure because of the short acquaintanceship, separations, and lack of preparation that characterized them. On the other hand, such negative factors unquestionably complicated the adjustment of a large number of these young people.

The continuance of military service requirements created uncertainty for the young persons of the 1950s and 1960s in planning for education, for employment, and for marriage. But the majority of youth in those two decades had the advantage of knowing that jobs were relatively easy to obtain. Most of them could not recall a time when it was difficult to procure work. The pattern of married couples attending college became prevalent in the post-World War II period, undoubtedly spurred by the availability of veterans' educational benefits. But many couples were supported by their parents, and in many instances the wife worked while the husband attended school. Marriage and higher education no longer were considered mutually exclusive goals. In contrast to the 1930s, young couples usually began their marriages with some resources—gifts of money and goods. In a study conducted shortly after World War II, August Hollingshead found that the average New Haven, Conn., couple began married life with the equivalent of $1,400 in cash and merchandise gifts. (No similar recent study appears to have been made, but converting the costs of those gifts to today's prices suggests at least doubling of the value.)[2]

The sailing was not so smooth, however, for all young people in those years, especially if they were members of ethnic minorities, lived in ghettos, and had limited education or job preparation. Even military service did not yield for them the same level of educational benefits as for veterans of the two World Wars and the Korean military experience. Substantial numbers were unable either to find employment or to effectively pursue educational or job-training programs. Some remedy resulted from affirmative action programs that aggressively assigned certain priorities to minority-group members for jobs and school admissions, but unemployment and low educational achievement have remained relatively high among these groups. Marriages among these people have not tended to have either a compelling goal of education shared by the couple, or the financial support of parents able and ready to supply such help at the beginning of the new marriage.

Today's young couples manifest behavior reminiscent of the depression of the 1930s: delay in marriage and the postponement of having children. The reasons are different, of course, and so are some of the other discernible patterns. Some do not marry at all, but live together as though they were in a legally formalized marriage. In many instances, whether married or not, the partners are students. Some are supported entirely by the work of one or both, sometimes in combination with scholarship assistance. Some partners take turns supporting each other for the duration of the educational experience. A common pattern is that both are fully employed. The 1970s recession, however, has markedly affected the employment opportunities of young men as well as young women, with the consequence that only one may be employed at all, or only one may be employed in the field for which he or she has prepared —teaching, for example.

Some couples, their numbers open only to speculation, have no "visible" means of support. They may be part of a communal or other alternative to traditional marriage, the arrangement sometimes including legal marriage. Whatever the alternative, however, like traditional marriage, its durability as a union is based on the complementarity of needs and wishes, and it must take into account the economic realities of survival and the more or less subtle impact of money on daily living and feeling.

Economic conditions and social customs of a society at any given period directly influence the circumstances under which couples marry or live together without formal marriage. Although the earlier concept of marriage as an economic arrangement has been radically modified, *each* partner still brings to the union, whatever its form, a "dowry"—

not necessarily of material possessions, but of attitudes, expectations, and potentialities that can contribute to the health of the union.

INCOME EXPECTATIONS
The average couple enter into marriage optimistically, with high hopes for a future that will bring security, independence, and personal satisfaction as well as a reasonable degree of approbation from others. And to a remarkable degree this optimism is justified. Their youth, their resiliency, their love, and their newly established partnership combine to form a strong motivating force for achieving their goals. Their confidence in their capacity to acquire the income essential for meeting their present material needs and, to some extent, for preparing for the future also helps them to attain those goals.

Understandably, this optimism is less apparent in informal unions that are social rather than legal. Marriage denotes trust in oneself and in one's partner and commitment; readiness of each partner to rely on the other and to be relied upon, and willingness to share, in whatever ratio suits them, the fulfillment of their life tasks—especially the providing and managing of income for protection in the present and preparation for their future. There are, of course, situations in which at least one of the partners is not legally free to marry. There are also many situations in which risking themselves in the establishment of a long-term arrangement is less a factor than experimenting per se, or conforming to a peer pattern. For many young people, depending on their responsiveness to an older value system, such liaisons actually reflect a high degree of self-trust, and a readiness to take risks in combination with the acting out of some rebellion. By and large, however, whether the informal union is expected to be of either short or long duration, there is a significant reduction or absence of the optimism which is inherent in mutual trust, and such goals as are shared tend to be limited and tentative.

Although the goals of young couples are similar in some respects, the meaning of the goals varies with the individual. For some, the goals are a nebulous wish that has little connection with the social and economic realities of their lives; for others, the wish can become a reality.

What, then, is reality for the young family? When is an expectation merely a wish that cannot be transformed into an actuality? The wish element, as well as the reality element, is apparent in the way the family manages its present income, its income expectations, its assets, and the way it uses credit. Few couples in the early stages of marriage have reached their peak income. Those who marry somewhat late in life may have. The income patterns of young couples vary as to both level and source. Today, an increasing number attend school, usually college; some secure their income in the form of transfer payments, often veterans' benefits (sometimes supplemented by food stamps), and others are supported by the parents of one or both spouses. There has been a persistent and decided trend among middle-income parents to continue to provide funds for their children in their late teens or early twenties, either for schooling or for maintaining a home. Many couples, however, undertake an educational plan on their own, recognizing that educational achievements will be personally enriching and are the gateway to increased earnings.

Among the young couples who are not involved in educational plans, both spouses often work. As was previously noted, in almost three-fifths of the young childless couples in the United States the wife receives income from wages or salary. Thus, the wife helps to accumulate the resources and possessions desired for their family lifestyle long before the family's income peaks, which generally is not before the husband has reached the age of forty. They may acquire goods and assets, or enrich their lives by travel or other activities that might not be within the reach of a single salary.

Certain extra expenses, of course, are involved when the wife works, and her working may create problems of adjustment for herself and her husband. The counselor, in evaluating a specific situation, should keep certain questions in mind. Is the wife working primarily to increase the family income? Is her employment a way of filling time because her homemaking responsibilities are light? Is she working because she finds personal satisfaction in being engaged in a profession or career, or because she likes to work, to interact with others in the business or professional world, to have the sense of fulfillment and reward the activity and the income may supply? Is her employment the direct or indirect result of a desire to escape from domestic responsibilities or strains in the marital relationship? Or does she work to exercise freedom of choice about how she will live her life?

In our culture there is general acceptance of the idea that women, especially if they are childless or if they are mothers dependent on public welfare aid, should work outside the home—provided there is no compelling reason for staying at home. Nevertheless, the long range economic aspirations and expectations of most families continue to revolve around the husband's income. His earning capacity is influenced to a considerable degree by the financial and social status of his parents. The social and cultural norms of his family often contribute to his choice of vocation and determine, to a large extent, his values and business or professional skills. Ethnic and geographic factors may also limit vocational choices. Children of professional parents are likely to choose a professional career; businessmen's sons are likely to enter the business world, although they do not necessarily select their father's kind of business. If the father is an unskilled worker, his sons may take related, but skilled work; or they may be propelled sharply away from it because their own or their wives' sights are focused on white-collar careers.

The level of aspiration, therefore, determines the way a man will earn his income and his expectations for the future. According to George Katona,[3] the level of aspiration is, in turn, determined by a number of factors. An important one is the person's own past performance, together with the appreciation he has received from his family and friends for his earning capacity. If his income has gone up in accordance with his aspiration, he will expect it to go up still further. If his efforts to increase his income have been unsuccessful or if, contrary to his expectations, his income has declined, he will not expect a higher income in the future. Accomplishing what one has wanted to do, approaching or achieving his level of aspiration, brings satisfaction and inspires further striving. On the other hand, lack of motivation or absence of striving toward a goal is generally the result of frustration. Failure and disappointment may cause the individual to think that his limited earning capacity is attributable to factors other than his own shortcomings.

In point of fact, however, the limited earning capacity of many individuals, particularly members of ethnic minorities and women, may indeed be unrelated to the person's qualities and qualifications. Enactment and implementation of civil rights and nondiscrimination statutes have advanced the causes of women and minority-group members in their efforts to obtain education and work suitable to their interests and talents. But there continues to be more or less overt job discrimination—with some cases currently being brought to courts or other regulatory bodies as the numbers of unemployed grow and cast a spotlight on such issues as seniority, affirmative action programs, and so forth. It therefore behooves the counselor to distinguish carefully between the discouragement that arises from factors that reflect reality and those that center in the individual's own personality and behavior.

Ordinarily, the young couple can expect the husband's real income to increase, irrespective of his vocational choice or the degree of success in his work. Similarly, if the wife plans to continue to work, particularly on a full-time basis, her earnings can be expected to rise as skill and experience are acquired. As the number of **dependents** in the family grows, the take-home pay (after tax deduations and other withholdings) of each parent working full-time grows too. At the same time, however, there will be some beginning protection for the family's future economic situation through mandatory coverage in the social insurance system.

EXPENDITURES

The spending and saving behavior of a young family is related not only to its current and future earning capacity but also to the positive or negative responses provoked by social expectations. The pressure of friends and relatives may influence or dictate the nature of the couple's expenditures. If the couple's associates own cars, they will probably buy one. If, like their friends and relatives, they enjoy concerts, they may purchase season symphony tickets; or bowling or attending baseball games may represent their choice in recreational expenditures. If their recreational activities take the form of entertaining at home, spending for food and beverages will be related to their group's standards for such hospitality. Lack of experience in managing money prior to marriage as well as patterns of saving or nonsaving in their own parents' homes will be reflected in the young couple's handling of their income.

In young families today certain living patterns and corresponding spending patterns are noticeable. There is a higher geographic mobility among this group than in others, for they are not yet encumbered by the responsibilities of raising children and they are relatively free to follow employment opportunities. There also is higher residential mobility, particularly among nonfarm couples. They move from apartment to apartment, changing to be conveniently near friends, shopping centers, or place of work.

For most young couples less housing space is needed than for other family groups. The house or apartment may be selected because it offers comfort and the opportunity for homemaking or for entertaining. An employed wife may choose an apartment small enough to enable her to manage it, as well as her job responsibilities, with greater ease. Or an employed couple who expect to share the household tasks may elect housing that they find especially satisfying in terms of spaciousness and amenities.

Young couples generally do not initially select their housing to accommodate children but, rather, to meet their own immediate needs and interests. Therefore, expenditures for housing and household operation are inclined to be at a lower level than in later phases of the family cycle. Approximately three quarters of the childless couples rent their homes.[4] However, a larger proportion of older childless couples—about 80 percent—purchase their homes. This fact undoubtedly is related to the probability that their income has already moved upward and there is less geographic mobility in this older group.

An interesting change in housing patterns of young married couples is becoming apparent. There has been a discernible trend among young childless couples to rent single-family houses or apartments in structures with no more than four family units, or to live in trailers. The latter type of arrangement is less common among black families than white—less than 1 percent of the former, and 5 percent of the latter.[5] Perhaps this is occurring because the couple plan to have few (if any) children and thus reach an early decision to settle into housing that can later accommodate a small family; or they may place a special emphasis on maximizing privacy.

Expenditures for food and entertainment may be relatively high among childless couples, particularly if both partners are employed. More meals are taken out, and in better restaurants. More trips are made. More commercial entertainment is utilized, such as theater, movies, and ballgames.

A fairly common sequence of expenditures is apparent in the consumer behavior of young couples. Car ownership is a top priority. If neither spouse owns a car at the time of marriage, the purchase of a new or used one is given early consideration. In fact, 71 percent of young married couples with no children own a car, and more than 33 percent own two cars.[6] Growing in significance is the number of childless couples who also own various kinds of recreational vehicles, including boats. For example, Bob and Sheila, in their mid-twenties, have been married for four years. Both are employed at work they enjoy, and have agreed that they will have one or two children *sometime.* For the present, however, they will add to the enjoyment of their childless freedom by investing in and maintaining their two cars and a small motorboat. More than 30 percent of their combined income is absorbed by payments for just these three items.

The percentage of those owning television or stereo sets and tape recorders reaches a high level at a later stage than car ownership; nevertheless ownership of these items is accorded an early priority. Neither very young couples nor fairly elderly childless couples are likely to own color television sets—only some 17 percent of the former. The proportion of television ownership begins to move upward during the wife's first pregnancy, possibly related to some curtailment in her activity; but television ownership precedes homeownership. Among the household items, refrigerators and stoves are important early purchases in those communities where these two items are not routinely provided by landlords as a condition of the rental of housing. Washing and drying machines are usually not purchased until a child is expected.

Childless couples in which the man is under twenty-five years of age have the lightest fixed payments for such items as rent, property taxes, mortgages, life insurance, and retirement and pension funds. But families (with children) with heads under age twenty-five are more frequently involved in instalment borrowing and a large ratio of debt-to-income.[7] Moreover, they are apt to have greater difficulty in meeting the financial obligations they have incurred. Young families are particularly likely to use credit, because consumer needs or desires are greater in the early stages of the family life cycle and, at the same time, young families probably are in the early stages of their occupational careers when income is relatively low. This combination of felt need and limited resources may lead young couples to overextend their resources more often than do older, more experienced families who are less vulnerable to the blandishments of sellers. But contrary to popular mythology, according to Gary Hendricks and Kenwood Youmans,[8] low-income couples are rather cautious in their use of instalment debt, and on the average maintain instalment-debt balances that are a smaller fraction of their income than do middle-income couples.

These spending patterns suggest certain social trends. One is that today's young adults value many, if not most, of their parents' goals: education, careers, marriage, home purchase, children, education of children, financial security, and time for leisure activities or travel. However, many are not pursuing these goals in the same sequence as that of their parents. They are reordering the priorities among these goals over the life cycle and pursuing them in a way they see as compatible with their interests. Material goals are important to many young couples, and they consider as basic to their lifestyle some items that were unknown or unavailable just a few years ago. In general, however, the spending patterns suggest that a large number of young couples, at the beginning of their marriage, want the comfort and luxuries their parents obtained only after a lifetime of work, thrift, and self-denial. There is reason to believe that the parents, consciously and unconsciously, foster this attitude, which is further reinforced through the commonly advertised avenues for utilizing credit.

A second trend is that heavy purchases are made at the time when the income from either the husband's earnings or the combined husband and wife earnings is still rising. These commitments reduce the family's current liquid assets and also forestall the accumulation of reserves. The young couple tend to relieve the strain by the use of consumer credit, including gasoline and other credit cards. The economic behavior in the beginning phase of the family cycle is characterized both by increasing income and by increased spending for durable goods.

Two other trends are of particular significance to counselors. The first is that the young couple's involvement in expenditures is usually geared to the total family income, which often includes the wife's earnings. When the wife stops working because of pregnancy and child rearing, not only is the income curtailed but the couple is faced with new and heavy expenses. If the wife stops working for other reasons, the couple is also faced with the necessity of adjusting to a lower level of living unless the husband's income has increased to the point where no deficiency exists, or the less likely possibility obtains that their living expenditures have been geared to the level of his income alone. With unskilled and certain blue-collar or low-paid white-collar workers, the likelihood of such an increase in the husband's income is not great and, as a result, these families may face particularly severe problems of adjustment.

The second of this pair of trends is that many young couples are unsophisticated regarding moderately effective and compatible ways of handling their income. Often contributing to this situation is the combination of early marriage and economic independence for the first time, without prior opportunity to gain any experience in decision making with regard to how income and outgo are maintained in reasonable balance.

MONEY AND MARITAL CONFLICT

In our money world, a young couple's personal relationships are constantly being tested as they move from the warmth of the honeymoon stage into the stage of practical planning to meet their current needs and to acquire a cushion of assets. They may expect a rise in income and a corresponding rise in expenditures. Generally unanticipated, however, is also a rise in temper and tension. The temper flare-ups may not necessarily stem from money matters, as such, but money nonetheless often precipitates them.

The personality development, the emotional maturity, and the mutual expectations of the husband and wife determine, in large measure, the way each partner deals with strain or conflict. A healthy marriage is more than the union of two individuals; it encompasses tasks and functions that feature the dynamic interplay of needs, wishes, and goals toward becoming a new family unit that will move through a series of normal transitional crises in the stages of the family life cycle. In the early years of the marriage, the tasks and functions of the new couple include emancipating themselves from their respect've parents and reorienting themselves from the status of two utterly separate and often financially independent individuals to that of a unique partnership central to a unique family life. They must learn many things: to understand and deal with each other sexually; how to carry the different roles that each must assume at different times and under different circumstances; to understand and respect each other's individual freedom and differences; and how to jointly manage economic and household responsibilities. Difficulties in carrying out these marriage tasks may be evidenced in anger, in withdrawal into sulky silence, or by other signs that are expressed in money terms or about economic matters.

Economic problems thus may serve as a safety valve for unleashing outbursts of feeling related to issues other than money. Economic problems may also be used as a vehicle for provoking negative feelings and attitudes in the partner or for precipitating disagreements and quarrels. Such displacement of feeling onto money matters, if allowed to proceed without understanding or control, may spell unhappiness or even disaster for the marriage.

Money itself does not bring happiness. Nor does its limited availability inevitably bring unhappiness. Its absence may produce anxiety and tension, but the reasonably well-integrated man and woman will develop devices for dealing with this absence, without directing negative feelings toward themselves or toward each other. But attitudes and feelings are very much entwined with money. Money is a powerful symbol, representing love, protection, and the gratification of normal dependency needs. It is an equally powerful means of gratifying infantile wishes and of expressing hostility.

Because money has such deeply personal meaning to everyone—for life cannot be maintained without it—there is a natural tendency to think of money problems as the cause of most marital conflict. It is true, of course, that an unexpected loss of the husband's job or a reduction in his income may create tensions for both husband and wife. Similarly, if their planning and management have centered in part around income she provides that unexpectedly comes to a halt, stress may be felt by both. Strain may arise, too, if the husband's work involves him in travel and long periods away from home, or simply keeps him out a number of evenings or weekends, leaving the wife alone. But if the marital partners are mature and realistic, when the complementarity of their needs is gratifying and active, they usually can move together toward making an effective adjustment and assuring a reasonably healthy marriage. They may adopt measures for financial retrenchment until more income becomes available. They may utilize personal or community resources to tide them over. They may take steps to find other or more satisfactory jobs; or, if the latter is not practical, they may adapt themselves to the reality limitations and work out acceptable compromises.

The immature, hostile, or generally unhappy person, when confronted with such practical problems, has difficulty in finding a satisfactory solution and in making the necessary readjustments. If the spouse, too, is immature or demanding, their separate and combined feelings serve to exaggerate the negative aspects of their partnership and add to their discord.

Money is used in a variety of ways by both marital partners to exacerbate marital discord. One partner often uses personal ingrained habits of spending as a means of attacking the other. For example, a husband may be controlling about money, holding his wife rigidly to a tight budget or doling out an "allowance" to her. This may be a role expectation, culturally determined; he may come from a home in which his father, like others in his social circle, was the authoritative, thrifty provider. Alternatively, such controlled disbursement of money may stem from the husband's recollections of hunger and deprivation in his youth. In today's climate which encourages independence in women and their freedom to exercise choice in relation to education, vocation, and manner of self-realization or self-fulfillment—whether as homemaker or breadwinner—the husband may express his resentment over this changing role through criticism about the quality of the wife's management of household finances and chores.

To certain neurotic husbands, money may be an unconscious symbol of masculinity and power. The wife's retaliation against his money behavior may take several forms. She may spend money wastefully as a way of expressing hostility toward him or as a means of maintaining a dominant role. She may make no effort to operate within the budget he has prescribed, or she may respond by setting limits of her own in meeting his sexual, physical, or psychological needs. She may even bring charges against him of inadequate support.

Some women often irrationally apply family or social standards for the purpose of attacking their husbands' inadequacy in earning. Other women with insatiable dependency needs displace their feelings onto material things and make excessive demands on their husbands. The husband's need to placate or hold a demanding wife may result in overspending and accumulation of debts, and both husband and wife may use money to "buy" the other's love.

Considerable marital tension may be aroused because the wife works outside the home. Problems in this situation are minimal if both marital partners have common goals and an acceptance of a jointly developed plan for the family income. Discord may develop, however, if the wife takes employment against her husband's wishes. He may not verbalize his feelings about her working because he is unwilling either to incur her anger or to appear to be "old-fashioned" when the "modern" husband is supposed to accept the equality and emancipation of women and their expression in her working and earning. But he may in various ways restrain, injure, or upset their joint plans in managing work and home, often with the excuse that it is in the woman's best interest. The pressures he puts on her to remain occupied with their home may elicit strong reactions on her part to the idea of giving up her employment and the status, independence, and satisfaction it provides her.

If the wife works because family needs require that she supplement the husband's income, she may add to his already existing feeling of inadequacy—whether she finds the work enjoyable or satisfying, or dislikes having to work but feels that she cannot afford to quit. The husband may feel that he is deprived compared to other husbands he knows: that she is not available to promote his own success in a competitive world of work; that she should be ready for business entertaining or to free him from time-consuming tasks like engaging in household chores, shopping for clothes, or maintaining links with relatives. And marital discord may center around her working and earning—and spending or saving—because the husband feels threatened by the possibility that his working wife may outrank him in earnings or level of success. In American society, the man whose wife exceeds him in prominence or earnings is still often pitied.

Overly strong parental ties often contribute to strain between spouses, and between them and both sets of parents. The ties themselves may be fashioned of money, woven into a knot too tight for the young couple or either sets of parents to sever easily. The ties are strengthened when parents support an adult child who marries but continues in school. The same kind of dependency role is created when a young married couple continue to live in either of the parental homes. Rivalry between the two sets of parents, often expressed in outdoing each other in their gifts, tends to enmesh the young couple even further. When grandchildren arrive, the relationship problems become heightened.

The balance in a marital relationship may be disturbed not only by loss or decrease of income but also by a sudden upward change. Either the husband or the wife may be unable to tolerate the power that comes with enhanced income. Sometimes, however, a marriage can be maintained only because the husband's good earning capacity enables him to meet his wife's narcissistic needs, or because her work channels some of her anger away from her husband into constructive paid activity, with the dual consequence that her sense of independence (concretized by a paycheck) enables her to tolerate serious marital discord. Severely compulsive people frequently have difficulty in marriage because their basic rigidities in personality are reflected both in their use of money and in their demands as to how the spouse must handle income and expenditures.

Emotionally immature people who have no concept of money management are likely to encounter serious difficulty in marriage. Often one competes with the other, even fighting with the spouse on a sibling-rivalry basis. Because of these competitive feelings they are unable to share money realistically. Sometimes the husband's immaturity is so basic that he has never succeeded in making a satisfactory vocational adjustment. His inadequacy prevents him from earning an adequate living and his failure fans the hostility and resentment of his dissatisfied wife. The husband's immaturity and his hostility toward his wife may be factors in his unwillingness to seek more remunerative work, especially in instances where the wife is ambitious and has high socioeconomic aspirations.

It is in the beginning phase of the family life cycle that the first tests of the quality of the partnership are made. The kind of relationship that the husband and wife establish then will largely determine the quality of future family relationships. Marital harmony is made up of many elements, and the same is true of marital discord. If the marriage partners do not recognize their basic conflicts and endeavor to reduce and resolve them in the beginning stage of their marriage, before the arrival of children obscures and complicates their personal conflicts, the entire family structure is placed in jeopardy.

Money, commitment, and nonbeginnings

The courtship may have been short or long, turbulent or smooth, built on "love at first sight" or propinquity or someone's matchmaking. Its culmination in marriage symbolizes the partners' commitment to each other and their readiness to engage in the giving, taking, sharing, emotional and financial supporting and being supported so important in a healthy marriage. The legal act of marriage not only serves to define tasks that are part of this beginning stage in the cycle of family life. It also serves to protect legally the reciprocal financial and property obligations and privileges of the partners, as well as the legal status and rights of possible children.

There is a prevalent belief that only one kind of marriage is legal: marriage by license and legal ceremony. But other methods also exist that *may* be legal in the United States and that carry the same economic sanctions and protections, although they may be harder to establish as a matter of course. Common law marriages and marriages by ratification or by presumption are phenomena that are found primarily in lower-income groups of white as well as of ethnic minorities ,[9] and the prevailing statutory trend in the United States is to abolish common law marriages. The number of such marriages is not recorded, but there is ample reason to believe that many are as enduring and healthy as unions officially noted in public records of vital statistics.

The socially-arranged unions, which do not in fact have legal status, constitute another kind of situation. They too may be only as enduring as marriages of young couples that end in divorce. They may be longer-lasting or transitory. They may be transformed into legal marriages, sometimes because children have been born, sometimes because of reason or combination of reasons unique to the given couple. Ordinarily, however, the very tentativeness and initial questioning of the permanency of the relationship may fall under the rubric of the self-fulfilling prophesy, with the economic aspects of the relationship a vital force affecting the union's stability and continuation.

There are, of course, no figures to indicate either the number of such social arrangements that exist or that have ended. It is fairly well accepted that a high proportion of the young married couples who turn to divorce do so because they either lack money or have not learned to carry adequately the marriage tasks of managing money and what it represents. It follows logically, then, that the absence of a legal bond will facilitate the separation of equally young couples who are similarly confronted with problems centering on money and who do not in fact have joint ownership or legal interest in income or property belonging to either of the participants in the union. Indeed, the role and function of money take on special significance in these nonlegal household arrangements.

Some people enter the nonlegal union because they do not like the idea of marriage or do not feel ready for it. Some face financial problems or, as was previously stated, are unable to marry because of legal problems with a prior marriage. Some do not want to be "tied down." Others avoid marriage because they believe, at least to some degree, that fewer problems will result if they simply live together without legal ceremony.

Some of the problems faced by unmarried couples are similar to those faced by married couples: What money and responsibilities for the household are his, hers, or theirs? How should accumulated property be divided in the event of a separation? Other problems are different: discrimination in housing; insurance; credit when the nonlegal status of the union is known; and separate income tax assessments on the two persons as single rather than as married.

Other kinds of problems also arise. The young couple's parents and their contemporaries, for example, may not find it too difficult to accept the fact of the unmarried lifestyle of the young people, especially if they like the companion their child has chosen. But how do they introduce the son's or daughter's housemate to their own contemporaries? What is protocol in giving gifts as would be done for a wedding? What kind, if any, of parental assistance should be available to the couple? The parents may be torn between a value system that is affronted by the nonmarriage and concern about alienating a beloved child. Such conflict may lead one or both sets of parents to be withholding, thereby arousing resentment in either, or both of the young people. Or the parents may compensate for their own distress by overgiving, thereby provoking in the couple some anger over what may be regarded as pressure to change to a more traditional marital arrangement.

Most unmarried people who live together do not sign a contract before entering into this arrangement; after all, the usual purpose for the social arrangement is the avoidance of the contract concept a marriage license symbolizes. They join forces because they like each other, it is convenient, and "details" can be handled as they arise. The keeping of accounts of what has been or should be spent for food, household items, entertainment, and other matters is inconsistent with the freedom sought in the relationship. Debt that is accumulated in the interests of either or both of the union's partners must be discharged by the individual who accrued it. If property is commingled, however, anger and resentment may arise because the separateness of the property cannot be easily established and may be claimed by the creditor of the indebted individual who does not in fact own a share of the property (joint savings, television set, furniture, and so forth). If each person views the financial or property contributions of the other as being in some acceptable proportion, there will be less potential bitterness about what each puts into and takes out of the relationship. There will also be less occasion for one partner to use the giving aspects of the relationship as a tool for control; in fact, it is the avoidance of such control that frequently is the rationalization accepted by the couple for the looseness of the relationship characterizing the social union.

But a major difference between married and nonmarried couples lies in the fact that the latter may separate on far less provocation than is true of the former. This fact may govern to a considerable degree the quality of freedom and security the couple feel in relation to each other, the tolerance they have for taking normal errors and anger in stride, and their ability to move ahead through the beginning stage of the family life cycle in preparation for the next phase. The social union remains a nonbeginning in the cycle of family life unless commitment of the partners to each other is formalized by legal marriage, which presupposes at least a degree of planfulness for a future together.

DEVELOPING ATTITUDES ABOUT MONEY

The modern family reflects the values of our democratic society in the ways that family members relate to each other. Cooperation and sharing are increasingly typical of today's family. The interests and well-being of all family members are considered and each has a share in the planning and carrying out of the life tasks that are central to a healthy marriage. The marriage relationship is less rigid and institutionalized than in the past, and is an increasingly mutual search for fulfillment of deep human needs for love and security.

The family's way of living is determined by the marital equilibrium that is established and maintained by the marital partners, and by the goals they set for themselves to form a framework for the structure and standards that will govern the family throughout its life cycle. These goals—cultural, social, and economic—will influence the expenditure of the beginning family's money, time, and energy. They will be reflected in the kinds of housing, food, clothing, recreation, and self-realization that absorb the interest and funds of the couple. Socioeconomic factors beyond the control of the individual couple may limit the attainment of some goals. The development of sound family attitudes toward money depends, however, not so much on the amount of income as on how each partner uses it, both psychologically and to meet reality needs.

In our culture young couples normally anticipate a steadily increasing income; at the same time they anticipate a corresponding increase in expenses. Thoughtful planning, based realistically on actual and potential income and on present and future responsibilities, is essential if the family is to progress smoothly through the various stages of the life cycle. Such intelligent planning jointly engaged in by husband and wife will enable them to make constructive use of the economic devices that our modern money world has developed. It will also free them to use money creatively and help them to escape being governed by the pressures and anxieties that come from its misuse.

NOTES

1. Frances Lomas Feldman and Frances H. Scherz, *Family Social Welfare: Helping Troubled Families* (New York: Atherton Press, 1967), pp. 63–96.
2. August B. Hollingshead, *Elmtown's Youth* (New York: John Wiley & Sons, 1949), pp. 83–120.
3. George Katona, *Psychological Analysis of Economic Behavior* (New York: McGraw-Hill Book Co., 1951), pp. 87–126.
4. Lewis Mandell et al., *Survey of Consumers 1971–72: Contributions to Behavioral Economics* (Ann Arbor: University of Michigan, 1973), p. 28.
5. Ibid., p. 30.
6. Ibid., pp. 38–40.
7. Ibid., p. 6.
8. Gary Hendricks and Kenwood C. Youmans, *Consumer Durables and Installment Debt: A Study of American Households* (Ann Arbor: Survey Research Center, Institute for Social Research, University of Michigan, 1973), p. 20.
9. Sanford N. Katz, *When Parents Fail: The Law's Response to Family Breakdown* (Boston: Beacon Press, 1971), pp. 15–20.

5
The Expanding Family

The life cycle of any family is marked by a series of dramatic changes. Perhaps the most radical of these is the arrival of children, no matter whether the first child is born a year, two years, or ten years after the marriage—or even before the parents marry. The relationship between father and mother is likely to alter, more or less subtly; their priorities and values are modified, and they make new plans for the future and set new goals.

Their new roles as parents call for focus on certain life tasks that, with the tangible presence of a child, become realities for the first time. The need to fulfill household and economic functions, previously merely contemplated, now is explicit and assumes definite shape.

Among the roles the father is expected to carry—whether or not he is married to the mother—is that of primary provider and protector. Changing family patterns may be bringing more mothers into the work world, but if the father is in the home, or available in the community, he is expected to meet the child's economic needs. He is expected to protect his children's economic future until they enter adulthood. He is expected to establish a model for the paternal role and, with the mother, a model for sexual role differentiation and socialization. And he is expected to protect the children from the spectrum of crises to which every family may be subject.

Heretofore, the father has been universally expected in our culture to be the role model of the primary breadwinner and provider. In today's money world, new role models have been emerging, with the father and mother increasingly viewed as coequal participants in the development and socialization of the child. According to these new role models, the mother has the right to choose homemaking or augmenting family income through work—or to combine them—and to seek and experience self-fulfillment as a person. Moreover, the father and the mother have the obligation to share in household responsibilities and to set and carry out the rules that will govern the children's role performance. The roles assumed by parents today and the patterns they create for their children to follow revolve significantly around which parent earns money, why, how, and how much; what decisions, if any, are made—and how and by whom—as to money management; and whether one or both implement those decisions (if actually implemented) and in what ways.

The beginning period of the family cycle, if not shortened by the early arrival of children and when appropriately and effectively used, is a period for establishing healthy marital equilibrium. It provides the time needed for the couple to mesh their interests, needs, and wishes, and to prepare for the arrival of children. It is in this period that clues as to the quality of the parenting role become discernible. The first-born child enters a milieu that is a blend of the responses of each parent to his and her own developmental experiences throughout childhood, and how each has dealt with and been affected by the performance of the marriage tasks in the beginning stage of the family cycle. The couple should have worked out such seemingly small matters as how the paycheck of each will be banked, cashed, or disbursed, and when to consult together about the implications and solutions of a problem one or both experience. And, indeed, most couples do this reasonably satisfactorily.

> When June S insisted all through courtship and the first year of marriage that she "simply could not budget for *anything*" and that Jack would "just *have* to take charge," he did. He established checking and savings accounts in his name, deposited from their individual earnings in each account the amount he thought appropriate, handed out to his wife the sums she requested for daily use, and unquestioningly paid the bills for the charge accounts she used.
>
> June gave up her job during pregnancy. No adjustments in their money management pattern were made to accommodate to the new income level and June's new role. Items for the coming baby were charged; health insurance would pay a portion of the obstetrical and hospital care.
>
> Jack had been transferring funds from the savings to the checking account. When both were depleted, he borrowed from his credit union. He did not "bother" June with the "details." Suddenly he was angered by the pregnancy, refused to look at his new son, and declined to have any part in naming the child.
>
> Overwhelmed by the growing burden of debt, by his failure to carry out what he perceived to be his role as the strong husband on whom his wife could lean, and by the loneliness of his position, Jack thought about how to extricate himself from this situation. Should he leave? Should he tell June he wanted a divorce? Should he just go and say nothing?

Could June really *not* handle money? Was she "helpless"? Did the couple ever discuss their changing financial circumstances? It was evident that elements other than money were operating to put this marriage on a shaky foundation, among them lack of communication and clarity about their individual and shared roles. But their money management in this instance offers the social worker both a window to the nature of the trouble and a handle for opening the window.

For the most part, families in the expanding stage of the family cycle approach the childrearing responsibility and role appropriately and well, although not necessarily identically. The family with an adequate capacity for social functioning may find that its pattern is temporarily disrupted by a major change, even when the change has been anticipated and does not take on overwhelming crisis proportions. Some counseling help for a short time may suffice to enable the family to regain its equilibrium and to manage its affairs thereafter. In some instances all the family needs in order to cope with the stressful or critical event is knowledge, and the counseling experience prepares the family for dealing satisfactorily with other stressful situations they may encounter later. Sometimes limited intellectual or emotional endowment, or the form and direction of personality development and interactions, complicated by individual and societal expectations, become obstacles to the family's smooth functioning as it expands. Counseling help of a more complex order may be required to bring such families through a troubling experience. It becomes important to determine, as in the case of the S family, whether the explosive marital situation can be eased sufficiently by education about the use of communication in the marriage relationship and about the management of money, or whether the financial symptoms mask deep-seated personality problems that would be responsive to skilled intervention.

THE MONEY CLIMATE OF THE EXPANDING FAMILY

In our society, the family is most likely to have children when the father is between the ages of twenty-five and forty-five. The maximum size of the family, usually with two or three children still under the age of eighteen—an average of four or five persons—is reached when the father is between thirty-five and forty-five years. The maximum family income, however, generally is attained when the father is between forty-five and fifty-four years old[1] (a little earlier in white families than in nonwhite). In most families, especially if only one parent is an earner, the low-income period is apt to exist while the children are small and they and the expenses grow together. Moreover, in many instances in which an employed wife gives up her work for a period of childbearing and the husband's income expectations have not yet been realized, the family simultaneously faces a time of heavy expenses for child and health care, and reduced income.

Indeed, the medical obligations are likely to be heavier in this phase of the life cycle than in any other period, except during old age. They include costs of obstetrical care and payments to doctors, dentists, and hospitals for medical services to children in their physically vulnerable years, as well as to parents. The medical bills constitute an early and pointed reminder to new parents of their growing responsibilities and diverse obligations. Available evidence also suggests that in this stage of the life cycle more of the family income is absorbed by fixed payments than at any other stage of the cycle, including both shelter costs and instalment payments, as well as other commitments. It is therefore reasonable to conclude that monetary problems are particularly pressing.

As the family expands, residential stability increases and, with it, the likelihood of home ownership. This trend toward home purchase is influenced by many factors, including the need for more space, the importance to the children of "settling down," the unwillingness of many property owners to rent to families with children, the desire of many for suburban life, and the general belief that buying is cheaper than renting. Certainly the unprecedented building of small homes after World War II and the then relatively liberal mortgage terms for a long time encouraged this movement toward homeownership. Thus, more than 50 percent of the nonfarm families with heads in the twenty-five-to-thirty-four age group have purchased homes, and more than 71 percent of those in the thirty-five-to-forty-four group.[2] The period of the 1970s, however, introduced a new era in home purchase costs: rising interest rates, mounting costs for building or purchasing housing, and reductions in the amount of construction. All of these factors combined to put the purchase of housing out of the reach of lower-income families and many middle-income family units. Nevertheless, 62 percent of the families with the youngest child under six years old own their homes, while 76 percent of those whose youngest child has passed the age of six own their homes, marking an upward trend in homeownership as the parents and the children advance in age. Nearly three-fourths of the white home-owning families live in single-family houses, whereas half of the nonwhite home owners occupy duplex or other multiple-unit housing.

Undoubtedly there is a relationship between the time of acquisition of a home and the peak in the purchase of major household items in these homes: stoves, refrigerators, washing machines, dishwashers, air conditioners, furniture, and so forth. The *Survey of Consumers 1971–72* reported that 62 percent of families with the youngest child under the age of six bought durables, 52 percent doing so on credit; 56 percent of those with children over the age of six bought durable goods, most of these using credit.[3] Some of the parents in these expanding families, of course, were acquiring durable and necessary goods for use in homes they were renting rather than purchasing.

One of the early purchases of the expanding family is television. This investment is made not only because of the generally expressed desire of the children, but also because it provides a form of recreation in the home for parents and, often, serves the parents as a child-caretaker! Television is an increasingly important medium for culture, education, and observation of current events. Reference was previously made to the fact that car ownership is fairly standard among beginning families. This also is true among expanding families, although in this group the automobiles on the average tend to be of slightly older vintage. Ninety-three percent own one car, 42 percent two (at least one of which is new), and 29 percent own more than two. Among the families with older children, 41 percent own three or more cars. This multiple-car ownership occurs more frequently among suburban families than among those in central cities.[4]

The amount of instalment debt carried by parents in expanding families is not as high as among childless couples. The amounts, however, are larger when the children are younger; the instalment obligations decrease as the children grow older, dropping from a total indebtedness of as much as $2,000 to less than $1,000.[5] Not clear from the available data is whether the obligations were incurred when the children were young (or before they arrived) and were being discharged as the children grew older, or whether the parents, because of greater caution or tighter money or reduced need, simply did not purchase as much with the passage of time.

> Mrs. A, a 30-year-old Guamanian mother of four children from 7 to 12, explained that she had tried to "stretch" her husband's earnings, now $650 per month, during their 14 years of marriage, by keeping instalment purchases at a level where the payments amounted to $50 to $75 per month with fair regularity. But now, with the added costs of meeting the needs of her growing children in times of inflation, with her husband's earnings having remained at the same level for two years ("and we're lucky he has them!"), she was paying off the obligations accrued, adding only "emergencies" of clothing items. Her husband's role, she reported, was to earn, hers to meet

the family needs with the earnings; if he thought she was not "buying enough," he would have to bring more money home!

The instalment debt pattern of the As is not unusual, and it had not perceptibly altered during the years they lived in Guam and the past several years since they had moved to the mainland. The *Survey of Consumers 1971–72* disclosed that 14 percent of families headed by a twenty-five to thirty-four-year-old man made monthly debt payments of $50 to $75; 13 percent paid $75 to $99; and 19 percent paid $100 or more.[6] The annual income of these families tended to be well under $10,000. Although Mrs. A uses no store credit cards, 43 percent of families with incomes under $10,000 do "stretch" their incomes by the use of such credit cards, a smaller number also using bank credit cards. As the age of the family head rises, the percentage of families using credit cards also increases.[7]

All expanding families are confronted with certain additional expenditures, such as for food, that are related directly to the increase in the number of family members as well as to the nutritional needs characteristic of certain age groups. In order to meet these basic daily costs, families often resort to the use of credit devices to meet other financial obligations, as noted above. Some families also have other demands on their income which are not universal. Increasingly common among these are costs for child care: babysitters, housekeepers, and nursery school or day care facilities. The growing phenomenon of mothers entering the labor force full- or part-time has increased this demand on family finances, even though the parents may have worked out a plan they regard as highly satisfactory in terms of dividing and sharing child care and household responsibilities. There may also be costs for foster family or institutional care that arise out of such circumstances as the mother's employment, the physical or mental illness of a parent, or relationship and other problems. A high proportion of the parents of expanding families buy health and life insurance for themselves, for the children, or for the family unit, to provide some protection against common hazards that confront all families.

When the children are ready for school, there is another upward spurt in expenses. Costs related to education and the clothing needs that accompany school attendance account for this rise. Recreation costs, too, move upward as the children do, and so do myriad other expenses associated with growing up. To balance the expenditures with the income, the family's income may be distributed differently: less may be used for recreation or meals out, more spent for health and life insurance.

More income may be allocated to transportation and instalment purchasing; less to savings. The wife may go out to work part-time; she may reduce family expenditures by sewing instead of buying clothes for herself and the children, or by doing more laundry at home than she did in the past. The husband may invest in tools and supplies that will reduce expenditures for repair and other services. Or help may be received in the form of gifts or services from relatives, especially grandparents; their gifts of cash or clothing and their babysitting services all help reduce outlay when income is limited. By the early 1970s, many families, previously economically independent found their resources no longer a match for inflation, and were led to stretch their earnings or other income by the purchase of food stamps. Relatively few of the younger expanding families have substantial cash assets on which to draw: a third of these families have less than $1,000 in reserves, and approximately 40 percent have none.[8]

MONEY AND WORK

When there are children in the family, the psychological pressures upon the husband to earn at a level satisfactory to himself, to his wife, and to other family members are multiplied by the number of people affected and by their individual feelings and attitudes. The young father who has had opportunity for vocational choice and training may already be embarked on a career of sustained, useful work which furnishes part of his motivation. The other part of the motivation comes from his gratification in providing for his family. The satisfactions in working and providing are related to and based on earlier learning, the challenge of competition, and the desire for creative expression. In our culture, too, there are numerous recognized social and economic advantages that accrue from hard work.

The wife may likewise be employed but, with few exceptions, society does not expect that her earnings will be the mainstay or the permanent income source for the family's basic survival needs. Like her husband, she may find her work satisfying and self-fulfilling, whether she chose her vocation deliberately or whether her working merely reflects her view that employment is a happier alternative to household management. She may be gratified by contributing to the family income, by the sense of equality she experiences from the freedom to make and carry out a career choice, and by sharing household tasks with her husband so that she does not feel relegated to the "lesser" role of homemaker.

In order to be happy, people must have a sense of conviction about their own worth and dignity. In our culture the individual's sense of worth receives major nourishment from work and the rewards that it brings. The parents' own sense of worth and of being rewarded for their labor is reflected in their ability as parents to develop in the children a sense of trust in the future and convictions about the worthwhileness of work. The children, as were their parents, are exposed from their earliest years to pressures to "do your best," "get ahead," "measure up." The child is taught that effort is rewarded and that success comes to the individual who tries hard enough. Implicit in such maxims is the corollary idea that failure to succeed is somehow the child's own fault.

Belief in this concept of success is of special importance to the family in which the husband's earnings are not enough to meet the family's needs adequately. This concept is meaningful also if the wife is earning either more than the husband or, together, their earnings are not sufficient. It takes on particular significance if the family must apply to a public agency for financial aid. In other words, although economic history and economic reality have established the fallaciousness of the idea that failure is the penalty of "shiftlessness" and "unworthiness," this belief is still held by many persons in this country and finds its target in the individual who fails in a monetary sense.

Nevertheless, the earning and management of money are criteria of adequacy and maturity in this nation, and economic independence is a major measure of both. Unless the family income derives from secure investments or other private sources that render the family economically independent without an evident need to work and earn, there is expectation that the father, and often the mother, will work. The essence of personal independence and self-sufficiency for the individual lies in the person's capacity to determine and meet his or her own needs through his or her own resources, and to identify and meet the needs of dependents. How parents in an expanding family regard the place of work in the life of either or both parents is of continuing importance in the care and development of the family's children; it affects the child's own later perception of the importance of work in the production and management of income for survival and other purposes.

PARENT-CHILD RELATIONSHIPS

Marriage and parenthood and all relationships within the family are colored by the inescapable psychosocioeconomic demands of a money world. Attitudes are developed within the framework of each person's own immediate family as the individual grows from infancy through childhood and adolescence, and emerges into an adult world with adult responsibilities. The child's experiences during the growing-up years, the economic and social position of the family, the attitudes and feelings of the family about money and social position, the way money is handled with the child, inevitably have an impact on the child's own attitudes throughout life.

Roughly the first twelve years of each child's life span comprise the early childrearing phase in the expanding stage of the family cycle. An important parental task in this phase is to develop in the child a healthy trust (and healthy mistrust), healthy love capacity, self-control, and the ability to learn. Childrearing is a continuous learning task for the parents and for the children; it is partly intuitive and partly learned, and the process varies with each child. It has two essential aims: to develop individuation or healthy separateness; and to develop healthy interdependence. These aims are achieved by a process of conflict and resolution between the parents and the child. Throughout the process, both the marital and the family equilibrium are frequently tested. But in a healthy family (and most families are healthy), the balance is maintained or fairly quickly restored.

Adolescence begins about the thirteenth year of the child's life and lasts until the beginning of adulthood. Although this period is fraught with anxiety for the children and insecurity for the parents, most young people succeed in growing up without special problems, and most parents take in stride the vagaries, erratic behaviors, and demands that are characteristic of this stage. The key task in this period is the adolescent's establishment of identity, and the foundations for this task are laid in the early childrearing years.

At the beginning of life the child is completely dependent on the parents or parent substitutes to provide sustenance and the means of survival. The quality of the diet received early in life is an important determinant in the child's physical health. Sturdy health is a more important value in our country than it is in those nations where the general living standard is lower. The financial security of the family also contributes to the child's opportunity to develop personal stability and individual abilities to their maximum potential.

The infant born into a family where there is poverty will experience privation in having its physical needs met. This in turn affects the child's feelings about self and others: to be hungry and cold is to feel unloved and insecure. In this regard, Charlotte Towle states, "The malnourished infant is one who experiences a deep affectional starvation. Undernourished infants have been noted to be restless, irritable, hyperactive, or, in extreme cases, apathetic, and these symptoms begin at once to influence their total experience in relationships."[9]

> Gary is the sixth of eight children whose Puerto Rican busboy father earned barely enough to pay for shelter and minimal amounts of food. When she was not pregnant, Gary's Haitian mother worked long hours as a janitress, leaving Gary and the younger children in the care of the oldest child, eight years his senior. She did not mind caring for Gary, for he was quiet and did not "fuss" about when or if she fed him. Gary, now 9, thin and rickety, is a passive nonlearner of normal intelligence (according to standard tests), always late to school in the morning, late in returning from recess or lunch, unable to join in when the class plans an activity for a week or two later. He cannot trust the future that is out of his sight, for he cannot trust the present or those who share it with him.

Gary's developmental experience can be replicated in any poor family unit struggling to survive in a harsh economic climate, regardless of ethnic identification or geographic location.

Because of its importance to the very existence of the child and the family, money assumes a major position in the strivings of the economically deprived to meet psychological and biological needs. It is the focal point of their anxieties around survival in a world that not infrequently places upon their shoulders the blame for their situation. Allison Davis reports on the anxiety of persons living in slums about having enough food, clothing, shelter, heat, and light: "Just as their deep anxiety about starvation leads them even in good times to glut themselves, as middle-class people view their eating, so does the learned fear of deprivation drive lower-class people to get all they can of the other physical gratifications, 'while the getting is good.' It would be more rational if they saved and budgeted their money, but human beings are not rational."[10] It is difficult, indeed, for those who have not experienced deprivation to understand truly the fear accompanying it.

Real physical deprivation, which results when money is lacking, may cause the child to view money as a tremendous source of power for the gratification of needs and wants. This is reinforced for boys and girls whose schoolmates come from families more affluent than their own. The affluent child has money for treats; the poorer child has none for necessities. Children who need to make friends among peers and to establish some substantial relationships outside the immediate family may feel that they are different from those with more money, and may find it difficult to make their way in their social world.

Just as poverty interferes with children's opportunities for healthy emotional growth and development, so too there are special emotional strains that affect children in families of greater wealth. There is pressure for achievement, sometimes beyond the interest and capacity of the child, but in keeping with the parents' social norms and economic ambitions for the child. There may be denial of the mother's personal care in accordance with the family's social values. The overemphasis upon money and social position, competition with the neighbors in a material way, the feeling that money is evidence of superiority—all these attitudes are easily conveyed to children and may hinder the development of a sound and realistic scale of values.

There has been considerable speculation that the "flower children" of the sixties and the many young people who joined the Hare Krishna movement acted out their rejection of parental "material values" by affiliating with such movements. The middle-class successes of ethnic-minority families are also criticized by younger family members who "are losing their respect for work and their will to succeed because they think success is 'bourgeois' and have somehow gotten the impression that struggling to get to [a middle-class residential district in a large metropolitan area] is bad."[11]

Children are especially sensitive to parental anxieties about money. They sense the tension that is created when the father brings home a smaller paycheck or is laid off. They quickly become aware of dissension centered around money matters. Their own feelings are aroused when one parent depreciates the other in terms of the earning and of the management of money. An aura of awe and mystery surrounds money; because it has such importance for the parents, it creates in the child feelings of happiness and unhappiness, security and insecurity.

Our American culture equates money with security, love, and achievement. Its absence is equated with deprivation. Some differentials, however, exist within the culture. In the working class group, the lack of money is likely to be brought much more directly to the child's knowledge. When the parents are worried about money, the child may have feelings of insecurity but also understands fairly clearly that the insecurity is associated with money and not with the relationship with his or her parents. This reduces the confusion that might otherwise arise, for the reality can be understood. However, the relatively free spending in this group when money is available, and the tendency to buy the children impractical or expensive things create problems for them concerning the spending of money and distort their values about necessities as opposed to luxuries.

In the white-collar, middle-income group a different kind of confusion arises. Parents tend to conceal money difficulties from their children. But they use money to show love and approval, and to mete out punishment. Material acquisitions are seen by the parents as signs of achievement, success, and status. The young child translates money and material things into symbols of love. Some parents may alleviate their guilt about negative or rejecting feelings toward the child by material overindulgence. This also is true in many situations where both parents work, particularly if the mother is working to buy "nice things for the home," or if she and, perhaps, her husband have not come to terms with the overt and covert reasons for her working. The guilt felt by these mothers often is handled by overgiving, even to a very young child.

Because of their personality structures, parents sometimes are unable to meet the child's emotional needs or to handle child training problems constructively. Money may then become a substitute for love, or an instrument for manipulation and control, or a weapon for punishment. The use of money as a bargaining agent to secure the children's cooperation in doing their share of the family tasks is a poor substitute for helping them achieve a sense of their importance, both as receiving and contributing members of the family. Bribing children with money to put forth more effort in their school work or to practice their music lessons sets up false motivation for achievement. It emphasizes the reward rather than personal development and the increased satisfaction that comes with accomplishment. This is equally true of putting a monetary price on good behavior or willingness to go to the dentist. Depriving children of money on a routine basis in order to force atonement for a misdeed, for carelessness, or for an injury to another is likewise inappropriate. The payment of money cannot in fact compensate for such actions and may lead the child to believe that any kind of conduct is acceptable as long as it can be paid for with money. Of course, this does not preclude as eminently appropriate the careful and selective assessment and decision by parents that a particular incident of property damage should at least in part be paid for out of the child's allowance.

These parental uses of money, while far more common in middle- and upper-income families, are also to be found among lower-income families. Indeed, some families with very limited means but a high regard for education or for other forms of achievement may deprive themselves or other children in the family in order to "reward" a child, not just for doing well in school but for remaining in school. Such a child often comes to view money as the goal (which may also be the parents' goal, achievable through education) rather than the total package of personal benefits that education can be expected to make available. The inappropriate use of money or its substitution for the basic elements in the parent-child relationship obscures the child's view of the real relationship of money to life and this obscurity becomes a handicap in later years.

The parents' differential use of money with siblings provides a healthy growth experience for each child. The provision of clothes, allowances, and money for recreation should be related intelligently to the needs of children at their respective ages. Problems occur when money is used by parents, either as a special reward or punishment, to play off one sibling against another or to stimulate competitiveness. Competitiveness is frequently fostered in connection with school achievement or in the performance of household tasks, as one child is compared with another. The use of money to stimulate performance arouses a variety of feelings in the child. The money thus received assumes unwarranted magnitude: it symbolizes parental acceptance or rejection. It stimulates sibling rivalry and develops demanding attitudes in the child struggling to be the most favored one. It may become a negative force in the relationship with brothers and sisters when money or other gifts are used by one child as evidence of his or her superior position in the sibling rivalries. Although it may assure the child of a favored position, it also arouses concomitant guilt.

When marital discord is present, the parents may vie with each other to buy the child's love by giving money or material things, each parent pointing out to the child how depriving the other parent is. If separation of parents has occurred, the child frequently is sent as a messenger to the father, demanding money in the mother's behalf. Or the mother may complain that the father's failure to give money is tangible proof of his lack of interest in the child. In instances of remarriage of either parent, demands for support often incorporate irrational elements; these demands may be used in an effort either to hold on to the ex-partner or to destroy the new marriage. The child, as devil's advocate, can be a disruptive factor in the new home by making excessive demands on the father or by accusing the stepmother of depriving both the child and the child's mother.

If the mother has remarried, the success of the marriage often can be measured by the manner in which money is handled with the child. The mother who is unsure of herself in the marriage may tend to protect her new husband by not permitting the child to make realistic demands on him or by refusing to let the husband assume the father role in the provision of money. If the family is receiving public assistance, especially Aid to Families with Dependent Children (AFDC), agency policies with reference to the financial role of the stepfather in the home may perpetuate this unhealthy type of interpersonal relationship.

If the mother's new marriage is not going well, she may blame the child for being an expense, or berate her husband for his refusal to accept the child. This kind of situation becomes particularly complex when support is being paid by the natural father. His contribution is seen as "belonging" to the child and is handled as a separate item, not to be put into the family's income pot. The common consequence is that this form of management gives the child a feeling of being an outsider or of being special or different from other children in the home.

MONEY AND THE YOUNG CHILD

The young child's awareness of money and feelings about it, as well as how the child uses or wants to use money, as has been pointed out above, are intimately related to the family's lifestyle, personalities, and relationships. However, there are certain patterns that are fairly common among children in particular age groups. It is of value to the counselor to be aware of these developmental stages in the child's ordinary relationship to money, especially because parents are often either concerned or elated by a particular form of behavior and, when the form changes naturally, there is a swing in parental reaction, which may be conveyed in anger, pleasure, praise, or punishment.

A child's first experience with money is likely to be a gift of money or an allowance, although for many it actually begins with foraging for coins, more or less secretly, in the mother's purse or the father's pocket. Their shininess and shapes are attractive and they may find their way into the child's mouth or under the sofa cushions or on the floor. But the very young child makes little connection between the coin and its use for the purchase of other items—although there may be very early awareness that older children are happy to be the recipients, by voluntary or forceful action, of the younger one's largesse.

By the time the child is five, in all but the poorest families or those remote from stores, the child has learned two things about money: that the coins appear magically from a parental pocket or other storage place and that the parent is the provider of the money; and that the coins can be used to procure satisfying items such as candy, bubble gum, and crayons. This has been demonstrated by the child's exchanging the coin for the item, generally under the watchful eye of an adult or an older sibling. Sometimes parents give the very young child money with the admonition that it is to be "saved," or not spent for another week or some other time period. The preschool child usually does not understand the concept of saving; moreover, postponement of self-gratification is not characteristic of this age group. The time concept may also be beyond the child's comprehension, for the sense of time—like that of money—has not yet been developed: days, weeks, and months appear endless.

With entry into the school system, although the child tends still to be careless in the handling or keeping of money, new vistas and opportunities are opened: money can procure sweets, comic books, entrance to movies, or additions to collections of toy cars. The six-year-old is eager to learn but the span of attention is relatively short and interest in the purchase may wane very quickly. The child likes praise but responds to correction with "No, I won't!" or "You can't make me!" even while heavily dependent on parental approval. Making choices is difficult, and saving is not one of the choices likely to be made. Yet, at age seven, the child is more persevering; and by the age of eight, the youngster has become "money-mad," hoarding money in a miserly fashion, bartering or "investing" in collections of baseball cards, bottle caps, matchbook covers, model airplanes, dolls, or other items with either pecuniary or "collector" value.

Eight- and nine-year-olds can begin to use time, to postpone to the next week the making of a purchase. They can be unrealistic about purchases and make mistakes in what they buy; their belief in magic persists. They are very preoccupied with fairness: why can't they have what others have? Their feelings are easily hurt, but they tend to respond to reason and can accept blame. By age eight, children know how much they have in money or bottle caps or marbles, how much is due them, what they want to buy, how much it will cost, how to save for more expensive things, how to barter. And by age nine, they like the idea of having large amounts of money or special items to look at, to show, to count, to talk about.

Many parents worry about the "closefistedness" of their child in this period, and then become bewildered when the miserly child suddenly becomes a "spendthrift," as many children do in the nine-to-twelve-year-old period. Their needs for and uses of money have undergone considerable change. They now understand time and can project into the future, planning and saving. They like to argue with adults and are beginning to display some independence about making decisions for the use of money. Conformity, to be a part of a group, becomes increasingly important. Children left out of a group may spend money in odd ways to work themselves into the circle.

Children in this age bracket spend more for recreation: club dues, games, and special events. Hobbies become more intense preoccupations for many. They can also handle more responsibility. It is among these children that there is greater demand to be "paid" for tasks performed. And it is in this age group that children from poor families and enterprising children from other families begin to seek ways of earning; the former may shine shoes or sweep the neighboring shopkeeper's floor, and the latter may sell lemonade at curbside in front of their homes.

Throughout these preadolescent years, the child's normal experiences with the role and uses of money shift and change. The money climate in which the child grows, however, in many ways affects the attitudes that are developed and the behavior that is displayed regarding its meanings and uses. Feeling responses to the money behavior of parents or others in the household may contribute to the child's retaining the behavior pattern consistent with an earlier age level and influence lifelong patterns of obtaining and managing money.

Money and the Adolescent

An expanding family frequently contains children in different stages in their development, ranging from infancy to young adulthood. All developmental stages have certain similarities but they differ from one another both in general psychodynamics and in the specific psychodynamics of money. The greatest changes come with adolescence. This stormy stage is marked by a conflict between continued dependence and strivings for independence, and by some special problems in relation to money. Young persons at this stage may be high school and college students, or new employees finding their way in the economic world.

The adolescent still attending school has sharply increased expenses for social and personal obligations. The availability or unavailability of money plays a strategic role in the young person's struggle to attain independence. Considerable anxiety is felt about the future—education, career, and marriage. Support, control, and freedom of choice are all needed. It is through money that the adolescent most commonly evidences normal conflict about dependence and independence.

Adolescents are likely to express part of their healthy rebellion against the family by strong reaction against all family patterns, including those of thrift and expenditure. Money is used as a way of measuring the parents' standards and behavior and as a way of depreciating them. Adolescents may be extremely critical of parental economic failures and may be unable to see other merits in parents who lack money. On the other hand, adolescents whose parents have been economically successful may tend to deny or denigrate the importance of this success, to be critical on ethical grounds; or they may leave home altogether to seek or practice a "better philosophy of life."

Some adolescents' normally exaggerated reactions may be magnified even further by sensitivity to real or fancied inferiorities of their parents' social class, their foreign background, the particular religious or ethnic group in which the parents have membership, or the offsprings' conviction that the parents lack experiences with today's problems and tensions and therefore "cannot possibly understand" the needs of today's youth. And, indeed, today's middle-aged and even older parents often do lack experiences that can be coping models for youth in the faster-paced world of their children, for many of today's circumstances and demands have no parallels in former years. This reality may compound the frustration not infrequently felt by parents with fractious adolescent children.

Adolescents usually demand more money than their parents provide, and want no control over their spending. They want to buy what they please, and they are likely to spend money defiantly for things that the parents deem useless but that the adolescents want in relation to peer standards. They neglect buying what their parents consider to be important, and they may be alternately tightfisted and wildly spendthrift. Often, at the same time, they are actually resentful when their parents place no control on spending, and the parents become a target for the anger of the children who make poor purchases. Because such inconsistency is part of the normal development process, great flexibility on the part of the parents is required if the adolescent is to be given some freedom and provided with some controls. Parents must not be too critical of failures or errors in spending, and must be approving of good use of money. Such a balance is not easy to achieve or maintain! If parents are too rigid in their controls, the adolescent may capitulate and never be freed from parental ties; at this period, ambivalence is at a high peak, and the young person fears the loss of their love. Or the adolescent may become too rebellious ever to learn to manage money. In the demands for money, the adolescent may be expressing a frustrated need for love. The fear of loss of parental love as expressed in the use of money is sometimes overshadowed by the problem of dependence-independence. Yet both aspects must be understood and dealt with if the adolescent is to be helped in becoming emancipated from infantile ties.

The children's adolescence is a difficult time for the parents, too. They often maintain rigid controls because they cannot face the process of their children's growing up and growing away. Parents therefore often resort to defensive behavior and rationalize that the young persons will squander their money. The need to control is sometimes further reinforced, especially among foreign-born or deeply religious parents, by the fear that the adolescents will "forget the old ways."

At the other extreme are parents who act out their feelings about their own deprivations by permitting their adolescent children to use money in whatever fashion they wish. Also, some parents may be overcontrolling or overpermissive because their own security is jeopardized. For example, it is not uncommon for a father whose status or authority is threatened by his son to attempt to set up rigid controls and accuse the mother of overindulgence. A mother may react in the same way to her blossoming young daughter. The mother may try to compete in appearance and to control the girl's selection of clothes. And the mother is likely to accuse the father of overindulging the daughter. To a certain extent these family rivalries are normal. But if the controls stem from deep-rooted conflicts that have never been resolved, the effect on the adolescent may be serious. Parents may successfully repress or suppress hostile feelings toward young children but, as these children reach adolescence, the parents tend to be more open about their own feelings. Hence, a father may insist that a teenage son start to earn his own way, even though this may not be necessary from an economic viewpoint; a mother may press a daughter to think about marriage.

Parents should endeavor to stand together on major decisions about an adolescent's use of money. In minor issues, they should permit each other to guide the adolescent of his or her own sex, so that the boy can identify with his father and the girl with her mother. The father may be a little indulgent with his son, and engage in a little foolish masculine spending. The mother should be permitted to do the same with her daughter; the parents can allow some mild playing-off of one parent against the other, if they both understand their roles and the needs of the adolescent. Strengthening the identification of the adolescent with the parent of the same sex not only fosters the emancipation process but also helps to prepare the boy and girl for their roles and responsibilities in marriage.

During adolescence, children begin to branch out for themselves, to develop many interests separate from the family, and to think seriously about their career goals. Adolescents who receive no support from parents in pursuing their ambitions are likely to pay for whatever success is achieved with some degree of emotional maladjustment. Children in families with limited income commonly encounter greater problems in becoming emancipated than those in more favorable circumstances, for often they realistically must carry some family burdens. Or, out of despair or frustration, they may escape from the family abruptly and prematurely. The adolescent who breaks away from the family under unfriendly circumstances also carries away a residue of emotional dependence and hostility. Because the basic emotional needs of such an adolescent have not been met adequately, some distortions of personality are to be expected. One of these distortions will be in the meanings of money and the uses that are made of it in adulthood. On the other hand, the adult who has had reasonably secure and satisfying experiences through those emotionally charged adolescent years can be expected to respond realistically to financial responsibilities and opportunities.

Normal money behavior of adolescents may be trying for parents and other adults in the adolescent's environment. There is the comfort of knowing, however, that despite the criticisms, the demands, the anger, and the inconsistencies, improvement almost inevitably arrives with maturation. Counselors, however, need to be watchful for danger signals discernible in the adolescent's attitudes and practices in the handling of money. The signals are broadcast in observable consistent patterns of behavior that include neurotic uses of money.

The "big spenders" are the boys or girls who are constantly the center of a group in the school canteen, the nearby sweetshop, or the neighborhood drugstore or billiard parlor, ready to draw on a seemingly inexhaustible supply of funds to "treat" everyone. These young people seek to buy friendship and affection they do not know how to obtain otherwise. The "borrower" bids for affection and attention from peers, teachers, or younger students by borrowing lunch money, snack money, pencils, paper, items of clothing, or other possessions. Borrowers grow angry when they are rebuffed or receive no response to this unsuccessful effort to learn if they are lovable and loved. The "hoarders" carefully secrete from others whatever material possessions they have. This young person constantly tries to add to his or her money supply and is unable to part with any. For this adolescent, the tangible form and value of money are evidence of strength and nurture self-esteem. Or the girl or boy may cling to it because it was a gift from an absent, possibly deserting or divorced, parent and symbolizes the love and care the adolescent may not actually have been receiving. Even if the money were involuntarily provided (by a court order to a reluctant parent, for example) it nevertheless is perceived by the adolescent on an emotional level (but who may tell himself or herself otherwise) as a sign of affection and caring.

The "pilferer" sneaks money and other items from the purse or desk of the teacher or from purses or pockets left unguarded in school dressing rooms or lockers, or at home. The consequent attention accorded the apprehended pilferer is tantamount to recognition that the adolescent as a person has found a satisfying way of striking at meaningful adults; the pilferer is "getting even" with those regarded as discriminating or who in some way have been belittling. (Some of the same dynamics are present in the youngsters who vandalize schools.) If the pilferer is not caught, he or she may feel a sense of omnipotence. The "cost pricer" is the unhealthily competitive boy or girl who demands to know the exact cost of a schoolmate's possession in order to acquire something better or costlier (even at some financial sacrifice on the part of the family), thereby demonstrating "superiority" that bolsters or masks limited self-esteem.

The "rationalizer" is the intelligent high school or young college student who uses the need to earn money to help the family or to maintain himself or herself as the reason for leaving a school situation that is unsatisfactory in some fashion. There may in fact be no economic pressures on the student or family, either because sufficient scholarship aid has been made available or because the family's own financial means make further schooling quite possible; but the need to work and earn is a socially acceptable reason for withdrawing from a stressful situation. This also may be the young person who espouses a cause or ideology or lifestyle in opposition to that of the parents, and rationalizes leaving home on the basis of a philosophical difference—most often, that the parents are preoccupied with materialistic values. This rationalizing behavior often stems from faulty development of trust, self-esteem, and identity in combination with an unrealistic response to the meanings and uses of money.

MONEY AND THE CHILD IN PLACEMENT

For a variety of reasons, children are placed in the care of a foster family or in a child-caring institution. Placements are made because of physical or mental illness or absence of one or both parents. Personality or other problems of the parents may indicate that the child's interests will be better served if there is an out-of-home placement. The child's problems or disturbances may not be as responsive to adequate treatment in the family's home as elsewhere. The placement may be voluntarily arranged by the parent with or without the help of an agency, or it may be ordered by a court.

The child in a foster family is exposed to a complicated set of experiences that will color the child's attitudes toward money. Not only are many persons important to the child involved in the placement, but each person has a set of attitudes about the placement, and all have various reactions to each other. In addition, each natural parent and each foster parent has a complex of feelings about money; the same is true of the social worker and the agency arranging and supervising the placement.

The parent who asks for the placement of a child experiences the conflicts that naturally accrue from running athwart tradition and convention. Guilt usually accompanies the relinquishment of responsibility the parents may not wish or be able to carry, yet which they know society expects them to carry. When a high degree of guilt accompanies the placement, the parent may be overgenerous with money, giving it to the child as a sign of love or as a placating device. Or, in competition with the foster parent, the natural parent may give money as "proof" of the superiority of a blood relationship. In the effort to prevent the child from establishing a positive relationship with the foster parent, the own parent —especially the mother—may be openly critical of the agency and of the foster parent. If she pays all or part of the cost, she may complain about the way the money is spent. She is particularly inclined to complain about the child's food and the adequacy of the physical care the child is given.

Often the child, on returning from a visit to the natural parents, is ill from overindulgence and laden down with things that are impractical for the youngster's daily living and beyond the income or normal standard of the foster family and its own children. The parent may remove the child from the foster home, alleging "misuse" of the money paid for board and care, thus adding to the number of homes in which the child must live, and reducing opportunity for the child to develop sound identifications with family members and family life. Such action often is taken by the unmarried mother who can neither keep nor give up her child; it is also evident among mothers who, for illness or other reasons, do not keep the child in the family home.

Parents who are self-punitive, guilty, or rejecting often deprive themselves in order to meet the financial obligations for the child's board and care. The parent who has always assumed responsibility for the family, as well as the one who wishes to gain prestige in the eyes of the child or foster parent and agency, may also meet the child-support obligations. In contrast, the emotionally dependent parent will expect the social agency to carry the financial burden of the child's care. Money is only one aspect of the placement experience for the parent, but because of its concreteness the parent understands it and responds to it with special feeling, often begrudging suspicion and hostility. The feeling expressed may typify the parent's feelings about other aspects of the placement.

The child in placement also translates various feelings into money terms. Inner conflicts may be expressed by demanding material things from the agency or social worker, or gifts and money from the parents to test their affection or to punish them for their seeming rejection. To the child, assumption of the board payment by the parents may constitute some evidence of being loved. Or it may be used as a device for gauging their love, measuring their payments against their ability to pay. The child may use the knowledge of their payments aggressively with foster parents and with other children in the home, as a source of courage and status. Because to "pay one's own way" is an important value in our society, the older child who is aware that the parents are not providing for the child's support may be burdened especially with feelings of guilt, worthlessness, inadequacy, and resentment: their failure to be independent and "powerful" intensifies the child's dependence-independence conflict.

Money also has special significance to foster parents. Although competence in parenting is a primary criterion in the evaluation of foster parents, altruism is also stressed. Some emotional need undoubtedly leads many foster parents to take on this responsibility. Yet a financial motive may also be present even though board rates generally are not high enough to justify the investment of self that is required of foster parents. If the motivation for foster parenting is to augment income, the payments and costs should be evaluated as well as the potential foster parents' reasons for having selected this way of earning money. This is not to question the value or validity of earning money by rendering a constructive service; rather, the foster parents' perceptions and handling of money become an additional influence on the child's developing views and feelings about the role and value of money in the child's own life.

Foster parents sometimes ask parents to supply money or material things. These requests may arise because the board payments are not commensurate with the cost of caring for the child and meeting certain uncovered needs. Other requests may stem from the foster parents' inability to accept the inevitable disappointments that are inherent in the fostering of children. Such requests may be charged with judgmental feelings or with rivalry and hostility toward the natural parents—or even be a defense against the hurt that will be felt by the foster parents when the child leaves them.

The child in placement ordinarily experiences many more affectional deprivations than does the child who has remained in the family home. The placed child is likely to magnify money as a symbol of love in much the same way as the adolescent magnifies it as a symbol of independence. To the child removed from the proximity of the natural parents, money spent on his or her behalf comes to be regarded as a measure of the affectional ties between the family and the child.

DEVELOPING CHILDREN'S ATTITUDES TOWARD MONEY

It bears reiteration that, inevitably, the adult's attitudes about having, earning, and using money are the products of a constellation of experiences and influences touching the individual during the growing-up years: the family's economic and social situation and location, the social system of which the family is a part, the feelings and attitudes of the family members about money and social status, whether money is scarce or plentiful in the household, and how its giving or withholding is handled as the ages of the children change. The most important impact is that of the parent (or substitute parent) model; closely related to this modeling are the skill and wisdom that children acquire by managing money of their own.

ALLOWANCES

A regular small cash allowance gives children opportunity to learn realistically to plan the spending of the money according to their personal choice. This is a valuable experience, even for the young school child, provided there is clear understanding between the child and the parents regarding what the allowance is expected to cover. Money that the child is given for carfare, lunches, or Sunday School collection or other prescribed purposes should not be confused with the child's "own money," for the youngster usually has no discretion over these parentally prescribed expenditures. It is instructive for children to have the experience of disbursing earmarked funds, but this is a limited kind of learning. The concept of an allowance, which is quite popular even with adults, means that each family member can have at least a small sum of money for personal use, to spend freely without having to account for it. This enhances the prospect that the children will learn realistically to get the greatest amount of satisfaction for themselves from the use of their own money, and will acquire the sense of independence that comes with spending one's own money. And the element of choice even a very small allowance affords contributes to the process of ego development.

In *Parents, Children, and Money,*[12] Sidonie and Benjamin Gruenberg tell of a mother who complains that her children invariably ask for pennies on wash day, when she has no time to defend a refusal. Another mother finds the children in sudden and immediate need of funds when there is company. In both cases the appeal simply cannot be denied. The Gruenbergs report that the extremes to which children will go in cajoling their parents into paying toll are almost without limit, and every human weakness—as manifested in parents—is a subject to levy. One cute little girl, after teasing her mother while they were out shopping together, until she exhausted her wiles, suddenly pulled away and stepped into the street gutter. Turning to the mother, she said, "Now I am going to lie right down here and get run over if you don't give me the money!" Could the mother calmly weigh one value against the other? Could she bargain? Could she take a chance that the child would yield from fear? . . . Could she apply major force? In another instance, the child called and called for a penny until the mother yielded with the explanation, "Because the neighbors might think I didn't have it."[13]

These are common and traditional forms of blackmail, today's situations differing only because inflation over several decades has affected the value and denominations of the money being extorted. But the examples are indicative of stresses and strains in relationships that go far deeper than the overt demand for money.

A weekly allowance (or on some other time basis) is not an answer to all children's problems. It is, however, an important tool in their healthy emotional and economic development: it is an important investment in the child's total education. Its purpose is to provide the child with experience in the art of making choices, exercising judgment and restraint about when and what to buy—if anything. It begins with a very small amount, thereby allowing for small mistakes. As the size of the allowance grows, so should competence in its handling; and the learning is gained increasingly less from mistakes than from successes.

Many times parents are reluctant to give a child money that is truly the child's own. They do not trust the youngster not to squander it, lose it, or just give it away. It is not merely that they think the child cannot or will not handle the money appropriately: many of these adults manifest their own need to retain what they have struggled hard to earn and that is hard for them to share; moreover, they often maintain that money should be earned before it is spent. However, generally, they also recognize that the young child's need for money or education as to its use may occur long before most children can earn it, even for chores at home.

As mentioned previously, parents sometimes withhold a child's allowance as a disciplinary measure. This practice, like the payment of a reward for good behavior, strengthens the child's tendency to think of money in terms of love and to feel disliked or rejected by the withholding of the allowance. Mortgaging the allowance—making advances from future weeks' allowance and requiring repayment so that the child never really has the full amount of the allowance available or does not have occasion to live within the established limit—reduces the effectiveness of the money-management learning experience. It is only with experience in having the allowance *as an allowance* that the child can begin to understand its use.

Money itself becomes more significant to children as they grow older and have more direct need for it. Although, after the youngster reaches the age of five, money is recognized as a means of purchasing things that the child wants rather than as a plaything, it is not until about age ten that the young person begins really to use it. Then the amount of the allowance—the part that is unrestrictedly for the child and not already allocated for specific items designated by others—should be in line not only with the family finances but also with neighborhood and peer standards. Although some guidance in managing the allowance may be needed, there should be no rigid controls. The money-payment principle should apply to progeny as well as to parents! Furthermore, as parents from one generation to another have learned, the child is not receptive to guidance as to how, what, and when to buy, or even where to keep money, until a mistake actually has been made that the child wants to avoid repeating. Like adults, children profit from negative as well as positive experiences in money management.

With increased experience in spending the allowance, the child develops greater awareness of values. Eventually the child will want an item that the small allowance will not purchase. Thus, something is learned about saving. Saving in itself, however, usually holds no attraction for children. It is only as they can see a real goal, usually a short-time goal, that they can become interested in saving. This point is apt to be of concern to parents who forget that it is only as people grow older and mature that long-term goals are either possible or meaningful. For the child's education, it is the principle of saving that is of importance—that is, to learn to postpone immediate pleasure in order to gain future satisfactions.

Even families of very modest means often can give their children allowances. Were they to keep track over a period of time of the amounts of money they actually give the child, an equivalent amount could be made available routinely rather than on an "as needed" or "asked for" basis. However, many families find it difficult to separate from their limited family funds, especially if their income is primarily some form of transfer payment, a sum that can be designated as an allowance for one or more children in the family. In such instances, it is particularly important that the children be aware that the realistic absence of money is the reason for no allowances and not an inferred absence of affection.

The difference may be hard for younger children to distinguish intellectually; they will, however, feel the difference.

For the adolescent who is not earning money or whose family is dependent on outside financial assistance it is particularly important that there be a clear understanding about the reason for not having an allowance. Indeed, the parents should enlist the help of the adolescent in examining the family income and expenses to determine whether even a small allowance can be provided without unduly disadvantaging other family members. Moreover, the adolescent and the parents should share an understanding that an allowance will be given when a positive change in family finances occurs.

Many parents sincerely believe that the most effective and generous giving of money to their children occurs when it is requested for a specific reason.

> Mr. D spoke with pride about his 17-year-old son, Jeff. "My boy is a *good* boy; he is a top student, a leader in his high school and in church. Best of all, no money 'jingles in his pockets'!" Whatever Jeff wanted or needed he had only to ask for, whether it was to buy five gallons of gasoline for his car, a corsage for his date, or money for a "soda or Danish" with his friends after school. The father, a credit manager in a department store with a large-volume credit business, was particularly sensitive to the many people who contracted to buy more than their paychecks indicated to be realistic; week after week they were self-deceived into spending more than their incomes justified. *His* boy would not be tempted like that!
>
> When Jeff was apprehended while burglarizing a gasoline service station, the father was beyond understanding either the boy's act or his own contribution to it. He was puzzled by his son's rebellion against the constant expectation that he had to "ask for money like a little kid."

Mr. A was unaware that he had deprived the boy of normal opportunities to learn to make decisions or to begin to manage his own affairs and hence to move from dependence toward independence and adulthood. Mr. A felt only the injury of his son's fight against the father's unwillingness to let him grow up, and the boy's calculatedly striking at his father's most vulnerable point—his fear about money "jingling" in a pocket.

It does not necessarily follow, of course, that all children whose parents prefer to consider each need individually as it arises will be in difficulties like Jeff's. In some families, particularly those with parents born in another country or with families whose cultural pattern places unquestioned authority with the father (or with the mother) to make all financial decisions both large and small, allowances are never provided.

In these families, the controlling and protecting role of the parent cannot allow for discretion on the child's part. In such families, the "value of a dollar" and emphasis on thrift are communicated by example only, unless the child acquires money from the parents or others as a gift, or until the child begins to earn and is permitted to manage part of what is earned.

In essence, the provision by parents of an allowance as a carefully observed matter-of-course act enhances its learning value for children. The size and frequency should be related to the child's age and interests, the neighborhood, the family resources, and the child's needs and ability to manage it. Changes in its amount and timing will be related to changing needs, experience the child has gained in using money, and what the family can afford and regards as consistent with its lifestyle and circumstances. Promptness and regularity in supplying the full amount agreed upon—with both the parents and the child understanding clearly the purpose of the allowance—are essential. If the young child spends the allowance too fast and thus is unable to buy something of value which the parents agree the child should have, they might find it wise to give the "missed" item to the child as a gift. Wisdom also would dictate that it is inadvisable to repeat this process. The older child, with some practice, should face realities, including looking to earnings to make up such a loss.

Parents should not give or withhold the allowance impulsively as a response to either wheedling by the child, or coercion or collusion by the child with one parent against the other. Nor should the youngster be expected to account for how the personal allowance has been used: this defeats the objective of instilling responsibility and judgment in decision-making, as well as respect for the property of others. How parents approach making an allowance serves in itself to give the child some idea about orderly management of money as a means to an end rather than as a symbol of, or substitute for, affection and approval.

EARNINGS

Learning what money will buy and how to use it are first steps in the child's financial education. The experience of earning money gives a third dimension to the youngster's education—namely, that effort must be put forth to acquire funds. In today's world, earning opportunities for children are limited, especially in urban areas. It is possible, however, that parents overlook certain opportunities for introducing children into a meaningful role in the household economy. The young child can earn money by doing clearly designated chores around the home, and in some communities, by doing chores for neighbors. In the latency period, the child usually develops habits of industry and takes pleasure in acquiring new skills and completing tasks. The child who learns to feel adequate in a work role has achieved an important step in psychosocial development.

Beginning experiences in working and earning are an important component in child development, and there is really no time when it is too soon for this learning to commence. Practically speaking, the role of the child within the family involves work elements; but because so much of what children are expected to do is in the context of its being "for their own good," their work or service that benefits parents and siblings is not regarded as producing economic values for the latter or an investment in themselves as human capital. In a more religious age, work in the household performed by the child as part of socialization was viewed as work performed for God. Work experiences, as a part of today's socialization process, should give children the sense that the work is productive according to the standards of significant persons around them, expressed by words, affect, or money. Otherwise, when these children become adults they too readily come to believe that they are unlikely to have something of value to offer on a social labor market.

The parental motivation for encouraging such work experiences, as well as the nature and timing of the tasks to be performed are of paramount importance. The purpose should be the child's learning, *not* earnings to accrue to the family even though the family may have only marginal income. A young child cannot be expected to carry a burden of financial responsibility for a family without severe impairment of later social or psychological functioning. This is not to say that there are no circumstances in which the very young child can be an earner: the entertainment industry, for example, offers important opportunities to some children. But certain protections must be supplied to ensure that the child is not exploited, that healthy development for adulthood is not thwarted, and that the child's allowance should not be dependent on or related to earnings. Certainly the youngster might be paid for tasks not otherwise normally performed by himself or another family member, and for which payment would be made to an outsider. Children should be encouraged (not pushed) to take available work such as lawn mowing, babysitting, newspaper delivery and so forth. Such encouragement should be accompanied by a decision in advance, reached by parents and child, as to how the earnings will be handled. Saved for some special purpose? toward the family's support? hobbies? future education? or unrestricted like the allowance? or to substitute for part of the allowance?

One of the adolescent's exciting new powers is the ability to earn money. In families of nearly all economic levels, the adolescent has a keen interest in part-time and vacation work. The young person also comes gradually to recognize that work is essential for survival and therefore thinks of future occupations with more reality and less fantasy than is characteristic of the younger child. An adolescent who is under strong parental pressure to select a particular vocation is faced not only with a narrowness of choices of occupation but may also experience considerable confusion and rebellion. If compelled by poverty to work full-time while peers continue to attend school, the adolescent is placed in a disadvantaged position. By losing the opportunity to develop latent capacities through continuing education this young person is forced to sacrifice later earning power to immediate need. The problems are further complicated if the adolescent leaves school only to discover that work is not really available, especially in a period of economic recession.

The adolescent's jobs are part of the preparation for later life work. Both through working and through managing earnings, the adolescent is meeting important developmental needs. The standards about ways of earning and spending money may differ from that of the adult, but the adolescent learns through trial and error. The way a young person earns and spends money often reveals the personality problems as well as the strengths that are present.

Adolescents have some tendency to cling to earnings, regardless of the family's financial circumstances, thereby expressing a basic drive for personal survival. If the adult world forces these young persons to surrender most of their earnings to the family, their reaction is likely to be one of hostility, the intensity of which will depend on their past experiences and on their family relationships. The adolescent who has had some opportunity to gain gratification and recognition by assuming responsibility will be better able to handle such family-support demands. Conflict and rebellion are to be expected, however, if adolescents are asked to take an adult role in supporting the family and, at the same time, are controlled like young children in other areas of their lives. They may leave the home in anger or, if they remain, become extremely bitter.

Social workers should be particularly aware of the dynamics involved in the economically dependent family with an adolescent breadwinner. In private agencies, some flexibility of budget and some individualization of need have been possible. But in public assistance agencies the obligations of the adolescent, as a contributor to the family, generally are set by statute and regulations that do not always take into account their effect on the adolescent's personal development. Rather, these policies express outmoded social and economic attitudes. The adolescent's economic contribution—whether the family is self-supporting or receiving public assistance—should be based on the needs of the adolescent as well as those of the family. The balance between the two can be established only on an individual basis. A helpful baseline for the decision can be drawn if the parents review the family budget plan with the adolescent, and then decide together what proportion or flat amount of the adolescent's earnings would constitute a reasonable contribution, and even what fraction and form of the family expenditures this contribution would cover. Some parents are reluctant to let the children know the amount of family income or how it is apportioned and spent, fearing that others might too easily become privy to this information. Even without discussing specific amounts or sources of income, parents can involve adolescents and younger children in understanding how income is allocated for the family's maintenance.

Adolescents who are wage earners should be expected to meet their personal expenses and to pay, to the extent feasible, for room and board. If the family has a limited income, the adolescent should contribute a specified amount to the total family expenses, but should be left free to manage, without parental criticism, the rest of his earnings: to spend, to save, or to apply earnings toward education, career, or marriage. Much damage has resulted from the insistence by parents and social agencies that an adolescent make relatively large contributions toward the family's support. In families where the father is dead or absent, the adolescent boy or girl is sometimes expected to assume the paternal economic role, an experience that may have deleterious psychological consequences. Many of these adolescents, for example, never truly emancipate themselves from their families. At the same time, it is equally undesirable for employed adolescents not to participate in paying for their own living expenses: learning to pay one's way provides a foundation for development toward mature independence and for later responsibility in marriage or heading a household. In order to be able to assume responsibility for others, a person must first have experience in taking responsibility for self.

Preparation for the Money World

Parents who are able to meet their children's need for love and affection, for recognition, and for freedom to grow up do not have to use money to accomplish these ends. For them money becomes a tool for meeting reality needs, and the children grow into adults who understand the role of money as the medium of exchange and as a symbol of value. But the irrational use of money by parents during their children's growing-up years presages many unfortunate consequences, albeit the consequences may differ from child to child even with the same parents. The confusion between love and money is the most common outcome, but it is closely followed by overevaluation of material possessions, feelings of inadequacy often masked by undue competitiveness, and overcompensation expressed in undue striving for money.

There are several common practices to which parents concerned about their children's welfare in a money world need to be alert. One frequent hazard lies in the small and sometimes obscure kinds of cheating in which parents indulge and in which their children become active partners. Lying about children's ages to gain cheaper admission to entertainment or transportation facilities is an example. Such dishonest practices modeled by parents become incorporated into the child's superego and contribute to a corruptible conscience.

More difficult for parents to deal with are the often highly publicized situations external to the family that influence children's attitudes toward money and justice, through an implied acceptability of the game of "getting away" with bettering others, especially in government or big business. Thus, a recipient of public assistance or a beneficiary of unemployment insurance payments may deliberately or inadvertently make statements that lead to an increase or continuation of such transfer payments in amounts beyond those to which the individual or family may be eligible. A wealthy taxpayer or highly placed official may fail to file an income tax statement despite having considerable seemingly taxable income. An executive of a large corporation entrusted with the savings of many small and large investors may doctor the accounts to his benefit and the loss of the investors. Similar kinds of psychodynamics are present in each of these dishonest acts, but public reaction as expressed in statute or in administrative or judicial interpretation treats each differently. The ineligible recipient of the transfer payment is prosecuted and may thereby trigger a public clamor for ferreting out and publicizing "fraud" among those dependent on public sources for their survival needs—and who, ipso facto, cannot simultaneously be poor and honest. The taxpayer or official may be permitted to negotiate and settle the claim without any particular punishment; the executive may be subjected to a fine or short imprisonment. To the growing youngster whose value system is being formed, the lesson regarding the fraudulent and immoral poor is clear. Equally clear is the conviction that when the financial stakes are high, the negative costs constitute a small price to pay for the ultimate profit. The burden falls on the parent to explain effectively these inconsistencies in society's attitudes toward money and morality.

Of a different order is the credit-card mentality that is steadily encompassing larger and larger segments of our population. The convenience of credit-card usage has led to some shifting of responsibility from card-holders to card-granters for day-to-day money management. Some adults carry little cash, tend to write few checks, and rely on charging arrangements for payment of practically all their bills. Now that it is possible for an individual's salary check—or transfer payment, such as Social Security benefits—to be deposited automatically in a bank, and to have bills forwarded to the bank for payment, some children may grow up without having observed parents receiving, planning, and managing the disbursement of their income. How will these children gain experience in decision-making and management of their financial affairs? Many are authorized to use parental credit cards and charge accounts. Will the future adult be able to distinguish between the magic of charging an item, and the reality of assuring that the money is available to cover its costs?

Just as it is essential that the beginning family formulate goals related realistically to actual and potential income and to actual and potential expenditures, so it is necessary for the expanding family to establish its goals. Effective attainment of goals requires a constant reevaluation of needs and resources when the family changes in size and structure as new children are born, as each child moves from one stage to another, and when the family income changes. The parents' attitudes and feelings regarding money and social position, their values and aspirations, as well as their realistic and symbolic handling of money with their children will be paramount in determining the kind of adults the children will become. Parental attitudes regarding money constitute the primary source of their children's attitudes about it. The children learn much from just being members of a family group, living together day after day in the same household. As the children grow older, they can be helped to develop sound attitudes about money if the family engages in planning as a family. The children then become economic planners and participants, and learn how to live effectively and satisfactorily in today's money world.

NOTES

1. U.S., Department of Commerce, Bureau of the Census, *Statistical Abstract of the United States 1975: National Data Book and Guide to Sources,* 96th ed. (Washington, D.C.: U.S. Government Printing Office, 1975), p. 397.
2. Lewis Mandell et al., *Survey of Consumers 1971-72: Contributions to Behavioral Economics* (Ann Arbor: University of Michigan, 1973), p. 28.
3. Ibid., pp. 51-55.
4. Ibid., pp. 39-40.
5. Ibid., pp. 25-34.
6. Ibid., pp. 12-13.
7. Ibid., p. 19.
8. Ibid., pp. 59-60.
9. Charlotte Towle, *Common Human Needs,* rev. ed. (New York: National Association of Social Workers, 1965), p. 3.
10. Allison Davis, "Ability and Survival," *The Survey,* 87 (February 1951): 62.
11. J. K. Obatala, writing in "Opinion" section, *The Los Angeles Times,* June 16, 1975, pt. 2, p. 7.
12. Sidonie M. Gruenberg and Benjamin C. Gruenberg, *Parents, Children, and Money* (New York: Viking Press, 1933).
13. Ibid., p. 29.

6
The Contracting Family

At what point is a family contracting rather than expanding? The age range of children in the family may be spread so wide that one child may be born and another married within a relatively brief span of time. It is when the family unit no longer contains young children that the family is really in the contracting stage of the cycle of family life.

THE MIDDLE YEARS

The altered composition of the family in the contracting stage affects its economic situation. It usually is at this stage that the father's income from earnings peaks. In today's industrial world, except for the relatively small group in executive and managerial positions, most men reach the top level of their earning power during middle age. Also, about half of the married women in the work force are in their middle years (forty-five to fifty-four),[1] a sizable proportion of these having no children in the home and presumably also at their peak earnings.

The attainment of peak earned family income commonly coincides with the lessening of responsibilities for the care and education of children except, perhaps, for those still pursuing a college education. Other children who may still be in the home generally are old enough to meet their own financial needs and sometimes they contribute to the family income. As each child leaves home there is a proportionate net increase in the funds available for the remaining family members from the parental earnings. If the wife had been working only part-time while children were still at home and now, on their departure, increases her work time and earnings, the couple may have more money for their own use than they did even before they had children.

At this stage, the family has long had an established home and, if they have bought a house, the size of the mortgage has steadily declined. Many parents tend to move to smaller quarters as children depart, but this move does not necessarily reduce shelter costs. In fact, the number of single dwellings owned increases among the married couples between the ages of forty-five and fifty-four, especially when there are no children under eighteen in the household. In this stage it is not uncommon, too, for parents to replace furniture that shows the battle scars of their children's growing-up years. Expenditures for durable goods such as washing machines decline, but are increased for television sets, air conditioners, and dishwashers—items that represent greater comfort in living.

Several trends signify that money problems are less pressing in this stage than in earlier stages of the family cycle. The proportion of income committed to instalment payments declines sharply in the contracting stage: about half of the families have no such debts, and only 16 percent have as much as 10 to 19 percent of their income obligated for consumer credit. Use of gasoline and store credit cards is at its highest level in the parents' middle years, and ownership of one car (97 percent) and two cars (43 percent) is up. Also significantly higher is the amount of assets owned by married couples over age forty-five, with the amounts that had increased when the children passed eighteen years going still higher when there are no children in the home.

Parents now replenish their wardrobes. They go more frequently to the theater, concerts, ball games, and movies. They more often dine in good restaurants. And, they take more trips. There is also greater emphasis on saving and planning for their retirement years as a couple, as well as for the probability that one partner, usually the wife, will be widowed for five or more years.

The leveling off of income and expenditures, which should have the effect of stabilizing the family's economic status and removing marital tensions, sometimes acts in reverse. The loss of the gratification previously provided by the children, and their absence as buffers to absorb the emotional and physical energies of the parents or to serve as a bond of interest between the mother and the father, often stimulate new (or aggravate old) marital problems which are then displaced onto money habits and patterns of spending and saving. The division of labor in the home alters. With the children gone, the parents must find new ways of living, communicating, and establishing a new balance with each other —one in which the marital partners turn to each other and not to the children.

Because these changes so frequently take place concurrently with the climacteric, the parents need to support and protect each other against anxiety, depression, and even regression. Often, however, they find fault with each other about earning and managing money: it is easier for them to talk—or quarrel—about money matters than about sexual needs and adjustments. In earlier years, the complaints and accusations centering around money could be connected with the needs of the children. Now the children are not present to provide a mask for other concerns. One or the other may overspend, or just spend without consulting the partner. The spending may be frivolous and for items beyond their means. Its covert purpose may be to demonstrate continued adequacy as an individual—or to place the partner in a defensive position as an inadequate provider or manager and, consequently, clearly the less adequate person on the marital team. The elasticity so essential to maintain equilibrium in a healthy marriage is disturbed. Not uncommonly, divorce results, surprising relatives and friends who had always regarded this long-time marriage as "happy," and who find it incomprehensible that the wife or the husband might be seeking in a new partner the emotional support that the economic resources do not provide. As often, however, the elasticity is restored and a new equilibrium established, without thought of divorce. If there has not been a legal marriage the equilibrium usually remains tenuous.

The departure of the children can bring other unresolved differences into the open.

> After 29 years of marriage, 51-year-old John S wanted a divorce. He'd "had it" with his wife's spendthrift behavior. While the children were at home he could understand her spending every penny he made to give them a good home and education; they all married well and were in good financial shape. But even though the excuse of children was gone, Mrs. S was still exhausting their resources, constantly looking for things to buy. There was no looking ahead to the future. He thought his wife was *deliberately* squandering his earnings to "keep my nose to the grindstone until I drop." His long-time secretary understood how hard he always worked to support his family in good style. She was pleasant to be with, undemanding, and concerned with his welfare. *She* appreciated his success.
>
> Marge S described herself as "in shock" when her husband announced he was moving out and would seek a divorce. She had been a good wife to him, standing by when business was poor, and encouraging him so that he "had the heart" to continue until good times returned. True, their interests had always been different: he thought her attendance at concerts and civic events was "putting on the dog," and he was angry whenever she went shopping or bought a ticket to a community event, even though he and his business would profit in the end by her participation in community affairs.
>
> John S's widowed mother had worked hard to rear him and his four

siblings without welfare help. She had earned barely enough for them to "get by" and then only by conserving every penny and every "rag." "Believe me," he told the counselor, "we knew the value of money. I'm not about to go through that kind of hell again."

"Ridiculous," Marge S said. "His income is good, and plenty has been put aside for the future. But money is for *spending*, for making life richer, for living graciously *now*. Not spending it now won't make his childhood any easier!" She thought he had always tried to control her by nagging about her spending. Now, his nagging having failed, he was threatening her with divorce and the idea of marrying his secretary, who "is as skinflinty as he is."

The Ss came from widely divergent backgrounds and neither could understand the other's internalized attitudes toward money.

Some new or additional marital tensions may center around the work and earnings of the wife, particularly if she is working outside the home for the first time since the children came, or if there has been some change for the better in her work situation. Discord may arise because the husband is not accustomed to what may seem to him to be the competition of her work, whether in earnings or status or just in its taking her away from the household's daily operation with the expectation that he will share household responsibilities. He may see the combination of her working and her new expectations of him as demeaning, as questioning his adequacy. His threatened self-esteem may cause him to insist that her work is too costly (witness the higher income tax bracket to which they have moved) and that she really cannot manage adequately both a job and a household. She may react with anger to his depreciation of her capacity to carry her responsibilities, resenting his "selfishness" and resisting the idea that she forego the independence and other satisfactions that she derives from her work. Problems may be exacerbated if economic or other conditions, such as health, have affected the husband's work and earnings.

For many contracting families, however, the easier financial situation brings a peaceful plateau. It is a period of relaxation and of freedom from the anxieties and tensions associated with child rearing. The marital partnership takes on additional comfortable qualities of companionship, planning, and sharing. The joint undertaking of planning and sharing minimizes problems that arise concerning the wife's working and how household and money management tasks are to be carried out.

The structure of the contracting family assumes various forms. In addition to parents, the household may contain an unmarried adult child who may be either employed or economically dependent. Or the adult child may be physically or intellectually handicapped, and require the continued care of the parents. Sometimes a married son or daughter, with or without the spouse, and with or without children, may live with the parents for convenience. They pay their own way and are free from parental control; the living arrangement is not the outgrowth of problems of emotional dependence.

It is not unusual, however, that parents are unable emotionally to give up their children. They may try to keep their adult children at home or, if the children live elsewhere, to dominate and control them. The present social pattern, mentioned earlier, of early marriage and parental subsidy of higher education for their children tends to perpetuate a close emotional tie. Although on the whole, this pattern is healthy, it contains certain psychological risks. Mature independence on the part of the child is delayed, and the young couple may have considerable resentment and guilt about the continuation of parental control.

Because they are lonely and emotionally dependent, some parents seek to exert control over their grown children by sizable gifts. Conflicts sometimes develop in the older couple because one of them gives secretly to the young family. The adult child may strive to be freed from this form of control, but may succeed only in gaining a little freedom at the cost of considerable anxiety. There then may be an effort to relieve this anxiety by spending money freely to bolster self-confidence. The adult child's overspending often results in an overextension of consumer credit.

Parents who are mature people have unique opportunities in this stage of life to find satisfactions and fulfillment. They still can play an important role with their children and grandchildren, and gain a sense of real achievement in watching them grow into useful members of society. The parents, too, have a future—a time for new activities and new personal relationships. Their contribution to their families and to society will reflect, in both tangible and intangible ways, the quality of their past achievements and their financial planning. As these parents move from the middle years through the last stage of the family life cycle, the effectiveness of their planning is tested constantly by personal and environmental problems that become more prominent with advancing years.

THE OLDER YEARS

The terms "elderly," "old age," "older years," and others used to describe the inexorable advance of time in an individual's life cycle are relative. Age depends in large measure on the perspective (and, often, feelings and attitudes) of the observer. An eight-year-old girl thinks of her forty-year-old mother and her mother's contemporaries as "old." In recent years youth have loudly proclaimed that any person over thirty years had passed the peak of understanding, creativity, and contributions to society's thinking. A sixty-year-old man may perceive a forty-five-year-old as "young."

In some industries, despite legislation that establishes age discrimination as illegal, old age is considered to begin at thirty-five years for women (usually because the last child is in school by then) and forty-five years for men. The general pattern for retirement is at age sixty-five. Indeed, this practice of setting sixty-five years as the retirement age developed as mere expedience rather than the point of demarcation between the middle years and old age. Even though some modifications have been made in various quarters regarding the magical aspect of retiring at age sixty-five, it continues to be accepted by most people as the age for retirement from business, or industry, or other employment —or even from life itself.

Persons in the later part of the contracting-family stage of family life are the elderly who tend no longer to work outside the home, and whose children long since have moved away. Ideally, the material needs in the contracting stage can be met by income from property, savings, investments, annuities, or private or public retirement systems (including the Social Security Act programs); and the satisfactions that should follow the successful rearing of children will provide considerable gratification in these later years.

While such is the case for many of the more than 20 million persons in our country who have passed their sixty-fifth birthday, it is not so for all. For one thing, more than a half-million fathers in this age group still head households in which there are children under eighteen years of age.[2] For another, the median income for families with heads over sixty-five years is about half that of their younger cohorts. In fact, about 19 percent of the total older population—those over sixty-five—is judged to be poor by official standards; among the older blacks, the proportion rises to 41 percent.

Ordinarily, by the time the family head is sixty-five, the income and spending patterns as well as the composition of the family will have undergone marked change, and earlier attitudes about the meaning and management of money now take on dimensions and forms that either facilitate or impede healthy accommodation to and coping with the changes.

Formerly, many elderly people expected to be cared for by their grown children, as recompense for their rearing. Changes in the social and economic conditions in this country have made this expectation unrealistic. Smaller families have resulted in fewer adult offspring among whom the burden of maintaining an aged father or mother can be spread. These younger families also have been affected by the ever-rising standard of living that absorbs a steadily growing proportion of the income available to meet the needs of their own spouses and children. The most recent census data report that more than 10 percent of the people in the United States are over sixty-five years old. If the present low birthrate should decline further, this percentage will rise still higher.

Not only are there fewer adult children and a larger population of elderly persons, but the life expectancy of persons who have reached their sixty-fifth year is now 12 years, and the life expectancy of those born in 1970 is 70.9 years. However, in spite of this projected increase in longevity, life expectancy in the United States has remained almost constant since 1955, with a slight drop-off for older men.[3] It was expected that whites born at the turn of the century would outlive "all others" by nearly 15 years, and those born in 1973 by approximately 6 years. However, the future life expectancy for blacks surpasses that of whites at about age seventy, and the black man or woman who reaches age eighty-five will probably live one or more years longer than the average white of the same age. Similar differences exist with some other ethnic minorities.

Such statistics point to the unreality of expecting children to support their dependent elderly parents. For example:

The Js had provided a monthly allowance for Mrs. J's parents—now in their 80s—to enable them to meet tax and upkeep costs on the home in which they had lived for 40 years. A small retirement income supplementing Social Security benefits enabled the parents to meet their other living costs. But now Mr. J had reached the age of 65 and mandatory retirement. His 63-year-old wife had no work experience or income of her own and they would be totally dependent on payments from Social Security sources and approximately $300 per month in dividends from investments. Their total income would not permit either the continuation of contributions to Mrs. J's parents or the maintenance of their second car. Tim, the Js' elder son, like his younger sibling Roger, was deep in mortgage debt, trying to help two of his children through college and to keep a third in high school. The illness of the sibling's wife had added heavy medical bills so that this family was considering filing for bankruptcy proceedings. Tim and Roger had both been helped with gifts of money while Mr. J was employed. Neither in the foreseeable future expected to be able to help the parents in turn.

The shift in population from rural to urban living, with the consequent dependence on wages or salary, and the increasing use of small dwellings have added to the mounting difficulty for children to provide either funds or living space for dependent parents. Additionally, there are changes of other kinds taking place. For instance, there long has been a general acceptance that Asian Americans "always care for their own," that the strong family system and veneration of the elderly are evidenced by the economic and physical care given older Asians by relatives. That this tradition is rapidly being altered is noticeable among the growing numbers of Chinese elderly who are living alone in inner cities at economic, psychological, and physical risk. The economic and health resources available to all elderly now are being more readily and frequently utilized by these elderly persons who, a few short years ago, would not have dreamed—nor would their children—of turning for help outside the extended family system.

Despite these trends and a general impression that the generations are alienated from each other, however, available data indicate that multigenerational families in the same household appear to be no less common today than they were a century ago, amounting to about 8 percent of all American families.[4] Such families develop primarily when the nuclear family is disrupted by death or divorce, but financial expediency or child care needs may also encourage such living arrangements. Thus, when Roger J's wife died, he and his three children all under ten years of age moved into his parents' home where his mother could manage the three J generations.

By the time they reach sixty-five, however, most people are living either with spouses only or alone. As is true of other adult age groups, most older persons in this country are married (71 percent of the men and 37 percent of the women), and most of them have living children (80 percent of the men and 76 percent of the women). As is not true of other age groups, more than 50 percent of the elderly women and 20 percent of the men are widowed. Many older persons have lost a spouse through death, but some of those widowed subsequently remarried, and others have been widowed more than once.[5] Nearly 80 percent of older men and nearly 60 percent of older women live in a family unit, most often consisting of husband and wife. Fewer elderly people lived with their children in 1970 than in previous census years, even though this independence often had to be purchased at considerable financial sacrifice.[6] For many, the cost was more in emotion than in money.

> Mrs. D, 67, had been twice widowed and had herself retired from a teaching post two years ago. Her married daughter had invited her to live with the younger family, but Mrs. D prized her independence and, although on good terms with the daughter and her family, thought this warm relationship would be better preserved if they did not live together. She moved to a retirement community where she retained her active and stimulating social life. Nevertheless, she was lonely. Friends introduced her to Ralph S, 70, and also twice widowed. They had many common interests and found themselves less lonely when they were together.
> Mr. S has two married daughters, neither of whom is married to a man their father likes or trusts to support the daughters and their children. Mr. S worries about the daughters; he believes it will be up to him to see to it that his grandchildren will go to college. In order to prepare for this eventuality, he has tried to avoid using any of his limited accumulated resources and has managed only on his Social Security benefits, amounting to little more than $300 per month. Mrs. D also has Social Security benefits in addition to her small teacher's retirement payments and the proceeds from the insurance left by her two husbands.
> Mrs. D and Mr. S decided to live together, thereby assuring that the transfer payments each receives will not be reduced and, at the same time, that their respective accumulated resources will be inherited by their respective children and grandchildren. They have not told their neighbors they are not married, but their children know and have been very critical of this "cheap behavior." The couple is convinced that marriage will create eventual estate and income problems; however, both are uneasy about what they laughingly refer to as "living in sin," and both have stopped attending church.

Out of every 100 persons over the age of sixty-five, thirty-one of the men and twenty-five of the women live in their own homes, four men and ten women live with relatives, six men and nineteen women live alone or with a nonrelative, and two men and three women are in institutions.[7] Financially, the elderly woman with a husband is better off than the woman without one, which suggests the existence of unmet needs among the many elderly women living in homes of their relatives. Practically speaking, women are absorbed into the homes of adult children somewhat more easily than are elderly men because they are more able to perform small services. In effect, then, women can be economically productive longer than men, which is probably fortunate in view of the fact that their life expectancy is longer than that of men.

Most elderly couples are reluctant to live with their married children and prefer, if necessary, to scrimp along at a reduced level of living in order to maintain their own homes and what these symbolize in terms of independence, sense of competence, privacy, and self-determination. About 76 percent of persons over sixty-five own their homes.[8] Many of them are not heads of household; many do not live in the homes owned; and homeownership does not imply adequacy of housing. A high proportion of these homes are extremely old and often run-down. Rising property taxes often take a substantial portion of the older person's income, leaving no money for repairs. Many are located in high-crime areas, where older people are especially likely to be victimized. They often remain in these homes simply because they have no adequate alternative. Sometimes the elderly owner rents out the owned home and leases smaller living facilities with the rental money. This is not always a practical financial or housing solution, however, because as the latest available (1972) data show the average value of the home then owned by a person over sixty-five is $15,000 and even allowing for inflationary factors the rental income from such a property is not likely to be substantial.

Because both income and expenses decline in this closing stage of the family life cycle, it generally can be expected that a balance between them will be achieved—although sharp inflation makes this difficult when the income remains fairly fixed, as it tends to be for most elderly people. With advancing age, there is increased need to purchase some personal services and to meet larger medical costs, not all of which are covered by Medicare. At the same time, other kinds of expenditures drop. Whether the home owned produces rental income or is the residence of the elderly couple, it is likely to be free of mortgage. Other fixed payments, too, decline. Life insurance generally is paid up, Social Security contributions decline or stop, and the amount of tax exemptions increases. The use by people over sixty-five of consumer credit, slides sharply downward, and amounts owed, if any, including gasoline, store, and bank credit cards, are very small. This reduction is related not alone to lower income and to the attitude of an older generation toward consumer credit, but also to the fact that generally they already have the durable goods they need.

Although the ratio of car ownership drops only a little from the level of middle-years couples, fewer than 15 percent of elderly couples own more than one car. Limited income and physical abilities combine to account for the lower percentage of car owners among the elderly. Continued ownership, however, does not necessarily mean that the car is in use.

Bill W, although 93, is still called upon to give consultation in his engineering speciality. The companies asking his help arrange for his transportation to their plants. When he and his 80-year-old wife go out for social events, at least twice each week, they either take a taxi or someone calls for them. But the Ws still own an expensive car, which for the last three years Bill has carefully driven down his driveway and back once every week. Childless, he calls his car his "baby," dusting and polishing it regularly.

To this couple, the car in the garage represents their vigor and control over their own affairs.

Considerable attention has been directed to the nutritional needs of elderly persons, but relatively little to how expenditures for food relate to their actual or perceived need for food. It is evident that generally there is reduced expenditure for food by most older persons, for they require and use fewer calories. Food, however, has importance for older people beyond its nutritional elements, and many older couples find that their food expenditures do not in fact change. "Breaking bread" with family and friends, an ancient symbol of welcome and trust, is to be found among many groups in this country and has important social implications and cultural associations, which translate, for example, to the serving of rice among Asian Americans, and wine among families still close to their Italian heritage. Such social and psychological elements play an important role in the food budgets of many elderly persons.

The assets of couples entering this age-stage tend to be higher than at any previous time. Interest and dividend income from these assets constitute a major resource for supplementing work-retirement benefits. These assets may be drawn on to meet large medical bills not covered by health care programs or insurance. They may be the source for paying for a new roof or buying the replacement appliance. They may be utilized to give sizable gifts or loans to adult children in a financial crisis—or to be sure the children recognize that the parents continue to have power to influence the lives of others. Any number of needs, compelling or not, may arise that cannot be met from recurring income. The assets may be zealously guarded and not used even when the couple suffers because of this abstinence. Or the resources may be vulnerable to assault for many reasons, among them, cost-of-living demands associated with inflation, or downward business trends that reduce dividends. Thus, one day the elderly couple becomes aware that the reserve is almost or entirely depleted.

Productivity and Retirement

Arbitrary retirement at a specified age works to the disadvantage of many elderly people who are physically and mentally able to remain in the labor market. In a culture that stresses that survival is based on work and social productivity, involuntary retirement especially appears to some retirees to threaten survival itself. People react to retirement in different ways. If they are psychologically prepared, they may find it a means for obtaining many gratifications. The way a man relates to retirement depends not only on his income and financial needs, but on the kind of person he believes himself to be and his family expects him to be. If he regarded fulfillment of his function as family provider as the core of his manhood, he may now feel impotent and useless. It is true that his powers diminish somewhat and that he suffers other losses, such as deaths of family members and friends. His retirement, therefore, is inseparable from other psychological problems of aging.

For the woman who has been in the work force, retirement—her own or her husband's—also can pose a range of economic and psychological problems, separately or in combination. Many of these problems are similar to those facing the retired man. But in some respects there are differences. If she continues to work after her husband has retired, and the average difference in their ages suggests the likelihood that this might often be so, he may react resentfully because he fails to continue in the work role. This resentment may be expressed by depression and refusal to take any responsibility for performing even heretofore accustomed chores during his wife's absence. For example, he may simply fail to pay bills, like utilities—since she is the worker, she also should be the money manager! If neither husband nor wife is working, they may find it difficult to realign their household and management responsibilities without expressing criticism or displaced anger regarding the circumstances that keep them so much together and "underfoot." For the wife the transition to being at home may be easier, for the homemaking function is one that she is unlikely to have relinquished entirely during her period of attachment to the labor force.

Either, however, may have considerable anxiety about the reduction in income from earnings to pension. Retirement income almost always is less than the previously earned income, and although work-related and other expenses are less, either or both spouses may feel they are now poor regardless of the size of their dollar income. One or both may fruitlessly seek part-time work, even when they really do not have the physical energy to work. Or they may give up too quickly. These anxious persons tend to cling to their retirement income and to savings and insurance benefits, even at the cost of physical suffering.

The Hs had worked until each was 65, he full-time and she part-time. In addition to Social Security retirement income, the husband received a company pension equal to three-fifths of his average earnings for the last ten years of his forty-five years of service. Mrs. H had worked for only six years and the pension awarded her came to $40 per month. In addition, interest on savings and stock dividends provided $4,800 per year. In none of the seven years since retirement had they needed as much as half of their annual income, even though illness had boosted their medical bills to a substantial level in two of the years.

The national emphasis on the shortage of fuel and other energy, and the expectation that costs would move even higher for these items frightened Mr. H. Would they be able to buy the heating and transportation fuel with their resources? Fearful about availability of the fuel, he put in a large supply of oil, contrary to the published warnings that this was an unwise move in the absence of safe storage facilities in most dwellings. He refused to turn on the furnace even when the temperature dropped below 50 degrees in the dwelling. He rationed television viewing and forbade his wife to use the dishwasher or garbage disposal not in the interests of the national energy shortage, but to reduce the monthly utilities bills. When Mrs. H became ill with pneumonia and required hospitalization, he used neither heat nor light except candlelight until her return home and their son angrily insisted that he "stop this foolishness." At this, although permitting the use of the furnace and some of the stored oil, Mr. H became depressed, announcing that his son would do nothing to prevent the father from living out his days in poverty.

The knowledge that money spent cannot be replaced by more earnings is frightening to many elderly retirees. Old-Age, Survivors, Disability, and Health Insurance benefits (OASDHI) and other forms of transfer payments, therefore, have many positive values. They represent security on both reality and psychological levels. It is of interest to note that among some elderly groups the availability of transfer payments dependent on an age factor has apparently contributed to acceleration of certain cultural changes. Thus, for example, eligibility for social insurance or public assistance payments among older Alaskan Eskimos has given them an important economic status because their age and infirmity no longer make them dependent on scarce resources in a subsistence economy; sometimes the cash payment they receive is the primary source of money in an isolated village.

In a modern competitive society, the older person is often considered economically useless, just as was the case earlier in subsistence economies on this continent. It is true that some helplessness and dependency result from the regressive process of aging, but our culture has over-stressed these limitations. The older person's feeling of uselessness and of being superfluous is only partly attributable to waning strength and vitality. Much of it stems from the prevailing attitudes about elderly persons. Physically, a good measure of restitution takes place in spite of regressive processes. The elderly person, however, is often bereft of supporting relationships and opportunities to be useful at the time these experiences are most needed.

THE ELDERLY AND THEIR CHILDREN
A person's productivity does not necessarily end with retirement from a job, although monetary remuneration may. Elderly parents who share a home with their married children usually are far from idle; they carry some responsibility for cooking, gardening, baby-sitting, and nursing.

The very helpfulness of the elderly parents, however, may become a problem: it may be viewed by the young couple as interference, control, or even competition—and it sometimes is any or all of these. If the parents hold the purse strings, the young people are kept in a dependency role with resultant resentment and hostility. If the household costs are shared, the parents may use their own resources to help the young family meet emergencies. Indeed, elderly parents often exhaust their financial reserves in this manner and then are forced to become economically dependent on their children or on the community.

If a parent becomes partially or totally dependent on a grown child, family roles become reversed and this change may create problems for both families. Dependency conflicts can be rearoused in the older parent, who is likely to become demanding and hostile; or the parents may deprive themselves rather than ask their children for help. They may feel inferior because they have lost status in the parental role. Both the increased dependency and lowered self-esteem of a parent in such a situation often lead to guilt and depression. In this reversal of roles, the adult child may have considerable conflict about money. Are the latter's spouse and children being deprived when contributions are made to the older couple? Guilt may lead these adult children to make excessive contributions. If their hostility is aroused, the children may refuse to make any contributions. Social pressures as well as regulations that may govern public welfare programs in a given state or locality enhance the danger of developing negative relationships between adult children and elderly parents. Also, such contributions from a reality standpoint, whether voluntary or required by law, often create financial difficulties for the young couple. Hardship may accrue to the elderly parents, who struggle along on too little income rather than either take money from children who need it for their own children, or acknowledge to the agency representative that their children are not contributing the sums designated by law or regulation.

Older people feel happier and more adequate when they can contribute toward their own expenses either in money or in services that represent money. They like to buy or make gifts for their grandchildren. The young couple, too, find it easier to help the elderly parent who has some personal economic resources. The younger people seem more able to mobilize their economic resources—and their positive feelings—if the elderly person's needs and demands are not too overwhelming. Failure to resolve these problems of financial relationships with elderly parents can lead to serious marital discord in the younger family.[9]

MONEY BEHAVIOR OF THE ELDERLY

Money holds meanings for the elderly that are not manifest in the same way among younger persons, even though these meanings in this closing stage of the family and life cycle are rooted in early stages of the individual's development. The elderly person's diminishing physical capacities are mirrored in the death of contemporaries and, many times, of their own children in their older adulthood. Fears about the future and "security" become pervasive. The elderly person whose childhood included physical or emotional deprivation believes that security is measured by money. This person will live frugally, hoarding money and goods in a miserly fashion. Possession and refusal to spend now are assurances that life will continue. These dynamics hold some explanation of the behavior reported in the press about elderly persons like Bertha Adams.[10]

> Seventy-one and alone, Mrs. A died of malnutrition after wasting away to 50 pounds. Neighbors in West Palm Beach took food to her; she begged from some. But "she always used to tell me that she was 'no poor woman,'" according to a neighbor for 25 years. Neighbors reported Mrs. A's condition to state social workers. She was first put in a nursing home, then transferred to a hospital where she died.
>
> Her court-appointed attorney discovered a safety-deposit key and two safety-deposit boxes among her possessions; cash and valuable stocks amounted to $800,000. Widowed twice, Mrs. A had been a businesswoman; she had no children.

Elderly persons may become hostile and demanding in the effort to prove to themselves that they are still of value to our society, a value that is expressed in money and material items. Such persons will feel rejected, bitter and angry by the adult children's impatience with requests that seem to the latter to be excessive. The counselor has to be sensitive to the reasons for such requests for which no actual need can be observed, and will recognize that opportunity given these older persons to talk about the days when they were achievers or in their prime often serves to replace the unrealistic demands for tangible help.

Other elderly persons, in contrast to the miserliness of a Mrs. Adams, reveal their insecurity by signing blank checks, throwing their money away, or giving it to strangers: the power to control their possessions, especially money, props their sagging sense of self-adequacy and self-esteem. They may write punitive wills, disinheriting children or relatives for real or fancied slights. Or, bequests may be subject to bizarre restrictions which are designed both to punish and to assert clearly the continued control of the writer of the will. Literally, such behavior "is ordinarily the last opportunity a man has to express his contrariety."[11] And others in their declining years suddenly increase their scale of living in order to enjoy the luxuries and pleasures they (or their spouses) had denied themselves previously.

Forgetfulness and inability to recall recent events may cause older people to find it increasingly difficult to manage their economic resources successfully. The necessity for solving even a minor or a very familiar problem that centers on uses of money may provoke considerable emotional distress. Some long for a relationship in which children or others will take over their care and relieve them of any concern about money matters. For some of these elderly parents, arrangements for living with the family of an adult child works out satisfactorily, especially if the older people are passive and noninterfering. For many, an arrangement of choice is life care in retirement hotels or communities where a specified monthly payment—sometimes with a sizable advance payment—purchases complete maintenance and health care.

But other elderly become anxious, apprehensive, and depressed if they have to relinquish control of their funds. Money has represented power to them, and management of their own affairs has been the essence of their adequacy and independence in a society that values these traits. Even if the help of others is needed in managing their affairs, these persons want to feel that they are able to make the final decisions.

Increased dependency and lowered self-esteem of older persons who had always valued their self-sufficiency and independence may lead to guilt and depression so that they deprive themselves rather than ask for help, whether financial or for a service of some kind. Thus they avoid disclosing a diminished contribution to society. Elderly persons' handling of their income, no matter how large or small, is the last vestige of independence and symbolizes their continued capacity and ability to control their own affairs. This is an important reason why many people dependent entirely on some form of limited transfer payment—Social Security benefits or Supplemental Security Income, for example—fail to request available services from a public or voluntary social agency, a church, or other organization: they cannot afford to abuse their self-esteem by acknowledging the reality of difficulty in managing, even when they have insufficient funds for their basic needs, or health that is too impaired to permit them to follow through on money management tasks.

PLANNING FOR RETIREMENT YEARS

If the meanings and uses of money have been rationally handled in the beginning stages of the cycle of family life, a major step has been taken toward assuring life satisfactions in the later years. If earlier problems have not yet been resolved on arrival of the middle-years segment of the contracting-family stage, urgent attention needs to be directed toward determining the measures necessary to assure that these later years are economically, emotionally, and socially comfortable.

In today's money world, financial planning for retirement actually begins, albeit usually reluctantly, long in advance of the actual fact of retirement: with the first job and the first payment by employee and employer into the federal old-age and survivors insurance trust fund within the OASDHI program (Social Security benefits). Thereafter, it may be consciously planned in gross or fine detail; or it simply may catch up with the couple as the age of retirement comes close or actually is reached.

In recent years considerable attention has been directed toward possibilities for people to enjoy greater leisure and the fruits of their long years of work and earning by voluntarily retiring before age sixty-five. This "opportunity" offers mixed blessings. Certainly, it is possible for husband and wife to rediscover each other afresh in the "golden years" of their lives when children and other responsibilities are no longer primary. However, the great emphasis on defining adequacy, independence, and morality in terms of occupational productivity contributes to the adjustment problems men and women (but particularly the former) must face when their status-giving role as earner, provider, and protector must be relinquished upon retirement.

Many American families are not adequately prepared for retirement, for either what it means in change from work status or what it means with regard to the lifestyle possible as the family cycle and the life cycle move in tandem toward their endings. Many working-class families slip into poverty upon the husband's retirement. If the wife also has been employed, their circumstances may be somewhat better, but not much; most suffer severe reduction in real income. For upper-middle-class professionals and managerial or executive personnel, retirement rarely means impoverishment, but it does often call for radical readjustment and a lower standard of living. This significantly affects how the retirement years are passed: truly "in leisure"? in volunteer activities? in part-time or occasional paid work? Whether the couple in retirement is poor or moderately affluent, inflation severely affects the retirement income. Most men leave widows within a few years after retirement, and this increasingly longer period of widowhood in the lives of American women generally is accompanied by further changes, usually downward, in the level of retirement income.

The psychological readiness of a couple for retirement is rooted in personal and societal attitudes about the meaning of work and the earning and managing of money and other resources. These attitudes enable individuals, as they grow older, to respond appropriately to economic, social, familial, and personal changes that will occur without their volition. These attitudes shape their coping capacities and those of their children as parental and family needs change in the course of the family life cycle. Will the parents need to call on their children for emotional or economic help, or both? Will the marital couple be able to maintain their parental roles, and fulfill the marital tasks that change over the years?

Will they be able to remain together? Whether or not their life experiences together have been satisfying, elderly couples need to stay together. Often there has been a synchronization of their personalities so that they seem almost to be one. The death of either may spur emotional or physical change in the other. And the death of one may leave the other so overwhelmed by the tasks that now have to be carried alone, that previous coping capacities appear to be dissipated.

The planning process, whether casual, formal, or fortuitous, should include sharing by the couple of knowledge about what they own, what they expect, how their resources and income are protected and handled, and how they should be dealt with by the survivor. Such sharing and planning should also be incorporated in a will, properly executed, that will protect the interests of the survivor and reflect and observe the wishes of the couple. Many couples in younger years think a will is premature; in older years they are superstitious: preparing a will is "courting death," and the task of is postponed, and often never accomplished. The planful, rational couple, however, will make a will not only for the protection of the survivor, but to avoid undue conflict and competition among heirs in dividing an estate, regardless of its size. For the family in which parents have not married legally, the presence of a will is especially necessary, for the normal legal safeguards on which spouses and children ordinarily can depend are either denied or difficult to invoke in nonlegal unions.

Aside from the legal uses and protections afforded by wills, the preparation of the will holds special import for the elderly couple. Wills are tangible testimony to their continued control over their own destiny and decision making regarding the ultimate management of the evidence (the estate or bequests) that they have functioned ably in today's money world.

NOTES

1. U.S., Department of Commerce, Bureau of the Census, *Statistical Abstract of the United States 1975: National Data Book and Guide to Sources,* 96th ed. (Washington, D.C.: U.S. Government Printing Office, 1975), pp. 346–47.
2. U.S., Department of Commerce, Bureau of the Census, *Statistical Abstract of the United States 1974: National Data Book and Guide to Sources,* 95th ed. (Washington, D.C.: U.S. Government Printing Office, 1974), p. 43.
3. U.S., Department of Health, Education, and Welfare, *Health in the Later Years of Life: Selected Data from the National Center for Health Statistics* (Washington, D.C.: U.S. Government Printing Office, 1974).
4. J. C. Beresford and Alice M. Rivlin, *Occasional Papers in Gerontology,* Vol. 3, *The Multigenerational Family* (Ann Arbor & Detroit: Institute of Gerontology, University of Michigan and Wayne State University, 1968).
5. U.S., Department of Health, Education, and Welfare, *Health in the Later Years.*
6. H. B. Brotman, *Facts and Figures on Older Americans,* 5, An Overview, 1971 (Washington, D.C.: U.S., Department of Health, Education, and Welfare, 1972).
7. Ibid.
8. Ibid.

9. Frances H. Scherz, "Strengthening Family Life through Social Security," *Social Casework* 36 (October 1955): 352–59.
10. *Los Angeles Times,* April 7, 1975, pt. 1, p. 2.
11. William Hazlett, "On Will-Making," in *Tabletalk: Original Essays* (London: J. M. Dent, 1930), p. 113.

7
Variants on Lifestyles

Not every human being moves through life according to a prescribed or "normal" pattern. An individual's progress may be marked by disabling illnesses or by emotional disturbances. It may be terminated by untimely death. Nor does every family unit proceed logically and inexorably through each phase of the family cycle. Some people retain their bachelorhood. Marriages are disrupted by desertion, separation, divorce or death. Some remarriages take place and children find themselves with two or more sets of parents; parents may have several sets of children unrelated to each other. Some parents never marry; and an unmarried adult may adopt a child and remain single.

Persons who have lived through one or more phases of the family life cycle, or who have remained unmarried and hence never entered the initial stage, live in the same general economic, social, and cultural climate as the families described in the foregoing chapters. These persons are influenced by, and react to, the same forces. The problems they encounter have many similarities, although their form and depth may be different. However, particular problems arise for the adult whose living patterns do not follow the usual family life cycle. Special problems or exacerbations of common ones may be displayed by children affected by some of these patterns. Some of the psychodynamics of these variants merit consideration in the context of behavior related to money.

THE SINGLE ADULT

In this group are included adults who are "unattached" in the sense that they currently live with neither parent nor spouse nor partner in a social marriage (a union that has not been legalized). These men and women, referred to here as single adults, generally have never been married, or they may have been in a very brief childless marriage. This arbitrary classification is used merely for the purpose of simplifying consideration of certain presently unmarried persons with similar characteristics in relation to money. Individuals divorced after many years of marriage, childless or not, and individuals with children, married for a very short time or not at all, manifest some differences in the arena of feelings and behavior about money.

It is difficult to know just how many persons among those classified in census data as "heads living alone" fit the definition used here. The 1973 population reports[1] identify household heads living alone by age and sex, but these are not further characterized by marital status.

TABLE 5. PERSONS LIVING ALONE, 1973 (IN THOUSANDS)

Age	Male	Female	Total
Under 35 years	15,903	3,136	19,039
35-64 years	29,222	6,516	35,738
65 years and over	7,735	5,738	13,473
Total	52,860	15,390	68,250

It can be assumed that these are childless, or never-married, or no-longer-married persons. No data are available, however, to indicate how many in fact share their living arrangements with a member of the opposite sex or the same sex. And the data do not suggest, when such sharing occurs, if it is a platonic arrangement entered into for companionship or expense-sharing, or if it has a sexual basis. If the attachment is an emotional one, the meaning and management of money have the implications discussed as nonbeginnings in Chapter 4. If the emotional attachment is homosexual, there may be added emphasis on the use of money to keep the interest of the sexual partner. Gifts or money may be lavished on the dependent person. The latter may in various ways express dependency on the strength and generosity of the other.

Nor do the data suggest how many of the under-thirty-five group are still in college or recently out of school and emancipated, endeavoring more or less successfully to establish their emotional and financial independence. A phenomenon of the 1970s is that college students and other young adults living alone in rooms or apartments have found that the accelerating cost of living outstrips their resources for independent living. There has been, for example, an unprecedented demand by college students in urban centers for dormitory facilities, in contrast to patterns of independent living arrangements previously popular. The fixed costs for shelter and food reflect one way of coping with the impact of inflation. There has also been an observable parallel trend: young people giving up separate living arrangements to return to the family home.

The sources and amounts of income for single adults are usually the same as for others in the general population possessing similar education, capacity, and skills. In fact, many single persons, by reason of their lack of attachments, have a relatively high degree of mobility and are freer to broaden their work opportunities. The way in which they spend or save their income also, is generally the same as for the rest of the population having similar needs and standards.

Some differences do exist, however. One is the accessibility of credit to single women. It has been well documented that women generally have been subject to discrimination with respect to bank, gasoline, and store credit cards. Similarly, many single women have found it difficult to obtain mortgages regardless of their income or demonstrated reliability in payment of obligations. The experience has been similar for almost every woman endeavoring to use her own name rather than her husband's. When Dr. C's husband died, she thought her accounts should be transferred to her name. Although her resources were unchanged and her income continued unabated, she was refused credit until she reinstated the use of her married name. Professor J, a tenured faculty member of a large state university, applied for a bank credit card. She was asked to use her husband's name—but Professor J had never married. However, since the enactment in 1975 of the federal Equal Credit Opportunity Act, which forbids discrimination by creditors on the basis of sex or marital status, the same opportunities for obtaining credit have been made available to women irrespective of marital status.

Other differences have existed that are race- or sex-related, or both. Women have tended to earn less than men for the same work requiring the same qualities and qualifications. Similarly, blacks and members of other ethnic-minority groups have earned less than whites for the same work calling for the same qualifications. A single woman with membership in an ethnic-minority group, like her married counterpart, has had to manage on lower earnings than men. This situation also has been the target of federal efforts aimed to achieve equity. In the meantime, however, the earnings of single women and, especially minority-group women, lag behind those of men, single or not. This fact affects both women's economic behavior and their attitudes toward money, work, men, and justice.

Certain variations are discernible in the spending patterns of single men and women that stem from the personal meanings money holds for them. They often spend money for luxuries instead of necessities, the luxuries serving as substitutes for love, companionship, family, and children. What appears on the surface to be self-indulgence may be compensation for lacks in relationships and the normal gratification of dependency needs. Loneliness may result in undue preoccupation with extravagant living; and a fancy apartment and lavish entertainment may be devices to relieve the anxiety that loneliness engenders, and the denial that one is really alone. These persons usually have difficulty both in managing and in saving their money.

Loneliness, on the other hand, may make the person fearful of dissipating the security that money symbolizes. The intense determination to save funds to provide for old age may lead such a lonely and fearful person to deny present satisfactions, even gratification of some basic necessities.

Sometimes an adult moves into separate quarters and is economically independent but has not really been emancipated from the parents. This move may create considerable anxiety which the person endeavors to relieve by activities that cost money. Forty-year-old Tom L made such a change in living plans against the wishes of his parents:

> Although the cost of his apartment was less than the amount he had contributed to his parents (which they did not need for their maintenance) for his room in the family home, he soon was drawing on his savings. Payments on a new and high-priced car, extravagant purchases of clothing, and frequent and costly entertainment of his friends could not be covered by his earnings. He exhausted his reserves in less than two years and then attempted to consolidate his pressing debts. When he could not obtain a loan he became depressed and, rather than turn to his parents for help, he made an unsuccessful attempt at suicide.

It should not be inferred that all persons living alone spend money recklessly or are extremely penurious, or that all are lacking in healthy family attachments. But it is true that a person living alone, apparently quite well adjusted and functioning at a good level, actually does have additional spending needs. The lack of other persons with whom to share costs often means that daily needs cannot be met as economically as those of a family. Even the single-person income tax rates are higher!

UNMARRIED PARENTHOOD

Much attention has been addressed in recent years to the fact that many unmarried couples live together briefly or for a long time, with one or more children born of the relationship. There is a paucity of comprehensive data about the numbers. The general perception of its prevalence, however, is supported by widely publicized reports such as those that feature luminaries in the entertainment world who have out-of-wedlock children and undertake relatively frequent changes in partners-without-marriage, and by the fairly constant stress placed by some citizens and some public officials on out-of-wedlock births among families dependent upon public welfare programs for sustenance. When the extra-legal family unit remains together, its financial needs and behaviors usually are indistinguishable from legal family units, with the exception of the anomalous position of spouse and children regarding survivor's rights, support, and property ownership.

When, however, the unmarried parents do not maintain a household together, they are separately subject to a variety of social-legal expectations expressed in money terms. Stress and distress are often discernible in the ways they handle money, and may be intimately related to stress in the relationship of the two adults with each other, as well as in the relationships of the unmarried mother and father with the nonmarital child.

One of the fundamental obligations of parents toward their children is to provide financial support. This obligation derives from a general concept of moral responsibility—in natural law, in common law, and in statutes.[2] When children are living with both unmarried parents who are economically independent and who meet this financial obligation, our society does not concern itself particularly with their marital status except to deny certain financial protections that are generally assured legitimate spouses and children. When they are economically dependent on public sources, they become susceptible to community criticism not unlike that directed to anyone receiving public assistance, but with an added dimension of public censure and control. When parents live apart, an entirely different constellation of attitudes obtains, some internal and some external—the former, in large measure, responsive to the latter.

Illustrative of some social attitudes toward irregular relationships is the 1965 Opinion (64/63) of the California Attorney General holding that under state welfare law an AFDC mother was liable to prosecution if she willfully and knowingly used any part of the assistance grant for the support of "the *m*an *a*ssuming the *r*ole of *s*pouse" (MARS). The policy, which most affected AFDC recipients of racial minorities, pertained to a man in the home not the father of the children and not married to the mother. As long as he had a visible means of support and contributed some money to the maintenance of the woman, no action was required to compel him to leave the household. If he had no visible means of support or made no contribution, he was presumed to be using some of the grant intended for the support of the children, and their mother thereby became vulnerable to being formally charged with committing a misdemeanor. The "morality" of the situation depended on the exchange or absence of money.

Many reasons have been offered for the illegitimacy, some of these tangential to or stemming directly from economic factors. One is that the pregnant mother may not marry the father because they believe their income is insufficient for marriage. Until fairly recently, there was a concomitant in the low income of the mother that precluded her obtaining a safe abortion. Another reason often cited is that poor income opportunities reduce the economic importance of the male to the family: the family's income with the father in the house might be no higher than its income without him. The reduced male role is perceived by some to be a substantial factor in the rate of illegitimacy and marital disruption among some population groups, leading young people to regard the chances for a stable marriage as low, and illegitimacy and female headship as acceptable to the community.[3] Still another reason is that the girl in a large poverty-level family carries considerable responsibility for the care of younger children, and "becomes a slave" to their supervision while either or both parents earn their aggregate low income. With no money she can use as she wishes, she may elect not to marry the father of her child because she may have some income (from him or a welfare agency) over which she has sole control and which gives her a sense of mastery over her own destiny even while she continues to meet the responsibility of care for younger siblings.

There is far from total agreement with these economic reasons as causal factors for unmarried parenthood. But they point to a dual societal approach to parental support obligations—namely, the actual obligation of parents that enables a child to be housed, fed, clothed, educated, and given health care in a manner that satisfies minimum community standards or that at least meets survival needs; and the parent's responsibility to provide support that precludes children from becoming economic burdens on the state. Accordingly, all states have some form of "neglect and dependency" statute, the former referring to parental fault and the latter to the parent's inability to provide for the child. While "in theory the neglect and dependency laws apply equally to all parents and all children,"[4] states the U.S. Congress Joint Economic Committee in its study on *The Family, Poverty and Welfare Programs,* "These laws are applied most often to lower-class whites" and the help offered by these laws tends "to be greatest in the case of poor and illegitimate children, among whom are a disproportionate number of blacks."[5] Typically, the neglect statutes, though sometimes purporting to be concerned with the moral aspects of parent-child relationships, do not really tend to recognize the emotional components of the parent-child relationship nor are they concerned with the meanings of support other than in the context of parental responsibility (and, therefore, morality) and of relieving the state of an unwelcome charge for support.

THE NONMARITAL CHILD

Euripides,[6] the Old Testament,[7] and Shakespeare[8] prophesied that the sins of the fathers would be visited upon their children and, with few exceptions, our moral code has embodied this doctrine by specifying the denial of rights of the out-of-wedlock child in the realm of support, inheritance, and various other aspects of parent-child relationships defined with regard to the legitimate child.

The denigrating social and economic status of children whose parents are not married has tended to affect not only the adequacy of the financial resources available for these children during the developmental years, but the feelings of the children about themselves, the people around them, and the world in which they live. The legal and ethical definitions of fiscal roles and responsibilities between the child of a nonmarital union and the father are inextricably tied with the child's sense of identity, self-esteem, and trust—of self and of parents (the wrongdoing mother, the legally and otherwise noncaring father). These ingredients, so essential to effective social functioning, frequently are impaired or wanting. The denial and rejection may stimulate in the child the development of aggressive, exaggerated, and lifelong search by the child yearning for the affection and security ascribed to money and to material items that are tangible—that can be seen, felt, and held close, or defiantly cast away. Such a treasuring or discarding action declares that choice, and independence from others, are within the child's control. It is not uncommon for such children to withdraw from relationships with others and, both as child and later as adult, to cling tenaciously to money and acquisitions.

In recent years a few states have enacted legislation which aims to give the nonmarital child legitimacy or, at least, some legal protection of rights.[9] The potential number of out-of-wedlock children who could be affected by such public policy is, of course, sizable. Fewer than two-thirds of the states report illegitimate births, yet the most recent available estimates[10] show more than 400,000 for 1973, half of those born to girls nineteen years of age and younger. Because illegitimacy is closely associated with poverty and with race (nearly 60 percent were born to mothers with ethnic-minority membership)[11] the children most sharply affected by the discriminatory effects of laws governing financial and inheritance aspects of out-of-wedlock children are also in the same groups that traditionally have been disadvantaged in other ways. The white-nonwhite discrepancy is further underscored by the greater prospect of adoption (and presumed emotional and financial security) of the white nonmarital child than the nonwhite child. The addition of legal sanction of the out-of-wedlock child's social, economic, and emotional status to the other disadvantages aggravates the likelihood that such a child will develop neurotic behavior patterns centering on the significance, and the procuring and using of money.

The states that have moved to protect the rights of nonmarital children have tended to address themselves to instances where the paternity is known and acknowledged. Provisions vary considerably. There may be specified right to paternal inheritance; to support in the same way and to the same degree as the legitimate child; and eligibility for benefits under workmen's compensation laws. It also may be stipulated that "every child is hereby declared to be the legitimate child of his natural parents, and is entitled to support and education, to the same extent as if he had been born in lawful wedlock."[12] But with whom the responsibility rests for establishing the paternity; what the rights of the father are when adoption is contemplated; and what requirements are imposed on the parents to provide a home for the child—these either are unclear or cluster around the wishes of the mother rather than the interests of the child. Thus, in Arizona,

> Marta J decided that she would not bring a paternity action against married but childless Robert S because he *wanted* to care for the baby boy they both knew to be his son, and she would not give him "the satisfaction." He was "rich and spoiled, always getting his own way. Well, this time he won't." Marta earned barely enough to support herself and the child but she remained adamant in her refusal to let the father see or contribute to the support of little Bert. By the time he was seven, Bert and his mother had lived in nine dwellings together, and he had been in four different foster homes where she had placed him in order that she could be "free." She was obsessed with earning enough so that she and Bert would not have to request public aid and become a public charge, which would permit public authorities to bring the father into the support picture.

The counselor's awareness of public policies affecting out-of-wedlock children is likely to bring added useful insights into what may seem to be neurotic or irrational attitudes of the mother of the nonmarital child toward sources and uses of money.

The Unmarried Mother

The unmarried mother who decides to keep her child is confronted not only with the necessity of meeting the day-by-day needs of her child and herself as is any other mother without a husband, she also must deal with the complex of personal and societal feelings related to her unwed parenthood. And, for her, money takes on added significance. If she regards her unwed motherhood as a social disgrace, money may be compensatory or provide her with a sense of security about being able to keep the child. If she is relatively or totally unconcerned with the illegitimacy of the child, the availability of adequate funds to meet their needs may be "proof" of her self-sufficiency and competence as a parent without the support or presence of the child's father in the home. If she asks for support from the alleged father, she may be using her demand for money as a device for punishing him. Or, like Marta J, she may punish the father by refusing to let him contribute to the child's support, irrespective of the effects on the child's well-being and development.

If the mother carries the burden of support alone, she may use money in a restricted way as a means of self-punishment or because the need to conserve her resources grows out of her uneasiness: can she provide currently and in the future for the child? Rhoda A illustrates both situations.

> She had placed her two-year-old daughter in a foster day care home selected from many to which she had been referred by a placement service because she wanted little Brenda to receive "lots of attention to make up in part" for the long hours Rhoda had to work as a waitress. She paid a fourth of her gross weekly earnings, including her tips, for this care. Occasionally she received extra pay because of a special party handled by the employer. This money was carefully placed in a "rainy day" account.
>
> When Rhoda was temporarily laid off, she was unable to maintain the payments with her unemployment insurance benefits. Her anxiety mounted steadily—manifested in extreme gastric distress attributed by the doctor to "nerves" and controlled to some extent by medication. She was afraid that nonpayment would result in losing this particular child care placement, but could not bring herself to touch the nearly $200 in the rainy day account; things might get worse later! She sought public assistance to supplement the unemployment insurance benefits but was unwilling to consider the proffered replacement plan that would reduce her payments but mean that Brenda would be in a facility with larger groups of children. Instead, she borrowed money, with her car as security.
>
> Rhoda was called back to work; she also was able to locate a second waitress job so that the debt could be reduced. The longer hours of child care required additional payment. Even though this mother in effect had less time

to spend with the child and was paying out more than 60 percent of her total income for child care and the auto loan, she would entertain no plan that would call for less expensive child care: Brenda had to have "the best" and it was "up" to the mother to pay for it no matter how much else had to be sacrificed, even food.

Some unmarried mothers have a need to punish themselves. Through a tendency to overindulge the child, as though to compensate for the lack of social status and for the emotional deprivations, the mother finds it difficult to maintain a proper balance between giving to the child and giving to herself. The situation has many of the same elements that are present in other kinds of desertions, but her guilt intensifies her conflict. The symbolic import of money, in consequence, is also magnified.

The trend among young unmarried mothers to keep their children rather than to release them for adoption has been viewed by many with concern or suspicion. Some individuals and groups have interpreted repeated out-of-wedlock pregnancies as evidence of more "depravity." A 1975 statement by California's State Benefits and Services Advisory Board, reiterated in various forms since its original publication in 1972, illustrates trends in this area:

> It is the position of the [Board] that appropriate legislation should be enacted so as to . . . provide that a rebuttable presumption shall arise that a mother is, in fact, morally depraved upon the birth of the third child out of wedlock and the appropriate public agency be directed to commence legal proceedings . . . to terminate the relationship of parent and the third illegitimate child and any subsequent children so conceived so that said child(ren) may be placed for adoption.[13]

Some people have maintained that the unmarried mother deliberately bears out-of-wedlock children solely as a way of obtaining or increasing a public assistance grant.[14] This implies not only that such assistance grants are truly liberal but that the mother is planful and able to calculate with a fair degree of accuracy (or inaccuracy) the net financial benefit that will accrue when the cost of bearing and maintaining another child is deducted from the anticipated grant. The level of assistance varies state by state. Overriding, however, is the unlikelihood that the mother is a planful person, at least so far into the future.

Without regard for consistency, the same groups protest that the young unmarried mother is not fit to handle a welfare check, that she should not be regarded as a separate "family unit," and that the girl's mother should be the payee if assistance is to be provided at all. This has been an area of conflict between some official groups and welfare-client representatives, with the former proposing more controlling policy changes. They give no consideration to the fact that in large dependent or marginal-income families the adolescent girl, who later becomes illegitimately pregnant, may be the family member who has carried day-to-day responsibility for marketing, household management, and care of younger siblings while the mother works. As one Welfare Rights Organization leader stated, "Often these girls, Chicana or black, are far more capable of managing a welfare check and children than their own mothers are; after all, their own mothers didn't keep their daughters from becoming pregnant!"

Today it is not only the poor or the nonwhite unmarried mother who keeps her baby but also the middle- and upper-income girls. Because of family resources, the financial problems faced by these mothers and their children are likely to be of a somewhat different order. These mothers tend to have educational opportunities available to them that are not so accessible to girls from poorer families; they can more readily arrange to purchase child care while they pursue education or a career that will enable them to meet the child's financial needs.

While many unmarried mothers are neurotic or more seriously disturbed, this by no means is true of the majority. Some women deliberately establish living arrangements with a man with whom marriage is not viable. Though pregnancy may be unanticipated, the dynamics differ from those of the young unmarried mother who engaged in sexual experimentation or a "trial" arrangement. They may be similar to the situations in which a couple, though free to marry, undertake what they expect to be a long or lasting relationship, but rebel against custom that calls for a legal marriage ceremony. The meanings of money in such situations are likely to resemble those described in Chapter 4.

A more recent phenomenon among mothers who have not married is the single mother who has been influenced by, and sometimes is a product of, the women's movement. Her interest in the father centers only on having a child, and, this explicit purpose accomplished, she proceeds to rear the child without the feelings of guilt, resentment, and anger associated with unwed-motherhood in previous generations or with other unwed mothers today. Generally, she is self-supporting, although child support payments are received in some instances from the child's father or from public assistance.

Diverse living styles are utilized by these single mothers and their children: small group homes; boarding homes where a number of single mothers live together with their children; foster homes for mother and child; or their independent dwelling arrangement in their own apartments or houses. Usually those without a separate apartment or house have a sleeping room or a small unit of rooms for the mother and child, who share with others the kitchen, dining, and living quarters. Such arrangements generally provide child care for the working mother, and a variety of caretakers. This suggests that a high degree of trust in adults must be instilled in the child who can then turn to other than the natural parent for solace and emotional support.

There are no data as to the number of such single-mother family units. Nor has sufficient time elapsed from which to draw systematic understanding about the kind of adult functioning that will characterize today's children whose mothers rear them with an antisexist philosophy in social arrangements that seek to compensate for nonexistent siblings and fathers. Nevertheless, some behaviors have been manifest that are common to other nonmarital family units of mother and child.

> Phyllis D, 30, and her six-year-old son, Mike, have been living for four years in a group home containing five other similar family units. A single mother operates the home and provides care for the six children in residence while the tenant-mothers are employed. Previously Phyllis and Mike had shared an apartment with another single mother, and Mike was in a day care center during the mother's working hours. The present arrangement for room, board, and child care costs $100 per week, leaving the mother less than $100 of her net monthly earnings for clothing, transportation, health care not included in her fringe benefits, recreation, and life insurance.
>
> She has found the arrangement good, though costly, because Mike has companions his own age and she has friends who share similar concerns and ideas about child-rearing by single mothers. All of the women in this group home participate in consciousness-raising sessions and all are active in women's movement organizations.
>
> Phyllis was laid off because the plastics firm where she had worked for nine years was unable to continue operating in the face of oil shortages. Her union was unable to help her find other work. When unemployment insurance benefits were exhausted she sought public assistance.
>
> The requirement that Mike's father be asked to contribute angered Phyllis. *She,* not he, was responsible for Mike's care and support. She would not permit the father to be contacted, and withdrew her application for aid. Two months later, having depleted all resources for borrowing as well as locating work and now faced with the request to relinquish her place in the group home to someone "who wouldn't need to be carried by the rest," she returned to the public welfare agency, ready to sign the necessary documents. She phoned Mike's father to let him know he would be contacted by the agency. She was infuriated by his statement that he would give her "not a penny," but would be glad to take Mike, that a boy needs his father and Mike's father

was ready to fill that role even though he had never seen the child. Phyllis' response was to tell the social worker that she was ready to file a formal nonsupport complaint with legal authorities.

Phyllis was determined to be independent of Mike's father. She dealt with this need to be able to govern her own affairs by retaliating for what she viewed as the father's "depreciating" attitude, taking initiative in seeking legal help to force him to "put out some money, which he can afford to do, but he is very miserly and vindictive." When she was again employed, Phyllis refused to accept further payments that the father had made at the behest of the district attorney's office and which were paid through that office. She and Mike would not be "tied to him by money."

THE UNMARRIED FATHER

In the civil- and human-rights climate of the last few years, growing judicial attention has been directed toward the rights of unmarried fathers to participate in decisions affecting their out-of-wedlock children, particularly with regard to adoptive or other long-term care arrangements. The several recent cases before the courts have not changed the long-prevailing contention that such decisions rest with the mother and that the role of the acknowledged father is to provide support for the child—albeit, commonly, support that either in level or duration is less than that for the out-of-wedlock child's legitimate half-sibling. Indeed, in some states paternity actions are still subject to criminal prosecution, the criminal offense having been to cause a birth out of wedlock.

Fathers of nonmarital children traditionally have been excluded from having any legal claims to those children. Their standing is that of a stranger insofar as custodial rights are concerned. Nor, with rare exceptions, has their consent been required to release the child for adoption. They cannot inherit from the estate of their illegitimate child; similarly, the illegitimate child has been excluded, through intestacy laws, from sharing with legitimate siblings the estate of his biological father.[15]

Many fathers readily acknowledge the out-of-wedlock child as their own. They may marry the mother; and between 10 and 20 percent of unwed mothers, white and nonwhite, have in the past married the father after the birth of the child.[16] About 24 percent of nonwhite pregnant out-of-wedlock women and about 66 percent of whites marry before the birth. The decision appears to be determined less by economic condition than by the couple's commitment to marry made prior to or shortly after pregnancy. Many fathers deny the child is theirs, even when knowing it is: they resent being "trapped" into assuming unwanted responsibilities and they decline to contribute to the support of the child, thereby asserting both their control over their own lives and their punishment of the mother.

The age and social and economic status of the father as well as of the unmarried mother often combine to determine the role, if any, the father will be expected to take in relation to the child's financial support, and to the nature of the continued relationship with the child's mother. The mother's economic need may bring her to a public agency for financial assistance. She may or may not wish to institute support proceedings, but such measures may be legally and, often, socially necessary. The 1952 Amendments to the Social Security Act require that public assistance agencies notify appropriate law-enforcement officials when children who had been deserted or abandoned by a parent receive Aid to Families with Dependent Children (AFDC). The provisions are no less applicable to the alleged father than to the acknowledged father. The 1975 Amendments, with the creation of the Parent Locator Service, move far beyond the earlier provisions with respect to pursuing child support not just for women and children dependent on public sources for financial support, but also for those with higher incomes. The unmarried mother who is self-supporting probably will find in this recent statute a lever not just in terms of the child-support money that might result, but also for control, for retaliation, for punishment, and for venting other feelings on the father for real or imagined actions or attitudes displayed toward her or the child.

The middle-class family of a young unmarried father may wish to protect him from having to carry responsibilities of parenthood before his own education or vocational preparation has been completed and he is able to support himself. If he is an adolescent, or if he is immature emotionally and not ready to shoulder the responsibilities of parenthood, he and his parents as well as the young unmarried mother and her parents will need counseling help in understanding and clarifying the responsibilities of parenthood, regardless of whether these young people marry each other. Consideration of the place of money and attitudes regarding its sources and uses in the context of meeting survival needs as well as of its relationship to trust, self-esteem, and identity can be of particular value. Such consideration offers opportunity to channel a multitude of feelings into the practicality of meeting daily living needs, and opportunity also to relate the meeting of these daily requirements to the development of the child and to the child's compelling need for affection and for security that is both economic and psychological.

A substantial number of boys and girls in such situations do decide to marry and can reap the benefit from this premarital counseling with its focus on the money component. Irrespective of the reasons that led these young couples to become unmarried parents, their subsequent marriage has greater potential for succeeding than those of many other young people. The absence of money or the lack of preparation for earning or managing money are acknowledged potent reasons for the failure of many marriages of young couples. Social work and other counselors sophisticated about the meanings and uses of money can help such couples (even while they work on the question of whether to marry) to prepare for the task of supporting a family and for coping with the financial management tasks every marriage or nonmarriage must face.

THE BROKEN FAMILY

The family broken by death, desertion, separation, or divorce characteristically is headed by a woman and falls into the lower-income groups. At the latest count, about one out of every eight families had female heads and, as was discussed in Chapter 1, their family income lags behind that of male-headed families. The absence of the father in itself generally is an important reason for this lag, because these families must depend on other sources for support. An increasing number of mothers work, but their earning power often is handicapped by lack of training and skill —although today's women heads of household are younger (median 45.1 years) than even ten years ago (median 50.5 years), and better educated, half having completed at least high school in contrast with the 32 percent of a decade ago. Moreover, despite improvements that have occurred in opening job opportunities for women, and equalizing salaries paid to them, there remains a substantial differential between those wages paid men and women for many of the same jobs, and a high proportion of the women work in such lower-paying jobs as clerical or household help.

Some of the divorced or legally separated women family heads receive alimony or child support or other forms of payment from the father while, for the most part, widows with children under eighteen tend to receive Social Security survivor's benefits or veteran's pensions, sometimes supplemented by private pensions. Whether widowed, separated, or divorced, the mother may have income from savings, gifts, insurance, public assistance, or workmen's compensation. The family income may also be supplemented by earnings of adolescent children.

In essence, the widows' families with children under eighteen have somewhat larger core incomes than similar families headed by divorced and separated women.[17] Yet, when the youngest child has reached the eighth grade or beyond, the widow's family income on the average amounts to only 58 percent of the family's normal income in the full year prior to the year in which the husband died. Such families whose youngest child is not yet in school have 69 percent of their normal former income.[18] It is evident that, contrary to the picture of the expanding family, the family income in the widow's household does not grow as the children and their needs do, unless she and one or more children are fully employed. The situation of the deserted, separated, or divorced woman head of the family is similar, although the median family income for such family groups is lower than that of widowed families, the Social Security or other pension benefits largely accounting for any differences.

Just the fact that the father is absent creates a multitude of problems. In our culture, planning and decision-making about matters of family living and child rearing generally are joint parental responsibilities, although one parent may assume a greater share than the other. If the deceased, or otherwise absent father, because of cultural patterns or for personal reasons not only had been the primary breadwinner but also had taken major responsibility for managing the family's income and expenditures, the mother is forced to take over unaccustomed functions. Lack of experience or cultural or psychological factors may cause her to be unprepared to assume the new roles thrust on her, usually with little or no warning.

The number of broken families headed by widowers, divorced, or separated fathers has grown considerably in recent years. While more than half of these family heads are widowers, the number of divorced or separated fathers with children in their homes increased more than 70 percent in a single decade. Some of this increase is due to the greater frequency with which divorce courts now give custody to the father; some undoubtedly is because mothers desert the family, often to "find themselves" away from the disliked "binding" routines of household and family management. The father remaining in the home generally is faced with new functions to be added to the breadwinning responsibility which he probably already had. He must now assume the child care and household management tasks (or provide somehow for them) that had been the mother's.

Most of these widowed, separated, deserted, or divorced mothers and fathers have the inner strength to reorganize themselves and their lives, and to meet the new demands at a level of social adjustment that ranges along a continuum from minimal to optimal adequacy. Some are overwhelmed by the enormity of the task. They are able to assume the new responsibilities only gradually, sometimes at great cost to themselves and to their children. If the father has died, the finality of death forces the mother to make a new life; she often can mobilize her strengths more quickly than if he is away temporarily. If the mother has died, the father is similarly called on to accept the irreversibility of the situation and to take the measures necessary to cope with this permanent change. In the instance of the father's or mother's widowhood, the early mourning period is often critical from the standpoint of the survivor's need for and ability to make constructive use of proffered counseling. The usually urgent need to act on financial and estate matters makes the individual vulnerable to exploitation. Appropriate counseling, however, can help the bereaved person to channel emotional and physical energies into required actions, and thereby to acquire some sense that life circumstances and problems still are within the individual's control. The feeling of control and movement toward a goal, centering on fiscal day-to-day matters, is important in strengthening self-esteem and self-trust.

If the father is hospitalized because of a physical or mental illness, the mother not only must assume the added family responsibilities but also carry a heavy emotional burden (anxiety and, perhaps, guilt) about his health and about his opinion of her performance in managing the household, the children, and their financial affairs. The latter area takes on added dimensions if the illness has added to their financial obligations and their income has been or will be reduced by continued illness. The anxiety may be tinged with anger that is masked from the patient. Where will it be directed? To the children? Internalized?

If the long-term absence of the father is because of imprisonment, the anxieties about management are mixed with anger (and, again, sometimes guilt) toward him or, frequently, toward society or herself for "forcing" him to the act resulting in incarceration. The emotional burden now has another element: how the paternal situation is to be explained to children, or how children are to be helped to handle not only the father's absence, but also the reason for it. In most situations, it is far easier to interpret illness than misdeed.

The mother's long-term hospitalization for illness imbues the father with similar anxieties, but usually with some differences. Society still does not fully expect the father to manage housekeeping and child-care duties smoothly, even though he may in fact be highly competent in doing so. He may be uneasy about the care the children are receiving and the adequacy of his housekeeping, but guilt is not usually present. His uneasiness about his wife's illness and his new responsibilities can be at least partly dispelled by the demands of his daily work, which must be continued to assure family income. In a sense his daily work removes him from the continuous burden of household responsibility. He may manage household funds and marketing ineptly for a while but, again, aside from needing to be sure that there is enough income to cover the outgo and wishing to demonstrate that he can rise effectively to any situation, including household responsibilities, the quality of pressure he feels is likely to differ from his wife's. The key is in society's limited perceptions and expectations of the father's tasks, and the economical readiness of relatives, friends, and neighbors to rally longer around the "father left helpless" by the wife's prolonged absence because of physical or mental illness.

Many families who lose a parent, whether by death, desertion, divorce, or separation, find that their expenses are higher and their income lower, particularly if it is the father who is gone; and almost all such families are confronted with the necessity for making certain financial adjustments. The remaining parent is likely, for example, to start the single-parenting role with sizable debts.

> Louis M found that his wife's terminal illness of several years—cancer—resulted in more than $12,000 in medical expenses not covered by what he had regarded as "good" health insurance. A certified public accountant, Mr. M had good earnings. The proceeds from a life insurance policy covered a substantial portion of the medical and funeral costs. He was able, moreover, to pay for housekeeping services that would prevent the brunt of housekeeping tasks from falling on either him or his young teen-age daughter and son.

Most women who raise children by themselves are not as fortunate financially.

> Ruth B was widowed when her husband died from injuries sustained in a hit-run accident. The accident had prevented him from working for two years before his death, and he had required Mrs. B's almost full-time nursing care for most of this period. Mrs. B had been a clerk before the first of her three under-10 children was born; she had not worked since, nor did she have any job skills. Her husband had earned $18,000 per year as an air conditioning serviceman; he had been on full disability pay for six months, then on Social Security disability benefits. Mrs. B had drastically curtailed the family's level of living in the effort to manage their daily needs on the less than $400 paid under Social Security. She had used the $8,000 left in her husband's insurance (on which $12,000 had been borrowed earlier to cover mortgage payments and taxes, car payments, and other fixed obligations) to meet funeral costs and some of the outstanding medical bills. But she still faced an outstanding indebtedness of $3,800 for medical care alone—and no income to look forward to except her continued Social Security survivor's benefits.

Divorce can create similar problems, even for a woman who works steadily.

> The S's divorce decree awarded Mrs. S $300 per month child support for the three children, 8, 12, and 17; she also was given the family home on which an $11,000 mortgage balance was outstanding. Mrs. S earned $6,500 annually as a typist-clerk, with health insurance provided for her but not her dependents. Mr. S earned $18,000. He expected to remarry shortly and thought that the child support award and the house were all that could reasonably be expected of him, that Mrs. S should be able to manage with these awards and her salary. Mrs. S turned to a counselor for help: How should she budget to meet mortgage payments of $180 per month; car payments of $45; dependents' health insurance of $38 each month; car and house insurance; school expenses; instalment payments on furniture and house improvements—$90 per month incurred two years before; taxes, clothing, and daily living costs? And, when the oldest child would turn 18, ready to go to college, what adjustments would she need to make because child support would be reduced to $200?

The widowed, divorced, or separated man or woman often also faces expenses that either are new since the break-up of the family, or were not so demanding when both parents were in the home. The low salaries paid most women and the difficulty and expense of locating child care combine to form an almost insurmountable obstacle to the well-being of many such families. Fathers left with children may need to purchase child care, either the services of a housekeeper or a child care facility. Grandparents or older siblings in the family or other relatives may become available for the child care tasks while the single parent works. The relative may move into the family home (or the one-parent family may move into the relative's home) or provide day care only. For many, such arrangements are not only the single solution within the income constraints, but also the one that works out very well for all concerned. There are many households, however, where tensions of various kinds are introduced by the delegation or the fulfillment of the responsibilities, particularly when thrust on teen-agers or on grandparents who either physically or emotionally cannot meet the demands of the children and the expectations of the sole parent in the home.

Since 1971, Congress on several occasions has liberalized the income tax formula for day care tax deductions. These changes undoubtedly have eased the burden for some broken families. Nevertheless, the net cost for child care per se, plus the additional hidden costs attendant upon the working role of a mother, constitute a financial drain on the single-parent family that is more severe than on the two-parent family. (See the related discussion in Chapters 11 and 14.)

It has been less easy for many husbandless women to employ "normal" credit resources in liquidating or increasing some of the debts and in meeting added costs of household operation in the aftermath of the husband's death or other separation from the family unit. As noted earlier, the absence of a husband ipso facto has served to categorize the single mother as a bad credit risk, regardless of her financial resources or the fact that she may have been the only provider while the husband was still in the home.

The impact on the family made by the voluntary or involuntary departure of one parent reverberates long after the separation has occurred: roles, responsibilities, and relationships of the remaining members are altered. The quality and form of the remaining parent's adjustment to the absence of the spouse-parent partner profoundly affects the effectiveness of the adjustments achieved by the children. A mother may manifest her failure to adjust adequately to the father's absence by spending on luxuries to gratify her own emotional needs or to "make up" to the children for the father's absence and her own uncertainty that she can meet their needs. She may set no limits in responding to their requests, no matter how unrealistic they may be. She may spend recklessly to convey her despair and resentment; or she may gamble rashly or drink excessively. The father who is left without a wife in the home may react similarly. In addition, he may jeopardize his livelihood by rationalizing tardiness or absence from work, especially if it is not satisfying, in terms of being "needed at home."

The fact that more than 30 percent of the nation's children do not live with both of their natural parents[19] underscores the importance of counseling help being available to those newly single parents who want it, so that they and the children can be guided through the trauma of the changed status, whether the change was voluntary or involuntary. Realistic and unrealistic money concerns and behavior reveal clues to the parent's disturbance and adjustment. Similarly, danger signals are discernible in the behavior of the children. They may try to use money as a lever to wheedle money or treats from the available parent, as proof they are still loved. They may learn that money is a source of power; that it increases the ability to "buy" some people, or to withhold from them, or to influence relationships. They may turn from the ungiving, seemingly uncaring parent to other or antisocial sources for gratifying their essential need for attention and affection.

Although emotional hazards that relate to money are to be found in one-parent families no matter why the other parent is absent, some behavior forms are more likely to be precipitated by certain reasons for absence than by others. It cannot be overly emphasized that it is not the absence alone of either parent that is significant, but rather it is a complex of interacting factors that produce adverse effects. Primary among these factors are the coping ability and the personality structure of the parent who retains the caretaker role with the children, and the personality structure and environmental milieu of the living absent parent. (Do the children receive adequate parenting and supervision and attention consistent with their age and developmental stage? Are the parents still together at least in how they relate to and plan for and with the children? Is each parent more preoccupied with his or her own hurt, angry, or vindictive feelings than with the child's needs for parenting and consistent role-modeling?) Another factor is the economic situation of the family—the sources and adequacy of income and resources that enable the single-parent family to maintain an appropriate standard of living—and the intimacy and adequacy of the continuing role of the living absent parent in the family's economic picture. And the third interacting element is the cluster of community influences to which the needs and behavior of the family members, whether in or out of the family home, are responsive.

Death

The healthiest of families is vulnerable to grim problems if a parent dies. The substantial reduction in the family's income and, often, serious economic hardships that may follow the father's death, may be compounded by other problems relating to or resulting from the death. Even if the family resources remain adequate, the family may suffer because either the father had not put or kept his financial affairs in good order, or because he deliberately or thoughtlessly failed to acquaint his wife with how the estate could or should be handled. She may helplessly or unwittingly dissipate resources that could be used productively for the children and herself. The mother's death may leave the father with a sense of helplessness, especially because cultural and societal expectations and limitations do not readily give him the option, even on a temporary basis, of staying home to care for the children. Who then should do it? What should the arrangements be, and what is a reasonable cost for what services? What aspects of care should be retained by the father or delegated to others?

There are certain ages when children are particularly affected by a

Variants on Lifestyles 161

parent's death. Surviving parents of very young children are in a precarious situation, no matter how well adjusted they are and how honestly the total loss of the other parent is faced with the children. The young children feel abandoned by the absent parent who is failing to protect them. Was the child unloved? Responsible for the parent's departure? Secrecy may surround the parent's death—secrecy to the extent that it is not discussed with the child, who is "protected" from the knowledge of the illness or accident or other cause of death. The remaining parent may be so saddened, helpless, and preoccupied with personal feelings or with economic survival that the sustenance and emotional support the child needs at this time are just not available. And so the child's questions are unasked. The child's anxiety tends to be expressed either through aggressive behavior or symptoms, or denial that the event actually occurred. The former may be demands for sweets, for money, for things that, when granted, are felt to represent the affection, solace, and protection withheld by the absent parent. Or the behavior may be a test of the remaining parent's tolerance and acceptance (and, therefore, affection) when the child steals, or spends money recklessly and extravagantly for items that are then ignored.

During adolescence, vulnerability is again at a critical level. In the child's push toward maturation, both parents are needed as models for identification, and as models against whom to rebel. If the father dies, the mother has to avoid placing the son in a fathering role to other children or a husband role in relation to herself, perhaps thereby pushing him into running away from both roles and the responsibilities inherent in them. The extremes of depending on the adolescent son for producing and managing the family income, or of shielding him from any responsibility in decision-making about how the family income will be utilized, will have a bearing on how he carries out the provider-protector function when he is an adult with his own family. Similarly, the temptation to lean on an adolescent daughter needs to be avoided lest she be overburdened with responsibilities that could result in overcompliance or in destructive rebelliousness manifested not only in the adolescent stage, but also in the girl's own marriage tasks in the future.

The father whose wife's death has left him with at least one adolescent child must also be on guard. He must be careful not to shift to that child too much responsibility for the care of younger children and for the maintenance of the household. An adolescent girl often is sure that she can carry such an assignment; but unless it is a moderate responsibility, leaving her free to move with a reasonable degree of normality through adolescence into adulthood, she and her father may find that she is being used as a mother substitute, with the potential consequences already described.

Similar needs emerge in families where a parent dies, whether the family is rich, poor, or anywhere between. The family's material resources, available either before or after the loss of this parent, are not in themselves adequate to meeting the children's developmental needs. The poor face added problems: the lack of money resources limits the options available to the family in planning how they will cope with the future. Embarking on vocational preparation for the widow, for example, or continued education for the children; having choices in the widow's or widower's purchase of child care arrangements; ensuring that too great a household management burden is not thrust on the children—these and other circumstances are less controllable by the family with severely limited resources, including public assistance, than by the family in a more favorable economic position. But, most important is the fact that the bereaved father or mother who is impelled by the loss into preoccupation with the struggle to meet financial needs, or with attempts to meet the emotional needs of children through the use of money rather than self, may profoundly affect the child's attitudes regarding money in adulthood.

Disturbed relationships and deprivation of either warmth and affection or (often, and) economic security at critical stages of child development are important influences in shaping the adult "penny pincher" who is constantly fearful of being robbed or envied, who is secretive and miserly, who spends only what is absolutely essential and regrets each penny so spent. Such adults form poor relationships with others, including their own spouses and children. (A classic example is to be seen in the character of James Tyrone, so dramatically drawn by Eugene O'Neill in *Long Day's Journey into Night.*) They are psychologically well-guarded and not easily reached by a counselor: they regard their approach to money as a virtue highly respected in our society which reckons thrift and management of money as measures of individual adequacy and morality! The intervention of a counselor in such situations is less to help this compulsive nonspender than to help the spouse and children to cope with the reality of their situation and protect the development of the children.

DESERTION
The marital disharmony that leads to desertion often has an economic component. Although economic deprivation is not necessarily the major cause of family breakdown by desertion, it creates an atmosphere that

is conducive to the disruption. If the partners are incompatible and do not share the same ideals and goals, the tension between them is likely to mount when they live in a cold or overcrowded home and when they do not have enough to eat or to wear. Worry about the future, for themselves and for their children, adds to the strain. Desertion, therefore, may represent a desperate attempt on the part of the father to escape responsibilities he cannot meet and to find a means of personal survival. In the past few years there appears to have been an increase in the number of deserting mothers. There is a paucity of data but much speculation regarding the causes. Some feel that there is growing public acceptance of the woman's search for self-fulfillment and that many can achieve such self-realization only by escaping the daily responsibilities that commonly are part of parenting and household management.

"Desertion" also may be a deliberate action by a father who is unemployed and hopelessly without prospects for changing this situation. The only recourse he may see for support for his dependents is public assistance. If the family resides in a state which does not aid a family with an employable father, even when work simply cannot be found by or for him, he may leave the household in order that the wife and children become eligible to receive some form of income maintenance. In such situations, there tends to be continued contact between the absent father and the family, often clandestine; his "desertion" is understood by the children (angrily or sympathetically) to be in their interest even though it is not condoned by the community.

There are many reasons for desertion by the father, but the act cannot invariably be taken to mean that he is unable or unwilling to continue financial support to the family. For example, it is not uncommon for a father to leave the home during his wife's pregnancy. He may be afraid or unable to accept the role and responsibilities of fatherhood. The level of his own maturity is that of the young dependent child requiring the full attention of a mother, for whom, in this case, his wife is a substitute. The essential problem is the personality disturbance and the shift in marital equilibrium which occurs with the pregnancy. His economic functioning may not be impaired, but he may be unable to deal with the competition of a baby in the home. He may or may not be able or willing to support the family; assumption of this financial responsibility is only likely to follow counseling assistance that aims to develop his tolerance for the parenting role.

In general, desertion is not only a symptom of unwillingness or inability to assume a degree of responsibility for financial and emotional support for the family; it is also an expression of rebellion against the demands and expectations of society. It follows, then, that a deserting father, when located by law-enforcement agencies, usually has a high level of resistance to contributing money to the family. The same dynamics operating in his decision or impulse to desert will be present in his failure to support and his way of dealing with or avoiding legal or other devices that require that he contribute.

Research has disclosed that fathers subject to court orders for support, contributed less frequently than fathers who had agreed through other means to provide support, and that the more informal the nature of the agreement the greater the frequency of the contribution.[20] Further, the proportion among divorced or legally separated fathers who contributed was considerably greater than among fathers who had deserted and subsequently had been located. This finding is not surprising, for divorce or legal separation (except when instituted by one spouse following desertion by the other) is a more responsible way than desertion for handling differences. That there has been an agreement—legal or informal, but nevertheless an agreement—implies an acceptance of continuing responsibility for and an interest in family members. It holds a greater potential than desertion for some financial support, even though in small amounts. The study also revealed that deserting fathers tended to return to resume support of larger rather than smaller families, a point of some interest in light of the stereotype of the economically dependent family that has out-of-wedlock children as a means for procuring more public assistance.

Desertion always creates rage, resentment, hurt, and guilt in the deserted parent. Children feel hurt, resentment, guilt, anger, and anxiety. Young children especially may feel that they are responsible for the parent's desertion. If the desertion has been accompanied by a complete break in voluntary communication with the family, or if there is no financial contribution by a deserting father, either voluntary or law-enforced, the mother's hostility and bitterness complicate the practical problems she must face. Feelings of guilt about her part in the separation may serve to immobilize her in taking hold of her financial situation, or obscure practical ways of doing so. And the children may fantasize the father as strong or weak, become overattached to the mother, or behave aggressively toward her and toward the father if there is a later contact with him.

The child often develops ideas about the deserting father or mother that may bear little resemblance to reality but usually are quite specific; thus the deserting parent may be all good or all bad. The deserted parent tends to reinforce this attitude, overtly expressing anger over being rejected, or silently conveying righteous martyrdom. If the family is dependent upon public aid, the mother generally is required to file nonsupport charges against the deserting parent. Some social workers and other helping professionals consider this process detrimental to any potential that may exist to reunite the family. Certainly the process does sometimes contribute to further marital difficulty and intensifies the psychological problems of the mother. At the same time it gives her formal evidence to point out to the children, "See, he's just no good! He's irresponsible about us who depend on him, and he does not care about his own children; otherwise, the 'law' would not have to force him to give you what every decent father gives his children!"

Often overlooked by counselors is the fact that the father contributes *something,* no matter how he comes to do so, is representation to the young child that the father *cares* and that the child has really not been instrumental in the father's desertion. This feeling, acquired in early developmental years, may well be altered by later understanding of the actual facts when the reasonably healthy individual is better equipped to handle any resulting bitterness.

Unless the parent in the home can be helped to understand the effects on the child's development of the desertion and of this parent's way of coping with it, the youngster may create fantasies about the reason for the desertion that undoubtedly will have a direct effect on the developmental tasks that the child must perform. There is little prospect that some severe effects will be readily or ever reversed; the child's severed contact with the deserting parent, for example, usually precludes alteration or elimination of the fantasies. Many of the first conceptions formed by a child about money and the division of labor within a family derive from the example set by the father as the provider of money, and the warmth, love, and food it connotes. The distorted impressions developed in regard to the absent figure bear directly on the child's share of trust, self-esteem, and identity. As older adolescents and later as adults, they incline toward spending and overspending to ward off depression, to demonstrate they are as good and powerful as anyone else, and to push their indebtedness to the limit that brings someone into the picture to call a halt.

Divorce

The finality of the spouse's death coupled with the knowledge that death generally is beyond the control of the survivor enables the widowed spouse to accommodate to the single-parent state without some of the deep-seated impeding feelings that are present when there is desertion—

even though the death itself may be regarded by the surviving parent as desertion. It should be noted that some attitudinal differences exist when the death is by suicide. The finality of divorce, of course, is of a different order. Unless the divorce follows desertion, or some other special circumstance intervenes, there is a continuing relationship between the divorced absent parent and the children. It may be regular or sporadic, frigid or warm, tenuous or close. Its very existence, however, regardless of its nature, introduces elements that markedly affect the family's economic and social functioning, and the interrelationship of these.

Marriages terminate in divorce for a broad range of reasons, sometimes after a brief period, sometimes after decades of marriage. There may be a legal separation rather than a divorce. To all intents and purposes the outcomes are the same except for the prohibition in the former against a subsequent marriage. In this discussion, no distinction will be made between legal separation and legal divorce, for the dynamics of money behavior are essentially the same in both. One difference, however, is to be found when the religious reason offered in opposition to divorce is used by one spouse to prevent the other from remarrying, thereby complicating not only the emotional relationships in nonlegal unions, but the financial aspects as well.

> Mrs. M refused even to hear the word "divorce," but did agree to a formal separation and a court-determined financial support agreement and delineation of her property rights. She refused to let the two children visit their father who was "living in sin" with "that woman and his two bastards." When he threatened to ask the judge to renegotiate the support order unless she complied with the visitation stipulations, she compromised: he could visit the children in *her* home or take them to a public place for lunch or recreation. It was "bad enough that tainted money keeps their stomachs filled and a roof over their heads."

Money plays an important part in the circumstances that lead to divorce and that emerge from it. Earnings, expenditures, priorities, and values governing meanings and uses of money for meeting needs as well as in relationships—these and many other factors may be symptomatic or causal, as was noted earlier. There may be realistic economic stress in the family, either because income is inadequate, or because one or both parents have managed it ineptly. Both before and after the divorce, adequacy in amount and management of finances may be a weapon used by either spouse directly against the other. It may be the weapon either or both parents use to attack each other because they cannot speak openly about other basic problems like sexual incompatability. Either or both parents may wield the money weapon through the children. It also may be used by children to pit one parent against the other or to test the parental feelings for the child.

The mother may use children to seek out the father with requests for prompt payment of child support or for extra contributions to meet special requirements that arise. The mother may really need this money. On the other hand, the children and money may only be a way to maintain a link with the father: maybe he will come back when he recognizes how much he is needed. Or she may use this manipulative device to reinforce in the children the idea that they are not of primary concern to the father. (Witness his refusal to provide money on time or when additional needs occur. Can they have any doubt that their loyalty should be with her, who cares for and protects them and places them first in her life?) In 90 percent of all divorce cases, women are granted custody of the children. The mother may be an inadequate person, but unless there is substantial evidence of neglect or abuse, the court usually sees fit to place the children in her custody. This fact, together with the "stinginess" of his financial contributions (total sums which actually may be in compliance with the court's order), comprises incontrovertible evidence that the father is really the one who is inadequate, rejecting, unloving, improvident, unproviding, and uncaring. The father, too, may threaten to withhold financial help, as did Mr. M, if his "rights" are not observed by the mother.

Many children learn to protect themselves from the emotions of either or both parents before and following divorce. They may demand money, toys, clothes, and other age-related tangible "things" from the beleaguered parents, sometimes playing one parent against the other, sometimes competing with siblings for parental attention and gifts, testing to see how far each parent will go in giving. These are poignant efforts to exercise some control over the tottering family structure and to have tangible reassurance—reassurance that can be held and felt—that the conflict is between the parents and is not because the parents do not love the child. The security of children is shaken by divorce and all that precipitates it; their self-esteem and sense of identity are threatened. How can a child retain a sense of trust if the adults one should be most able to trust do not trust each other?

The divorced parents frequently have a mutual, readily observable attitude toward each other: distrust. The father may feel that the wife creates any excuse to prevent his seeing the children, and will "run him down with them." The mother may fear that the father will harass her with too frequent visits, disrupt the children's routine, entice them with treats and presents, and confuse or upset them, interfering with their discipline. The distrust may take the form of prescribed hours and days of visits—which the father may try to meet, and which the mother, who really is not eager to encourage visits from her ex-husband, discovers have actually forced him to become a regular visitor. The distrust may be anticipation that he will not meet the conditions of child support or alimony payments; so she harasses him by telephone and letters or by messages sent through the children in advance of the time the payments are due. In turn, the father may use the double threat of discontinuing support payments, especially if he is more generous than the divorce action had mandated, and of moving out of reach should she become "unreasonable" about his seeing the children.

> The divorce proceedings of the Ls involved a bitter courtroom battle over the children's custody, Mrs. L maintaining that her husband had been a poor provider because he had declined to accept a promotion in his company that would have required him to move to a city which he disliked but Mrs. L found pleasing. She insisted he deliberately gave her less money for running the household than was needed and he could afford; he accused her of being a poor manager of the family income. She wanted to have all of the money in the couple's joint bank account; he wanted to close out all the charge accounts. She wanted to keep him from ever visiting the children after the divorce; he threatened to leave town and send her only what money he wanted to, and never send her a dollar of alimony or child support. She insisted that he was deliberately presenting a facade of low income so that he would not have to pay for the support of his children.

Even when events leading to divorce have not centered causally or symptomatically on financial matters, the hurt sustained by children may affect their adult money behavior.

> Seven-year-old Nancy had witnessed scenes of violence between her parents from her earliest memories. She had seen her mother's eyes blackened by her drunken father; she had observed her mother swinging a golf club at her father while threatening to "knock his block off." After the divorce, Nancy spent her spring vacations and two weeks each summer with her father. He was lavish with gifts which, when she returned to her mother, Nancy tucked into dark corners of her closet and refused to take out or mention.
>
> When Nancy married at 22, her father attended the wedding, gave her a wedding check of $5,000, which Nancy put into a drawer, not cashing it or depositing in a bank. Two months later Nancy's husband came home from work one evening, having stopped at a bar "with the boys for a couple." Nancy went to bed without speaking to him. The next morning she spent the entire $5,000 on a car. Two miles from the place of purchase, crossing a street

against a signal, she collided with a truck. The car was demolished; Nancy sustained a broken arm.

The anger and anxiety of a seven-year-old child had not, years later, been mollified or dissipated by her father's gifts; she used them to "punish" first her father, then her husband. Without help in understanding the dynamics and consequences of her behavior, Nancy was destined to keep her own marriage off balance, if indeed she kept it at all. Nancy's dramatic reaction and action gave the counselor a handle, easily visible to Nancy, with which to take hold of her unhappiness: the significance she attributed to the gifts and their value, and how she used them to vent her anger.

Much of the acrimony that precedes and follows divorce is displaced on the level and form of financial contribution to be made by the father. There have been some instances in the past several years in which the divorcing wife is the one who pays alimony. Nevertheless, it is still generally expected that the father will support the children, no matter what the family circumstances. How much support he must pay for the children and whether he must also support the ex-wife by paying alimony are commonly areas permeated with bitter anger and resentment. There may have been no dispute about whether there should be a divorce. Agreements may have been reached in a sophisticated "reasonable-adult" fashion regarding custody of children and visitation arrangements, and even the distribution of property and resources. The matter of continuing support, however, is of a different emotional as well as financial order. It symbolizes dependence and independence of the caretaker parent as well as of the ex-spouse living away from the home. It is a measure of the latter's affection for the children and respect for their mother. And it represents his adequacy and generosity, or determination not to be "played for a sucker." Divorce means failure of the marriage. The handling of financial outcomes of the divorce (which of the parents "comes out better"?) is an important, though not necessarily conscious, index as to who is the adequate one and therefore blameless in the failure of the marriage.

The very fact that continuity is expected in the financial arrangements, at least until the children have reached their majority, is a constant and often rancorous reminder to the children of money's important part in the quality of the adult and parent-child relationships. Husbands and wives generally hold different views of what is "generous." Men often see the divorce system as an ally of women, their instrument to punish the husbands and "get all they can" from them. Women often blame their need to work after divorce on a male-dominated court or an ex-husband whose living away from home is perceived by the mother as "having it easy" and whose freedom is to be envied—even if the "freedom" may in fact relegate the absent parent to living in a dingy furnished apartment, spending much of his salary to support the children.

It behooves the social worker to have some special understanding of the implications for families of the kinds of financial arrangements developed where divorce is pending or has been made final. The adequacy of the predivorce family resources is not necessarily an index to their adequacy for maintaining two households. The fact that more divorces take place among families in lower- rather than higher-income brackets suggests, for one thing, that greater income offers the parents more options and channels for dealing with their incompatability, with possible consequences and accommodations not easily available to less affluent couples. It also indicates that more financial adjustments will be required after the divorce to stretch the less-affluent family's income and resources to meet the needs of two households, particularly if the father remarries and heads another family requiring his financial support.

Regardless of the feelings that inevitably affect the financial arrangements in a divorce action (charges, for example, that the husband or the wife is "guilty" of some callous, blatant, or offensive misconduct and should therefore be punished by paying, or by foregoing payment), two key questions need to be addressed. What will be the needs of the wife and children, and of the father, after the divorce? How should or can these needs be met? A concomitant question is whether payments will include alimony and child support, or only the former or latter.

Child support generally continues until a specified age is reached by the child and it continues regardless of whether the mother works or remarries. The cut-off point for child support most often has been 21. However, with the change in majority age to 18 in many localities, some shift is being observed in regard to continuity of child support after that age. Alimony payments made to the divorced wife, terminate as a rule when she remarries, as eight out of ten women do. If she becomes employed, the ex-husband may be able to prove that she is self-supporting and no longer needs the alimony; such payments may then be discontinued. If, however, she neither remarries nor becomes self-supporting, she not only will receive more money over a longer number of years, but she will have some income from this source in her old age, provided the ex-husband is still alive. Tax advantages also need to be weighed by the divorcing parents. Alimony payments have been acceptable deductions from the husband's taxable income both federally and in many states, whereas child care payments have not. On the other hand, the wife has been expected to include alimony in her taxable income, but not child care payments. Other tax aspects have importance, as well. If there is reason to anticipate that the mother is unlikely ever to become gainfully employed, alimony might be perceived as part of her future retirement income. In addition, some of the husband's resentment at having to support the children and their caretaking mother may be tempered by any satisfaction he may derive from reduced income tax payments.

> Tom R has a taxable income of $20,000 a year. While married, he paid taxes in a 32 percent bracket. He found he would be in the 38 percent bracket after the divorce. He was concerned about having enough free cash left each month, after providing for the children, to meet his own needs. He agreed to pay $200 per month in alimony, all of which could be deducted on both his federal and state income tax returns. This meant a saving to him of about $70 per month. By paying $2,400 a year in alimony, he saved nearly $850 a year in taxes.

In this instance, both the father and the mother used their financial agreement to assure their two teen-aged children that the parents could still plan together toward their common interest in the well-being of the children and each parent. The mother's small earnings were not likely to place her in a position of paying tax on this alimony; she could afford both financially and emotionally to be fully cooperative with her former husband and be viewed by the children as a "good sport."

But no matter how well-intentioned a divorcing couple may be in reaching a financial solution as part of the domestic solution, it is unusual for the two segments of the family to be as well off as before the divorce. The caretaking wife will need almost the same amount of money to support the children herself as was needed when the husband was still with them. The one less mouth to feed will not greatly decrease the food budget. Nor, if they remain in the same house or apartment, is there likely to be reduction in the cost of shelter. Clothing costs for the mother and children may change little if the mother does not take a job; if she does, there may be added clothing, transportation, and food expenses connected with maintaining her work, as well as other expenses connected with child care and household maintenance (see Chapter 11). If the two households are now to be supported without change in the amount of income that had carried one household, the probability will be that neither will be as comfortable without some sacrifice or compromise by one or the other parent. To reduce the impact on both segments of shared and, therefore, lower income, while being certain that the protection of the children's present and future interests is not ignored, requires careful planning by the parents undergoing the divorce process. They need to consider not only the survival needs (food, shelter, clothing) but also providing for protections that are to be found in medical, hospital, and life insurance, as well as meeting the costs of educating the children to whatever extent is suitable to their individual needs and the family's standards.

Particularly necessary in contemplating any divorce action is awareness of the impact that the divorce will have on the rescurces and on the management of the resources available to the fractions of the whole. The planning must be as comprehensive as possible to assure that the divided resources will be utilized most effectively. In many instances, of course, the mother and children will be unable to expect enough support from the father to permit them to manage without either public aid or employment of one or more members of the family. But when child support, or alimony payments, or both are arranged, it is of utmost importance to the healthy development of the children and the parents' interests that these payments be made with prescribed regularity.

In many families broken by divorce, desertion, or death, the sheer necessity to survive stimulates the members to develop tremendous resourcefulness in managing on a limited income. The attitudes and values as well as the psychological strengths of the remaining parent will mold the attitudes of the children toward money—in both its reality and relationship uses. Often there is an increase in family solidarity and an unprecedented amount of sharing among those left in the family. In other instances, family members may displace their feelings of hurt and anger onto money. The mother who fails to make an adequate adjustment to the absence of the father may express her disturbance in her handling of the family money, thereby also influencing the patterns the children will develop in their adulthood regarding money and all that it represents to them. By his absence as well as his accessibility to them, the father likewise influences the way the children perceive the meanings and uses of money. The quality of his relationship with the children and their mother, and the way he continues to fill the paternal protector-provider role with regard to the children affects the quality of their own relationships with others and the part money has in those relationships. The way in which the parents continue to fulfill parenting tasks following divorce is, of course, strongly influenced by the remarriage of one or both of the natural parents.

REMARRIAGE

The family containing a stepfather or a stepmother usually falls into one of the previously mentioned stages of the cycle of family life: the beginning, expanding, or contracting phase. Remarriage following a period of widowhood or divorce status may in fact return one or both members of the new marital team to a stage where they had already been. Either or both marital partners may have children from the prior union, now living with the former spouse or grown and living away from either natural parent. The newly married couple again may be in the beginning stage. If they have children by this union, regardless of whether children from a previous marriage also reside with them, they may be in the expanding stage. Or, there may be children from the present or a former marriage who no longer depend on the couple or on either of their natural parents, so that the new marriage partners now have come to the contracting stage of the family cycle.

It was noted that a high proportion of divorced and widowed persons marry again, that the second and third marriages tend to endure, and that it is estimated that more than 30 percent of children in this country do not live with both natural parents. The sheer volume of individuals involved in the numbers of such children and the numbers of the remarriages points to the importance of the counselor's being alert to the implications for the development of children who are placed in a set of active personal relationships with two or more families. Despite the continued semibelief in the fairy-tale stereotyping of stepparents as selfish and wicked, always placing their own natural children's interests above those of their stepchildren, children by and large accommodate reasonably well to the world in which they find themselves with more parents than the average child. In some situations, however, they are profoundly affected both as children and as adults by their own responses to their situation and by the feelings and attitudes of the adults they encounter in and outside their immediate environment.

A divorced father who remarries has multiple family responsibilities. If he is fortunate enough to have a high income, he may be able to keep his money-charged relationship under control; his financial ability to support two families adequately removes a frequent source of emotional pressure. If his income is average or low, his money and relationship problems may become extremely complex. His first wife and her children are likely to consider his contribution meager and to interpret it as rejection of them, or as reflecting the likelihood that the new wife is a scheming and depriving woman. The man's new wife may view his contributions to the first family as an unwarranted expenditure which deprives her and her children. To alleviate his guilt feelings, the father may actually give more to the wife and children he abandoned than he can really afford. Sometimes he may refuse to make reasonable payments, thus expressing his resentment of the pressures they put on him for money.

In such remarriages, where does the divorced father's first responsibility rest? With his new family? Or with the earlier family? On what basis can he—or a court—determine the proportion of income that should be allocated to the respective families? The reality of the need of the first family must be objectively appraised. There is always a risk that the demands for increased support by a divorced wife may represent efforts to regain the ex-partner, to destroy the new marriage, or to gratify dependency needs. The divorced woman, like the widow or the deserted wife, is often helped best if she is aided to mobilize energy for new activities and a new way of life, which may include employment or remarriage.

If a divorced woman remarries and her first husband contributes to the support of his children who remain with her, another set of problems arises. The father may vie with the stepfather for the affection and respect of the children. He may competitively overindulge them, buying them gifts that are impractical or beyond the means of the stepfather. If the mother has children by her second husband, her ex-husband may stir up strong sibling rivalry between his children and their half brothers and sisters. He may press his children to tell him if their mother is diverting his contributions for *their* support to the care of the other children.

> Tom, 14, lived with his mother and stepfather, Al G. They had married five years before, two years after the mother had divorced Tom's father on charges of cruelty: he had twice been apprehended by police, on complaints of neighbors, for wife-beating. Per court order, Tom's father paid $80 monthly for child support; he brought this money regularly to Mrs. G with a flourish, asking for an accounting for the previous month's payment, insisting it was not to be used in any way in behalf of her two young children by her new husband.
>
> Tom's father demanded to know from Tom whether he was well-treated, whether the G children were given more care than he, whether Tom was being exploited by being expected to care for the younger children, serving as an "unpaid babysitter."
>
> Tom, fond of his stepfather and loyal to his own father, could not understand why his mother thought the latter unreasonable. She asked him not to come to the G home but did not decline to take the money he brought.

To Tom's question, she replied that after all, it was not Al G's responsibility to take care of him, but his own father's, who in fact should be paying more.

Tom ran away, financing his departure with money and a credit card taken from his stepfather's dresser drawer. When he was apprehended two weeks later in another state as a runaway, he told the juvenile officer that he was "in the way," his stepfather "hated" him and his father "didn't think [Tom] was worth much." Mrs. G could not understand why Tom was so ungrateful when his stepfather had been a "true and loving" father to him.

In actuality, the behavior of Tom's natural parents toward each other in their manipulation of the child support payments, with their complaints and recriminations swirling around Tom, was much the same as when they were married to each other. Therapeutic intervention was indicated to sever their tie and to permit Tom to work through, appropriately, his feelings about and relationships with the parenting adults in his life.

Where Al G was a loving but passive stepfather, John A was an angry father and stepfather.

His first wife had custody of their seven-year-old twin sons, toward whose support he contributed monthly, rarely without reminder from their mother and resentment on the part of his second wife. The first Mrs. A was employed as a secondary school teacher, earning a good salary. She shared housing with her parents, who gave devoted supervision to the children while she worked. John A complained that they gave "those kids too much" and "ran me down" by letting them know that the grandparents gave them more love and care than their own father.

Mr. A, a free-lance writer who contributed regularly to several weekly magazines and earned an amount he was not willing to reveal to his present or former wife, maintained that his former wife earned more than he.

The present Mrs. A had two sons from a former marriage, ages 13 and 15. Their father, whom they visited regularly, paid child support—a larger amount than Mr. A for his children—and frequently bought them clothes and other presents. Their mother wanted to bank the child-support payments for their future, giving them each an allowance for their personal use, but expecting Mr. A to support them along with her. He was infuriated: They wouldn't obey him, so why should he support them? They spoke to him only when it just could not be avoided. Giving them an allowance would also be tantamount to letting them know they could do as they pleased regardless of what he might say or think. Mr. A had never had an allowance and *he* had learned the meaning of money. Let their father take care of them! And if their mother thought so highly of her ex-husband that she wanted to save his money, why did she divorce him?

This man was carrying a burden of unresolved developmental tasks of his own which now affected not only his present marriage but his relationship with the children from the prior one.

Money is often the means used by the ex-wife or ex-husband to create strain and tension in the new family. Parents who remarry, therefore, have a special responsibility to try to help the children maintain a wholesome balance in their loyalties and affections to their parents and stepparents. In counseling with these families, there must be a sensitive understanding of the complex interrelationships and an endeavor to help both parents and children handle their feelings and their use of money as objectively as possible.

NOTES

1. Current Population Reports, *Population Characteristics,* "Households and Families, by Type: March 1973," series P-20, no. 251 (Washington, D.C.: Bureau of the Census, 1973), p. 3.
2. Harry D. Krause, *Illegitimacy: Law and Social Policy* (New York: Bobbs-Merrill Co., 1971), pp. 65ff.
3. U.S., Congress, Joint Economic Committee, *The Family, Poverty and Welfare Programs: Factors Influencing Family Stability.* Studies in Public Welfare Paper 12, Part 1, 93rd Cong. 1st sess. (Washington, D.C.: U.S. Government Printing Office, 1973), pp. 12ff.
4. Ibid, p. 267.
5. Ibid.
6. Euripides, *Phrixus,* fragment 970.
7. *Exodus* 20:5.
8. *Merchant of Venice,* act 3, sc. 5, line 1.
9. Alaska, Arizona, Minnesota, and North Dakota in particular according to Krause, *Illegitimacy,* pp. 297–306.
10. U.S., Department of Commerce, Bureau of the Census, *Statistical Abstract of the United States 1975: National Data Book and Guide to Sources,* 96th ed. (Washington, D.C.: U.S. Government Printing Office, 1975), p. 57.
11. Ibid.
12. *North Dakota Central Code,* 1969.
13. *Illegitimacy: A Position Statement.* In 1975 the Board altered its statement of position by changing the report to *Unplanned Parenthood: A Study of Unwed Parents and the Potentially Endangered Child* and insisting that all children born out of wedlock are at risk and require state protection, especially because unwed mothers tend to be abusive and neglectful mothers (Sacramento: State Board of Social Welfare, 1975).

14. The Joint Economic Committee of the U.S. Congress reports that "high welfare payments are not the overwhelming influence on illegitimacy." Ibid., p. 14.
15. Sanford N. Katz, *When Parents Fail: The Law and Response to Family Breakdown* (Boston: Beacon Press, 1971), pp. 3–17.
16. U.S., Congress, Joint Economic Committee, ibid., p. 134.
17. Lucy B. Mallan, "Young Widows and Their Children: A Comparative Report," *Social Security Bulletin* 38 (May 1975):3–21.
18. Ibid.
19. Report from Bureau of the Census quoted in *Los Angeles Times,* July 3, 1975, part 1, p. 4.
20. Saul Kaplan, *Support from Absent Fathers of Children Receiving ADC: 1955.* Public Assistance Report no. 41 (Washington, D.C.: U.S. Government Printing Office, 1960).

PART 3
MONEY
AND
COUNSELING

8
Money Counseling: Goals and Techniques

The amount of a family's income without doubt has a direct bearing on the living standards the family can maintain. It may enable a family to have housing near good schools, or to provide the privacy some family members may desire, or to purchase satisfactory child care services. It may crowd a family unwillingly into a ghetto dwelling, without transportation resources to reach more favorable job opportunities or educational, recreational, or diversified marketing facilities. Availability of income may permit parents and their children to channel time and emotional energies into socially and personally acceptable diversionary activities, away from interpersonal tensions in the home and family disruption or breakup.

The kinds and nature of life experiences available or unavailable to the family members to a considerable extent are governed by the level of family income. There is an inescapable interaction between the environment and the family or individual in it. Sharp upward or downward changes may alter the family living standards or composition, or both. Increased income may relieve stresses, removing strain from brittle adaptive capacities, thereby preventing family disorganization. Lowered income may cause an adolescent child to "go out on his own," or family "belt-tightening" that leads to less adequate housing or disrupts an educational or vocational plan—or encourages mental illness, as in the J family described in Chapter 1.

But at least as important as the size of the income, and often more important, is the way it is manipulated and managed. The Ss and the Ws illustrate this fact.

> They are close friends who bought homes in the same block in a tract housing development. The husbands are insurance adjusters employed by the same company, earning identical salaries. The Ss' three children are under 10, as are the Ws' two. Both mothers are active volunteers in the headquarters of their political party; each devotes a day a week as a volunteer driver for the

local cancer society. There the similarities end. The Ws are often in debt, either Timmy, 8, or June, 7, acting as courier in borrowing "until payday" from the Ss or other friends in the community. The Ws repay the loans promptly, but from time to time, after borrowing earlier and earlier in successive months, they turn to a commercial lender: the time gap between repayments to friends and the next paycheck is too great to cover the indebtedness out of regular income.

In our culture, the mature individual is expected to earn sufficient money to live comfortably and to manage money rationally. Modern economic theory is based on the assumption that the individual makes conscious rational choices about whether to save or to spend and about which of the myriad available goods and services will be purchased. Psychological theory, however, postulates that many choices are not rational but are made on the basis of unconscious drives and motivations.

The money problems that people bring to counselors may be those involving rational planning, or they may be outward expressions of emotional disturbances. In the latter instance, the individual may be aware that the handling of the money is nonrational and may ask for help in resolving personal difficulties. Often, however, the problem is emotional and goes unrecognized; the individual may need help in acquiring such recognition. Thus the nature of the services that counselors are called upon to give to people with money problems varies considerably. It is determined by the character of the problem, the resources available, the extent and kind of help the client is able and willing to use, and the purpose and program of the agency. Financial assistance, either full maintenance or supplementation of income, may be given. Counseling service, either alone or in conjunction with economic help, also may be provided. A social agency, for example, may be able to provide the needed services within its own organizational framework, or it may utilize other community resources such as legal aid.

In general, the money problems brought to social agencies fall into four groups. In the first are the problems of those families and individuals who simply have not learned how to make choices in the management of income through experience or models provided by meaningful adults or elsewhere, such as in school.

> The Ts, both 19, were married when they were graduated from high school a year ago. Bob is in college, his tuition being paid by his parents with whom he lived until his marriage. Mary is working as a secretary in the college and plans to do so until Bob has his degree. Her base pay is $500 monthly. The couple leased a nearby furnished apartment for $125, but added a small freezer and television set, which they arranged to buy on credit. From a

graduating student they purchased an old car; to finance this, they borrowed from the credit union in the college. Their credit payments total $84 each month. When they were notified that the freezer and television set would be repossessed, they could not understand why they were short; they were not living lavishly!

The second group of problems grow out of environmental factors: insufficient income or unexpected reduction in income because of layoffs, strikes, economic recessions, inflationary influences on fixed income, and other contingencies. The persons involved are usually reasonably competent in managing their financial affairs realistically. They may adopt measures for financial retrenchment or for utilizing personal resources planfully, taking steps that seem necessary for managing within the available income. Or they may find that the practical limitations of the low income force them to seek financial help from a public assistance agency or other resource.

The elderly Js found that the rising costs of maintaining their modest house, combined with large pharmaceutical bills not covered by Medicare, left them with insufficient money from their Social Security pension to meet their basic food and clothing needs. For several months they tried to reduce their food bills by having two meals daily, but the resulting savings still did not help them to keep their income and expenditures in balance. They could do nothing about the pharmaceuticals, or reducing their already minimal clothing expenditures. Although valuing their privacy highly, they rented out a room, the income from which at least covered the costs of their utilities and of the occasional handyman who was needed to do the chores Mr. J could no longer perform.

The handyman was their neighbor, Ralph A, an unemployed auto worker. He had worked for eighteen years for the same employer. When general economic conditions led to a series of layoffs, Mr. A found himself in the fourth round of those laid off. The union-arranged unemployment benefits plus the state unemployment insurance benefits maintained the family of seven for more than a year; careful husbanding of money obtained by a second mortgage on the small family home carried them for another five months. All their resources exhausted and prospects of returning to work very dim, the As turned to whatever work they could do—occasional odd jobs for Mr. A and baby-sitting for Mrs. A, with her husband sitting with their five young children while she worked. These earnings were not even enough to feed the family; they faced foreclosure of the mortgage. Mr. A finally applied for public assistance.

The problems in the third group develop from circumstances beyond the control of the individual or family, generally a crisis such as the death or catastrophic illness of the breadwinner. Most people who find themselves in such situations—more often the wife—have the inner strength to reorganize themselves and their lives to meet the new demands. Others are overwhelmed by the enormity of the task, or are temporarily immobilized by the nature of the crisis and able to assume the new responsibilities only gradually.

Clustered in the fourth group are money problems involving personality difficulties. Persons who have such problems may use money as a weapon in interpersonal strife, or they may incur heavy indebtedness because of neurotic needs or disturbed family relationships. Waste and extravagance on the part of one or more family members may represent the acting out of unconscious impulses.

> Don K's annual net earnings as a consulting engineer exceed $70,000. However, he is on the verge of filing for bankruptcy, the third time in as many years he has reached this stage without taking the final step. The house is large enough so that each of the six children has a separate bedroom and each pair share a bath; the house is sparsely furnished, although each of the four older children (the oldest is 13) has a television set, a record player, and a telephone. The Ks have three large foreign cars and a 30-foot sailboat, on which Mr. K entertains his—not his wife's—friends. They do no entertaining at home, but Mr. K picks up the check regularly for friends and acquaintances who lunch or dine in the same restaurant he happens to be in. He is an impulsive buyer of clothes, his closets full of suits and shoes worn once, always "the best." Mrs. K, on the other hand, withdrawn and inarticulate, has had no new clothes for several years, and the children wear clothes contributed by relatives whose children have outgrown them. Mr. K gives her an allowance for food and household operation, and a small allowance to each of the four older children. She "scrimps" to stretch the food allowance to meet rising food costs. He follows horse racing and boat racing, gambles heavily on them, drinks excessively, and is often cited for speeding in the car.
>
> When the school social worker talked with him about the truancy of the 13-year-old, Mr. K shrugged this off; he had often been truant as a boy, and his mother and father didn't care, so why should he? When the worker asked if he is aware that the next child has been "flashing" money around the elementary school and treating her friends generously, he replied, "Well, I don't know where she's getting the money, but I know where her generous nature comes from!" Moreover, it is up to his wife to know where the children are all the time and what they are doing. His attention and energy must be devoted to providing for them.

When the seminal problem of personality difficulty or limited intellectual endowment is coupled with environmental factors or crisis beyond the control of an individual, problems related to personality are likely to be in the ascendency. The environmental or crisis factors identified with the second and third groups, though important, may not be as significant as the developmental factors.

Any of the last three groups may include the problems of family members who lack knowledge of how to develop a spending plan, who are unable to agree on priorities in purchasing, who are unable to account for the expenditure of their money, who overexpend for home, car, furniture, or other items, and who have low sales resistance because they are in competition with their neighbors and friends. The problems in any of the groups may be affected by social and cultural pressures. Among these are intergenerational conflicts about appropriate ways of obtaining and disposing of income, especially when the parents are foreign-born or have a different level of educational, economic, or social achievement than does the younger generation of striving adults.

A family's problem may represent any combination among all of the groups. Environmental and cultural factors are complicated or even governed by psychological factors. For instance, an emotionally deprived man who is unable to earn enough to support himself and his family may have difficulty with both his wife and his children and may turn to alcoholism or gambling. In the same way, the individual whose intellectual or educational limitations narrow his work potential may fail to find satisfying employment and may express his dissatisfaction in his marital relationship. The woman too may express discontent with the marital situation when she feels spoken or unspoken criticism of her household management skills, and realistically or inaccurately avers that she is "tied down" to household and family responsibilities instead of fulfilling her potential in an outside job.

COUNSELING GOALS

Counseling with regard to financial management is provided by many professions, in many settings, and for many purposes. A stockbroker or a banker may advise a client about ways to invest money to increase its earning, or to conserve it through saving. A lawyer may help a client take legal measures to protect or distribute an estate or arrive at an equitable settlement in a divorce or support action. A tax accountant may suggest ways of utilizing tax shelters or other means for keeping to a minimum the amount of income that otherwise would be expended for taxes. An automobile salesman may help a potential customer design a spending plan so that a portion of the income can become available to meet monthly car payments. A credit union committee may review a member's outstanding indebtedness and assist in working out a plan for consolidation of the debts whereby the credit union loan permits liquidation of all the debts except the single one to the credit union. In the course of treatment a psychiatrist whose patient is a compulsive gambler may draw upon knowledge of the financial and emotional cost of this behavior to the gambler's family.

Within a social agency, counseling may be undertaken for several purposes and in several ways. In the earlier days of social work, counseling usually took the form of giving advice. As knowledge about human behavior has advanced, counseling in social agencies has taken on many new aspects. It now has the dictionary connotation attributed to it by Webster: "deliberation together"; and how the social worker and the individual or the family share responsibility in this process, depends on agency function, the goals sought by the persons requesting service, and the assessment of their motivation and capacity for moving toward the goals with some degree of success. This is not to say that counseling should not or does not include the giving of advice. Rather, a counselor's decision to give advice or utilize other techniques aimed toward enabling the client to reach an acceptable goal and level of social functioning should rest on an evaluation of the unique constellation of feelings, capacities, and needs brought by the person or family. The deeply anxious mother whose husband seemingly without warning "just quit his job and walked off" with another woman, leaving his wife with two small children and no knowledge of family assets or resources available for their maintenance, may need help to channel her anxiety quickly into action so that the family can manage while longer-range plans are being developed. Firmly offered advice may be the technique chosen to help this woman begin to take hold of her situation, to begin to think about goals.

Individuals and families vary greatly in their ability to plan their lives, to manage their economic affairs, to set realistic goals in planning their income and expenditures, and to ask for and use help for defining or refining and reaching goals—or for translating unrealistic or undesirable objectives into goals that are practicable. The counselor, therefore, must evaluate the nature of the request brought to the agency and its practicality in terms of the individual's goals as well as the potentials for realizing them. In addition, consideration must be addressed by the counselor to the compatibility of the goals with the welfare of the family and community, and with the agency's philosophy and function. The counselor, in consequence, may need to decide whether to help the individual move toward a delineated goal that appears impractical or endeavor to help the troubled individual or family transmute the original objective into a more manageable one. Mr. and Mrs. B's problem illustrates a need for service aimed at helping the family modify its goal.

> Ten-year-old Marcia, the middle child in the family, was four before the parents admitted that she was "slow." Although the child was admissible to the public school system, which has special education programs for the mentally retarded, Mrs. B maintained that the girl would suffer there, that she should have individualized attention at a private school to maximize her potential and to "protect" her from "misleading" influences. Mr. B's moderate salary as a meter reader for the local utilities company met the family's ordinary needs comfortably, but there was not sufficient income to pay for the costly educational program selected for Marcia. Mrs. B obtained a secretarial job at which she worked only in the hours Marcia was in the private school but her earnings did not quite equal the cost of tuition. Mr. B found a part-time job for evenings and weekends to help meet both inflationary living costs and the difference between Mrs. B's net earnings and the cost of Marcia's education.
>
> Not a robust man, Mr. B found the extra work physically draining and it was increasingly difficult for him to get to his meter reading job on time. He became depressed when his annual rating dropped from "very satisfactory" to "needs improvement." The company personnel officer suggested he go to the local family service agency.

The counselor's exploration with the Bs revealed not only that the father was working beyond his physical capacity, but that he supported the "school plan my wife worked out" because he felt in some way responsible for Marcia's limitations, even though it had been medically determined that Marcia's intellectual development had been affected by her mother's illness in the early gestation period. A family interview, which included the other daughters, was shocking for both parents.

> Thirteen-year-old Emily resented the amount of time she had to spend with "that dummy" and was embarrassed when friends came to visit, which she tried to avoid by meeting them elsewhere. The mother became aware that she did not know where and how Emily spent her time outside of school hours; the girl did her assigned chores and the mother did not look beyond this fact. Emily's unhappiness and the disclosure that she twice had started to run away was met by the mother with angry tears and by the father with an accusing "See what you are doing!" to Mrs. B. "After all, the other girls are important, too!" Doris also expressed hostility about "No one cares about me; I don't even get a new dress because I'm younger than Marcia, so her cast-offs come to me. At least Emily gets new clothes!"

Looking together at the needs of Marcia and the others in the family against the backdrop of available income with and without the moonlighting and the mother's outside employment, led the parents both to reexamine the public school program as a resource for Marcia, and to redeploy their attention to the children and to each other. The decision to reestablish the marital and family equilibrium involved the participation of all the family.

Of a different order was the problem posed by Phillip R, an American Indian, who was referred by his employer to the local consumer credit counseling agency for help in dealing with indebtedness exceeding $5,000.

> The father of nine young children, Mr. R was on a salary schedule of $12,000 a year as a truck driver for the local newspaper. He had been in heavy debt almost from the time he began on this job, had borrowed from the company's loan fund to the maximum, and now his salary had been garnisheed for the third time by creditors.
>
> The interview disclosed that Mr. R had traveled 3,200 miles five times within as many months, each time losing pay for days not worked; the last time, his car broke down and required the outlay of $750 before he could proceed home. His wife had borrowed the money from the employer and wired it to her husband. The trips were to the tribe on an Indian reservation, occasioned by the death or serious illness of individuals there. Although they were not his blood relatives, Mr. R's position in the tribal council caused him to feel obliged to return to the reservation whenever he was called upon to do so.
>
> The Rs had lived on the reservation until Mr. R decided to relocate his family to the urban center and see "what good this would be for the kids."

It was clear to Phillip R and to the credit counselor that even though a plan could be worked out with the employer and the creditors to reduce the indebtedness over a period of time, recurrence of the circumstances causing the present problem was likely. Resolution of the problem would have to take into account cultural, emotional, and financial factors and their impact on any goal that would be regarded as both reasonable and desirable. To help Mr. R work his way through to a solution, he was referred to the social service agency with identified interest in and sophistication about services to American Indians. Meanwhile, the credit counselor initiated a debt proration plan with Mr. R. (This kind of plan is discussed in Chapter 13.)

Short-term and Long-term Goals

As both the Bs and the Rs illustrate, it is important that the client (individual or family) and agency agree on the importance and nature of the goals toward which they will work together or separately in the interests of the family. The agreement may be expressed in different terms. The client's or client-family's motivation for achievement of the goals may be at higher or lower levels at various times. To be attainable in any part, the goals must be desirable to the family and compatible with the interests of the agency and the community. There must also be awareness that achievement of an ultimate goal often depends on reaching successive small or short-term goals, and is often the aggregate of small successes achieved on the way to the final large goal. Moreover, assessment of the accomplishment of an intermediate or short-term goal may suggest a modification in the long-range goal: a reassessment that realistically considers the demonstrated adequacy of family members in reaching the short-range goal; the nature and strength of cultural determinants; personal pathology that may contribute to problems or impede problem-solution; or enhanced self-esteem and confidence that resulted from the small success and now can be drawn upon to impel the family members closer to the ultimate goal.

Long-term goals tend to be comprehensive in scope and are aimed toward maintaining or developing family cohesiveness and stability, appropriate self-sufficiency (emotional) and economic self-maintenance (in part or in full) of families and individuals. Short-term goals, which are narrower in scope, may be attainable in a relatively brief time or may actually require a long time to reach, with the progress punctuated by the completion of prescribed small steps.

Whether budget or other money counseling is an end in itself or is used as a means for reaching other goals, depends on the counselor's understanding of the factors that created the problem. Budget counseling may be the only objective if an individual or a family, generally adequate in personality and in money management, is temporarily overwhelmed by debts that have accrued because of external pressures such as unanticipated medical costs, payment for education, or an unexpected work stoppage. A beginning family in particular, like the Ts, may use budget counseling as an end in itself if they have not yet learned to manage expenditures either as individuals or as a young married couple.

Budget counseling also may be the only service objective for individuals with marked personality limitations, and for families in which there is severe social disorganization. Often the parents in these families are very immature or have severe character pathology for which the prognosis for improvement is extremely poor. Such counseling requires that the parents learn how to use money, not intellectually, but through identification with a mature adult who offers support and encouragement but does not take over their responsibilities.

Short-term goals, therefore, usually are appropriate for the individual at either end of the range of personality development. For the mature person, brief counseling is probably all that is required. For the disturbed person, it may be all that can be tolerated. In working with the disorganized family,[1] the counselor should take into account the meaning of temporary acute stress, recognizing the concurrently heightened dependence. The family members usually require some gratification of needs before they can meet the demands that will move them nearer to their objectives.

Money counseling can be a device or tool in the long-range treatment of psychosocial problems for persons who fall in an "in-between" group —those who have interpersonal and personal difficulties and who have a tendency to displace their problems onto money. In working with this group, the counselor still starts with the request of the individual or family, and deals with it. The area of consideration, however, may be extended to causes and to the treatment of causes. The discussion of money troubles between husband and wife may lead to better communication between them and to discussion in regard to other areas of discord, and may help them develop a greater understanding of each other. It may be used as the focal point in discussing emancipation problems of adolescents and in helping parents permit children to establish their own identity. In other words, money discussion is often a way of dealing with a range of family or individual problems. In helping people to master a practical problem, the counselor touches on significant interpersonal relationships, personal attitudes, and modes of behavior which are inevitably influenced by the discussion. The gratification that comes with mastery of a problem is an incentive to further learning and personal development.

> The Es were launched on such a course when the reluctant father participated in a family conference with his wife, daughter, and the social worker in the family service agency. Mrs. E had been referred by juvenile authorities to this agency when 13-year-old Carol was apprehended while slipping costume jewelry from the store counter into her pocket. The social worker already had talked once with Carol, and once with Mrs. E.
>
> "I make a decent living, but I work hard for every dime I get and she spends it faster than I can bring it home!" Mr. E glared angrily at his wife. She kept her eyes fixed on the counselor, her fingers busily snapping the clasp

of her purse open and closed. *"Decent!* Not a woman I know has to struggle as much as I do to make ends meet. He can't understand what it costs us to live, and on top of that, he is just plain stingy! Now he's insulted because I got a job as a grocery checker and his dinner won't be waiting when he gets home from his cheezy job. Well, we need the money and its up to me to get it!" Pointing to Carol, crouched in a corner of the chair, her head bowed, the mother added, "If he was a decent father, I know Carol wouldn't have shoplifted."

Mr. E's hurt centered on his wife's working, and her anger focused on his "unrealistic" expectations about household management. When their feelings were brought into the open, the couple could look at the impact of their noncommunication on each other and on Carol. Their ability and readiness to separate reality from fantasy, to recognize the factors leading to their present situation, and to accept individual responsibility for the consequences of their separate and reciprocal behavior—these characteristics of maturity enabled the family to cope with the immediate stress (the short-term goal) and to subsequently return to the agency for another time-limited series of conferences aimed toward consolidating their gains and planning for the future (a long-term goal).

In contrast is the kind of situation more often seen in public welfare agencies as demonstrated by the M family.

Mrs. M, the mother of three very young children, has a history of care for mental illness, sometimes in a hospital. Her behavior often is erratic and she cannot tolerate frustration. She buys costly furniture on credit, fails to make payments—and the furniture is then repossessed. She then goes to another store, where the same process is repeated: buying on credit, threats by the creditor, and then repossession.

The worker helps Mrs. M deal with the recurring crisis, knowing that the woman lacks the emotional capacity to learn from these repeated experiences or to gain insights into her behavior that might lead to its alteration.

INCOME INSUFFICIENCY

It bears repeating that even in our present, high-level economy in the United States, the income of a substantial portion of individuals and families lags behind the amount indicated for the maintenance of a moderately adequate standard of living, and that a substantial fraction of the middle-income group, encounters difficulty in supporting a moderately good living standard without incurring a heavy burden of indebtedness. A family's income may be too low for many reasons: absence of a wage earner; the curtailment or suspension of income because of illness of the wage earner or labor disruption; transitional or long-term unemployment because of changing technology or economic recession; or inability to obtain employment because of age or physical or vocational handicaps. Other income sources for these families may be inadequate or nonexistent. Survivors' benefits and insurance payments (both governmental and private), child support or contributions from other relatives, and interest or dividends from assets may cover only a comparatively small proportion of a family's basic needs. The family must then apply for help from public agency programs—public assistance, food stamps, rent supplements, Medicaid—or to voluntary philanthropic agencies. Responsibility for meeting the economic needs of individuals and families is generally acknowledged to rest primarily with public organizations which administer the income maintenance programs. Their standards of assistance, however, may not coincide with the family's actual needs or with its concept of its needs. The income of most individuals and families receiving some form of financial support from public or private agencies is marginal. Many families struggle to increase their income through employment or sale of services.

Large families often have difficulty in managing on the earnings of the father, mother, or both. Even the earnings of children, when added to the parental earnings, do not necessarily alter the balance between bare survival and a moderate level of living. In recent years, legislative bodies and the general public have devoted considerable attention to debating income maintenance systems that would assure families and individuals of at least minimal funds essential to a decent and healthful standard of living; supplement the earnings of the working poor; incorporate work incentives to encourage them to continue working; induce others capable of working to prefer employment to economic dependency; and provide training and job opportunities so that the goal of economic independence might be achieved. Regardless of the kinds of income maintenance programs that might eventually be instituted, it is likely that an economic problem still would exist for wage earners with incomes in the middle or the upper-lower brackets, or for families at these levels whose income is derived from sources other than employment. Inadequate wages sometimes are supplemented by cash or kind (food stamps, medical care, homemaker service, for example) but this is not universal for either large or small families.

For families whose incomes are too small to meet basic maintenance, two long-range goals are indicated. The first is to raise public assistance standards and to increase social insurance benefits. The second is to help

Money Counseling: Goals and Techniques

the individual family increase its income, through retraining and change in employment of the wage earner, or through increasing the number of earners. A concomitant goal may be to help the individual family use its resources to best advantage.

Families with heavy indebtedness often must live on incomes too low to meet their needs. On the surface the income appears to be adequate, but debts or other obligations may absorb so much of it that the family actually has insufficient funds for its daily necessities. In counseling with these families, the goal is to help them bring the indebtedness under control to the extent that the uncommitted income is ample to care for the family's needs. In a sense, the goal is to increase the income, but it is achieved through increasing the amount that is available by more effective management of the total income.

Personal and Interpersonal Problems

Not all problems brought by individuals and families to public or private social agencies contain money factors, although money per se is an inescapable necessity in anyone's life. The size or source of the income, however, frequently aggravates existing problems; and, conversely, the size or source of the income is frequently affected by the existence of personal problems. However, families and individuals who turn for help to public assistance agencies or related programs, such as Medicaid, do have a problem that they see as a money problem; and the agency considering the request for help also discerns a money problem. To meet a financial need or a medical need that the family cannot handle because of limited finances is, after all, the reason for the program's existence.

Experiences of many kinds of social agencies have shown that it is far from simple to ascertain whether a specific problem stems from money attitudes or whether money attitudes create the problem. Nor is it always necessary to make this determination. Often, the psychological problems are intertwined with the money problems, and effective counseling calls for a psychosocial approach. The knowledge, skills, and processes required for money counseling are the same as those needed for the understanding and treatment of the range of psychosocial problems dealt with by counselors.[2] However, because money provides an index to family feelings and attitudes, the counselor should have a sound understanding of the use of money by a particular client and what it means to the various family members.

Effective budget counseling may be the major means of helping family members resolve their basic relationship problems. This was true in the case of Mrs. D.

A 27-year-old domestic worker, Mrs. D came to a marriage counseling agency for help in resolving her critical financial problem. She was earning $400 a month plus room and board. She was so deeply in debt that she did not know how to extricate herself and now her employment was in jeopardy because of garnishment for debt. She had been married only six weeks earlier, following a brief courtship. Mr. D earned $470 per month. At the time of marriage, she had $1,600 in the bank and owned a car. Her employers, for whom she had worked for six years, had encouraged her to acquire these assets.

Within a few weeks after her marriage, marital as well as financial difficulties had developed. On discovering that Mr. D was continuing an affair with a former girlfriend, Mrs. D had had a violent temper tantrum while driving their car, and had an accident which caused $900 damage to a new car that they were buying on credit. Their combined indebtedness exceeded $6,300, of which $3,500 was for the car, $700 for loans, and the balance for clothes and other merchandise. Except for the car, Mrs. D's bills were primarily for merchandise for which she had been a co-signer, both for her husband and for friends, before she was married.

In the subsequent series of four interviews with the counselor, Mrs. D was able to recognize that the loneliness that had characterized her life and her need for friendly relationships had led her, in effect, to buy friendship. The process of helping her to work out a plan for handling her debts also helped her to evaluate her marriage, and to reach a decision as to her continuance in this relationship.

Mrs. D had sought help from the marriage counselor in coping with financial problems associated with her new marriage. By contrast, Mrs. C turned to the family agency for marital counseling.

Mrs. C, 32, had married immediately upon graduation from college. Her husband, an account executive, encouraged her participation in Junior League and in civic affairs, for "the contacts are good." They lived with their two young children in a suburban development, with a swimming pool in their backyard and two cars in the garage.

Two years ago the Cs realized they were living considerably beyond their means; they made a joint decision that Mrs. C would use her education and personal qualities on a job. She found work as a secretary, was quickly advanced to administrative assistant to an executive, with sharp advances in salary.

Concurrently, Mr. C began to arrive home late, often drunk, with no explanations. He began to charge expensive and modish clothes, which his wife thought at first might be due to a "past-30 syndrome." Within a year, however, he did not return at all.

The supplemental income from Mrs. C's employment now became the only income source for her and the children. Because the Cs had discussed "in adult fashion" the prospect of her working, she was unprepared for the threat her job and subsequent advances would hold for her immature husband. She is now faced with finding housing and child care that, along with other necessities of life, can be provided for the children and herself from a single available income—hers.

Money problems may be a reflection of mental or neurological problems that are not recognized by the family. A careful evaluation of the earning and spending patterns of husband and wife may reveal incipient disturbances which can be brought under timely medical supervision. The H family is an example.

The Hs, a young couple with a five-year-old child, live in a large tract development, occupying a home they had bought three years earlier under a veteran's program. They had anticipated no problem in keeping up the $140 monthly payments from Mr. H's net monthly earnings of $700, which were supplemented by the wife's part-time earnings, averaging $250 per month, as a clerk in a nearby drycleaning shop. Also, they had contracted to purchase furniture and a late model, but not new, car. Then Mr. H lost his job. He soon found another, but lost some salary in the interim.

Again he lost his job. By the time the family applied to a social agency for help, Mr. H had lost a total of five jobs; the family's inability to maintain payments had led to repossession of both car and furniture. Mr. H was convinced that each job loss resulted from steps taken by some of his creditors to attach his wages.

He also accused his wife of extravagance. Her description of how she managed their finances, including meeting the monthly instalment obligations for furniture and car, displayed a realistic handling of their funds. In joint interviews with the counselor, Mr. H could offer no way in which he would have deployed their resources differently and admitted that he "left the money matters to her" because he always was impatient with having to tackle such details. Nevertheless, he persisted in complaining about her extravagance and mismanagement generally.

The joint interviews also disclosed her anxiety that "he's been changing," and how his behavior has altered from the time he lost "that first job" nearly a year ago. He angrily contradicted her statement that he seemed nervous and irritable, unable to concentrate on ordinary tasks. He reluctantly agreed to the counselor's suggestion that he have a physical examination—he had "had enough of those in the service." The beginning of a serious neurological disturbance was revealed. Subsequently, he was helped to pursue medical follow-up and vocational rehabilitation that enabled him to work productively despite narrowed capacities.

Indebtedness itself is not a major problem. It can be used creatively and constructively by most people for relieving environmental pressures and for meeting certain needs realistically. It has special significance only if it is a symptom of unhealthy relationships or of a person's incapacity to perceive cause and effect. Thus, the Ls agreed that it was worthwhile for them to go into debt for nearly $800 to buy an automatic washer and dryer set that would enable Mrs. L to handle more easily the laundry for her family of six, even though these appliances would take almost all the uncovered space in the small kitchen and obligate the family to struggle to meet the monthly payments of $40 from their combined net earnings of $680 per month. Careful examination of their income and fixed obligations gave them confidence in the reality of this plan, even though to carry it out would mean certain sacrifices.

The R family, on the other hand, purchased a second color television set, so that the two children could look at the programs of interest to them without "interfering" with the parental choices of programs. Monthly payments were to be $38 for three years; this obligation increased the monthly instalment payments of the family to 35 percent of their income, derived from the combined full-time earnings of Mr. R as a school custodian and the supplemental earnings of his wife as a babysitter. Mrs. R stated that she did enough babysitting on the outside so that she should not have to sit with her own "rotten kids."

YOUNG COUPLES

More critical than most other elements in the give and take of marriage, especially a new marriage, are the attitudes of the marital partners toward money and how these attitudes influence their handling of money generally and its use with each other. Attitudes about, and uses of money by each marital partner, are common precipitators of quarrels that test the marriage. The quarrel may be triggered by an inconsequential or quite ordinary expenditure. It may be the consequence of money handling, or the absence or paucity of money, that is a serious reflection of profound developmental or environmental problems, or a combination of both.

If the young couple can be helped to reach a balance in the division of responsibility and in the management of income, and its allocation for desired and necessary purposes, the outlook is good for the way they can handle other aspects of their lives together. This is particularly true if they have not yet learned to manage money but possess the mental competence necessary for such learning. If their behavior with regard to money is inadequate or faulty, the counselor may be able to give them the help they need to master their financial management problems—and perhaps other troubling problems as well. (All of this is equally true if the couple are not young but are in a new marriage in which for the first time each marital partner is faced with meshing individual established modes of behavior with someone else's.)

The couple that does not yet have children or the responsibility of other dependents is likely to distinguish more clearly the problems that are associated with money than when other personalities and relationships become part of the picture. The young Ts, described earlier in this chapter, quarreled constantly about the source and amount of their income and the priorities in its spending.

> Bob and Mary T thought that when they married they had planned all their finances for the duration of Bob's college program. His father would pay the tuition directly to the college and would give Bob $20 monthly for school supplies and books. Mary would be paid monthly and regularly, so they knew what income they could count on. She would pay the rent, buy the groceries, and spend whatever was necessary for household operation. Anything else they would decide on together, and it would come out of the uncommitted balance of Mary's earnings—her first. In this way, the couple decided to purchase the car and the television set.
>
> Before her marriage, whenever Mary had needed money for any purpose, she would ask her parents for it. She was given what she asked if they regarded the purpose as "o.k." Similarly, whenever her mother wanted to make a purchase, she asked her husband for the money. It was "up to him to bring in the money," and it was her responsibility to maintain the household. Mary had no assigned household responsibilities at home because she would have "been in the way, slowing down" her efficient mother.
>
> For the first two months in the marriage, all went well, even though they were disconcerted to discover that Social Security taxes, disability taxes, withholding taxes, and mandatory deductions for retirement benefits reduced Mary's take-home pay by nearly 20 percent. She asked her parents for a loan, which they readily provided. When the Ts found themselves short of money to meet their payments, Mary suggested that Bob put his monthly book allowance "into the pot" and use books from the library. He was furious, called her selfish, and suggested she ask her parents for some funds; they were not "putting in" as much as his. Angered, Mary said she might as well just live with her parents, packed her suitcase, and went to her parents' home. Her mother thought Bob was unreasonable, for after all Mary was supporting him; her parents would be willing to help her, but why him? Husbands should be the earners. Mary's father thought she should go back to her husband and work out their differences, perhaps with the help of a marriage counselor. To reduce the quarreling that developed between her

parents over the situation, Mary returned to Bob and they sought help in budget management.

In contrast was the situation of the V couple.

They had married 20 months before, when Mr. V was 38 and his wife 25. They had accumulated an indebtedness of $8,900, had thirteen creditors, and did not know which way to turn to extricate themselves from this situation that seemed to grow worse steadily. The husband earned $11,000 a year as a postal worker, and was in line for a promotion that would add $2,000 to his pay. Mrs. V was a receptionist, earning $6,000. The couple told the credit counselor that they did not gamble or drink or "squander money," that they did have trouble with "sales resistance," and that Mrs. V was deeply depressed even though her husband reiterated that he "was not about to divorce her." On the credit counselor's recommendation, the couple consulted the family agency worker about "how to control those buying impulses."

The worker's exploration revealed that Mrs. V had twice attempted suicide and was taking tranquilizers on medical advice. Her husband had been trying to please her by spending more than they could afford on a car, furniture, clothing, and gifts, without ever consulting her about any of the purchases. He could not bear to admit to her that his management of their income was less than perfect, and the continued spending angered her so that she withdrew rather than provoke the kinds of quarrels that had marked her parents' relationships and "ruined" her adolescence.

Budget counseling became the tool for opening communication between husband and wife, and for making them aware of the patterns of action and interaction in their relationship. They started to plan together for their expenditures and to work actively with the credit counselor on a debt repayment plan. As they began to view their problems realistically and conjointly, Mrs. V's depression lifted and her husband was able to accept the fact that he did not have to "buy" her mental health or full participation in the marriage.

PARENTS AND CHILDREN

Money counseling can be an effective tool in understanding and treating relationship problems between parents and children. The ways in which children use money, both practically and symbolically, provide many clues to the nature of their needs and problems.

Jimmy G, 10, began to steal from his mother's purse, to rummage in bureau drawers where his parents dropped change. Mrs. G mentioned this to her husband who said, "He'll grow out of it, just wait." This suited Mrs. G's inclinations, for she was very busy settling the family in the new home to which they had moved in their efforts to "protect" their three children from

Money Counseling: Goals and Techniques 199

the effects of a deteriorating neighborhood and to avoid having the children bused to a distant school in the movement toward racial integration in the schools. The new home was far above the family's financial level; they had drained their resources to buy it. The necessity to meet the large payments on the new dwelling meant that the family lived on a stringent budget. Mrs. G took a job to help out—her first outside employment since the children were born. The parents were so preoccupied with making ends meet that they withdrew some of their usual interest in Jimmy, content in the awareness that he seemed to be popular in the new setting, to have many friends.

The parents were asked to meet with Jimmy's teacher, and were appalled to learn that he had taken a $20 bill from the teacher's purse. He had readily acknowledged this when the teacher asked him about the disappearance during a time when only Jimmy was in the classroom. On referral from the teacher (to whom Jimmy had returned the money), the Gs and Jimmy talked with the school social worker.

The boy's wish to get along with his peers and his feeling of being neglected by his parents were both evident in the individual acts of stealing which simultaneously provided the means for buying companionship and comforting himself for his parents' seeming lack of interest.

Jimmy was younger than Jeff A (Chapter 5), and parental attitudes and circumstances were different. But the counseling goals were similar: to help the parents and the children understand the meaning of the signal emanating from the children's behavior—their psychological needs for appropriate development of the trilogy of trust, self-esteem, and identity so essential to their functioning as adults, and their resorting to inappropriate ways of obtaining money to substitute for the attention, affection, and trust not being provided by the parents.

The meaning of money to children in placement and to their parents was also discussed in Chapter 5. The counselor's understanding of their complicated feelings contributes to skill in helping parents to participate constructively in the placement process. From the point of intake throughout the contact, it is important to focus attention on the realistic aspects of placement—and one such aspect is money. Money, therefore, is an integral part of the professional activity with parents, foster parents, and children. Through discussions about money, parents can test their real desire for placement, and the counselor can acquire an understanding of the parents and the parents' needs and problems. The parents' attitude toward payment gives an indication of the degree of responsibility that will be assumed not only for the child but for other obligations.

Some parents, as indicated earlier, offer to pay more for the child's care than they can afford. Others endeavor to escape all responsibility.

In either event, discussion of the payments provides a means for parents to gain some awareness of their own attitudes and behavior.

For the children in placement, money can be the focal point of complaints and dissatisfactions and an indication of their adjustment and acceptance of the placement situation. Their use of money offers evidence of the nature of their feelings toward the parents, the foster parents, and the agency. It also reveals to what degree the placed children have accepted the many limitations that reality has imposed upon them.

A growing body of research findings in recent years has pointed to the association of many child abuse cases with parental pressures caused by inability to find work or to pay the mounting bills, or by a felt inadequacy of the father (or stepfather) to meet the expectations of the wife, even though income may be substantial.[3] Such parents not infrequently were themselves the child victims of abusive parents; and they deal with money and other precipitants of frustration by inflicting abuse on a child in their own family. The counselor will often find that discussion with these parents about financial matters is something which they can comprehend and which can be a bridge leading toward understanding the impact of their abusive behavior on their child and on themselves.

SINGLE PARENTS

Through counseling on matters that relate to money, single parents can often be helped to cope not only with financial management per se, but also with anger, guilt, depression, or other feelings that affect not only the single parent's well-being but that of the children—and, often, the parent who is not a part of the household. Paramount is the necessity for the parent (and the counselor) to help children regenerate attitudes that they already hold, to some degree, and that they could cultivate if given the opportunity. The parent, who may feel disadvantaged by not having a marital partner with whom to consult or share responsibilities about decision-making affecting the child, nevertheless has to convey to the child by expectations and demands that certain behaviors and abilities are to be developed. It should also be noted that when the parents of a divorced mother lavish excessive gifts on the grandchildren as compensation for the absence of their father, the grandparents in effect communicate to the children that they have suffered a tragedy and that their mother's divorce was a disaster that permits them to become exploitive. Similarly, either divorced parent's undue generosity with allowances and gifts may be a form of bribery to which the child succumbs.

This overgenerous giving to the children often becomes the focus of counseling with the parent. There may be anger because of someone else's giving which the single parent-caretaker does not feel able to match or control. Or an inability to make ends meet may be attributed to the consequence of atonement or competitive giving to the children because of the absence of the other parent.

The divorced mother is most likely to respond to counseling interventions and efforts related to child support. Loneliness, a sense of abandonment or martyrdom, deprivation—these and many other feelings can be expressed in terms of the adequacy, inadequacy, or irregularity of child support. Child support complaints can be an acceptable lever for demonstrating to the children and to the world that clearly the failure of the marriage was due to the inadequacy of the father, as witness his failure to meet the needs of his own children.

ELDERLY PERSONS

Money can become an extremely important factor in counseling in regard to living arrangements for elderly family members. Often, neither the adult children nor the older persons have sufficient funds to permit them to live comfortably in separate quarters. Or the older people may be unwilling to live independently because of fear of exhausting the financial reserves they ordinarily cannot replenish; and sometimes they have a strong desire to leave their financial reserves intact for the children or grandchildren. Adult children, because of guilt or fear of incurring the older person's displeasure, may be reluctant to arrange another living plan for a dependent parent even though such a plan would be in the best interests of all concerned.

> Mrs. F consulted an agency because her 15-year-old daughter, Alice, was morose, refused to have friends visit her, and refused their invitations to visit them. She had even threatened to run away from home. Alice resented the paternal grandmother who made her home with the family. The grandmother, as described by Mrs. F, was an irritable and controlling person. She openly criticized Alice's friends, embarrassing both her and them. Mrs. F said she had remonstrated with her mother-in-law but the elderly woman reminded them that it was her income that enabled them to live in such a fine house.
>
> The social worker, in subsequent contacts with the family, found ample justification for both Alice's and Mrs. F's embarrassment and resentment. Even Mr. F was of the opinion that his mother should not live with the family. The question of how to manage without his mother's subsidy arose. Careful analysis of the budget revealed that the Fs were not, in fact, economically dependent on the grandmother; the cost of her maintenance actually was as great as her contribution. Because her income was sufficient to permit

her to maintain herself independently, the worker suggested that the family consider frankly discussing the possibility with her.

When Mr. F broached the subject of her living in separate quarters, his mother agreed willingly. A few days later she had an asthmatic attack. After her prolonged and crotchety convalescence, Mr. F again brought up the subject and she had another asthmatic attack. Mr. and Mrs. F were helped to understand the relationship between her attacks and her fear of, and resistance to, being "put out" of the family. At Mr. F's request counseling was then begun with the mother.

She responded positively to the worker, and revealed her anxiety that her resources would quickly be exhausted. A realistic evaluation of her financial resources and a discussion of possible living arrangements enabled her to take pleasure in making new plans. She looked forward to her independence and freedom and selected an apartment near enough to visit the F's but far enough away to limit her interference.

A diversity of living styles and arrangements for elderly persons have been developed during the past several decades, from life-care programs in which individuals invest all of their funds in exchange for continuing full care, to retirement communities with a broad spectrum of individual and group-living plans including many variations in required financial arrangements, and board and care or nursing facilities. As was noted in the first chapter, an increasing portion of elderly persons, whether still married or not, retain their own homes or apartments, helping them maintain a sense of mastery over their own affairs.

There is a growing trend for elderly persons to utilize boarding homes, on a regular payment basis, instead of investing all their funds in life-care programs. This newer trend has the value of making the older persons feel that they are still able to govern their own destiny. Sound counseling, including budget counseling, can help elderly persons make appropriate choices about the type of care best suited to their respective needs. Direct counseling with elderly persons, whether living apart from or with adult children, is usually essential to sound planning. It may help them to deal more effectively with their own problems and simultaneously to alleviate some of the related problems of the children.

THE COUNSELOR

The personality, capacities, and motivations of the individuals seeking help determine to a considerable degree whether they will profit from money counseling. But the counselor's attitudes and quality of response to the requests for help are of equal importance. The counselor's own feelings about money may be extremely complex. It is possible that the counselor's own management of money affairs is haphazard or confused, that personal perceptions and experiences will impede the qualities of objectivity and nonjudgmentalism essential in the relationship with the individual or family being counseled. Moreover, the attitudes of the counselor about helping people with money problems may have been formed in the years when it was thought that such service was less "professional" and required less skill than helping with "psychological" or "relationship" problems. It may be some time before all social workers and members of some other helping professions come to terms with the fact that the same principles and skills that are applicable to the study and treatment of psychosocial problems are equally applicable to the understanding and advice in the handling of money problems. Indeed, people by and large are more guarded in exposing their feelings and uses of money than almost any other aspect of life, including sexuality. Money is an essential reality ingredient of family living and family relationships.

Inherent in the counseling process of "deliberation together" is the recognition that the troubled individuals and families will arrive at a more satisfactory solution to their difficulties if they do most of the thinking and planning, and accept responsibility for bettering their situations. This principle of maximizing the family's participation in the examination and resolution of the troubling problem applies with particular force to money matters because money is the key to improvement of many kinds of circumstances. The quality and productivity of this participation is contingent on both the counselor's and the client's clarity as to the purpose of the counseling, and the latter's understanding and acceptance of the kind of help and participation involved, and agreement regarding the goals to which the help is to be aimed.

This agreement may be based on initial partial comprehension, which suggests that the purpose requires mutual reexamination as insights are reinforced or gained. Or the agreement may center on an objective clearly perceived at the outset. The counseling process itself, however, may produce some changes. Indeed, change in some fashion and to some degree is an expected outcome of productive counseling. Hence, reexamination is in order to assure the validity of proceeding along the original course or now detouring in accordance with the altered circumstances.

There has been a marked trend toward a contractual arrangement between the troubled family or individual and the counselor. Such contracts have many demonstrated values, including the probability that there is clarity about the objective of the work to be done and agreement as to the course to be taken and the division of responsibility between the parties to the contract. Sometimes these contracts are verbal, sometimes signed. They may set forth the long-range goal or short-term or intermediate goals, with new contracts developed ad seriatum as each successive short-range or intermediate goal is achieved or abandoned.

One caution should be considered by the counselor who contemplates the use of the written contract when money counseling is involved. Anxiety will be exacerbated in some people who are fearful about putting their names "on the dotted line" and making an implied commitment which they are not ready to fulfill. Some will be uneasy because their trouble has been triggered by the signing of contracts obligating them to the payment of money, with subsequent overextension of credit. The idea of "signing" may be so identified with the unpleasantness of their financial predicament that they will refuse to enter the agreement, or, having signed, fail to return. Some persons evidence faulty perceptions of time and therefore find it difficult to adhere to the intent and terms of a contract loose as they may be. And the neurotic person who, despite adequacy of income or resources, fails to meet financial obligations and encourages repossessions, garnishments, and lawsuits, may find in this contract a way of testing others—in this instance, the counselor. For this person a credit-granting agency is something against which to fight, to rebel. If a suit for violation of the person's contractual obligations is brought, it may be countered by one brought against the creditor because of the kind of treatment to which the debtor was subjected. If such a person does sign the agreement, it is likely that this act will convoke efforts to circumvent the identified goals and measures for reaching the goals.

Whether the counselor plays a constructive role in the counseling process that includes some discussion of money will depend largely on the counselor's attitudes as well as knowledge about money behavior, common human defenses, and characteristic human ways of coping with stress. Counselors must develop awareness of their own attitudes and reactions to money. How do they feel about a person who is deeply in debt? What is their point of view about instalment buying? Is their attitude about loans disapproving, or do they think that all assistance should be in the form of loans? Are they comfortable about asking troubled people to pay a fee for a social service? This is not to suggest that the counselor's money attitudes must conform to a specified pattern or set of values. Rather, there must be sensitivity on the counselor's part about when and how the existence of certain personal attitudes may influence the family's or individual's reactions to and trust in the counselor's objectivity and acceptance of the individual as someone needing

Money Counseling: Goals and Techniques

help. There is no doubt that there are few things more difficult to achieve than to help other people, while at the same time leaving them free to manage their own affairs and live their own lives.

Regardless of the nature of the individual's or family's problem and motivation for coping with it, the counselor is likely to encounter some resistance. It may be a protest against actual or potential financial or other dependency, or against authority, or against being perceived as less than adequate because of insufficient income or faulty management of income, or against just being in the present unhappy situation. This places with the counselor the responsibility for distinguishing between resistance that is healthy and resistance that is retarding. Unhealthy resistance may take the form of apathy or inertia, and lack of knowledge; of open hostility and anxiety; of fear of tackling change; or of distrust of the counselor who represents an agency that can give or withhold help. Because the person affects and is affected by the family in a continuous flow of psychological interplay, each family member must be understood and considered within the context of family interaction as well as the individual's own personality structure.

Communication is vital in improving or healing many problems that are reflected by the nature or form of the resistance. Techniques for dealing with faulty or limited communication cover a wide spectrum of available skills and vary with the needs of each given situation. They may include suggestions, guidance, or advice in small amounts carefully paced, for the troubled individuals often know what should be done in spending or not spending money, but find it difficult to follow through. The techniques may be utilized to help persons separate reality from irrational feelings and actions, and to move toward understanding and dealing with the bases of the problems.

> The Ws, for example, built their own small house, to which they planned to add another bedroom and a family room. Mrs. W was PTA president in their midwestern state, was a highly efficient organizer both at home and in community affairs; she had occasional work as a substitute teacher. Her husband created various effective devices to simplify household operation, some of which were patented and were evoking interest among some commercial manufacturers.
>
> Mr. W was employed by a public utilities company. Monthly deductions were made from his salary to pay for savings bonds; otherwise, the family income was fully utilized for living, including purchasing of materials as needed for the completion of the house. When an opportunity arose whereby a bulk purchase could mean a considerable savings to the couple, Mrs. W proposed that some of the savings bonds be cashed; her husband refused,

giving no explanation. Their quarreling over this became more intense and open, with the two children (9 and 11) removing themselves from the angry sounds by visiting the paternal grandmother, two blocks away. She persuaded her daughter-in-law to consult the pastor, who referred the couple to the family service agency.

In his wife's presence, Mr. W simply maintained that he wanted to protect the family's future and he would therefore not cash the bonds. In a separate interview, he reluctantly acknowledged that he suffered from duodenal ulcers, a condition that he did his best to hide from his wife, that in fact there were no bond reserves to cash—he had cashed each bond when it became available, using the money to cover his medical expenses. He would not use the available group health insurance, believing that his employer might "think less" of him because of this "weakness." Mr. W had to be helped to tell his wife, and to bear her anger for his lack of trust and confidence in her. She had to be helped to understand the importance to Mr. W of independence and that he could be and was no less adequate as the family provider and protector because of his health condition.

The counselor's tasks included sifting misconceptions and distortions from reality, with the family members together and separately. In fact, as the family tested the counselor's reactions to their expectations, realistic and unrealistic, they were then able to test each other and appropriately plan not only the best way of meeting Mr. W's medical needs, but also how to modify their handling of both their income and their common expectations about completion of the house—and of themselves.

Communication constraints or inadequacies may require the counselor to use the technique of advocacy, wherein the counselor intercedes in behalf of troubled individuals or families, or collaborates with them in pursuing specified goals or actions. The person who is inarticulate, timid, frightened, or otherwise disadvantaged (by poverty, illness, location, or other reason) may not be able to mobilize sufficient strength or forcefulness to communicate a concern requiring redress or other attention. Thus, the credit counselor who works out a proration plan with the consumer's creditors and distributes the periodic payments to them in the consumer's behalf; the social worker who goes with the family member to the health department to request sanitation improvement; and the social worker who accompanies the single parent to the law enforcement agency in connection with child support or a client to the Social Security office to trace a missing application when the individual believes "I'm getting the runaround because I'm old" *or* "black" *or* "Puerto Rican" *or* "a kid" *or* "have an accent"—all of these are examples of advocacy. The communication needs here are not merely verbal. The intent is to accomplish the specific task, but also to provide a model that the family

Money Counseling: Goals and Techniques 207

or individual can utilize in the future without the intervention of the third person, a counselor.

Some of the same techniques used in improving communication outside the family are important also in deciding when and how to involve family members in separate or conjoint counseling, using the family interaction in helping clients improve intrafamily communication and in other ways gain mastery over their situation.[4]

Important counseling tools in the area of communication are sensitivity to nonverbal communication (for example, the way family members look at each other or refuse to do so, or the way Mrs. D's fingers busily showed her uneasiness), and patience and timing in the face of silence. To be articulate about failure to handle funds wisely is exceptionally difficult for many people—Mr. W, for example—because it may reveal one's inadequacy as a functioning adult. Silence may be the protective device employed with the counselor. The counselor, however, must be able to interpret the meaning of the silence. In a fairly remote Alaskan village,

> George A, an Eskimo, recently disabled in a serious hunting accident, found that the mail order company from which he had purchased his snowmobile on the instalment plan, planned to repossess it before the summer ended, and the area would be isolated by weather. This plan had triggered his request to a neighbor to write to the welfare department so that the family could receive disability benefits until he would be well enough to resume working as a guide and hunter. When the worker called on the family, the husband and wife sat wordless for many minutes, while the worker waited.

The counselor needed to distinguish among the possible reasons for the silence. Was it hostility toward a Caucasian social worker? Was it respect being shown by younger persons to an older adult? Or respect for the authority of the agency represented by the counselor? Was it unwillingness to risk speaking in broken English? Was it anger that George A had, at least temporarily, lost control of his own affairs?

To work effectively with individuals and families with a somewhat complex problem that has a money component requires that the counselor have considerable practical knowledge about the meanings and uses of money in creative daily living. There is the same need to add new understandings to this knowledge, including drawing on the material of related fields, as is true of counseling on other aspects of social adjustment and family relationships.

COLLABORATIVE SERVICES

Many situations in which money problems are involved require more than social work counseling. Often the persons need legal counseling or a combination of legal and other counseling. For example, clarification of or legal resolution of a man's liability for alimony to a former wife may be necessary before counseling on money management can be carried on effectively with either the man or the divorced wife.

In the same way, legal counseling about garnishment or indebtedness may be necessary before the counselor can deal with the psychological motivations for indebtedness. Credit counseling may be supplied by a consumer credit counseling service—either a free-standing social agency or one affiliated with a family agency—when the family needs help in working out agreements with creditors regarding acceptable programs for liquidating the debts. Such programs may involve formulating a proration plan or a plan to be carried out directly by the family with the creditors, or the filing for bankruptcy.

Whatever the division of responsibility may be between organizations collaborating to help a family or individual gain control over a vexing problem that calls for complementary expertise, the counselors in those agencies must understand clearly their separate and collaborative roles, and how long the collaboration should continue. It is equally important that the target family understand the respective roles and responsibilities. Otherwise, possible confusions among either counselors or clients may lead clients so inclined to play one counselor against the other and use the lack of clarity as rationalization or permission for doing little or nothing to take hold of the financial problem themselves. A parallel situation occurs when people, deep in debt, manipulate their income and creditors, now giving a little to one, then to another, failing fully and realistically to tackle either the indebtedness to any one creditor or the total indebtedness problem. Unless special care is exercised by collaborating agencies and personnel, the recently implemented separation of the system of financial assistance payments from the delivery of public social services—whether the latter are proffered by the public welfare agency directly, or through the medium of purchase of service contracts with voluntary or other organizations—may offer some economically dependent persons special opportunity to indulge or persist in such neurotic manipulative practices.

NOTES

1. For elaboration on work with the adequate, chaotic, neurotic, or psychotic family, see chap. 3 and pts. 4 and 5 in Frances Lomas Feldman and Frances H. Scherz, *Family Social Welfare: Helping Troubled Families* (New York: Atherton Press, 1967).
2. Ibid., passim.
3. *Los Angeles Times,* July 13, 1975, part 9, p. 1.
4. Further discussion of criteria, principles and techniques for counseling with the family group will be found in Feldman and Scherz, *Family Social Welfare: Helping Troubled Families,* chaps. 17–19.

9

Income Maintenance: Dependence and Independence

The amount of family income and the way it is earned or acquired profoundly influence the psychological development of the individuals in the family and the patterns of family life. The fact that all or part of income is derived from certain income maintenance programs may have a marked transient or long-range effect on the social functioning of the family members. The effect may be particularly significant, for example, if the source of income is public assistance, based on a means test, rather than a form of social insurance to which either recipient or employer or both have contributed to cushion the loss or reduction of earnings.

Both public and voluntary agencies, as was pointed out earlier, assume certain responsibilities for meeting the maintenance needs of people. The nature and degree of these responsibilities have varied over the years. For the greater portion of this century, however, the major charge for relieving problems of insufficient income has been placed with federal, state, or local units of government, separately or in some combination. Many voluntary agencies also have provided basic financial relief to needy persons, or supplemented public assistance with aid in cash, kind, or special services.

SOCIAL POLICY AND THE QUEST FOR INCOME SECURITY

In general, the public income maintenance programs take the forms of social insurance and public assistance, health and welfare services, and housing. The social insurances provide specified payments to persons who meet certain eligibility requirements for work-related transfer payments or for health care. The amount of the social insurance transfer payment generally is stipulated in the statutes and bears some relationship to the earnings of the insured individual. (Variations are more likely in workers' compensation programs which are a social insurance under the auspices and control of the individual states.) Moreover, the contributions to the funding agent (usually a trust fund) are for the particular worker who is entitled to the insurance benefits when the designated risk becomes reality, as a deferred wage payment.

Public assistance, however, whether for categories covered under the federal Social Security Act or for general assistance or relief in which there is no federal financial participation, is administered on a basis of need. This is true for the relatively new Supplemental Security Income (SSI: Title XVI of the Social Security Act). SSI endeavors to temper the traditional means test with a uniform, simplified, guaranteed income system containing a major characteristic of the social insurances, namely, that eligible needy aged, blind, and disabled adults are entitled to an established minimum income. It also is true for health care under Medicaid (Title XIX of the Social Security Act), food stamps, and low-cost housing or rent supplements.

Distinctly different community attitudes are noticeable with regard to these several programs and target groups. Nearly everyone is touched directly by the social insurance provisions—as a covered member of the work force, as a dependent protected by the coverage of someone now or formerly attached to the work force, or as a retired or disabled worker. There is general awareness that benefits are a return on the actual monetary investment made by the individual or someone in that person's behalf, and are related to earnings but not other income. Insurance benefits represent work, thrifty planning (albeit involuntary) for future contingencies. The universality and the other characteristics of social insurances just noted constitute incontrovertible evidence of adequacy; dependence on the benefits, therefore, can be accepted for what it is—a right. Support of the SSI program, though not contributory, is accepted by the public with some equanimity: many of the individuals aided have been in the work force and also receive some Social Security insurance benefits, although not enough for maintenance. Moreover, the incapacities of age, blindness, and disability (especially when obvious) generally are acceptable testimony to the individual's dependency due to inability rather than unwillingness to work.

Attitudes about others who are dependent on public financial programs tend to be less accepting. There is a continuing conviction among many taxpayers and others who contribute to the support of these programs that recipients actually enjoy their dependence, that relatively few make efforts to become self-sufficient, and that welfare costs constitute a tremendous tax burden upon those whose hard-earned money should be available for their own uses rather than for others who fail to meet their own needs. At the same time, recipients of assistance protest that their assistance grants are much too low to maintain even a minimal level of health and decency. These attitudes and reactions contain common elements. An articulate segment of the public resents the dependency, citing it as proof of inadequacy and immorality. The recipients resent being dependent and, as is common in many kinds of helping situations, the anger of the person helped is often focused on the helper—the witness to the fact of the dependency.

In general, the recipient and the nonrecipient hold similar views about the relationship of work and adequacy. Aside from the fact that the assistance grant in reality may be less than is needed for more than bare survival, many recipients of financial assistance, food stamps, or rent supplements rely on the low level of aid to explain away any questions or criticism about their inadequacy as money managers: after all, one cannot be expected to manage adequately with palpably inadequate resources!

To be sure that only the really needy are aided (generally those who obviously are in desperate need through no fault of their own), that their honesty is certified, and that they are not permitted to lapse into dependency on others who work hard to maintain themselves and their own dependents, two parallel developments have become integral components of the noncontributory income maintenance programs: complex systems for certifying initial and continued eligibility; and mandating of work requirements as a condition of eligibility. Sporadically, "declaration" or "certification" procedures have been introduced, aimed toward simplifying the application and continued-eligibility investigation process. With relative speed, however, these have been abandoned or superseded by detailed, fuller forms and stringent investigations. The requirement that the applicant register for work or training generally has made no obeisance to the possibility that work opportunities may not either exist or be accessible; or that there may be a shortage of such supporting services as child care centers—necessary to make it possible for some parents to relinquish child-care tasks in favor of paid-work tasks; or that a paucity of jobs in a depressed economy may result in "recycling" individuals through one training experience after another to ensure that they are at least making an effort to end their dependence on the public.

Such evidences of societal distrust of the needy person, especially when the request for help is met by rigid, cold, condemning affect in the agency, often serves to reinforce the applicant's self-pity, depreciation, and hopelessness. It diminishes self-esteem, sense of identity (as an individual with importance and dignity who merits respect), and readiness to trust others or oneself. It generates hostility that is directed outward as well as inward. In reality, the agency representatives—especially those without preparation for coping with such feelings—may utilize rigidity, impassivity, coldness, criticism, or other rejecting behaviors to defend their inability (either because of lack of knowledge or limitations by statute, agency policy, or regulation) to comply with the applicant's needs, either partially or totally. The applicant is likely to feel overwhelmed, to be immobilized by the extent of the personal crisis; or there may be a reduced capacity to become or remain self-sufficient or self-supporting, unless understanding intervention by a counselor breaks into this circle.

Traditionally, the organization and delivery of public welfare services included the provision of money payments and other services through the medium of one worker. Role responsibilities often were in conflict and confused, especially if the counselor's limited behavioral knowledge and skill and the agency's administrative climate were not conducive to carrying out the eligibility process in ways that could enable clients to deal appropriately with the critical need that brought them to the agency, to retain a suitable level of social functioning, or to prevent regression or deterioration in such functioning. While there can be little doubt that many economically dependent families received financial assistance and at the same time made productive use of the social services provided by the public assistance agency personnel, many recipients of public assistance were not given the opportunity to decide if they wanted to avail themselves of the services offered, and it was not uncommon for a public assistance agency to require the client's compliance with a particular plan as a condition for continued financial assistance. Reactions to such "coercion" and other factors, led to the system, implemented in the late 1960s, that incorporates the concept of the separation of the administration of assistance from the provision of social services.

It is not intended that the issues regarding adequacy or form of income security programs and policy be debated here, nor issues or mechanisms pertinent to the auspices under which social services are or are not provided (separated from assistance payments, directly by public welfare agencies or indirectly through purchase of services from voluntary or other public agencies). The focus of this chapter is on the money counseling aspects of transfer payments or social services per se. Social services, as used here, are those activities and programs that preserve or enhance the social functioning (including economic, emotional, and cultural) of families and individuals. This definition embraces the provision of financial support based on need as a social service in the same way that homemaker, child care, marital counseling or other kinds of services are made available in response to the request of the family or the individual for help in meeting the particular social need.

The new system is predicated on several (sometimes controversial) assumptions. One is that the determination of eligibility for assistance should be simple. Another is that the decision-making process regarding payments should be "objective," and that asking for financial aid should not automatically subject the applicant's life to scrutiny by counselor and agency. And a third is that the dignity of the recipient should be protected by providing a flat grant, instead of grants allocated on the basis of individually determined needs and budgets. In order to achieve this simplicity, objectivity, and impersonality, nonsocial-service personnel (frequently drawn from clerical or other nonprofessional classifications) should be assigned the income maintenance functions with the expectation that they will refer for social services those applicants or recipients of assistance payments who wished such help.

The experience of the past several years generally has shown effective coordination between the separated income maintenance and service programs to be elusive (perhaps also *ill*usive). Lack of sophistication about common human defense mechanisms and, sometimes, sheer insensitivity to the applicant's stated or affective communication often have resulted in nonsocial-work staff at point of intake being either unaware of possible needs or indifferent to giving applicants the opportunity to decide whether they wanted specific services.

> Susan McN, her two small children playing quietly on the floor at her feet for the two hours she awaited her turn to be seen by the application worker, burst into tears as soon as she sat down at the worker's desk. She did not know how she would "manage." She had learned this morning that her husband was dying of cancer and she did not know what to do. She "guessed" they had hospital insurance and she "supposed" her husband was on full-pay sick leave since his collapse three days ago in his office, when he was rushed by ambulance to the hospital. A draftsman assistant, he had been with this company for two years, earning $7,000 a year. Mrs. McN "guessed" she needed some "help." She had no relatives to whom to turn and no close friends. She had no available cash to meet immediate needs.

Each time Mrs. McN said she "guessed" she needed "help" the interviewer stated that she was not eligible. The interviewer at no time asked what kind of help was being sought or suggested that Mrs. McN might find it useful to discuss with someone—a medical social worker at the hospital, a personnel officer at her husband's plant, a services worker in the public agency, or another counselor—how she could cope with the crisis at this point, and plan the next steps she would need to consider taking with her husband or alone. Like many others, Mrs. McN was finding it hard to verbalize her fear and anxiety about the problem actually confronting her. She could, however, substitute the concreteness of money problems for the intangible but pervasive fear about her husband's illness and its implications for him and the family. She could extend a request for help in terms that she would expect anyone to recognize as real and valid, and at the same time she could magically obscure the reality of the seriousness of her husband's diagnosis by not dealing with it further at this time.

It is not just at intake that the personnel who meet with economically needy persons must be alert to the feelings that swirl around the immediate need of money. The union representing eligibility workers in a large public assistance agency demanded that the administration increase the security precautions to protect the workers and other personnel in X district from attacks by clients. The office was located in a "nice" community and was one to which personnel formerly had been eager to be transferred. Investigation by the local press as well as the administration disclosed that a malfunctioning computer system for two months had been rejecting certain welfare checks and that some new applicants had been without help as long as a week after their need was acknowledged. Moreover, when individuals asked the receptionists or eligibility workers about the delays, they would be gruffly told to sit down and wait; they might wait six or eight hours without learning the outcome of their inquiry. The four incidents of physical attack on the staff within one week had involved such waiting.

In these instances, the non–social work staff were not aware that the seeming indifference and lack of respect on their part served to fan the anxiety, rage, and panic of the waiting clients, who resorted to abuse as the only protective weapon at hand to demonstrate to themselves and others that they still had some control and independence. Awareness of the employees' and the recipients' normal reactions to stress and of ordinary techniques for helping individuals cope with it did not appear to be part of the agency personnel's armamentarium. The staff members were confronted not only by the physical need for the money, but also by the psychological need for understanding and information to reduce the ravages of fear and uncertainty, and to provide a basis for the counselor and client to see what steps could and would be taken—and when—to remedy the situation.

Similar dynamics are present in the approach to district offices of the Social Security Administration by individuals or couples who are requesting SSI cash aid. Factors of advancing age or physical or mental disability may exacerbate the anxiety and hostility these people already feel about seeking help. Lack of initial acceptance of them as persons to be accorded dignity and respect—a lack to be inferred from the interviewer's manner and language—may shut the door on the prospect of realizing the person's potential for continued self-care or management of his or her own affairs.

Evaluating need

It is to be expected that persons who seek help in a public assistance agency will present their problems in money terms. After all, the basic reason for the existence of these particular agencies is to meet economic needs of individuals and families. How the applicant designates the reason for being in financial distress holds clues to when and if the interviewer should acquaint the applicant with services that may be available for resolving or ameliorating the central problem, or for helping the applicant deal with the associated practicalities, especially if the problem does not lend itself to ready solution.

The application or intake worker administering welfare funds in either a public or private agency (whether a counselor, eligibility worker, or one having another title) must evaluate the nature and extent of the applicant's need and determine within the framework of agency regulation and policy, if financial assistance can be given and, if so, in what amounts. With relatively few exceptions, the individual who requests financial aid is uneasy about making the request. The usual reluctance to expose ineptness or failure to meet one's economic needs (because it suggests personal flaws or inadequacy) is magnified when the request is compelled not just because a few needs are not being adequately met, but because even basic survival needs cannot be handled by the individual without help. Indeed, in some families of Latin background, for example, where incapacity or unemployment of the father is the reason for the financial need, it is expected that the wife will ask for the help, not the husband. She is the supplicant in the church. She does not have to present a facade of strength. And for her the act of asking for help is presumed to be less demeaning than for the man. (It is likely that the women's movement will have some impact on such a culturally determined role assignment!)

Income Maintenance: Dependence and Independence 217

It is important for the interviewer to be sensitive to the factors that lead one spouse rather than the other, or both jointly, to ask for help. It is important to be aware of the significance and reality of the applicant's feeling about and phrasing of the request for help. "I'll pay it back." "It's just for a few days." "Look what he did to me!" "I just can't go on!" Such approaches contain useful clues to how the applicant may be expected or able to respond to and cope with circumstances that contributed to the dependency state.

For the application interviewer who has some comprehension of the psychosocioeconomic factors that affect the persons requesting financial aid, it is possible to differentiate between the emotionally adequate families and those whose personal pathology creates or contributes to their problems. And it is possible and essential to recognize how the reality environmental factors delineated in Chapters 1 and 2 impinge on and interact with the personalities and problems reflected in the presenting of the request for economic assistance. There is then greater likelihood of successful referral of interested applicants for services that may be effective in helping them to use this period of economic dependency to move toward and achieve independence. For the emotionally adequate group, the worker's aim is to meet their reality needs and to help them, through referral for counseling (or by providing it if this is within the agency's scope), to gain mastery over their economic problems. For the presumably less adequate, the aim may be the same, but the worker should be aware that certain protections may have to be provided and that rehabilitative measures often are required.

Individualization of both need and personal capacities is necessary in extending financial assistance in any agency, whether public or private, and can be accomplished without in any way jeopardizing principles of equity, uniformity, and rights. The extent to which the counselor is permitted to individualize the help that is provided, and the manner of doing so, however, depend largely on the amount of statutory and administrative discretion that is delegated. The degree of discretion varies considerably by locality, by type of program, and by administrative and community attitudes about dependency that are reflected in the program. The amount of the assistance may be the same for all family units of given size, but allowable or deductible income, or resources and other considerations may differ. The counselor must be cognizant of the nature and degree of flexibility permitted and should endeavor to exercise this flexibility in order to meet the particular applicant's needs. The approach in counseling should also be individualized. Some persons, if helped to come to grips with the limitations of a grant, are enabled to find new ways of managing and thereby to achieve a higher level of maturity. Other persons may benefit more by a rigid budgetary framework. It serves as a supportive device for persons who, because of immaturity or personality or other difficulties, are not able to make wise decisions about expenditures.

How much financial assistance should be given to a family for its maintenance when it has no source of income, or its income lags behind the family's needs? Should the amount be just enough to keep the family members alive? Should it aim to ensure a minimum standard of health and decency? By what norms should the standard be established? Should all needy families receive the same amount of assistance? Should there be a given standard by family size? by sex and age factors? Should the nonworking family be supplied as much income as or more than the poor family endeavoring to remain independent through work?

One of the most controversial issues in social welfare administration is the question of the amount of assistance to be extended, and the basis on which that amount is to be decided. Although standard scientific budgets have been developed by home economists and nutritionists, these are not always the criteria for establishing the grant level. The amount and source of available funds and numerous other factors influence the determinations. A state agency may decide that a given sum of money is required to meet minimal needs of families of certain size and circumstances. However, because of tightness of state revenues, legislator or citizen attitudes toward dependent people, or other subjective or objective reasons, there may be an across-the-board percentage reduction for certain basic items or for all family assistance grants. General assistance, which is supplied by state or local sources, ordinarily is much lower than grants to persons aided through one of the federally funded programs like Aid to Families with Dependent Children (AFDC) under Title IV of the Social Security Act, or SSI under Title XVI. Moreover, there is no universally established standard as to what ought to be included in such assistance. In some areas the same items are covered as in the federally aided programs. In others, assistance may be limited to rent when eviction is in the offing, or grocery orders, or other short-term or emergency help. It may be denied entirely to single men or women; and still other exclusionary or limiting features may be present.

These varying relief standards reflect myriad community and individual attitudes toward the social problem of and people with economic dependency. Some persons believe that welfare aid should be no more than the earnings of the lowest earned-income group. Others maintain that those in need should be taken care of by relatives. These and other

Income Maintenance: Dependence and Independence 219

outmoded theories contribute to the establishment of arbitrary assistance ceilings, rigid rulings about contributions of adolescents and married children, and many other restrictive policies. The counselor who must implement the policies often feels apologetic and even guilty because the agency permits little opportunity to individualize the client's needs and offers assistance at a level patently short of even a minimum standard of living.

When these conditions exist, the counselor, like the recipient, must work within the harsh reality imposed by inadequate assistance payments. The counselor has an obligation to discuss the budgetary limitations realistically with the family members and to endeavor to help them find additional resources to meet their needs. If their need promises to be of short duration, family members often but not always can make some adjustments in their living that will carry them through the emergency. If the need is apt to be long-standing and there is little likelihood that the amount of assistance can be increased, the problem is more complex giving particular significance to the counselor's attitudes and approach. An already discouraged man or woman, trying to meet family needs on an inadequate income, is likely to become more despondent, to be overwhelmed and immobilized if the discouragement and hopelessness felt by the worker are communicated to them. It is essential to the clients' ability to function as well as possible that the worker convey to them the expectation that some decisions are necessary as to the use of even realistically limited resources, and that some things must be accomplished however modest; and that the counselor must ask what measures they have thought of so far. By so doing, the counselor can reassure such persons that they still have some control over their own affairs. This confidence, albeit timid, is an essential ingredient in enabling such economically disadvantaged persons to keep going without utter deterioration in their mental health and social functioning, and to seek persistently to manage until other solutions become available.

> The Ps had maintained a comfortable standard of living in their suburban community until Mr. P was suddenly hospitalized because of cancer of the throat. For sixteen years he had been employed in a good position for a large aircraft manufacturer. After two years of successful chemotherapy and surgery he was well enough to work, but had lost his job. Even though his speaking voice was in no way impaired, in the eyes of many potential employers his medical history rendered him too great a risk, although the doctors and he maintained that he was well and employable. He could not find work. The couple had been buying a home and had accumulated a small reserve in savings and stocks. They owned a car and, until Mr. P's illness, had no

unusual or heavy debts. The medical expenses, not covered by group insurance, and living expenses soon exhausted their assets, including Mr. P's sick leave pay. They sold the car, borrowed money on Mr. P's life insurance, and sold the stocks at a loss in a depressed economy. Without training or experience, Mrs. P was unsuccessful in finding any work even though her husband would be able to care for the three young children.

When all the funds were exhausted, the family applied for public assistance. Mr. P was depressed, had given up his fruitless search for work, had to be "pushed" by his wife to have the periodic medical examinations necessary for him—what use was he to anyone, including himself? He could not even be classified as disabled for Social Security purposes and thereby assure his family of nonwelfare income. When Mrs. P realized that the total public assistance grant and the food stamps together were equivalent to her prior spending for only a half-month's food and household supplies, she reacted with panic. The worker recognized her panic, her inability to plan alone, and her husband's depression, which kept her from involving him in planning because "He just can't stand anymore!"

The worker discussed specific immediate expenditures with Mrs. P. This discussion helped her to focus on ways of handling the limited funds. It also gave her some confidence in asking her husband's help in management; after all, long-range planning had been part of his professional life and now he could bring his demonstrated planning skills to bear on their personal money management. He began to take some special interest in the challenge of finding ways to stretch the limited income, including comparison shopping. His anger with his former employer and other potential employers became overt as he told his wife and the worker that he *was* good for *something*, even if only to figure out how to save some pennies! He began again to search for work, to insist to potential employers that he was capable and competent, and that he could quickly prove this. He was hired on a "trial basis," then put on the regular payroll.

Mrs. P brought a note from her husband to the worker in a termination interview. Mrs. P said: "I felt absolutely hopeless until you told me you *expected* me to be able to get along, and I thought if *others* can, so can I and you must know it! If you had said to me, 'It's too bad, but you'll have to manage somehow,' I know I wouldn't have had the courage to go on. Nor would my husband. Because you believed in me, it helped me to show I believed in *him*, and that was the turning point." Mr. P wrote: "I have found unexpected riches: emotional strengths I did not know my wife and I had, health to cherish, and a good job. I have heard people who are suddenly struck with illness say, 'Why me?' And I said it too. But now I *know* why *me. I* could overcome the odds, and did."

Even if adequate assistance is not available, the counselor at least can offer hope that some solution can be found, and expectation that some steps can and will be taken. This differs from offering reassurance that is not realistic. "Everything will be all right" neither substitutes for the needed income nor strengthens the troubled individuals' ability to handle the problem. It drains off the rage and despair these people may need in order to deal with their problems. It prevents the forming of trust in the counselor, and this is a vital element in the client-counselor joint effort to find a solution to the family's difficulties. False reassurance by the counselor can only lead the troubled family to wonder about the practicality of the counselor's views and reactions, and further deepen their despair. Working toward solutions, though they may seem remote or minute, in itself may stimulate the individual to find ways of managing.

STANDARDIZED BUDGETS AND GRANTS

Equity and justice require that income maintenance payments be made on a formula that is applicable in comparable situations. The formulas vary with the kind of program and the objectives that program is designed to meet and the target groups it purports to help. SSI, in consequence, provides for a flat sum from federal funding sources for each individual or couple to meet the basic needs of food, shelter, and clothing.[1] This is uniform throughout the nation; the amount is stipulated in the Social Security Act. Individual states, however, may use formulas constructed in accordance with their own definitions of need and income in adding from state sources to the federal SSI grants. Grants to families and children under the Social Security Act's AFDC program are not specified as to amount, only the formulas for federal reimbursement to states for assistance payments and administration are defined. The amount issued per family, then, may be developed on the basis of the family size and composition, or just the size, or on the basis of itemization of allowances for various specified items. A degree of uniformity and equity is maintained, however, by observing the principle that all those meeting certain specified conditions of eligibility within a given state will be supplied the same amount and kind of aid. The budget basis may have been developed by experts on the basis of actual need, or it may be an adaptation.

Regardless of whether a flat grant or an individualized budget is the basis for determining the assistance to be provided, the counselor should understand it; what the grant purports to cover, and the degree to which actual need is covered by the amount allowed for the items included in the budget or leading to the flat grant. There should also be some understanding of the means used to develop standard budgets, for this knowledge often may be called upon in counseling with a family about distribution of the grant when the family asks for help in managing the money. For instance, a minimum standard budget for food is based on the nutritive needs of people in relation to their age, sex, and degree of activity, and is computed in terms of pricing done at particular times and places. Are these prices adjusted to take into account rising costs of living? How do the items and totals compare with the family expenditure standards described in Chapter 2?

The items in a standard budget require periodic review and adjustment, particularly at times of sharp fluctuations in living costs. Regular reassessment of living costs is advisable, for the budgets used by social agencies at best provide only a minimally adequate level of subsistence. Even a slight upward change in living costs can reduce the relief grant below the subsistence level. Federal social policy has recognized the special problems of the economically disadvantaged who rely on transfer payments for survival in inflationary periods. Accordingly, the Social Security Act contains escalator clauses and provisions for increased federal support for certain programs, but such adjustments are not applied in all transfer payments.

Social agencies, as was stated earlier, frequently encounter administrative difficulties in making the necessary upward changes in their assistance payments. Their welfare funds may be appropriated and allocated by boards or legislative bodies for a long period in advance of expenditures, and there may not be sufficient flexibility to cope with increases in living costs or even the additional costs of caseloads that are rising because of unemployment or general economic conditions. The rising costs may lead agencies to make the kinds of adjustments in their budgets noted previously (across-the-board percentage reductions, for example) in order to effect a balance between available resources and projected expenditures. The resultant policy rulings not only create hardships for the families receiving aid, but also create a poor climate for effective money counseling.

It is not unusual that the allowance for a particular family will not meet all its officially recognized needs. The counselor in these situations has a responsibility for utilizing the budget as a tool to help family members use their funds as efficiently as possible. This management experience often has the value of strengthening the client's capacity to handle other reality problems constructively and thus to achieve a greater degree of self-sufficiency.

In an agency's standard budget, food and clothing allowances are usually computed in terms of basic requirements which can be met only through the purchase of low-cost items. Allowances for personal needs and incidentals, household operation, recreation, education, and life insurance are also minimal and are more arbitrarily set. Few agencies

Income Maintenance: Dependence and Independence 223

include allowances for such items as automobile insurance or annual licenses, instalment payments for television sets and other "nonessentials," and payment of dental or other health care not met by Medicaid or other health care plans. It is sometimes possible for the counselor to use these budget limitations as a means of motivating the discouraged or fearful person to move gradually from complete dependence to a state of at least partial independence.

> Mrs. H, 32, became deeply depressed after the death of her husband. Alicia, aged 13, the oldest of her three children, became hostile to her mother, and complained about a lack of clothes and social opportunities that the mother could not provide on her limited assistance grant. Mrs. H became more despondent as Alicia became more demanding.
>
> When the social worker discussed with Mrs. H possible ways of improving their situation, the mother decided to try to do a few hours of babysitting, even though she was fearful about taking on such responsibility. When this experience proved successful and she dared to move beyond her own doorway, Mrs. H began gradually to seek other ways of earning money. With each small success she gained confidence in her ability to be a productive person and a responsible parent. She accepted, somewhat reluctantly, the agency's policy that a substantial portion of her small earnings must be applied toward reducing the budgeted allowance. As her earnings increased, she gave up protesting that the deductions were a "punishment for working" and took active pride in her growing independence.

When Mrs. H and Alicia talked with the social worker retrospectively about what this experience in beginning to work had meant to Mrs. H and the children, Alicia, now fourteen, volunteered:

> "I was always angry when my father died. She [Mrs. H] sat around and got sympathy from the neighbors and took it easy. Well, *I* lost him too, but *I* had to watch the kids, run to the store, make the beds. No one sympathized with *me*. Well, when she got a few little jobs, I thought, 'Wow! Maybe she's got something after all.' I realized she was as scared as me without my dad. She was trying, so I tried too. Now I'm pretty proud of what she can do and I don't mind taking care of the house and the kids. Not all mothers around here got what it takes!"

Mrs. H remarked: "I had never even thought of working. I was brought up to think this was the husband's responsibility; my husband wouldn't have liked me to work, he would not like any of this women's lib. And when I first worked, on those first few babysitting jobs, I was just glad to get away from Alicia—she was so unpleasant to be around! Now I am glad to work as much as I can and I know I can do almost anything"

Janet O, the unmarried mother of three elementary school children, asked the worker's help in finding some part-time work.

Her request was a surprise; for years it had been generally accepted by workers who had known her, that Miss O could not be motivated toward independence. She kept her little house in good condition and her children were always clean and well-behaved (*too* clean and quiet, one worker noted). Occasionally the father of the three children would send her a small check, which she would immediately use for clothing for them or to buy a small household item. She managed carefully on the assistance grant, from time to time complaining that her children did not get enough good food, for she could not afford it. She had asked how she could obtain a television set because it could offer her and the children some needed relaxation and entertainment; but she was informed that it could not be supplied by the agency nor could the money to buy one on credit. She had made an inquiry about obtaining credit, but had been told by several stores that they did not customarily extend credit to women without husbands.

When Miss O read several news reports that discrimination against women requesting credit would shortly be illegal, she again made the rounds of stores that sold television sets on an instalment basis. She realized now that the fact that she was totally dependent on public assistance weighed against her: she was regarded as a "parasite" unwilling to do anything in her own behalf and "living off others who work." If she could work part-time, long enough so that an employer could confirm her status as an employee, she would be able to establish credit.

Miss O was able to find a job as a file clerk for twelve hours each week. After four months, she applied to the credit department of a large retail store for credit; her employment reference was checked and credit was granted. Her immediate purchase was a small black-and-white television set and she needed to use all her earnings and part of her grant to meet the payments. Her employer noted the compulsive quality in her personality that made her very careful in performance of her work, and offered her a three-quarters-time job. Pleased with her success in her work and in her credit arrangements, Miss O accepted.

Sometimes an agency allowance provides a family with more income than the family members earned previously or may be expected to earn in the future. An evaluation of the individual family's problems and potentials may be important. The period of dependency, with its higher level of income, may be used by the family and the counselor to develop a vocational plan that will result in higher earnings and a better standard of living. Often the family can be helped to use its enlarged income to improve its living standards, even though the income will be subsequently reduced.

The I family, from American Samoa, had been in mainland United States for three years. Life had been "easy" in Samoa, according to Mrs. I, for they had "everything," and education was the only substantial item they had to pay for. Mr. I was able to get work as soon as he arrived on the mainland, as a busboy in a large public hospital. It was now harder for the family to manage, for costs were far above the island costs.

Then Mr. I, 41, was seriously injured in a hit-and-run auto accident. During his long illness and convalescence, his family, consisting of his wife and seven children, received public assistance. His earnings had been considerably lower than an assistance allowance for a family the size of his. Even though the agency had a ceiling on its maximum grant, the allowance exceeded Mr. I's maximum earnings. When Mrs. I received the first check, she set aside the equivalent of her husband's earnings and spent the balance on "extras" including an automatic iron for herself and a ukulele for an adolescent son. She described the expenditures to the social worker with considerable guilt. The worker's acceptance of her "fling," and particularly her need of the new iron, enabled Mrs. I to ask for suggestions about ways of managing her grant. They worked out a plan for the gradual acquisition of clothes for the children, anticipating their needs for some time ahead, and for the purchase of or replacement of needed household items. This planning led to discussions about marketing and the economies that could be made by purchasing basic provisions in quantity. As a result of this period of increased income, Mrs. I was able to purchase needed items and was helped to develop sounder buying and budgeting habits.

Noteworthy in this situation is the response of Mrs. I to the counselor's handling of Mrs. I's "fling." Had the counselor been critical, suggesting by word or tone that the money might have been better spent, it is likely that the woman would have become convinced that her action was right and good, and that she would not have sought or used help in managing the money. Criticism would have been equated with lack of respect for Mrs. I's ability to manage the household affairs; it would have been interpreted as disappointment in Mrs. I for having made an imprudent and even shameful decision in spending needed money for a frivolous item. It would have left no room to convey to this uneasy mother the empathy she needed in this critical time of her life, beset with doubts and fears. The resulting hostility would effectively have barred Mrs. I from using the counselor as a source of help. This is not to say, of course, that in situations where the grant is spent repeatedly in a way that fails to meet the basic needs of the family, the counselor refrains from criticizing. Rather, it is important to be sensitive to the feelings that precipitate or follow the action under consideration, and to assess them in terms of both the single action and the pattern of subsequent actions and reactions.

Unrestricted Money Payments

The principle of unrestricted money payments, officially established early in the life of the Social Security Act, had gradually been introduced in some public and private agencies before it had become official policy of the Federal Emergency Relief Administration, that first pattern-setting federally funded program to bring cash relief to the needy millions of Americans displaced from jobs for reasons beyond their control. Social workers and others in the human services professions also were convinced that "cash relief" had advantages over "relief in kind." This was predicated on awareness that providing cash assistance without restriction as to its use gives the recipients freedom to manage their own affairs, and helps them retain self-esteem and the sense of dignity and individuality, or identity, that are such essential ingredients for satisfactory social functioning. The fact that so many work-oriented adequate families needed financial aid was an important stimulus to the efforts of social workers and political decision-makers to help these families preserve their dignity and self-respect by supplying them with cash payments for which the recipient retained management responsibility.

The soundness of this principle generally is accepted today in social policy and among the helping professions of social work, psychology, and psychiatry. Many public administrators justify its use in view of the lower cost of issuing checks directly as compared with the several processes involved in third-party payment accounts or vouchers that go through several steps before returning to the agency of origin. Nevertheless, it is an emotion-laden principle that embodies issues involving fraud, morality, trust, and social control. Because opponents of the principle insisted that one cannot really trust social welfare recipients (again, the pairing of honesty and poverty), vendor and third-party payments for medical and pharmaceutical services were established in the mid-1950s. Their skepticism was marked by their generally stubborn insistence on utilizing food stamps and certain other in-kind services. Some states have begun to provide cash equivalents for some target groups, particularly in augmenting SSI with state monies. Although there is statutory authority to give aid in kind instead of cash in identified mismanagement situations, federal statutes restrict the number of such arrangements that may exist at any given time within a state, and require a periodically reviewed plan to protect individual or family assistance payments either from exploitation by others or from diversion from meeting survival needs to expenditures for such items as alcohol, drugs, gambling, or others. Cries of administrative or client fraud, generally unsupported by documentary evidence, are usually inspired by individual prejudice against welfare systems or by partisan political opposition. Complaints often result in the use of investigative procedures aiming to reduce welfare expenditures or to establish social, moral, and financial controls.

Aside from questions as to the validity of these accusations and the volume of misuse of assistance monies, with or without fraudulent intent, the impact of these attacks, for many economically dependent families, is tremendous, reinforcing their feeling of reduced self-worth. Problems, then, that inhere in the application of the money-payment principle often compound problems for both family and the agency. The family may be subjected to criticism and the agency may be the target of complaints because a dependent mother elects to purchase "good" clothing for her school children and seemingly neglects to buy necessary household items. A parent may place special value on living quarters and choose to live in a better dwelling or neighborhood, conserving on quality and quantity of food to do so. Or the parent may supply a child with money to buy lunch in the school cafeteria instead of carrying lunch from home.

One of the responsibilities of the counselor is to be able to respond to families living on the limited assistance payments who have expressed concern about using their funds most effectively. But money counseling does not mean control. The dependent family or individuals must try to manage the limited income and can learn best by accepting responsibility for the consequences of their decisions and their actions. The learning problem, made more difficult by these inflationary times, is the same for *all* families living on fixed and relatively low incomes—or even on larger incomes that do not accommodate readily to the lifestyle preferred by the family. The money-payment principle would be violated if the counselor tried to designate or control the amount to be spent for food, for rent, and so forth. The individual's or family's self-confidence and competence in managing their own affairs also would be violated, perhaps irrevocably.

The principle is not abridged when troubled needy persons request help with regard to ways of using funds effectively and economically. Such requests are sometimes made defiantly ("No one can tell me we can get along on this! I suppose *you* can!), not because the family believes the counselor can be helpful or because the counselor is perceived as someone to be trusted, but rather because the family is expressing anger that the grant is small, and despair about "stretching" it to meet the family's needs and society's expectations. Some requests are statements of *"You tell me what to do!"* with which the individual thrusts the responsibility onto the counselor.

The counselor must distinguish the language and affect, focus on the nature of the feeling that is being expressed to decide if the individuals really are asking for help. It is important that the counselor avoid defending the target of the person's anger—the size of the grant, how it is determined, and eligibility conditions—for this at once puts the counselor and client on opposing sides, without a bridge of trust that either can use.

Nor should workers attempt to defend the reality they may be unable to justify or change. The acknowledgement that the reality is harsh and that much is being expected of the client must quickly be followed with the question about what steps the person is thinking of trying. This question accomplishes several things: it assures the client that there is no depreciation of trust in his or her competence and adequacy; it implies that the reality must and can be met, and that thought and effort should be directed to this purpose; it points a direction to the client about which steps to begin or pursue in planning. Only then is it likely that the client will see the counselor as a helping person and make a real overture to obtain help.

The counselor needs to remain aware of the unwillingness of most people to take help, whether they ask for it directly or indirectly, unless they are in a crisis situation with some kind of imminent danger. Understandings gained from theories of crisis intervention can prove useful to the counselor engaged with a public assistance client in considering how to deal with financial need in the face of too-limited resources. The paucity of money to meet basic needs, with its negative implications for feelings of adequacy and morality in having and managing money, very often triggers a crisis, especially for the newly dependent family that has suffered some related personal or environmental trauma.

If assistance recipients are incapacitated or are minors, modifications in the cash-payment plan may be indicated. These modifications will be discussed in the subsequent paragraphs.

A modern concept of a public welfare system is that it should provide financial and other services to aid adults in becoming self-supporting and self-sufficient, and help parents maintain their homes and rear their children to become adequately functioning adults. People differ in their capacity to carry out these responsibilities, including the management of money. Persons who receive assistance and either fail to meet certain obligations or exhibit behavior that deviates from the approved norm of the community are likely to be exposed to more criticism and attack than are self-supporting persons who display similar behavior—their nonconformity is not at the direct expense of the hard-working taxpayer! The

Income Maintenance: Dependence and Independence

social agency, however, must take a firm position when attacks are made, difficult as this may be at times. There must be a clear policy that assistance will not be denied because of variant behavior. The psychosocial problems of such persons merit as much professional attention as the problems of others. Withholding assistance which would allow such persons to meet their survival needs offers no solution, only additional problems.

WHO RECEIVES THE MONEY?

In our culture, the father long has been expected to fill the role of the primary breadwinner, although in many families this function is either freely carried or shared by the mother. With this breadwinner role goes responsibility disposing of the family income, either directly or by delegating the responsibility to another family member. If the family is without a father, the earning and spending roles may be taken over by the mother or by an adolescent child. Social agencies, therefore, tend to assume that the father is the proper payee if he is in the home and is able to function. If he is absent or incapacitated, the mother usually is designated as the payee.

The determination of payee, however, requires consideration of several factors if a favorable atmosphere for counseling on money and other problems is to be created. The chronically ill father may have considerable feeling about his inability to support his family and may resent delegating to another family member the money decisions which are a traditional index to his capability and human value. His illness, even when chronic and physically incapacitating, may not preclude his participation in family planning for managing the income. On the other hand, he may be judgmentally impaired without his debility being acknowledged. But limiting the mentally competent man's participation in planning, and issuing checks in his wife's name sometimes intensifies the husband's feelings of inadequacy and guilt, which in turn stimulate resentment, self-depreciation, and hostility. His negative reactions may be particularly acute if he comes from a patriarchal culture in which the father is responsible for handling the family's funds. The feelings aroused may lead to marital conflict, retard his recovery, evoke resistance to rehabilitative measures, or impair his good judgment. If his judgment is realistically a matter of concern to his wife, she may need counsel in considering ways to help him function to his maximum capacity or to find the strength to assume money management responsibility despite his anger.

The counselor must be alert to the question of role. What management role has been taken by each family member? To what extent is the role culturally and psychologically determined? What are the implications, both for parents and children, if the mother becomes the payee? If the control shifts from father to mother, what are the possible effects?

Parents are sometimes incapable of handling their funds in a way that ensures proper care for their children. Usually it is one parent, perhaps an alcoholic father or mother, who dissipates the income to meet his or her own neurotic needs. Sometimes both parents have personality disturbances and neither can manage the money. Some agencies then may make certain in-kind payments for food and shelter or other basic items. The counselor, in these situations, must take responsibility for assessing the nature and causes of the behavior, and the possibilities for effecting behavioral changes. If the prognosis for improvement is poor, the counselor's service to the family may involve a supportive relationship that is designed to protect the children from neglect. This may eventuate in placement of the children, in foster homes or institutions, which at times is the only means of ensuring that they have adequate care and protection. Because placement creates an additional and complex set of enduring emotional problems for the children and parents, this remedy ordinarily should be used only as a last resort.

A person being aided by SSI or Social Security benefits may encounter problems in income management not unlike those found among individuals and families whose income is not derived from public sources or from transfer payments. Self-neglect to the point of emaciation and illness, as in the case of Bertha A (Chapter 6), may be present. Rather than using the money to meet survival needs of the individual and family, it may be diverted to unrestrained credit purchases, to buying of liquor, to gambling, to drugs, or to lavish entertainment of others. The unwary elderly or mentally disadvantaged person may easily be exploited by others: professional confidence men or women, or individuals who offer some form of affection or attention for which the yearning and lonely person willingly or unwittingly gives up available income or other resources.

Any of these kinds of situations may require protective interventions on behalf of the person or family. Most communities have some form of established procedures for meeting such protective needs, although they may be less than adequate. Arriving at a decision to employ protective devices should include exploring these questions among others: Is the troubling behavior masking a realistic anxiety that lends itself to resolution and, if addressed, would it permit a restoration or continuation of self-managed functioning? Is a level of functioning possible that, even though somewhat disturbing to others, would not endanger the person or others, and permit some degree of independent living? What supportive resources can be utilized on behalf of the person's continued functioning at the highest level of independence possible under the given circumstances? Would the use of protective, or in-kind payments where these are possible, enable the person to function with reasonable satisfaction in other aspects of daily life? Would homemaker service, shopping service, or a friendly visiting arrangement with an agency, church, or older person's organization suffice? Could the elderly or handicapped person maintain at least a minimal level of functioning by an easing of relatives' pressures and expectations regarding his or her money management?

Cognizance of two points in particular underpins such exploration. One is that increasing frailty due to age or illness may cause the individual to cling frantically to possessions, including money. This clinging represents a need to cling to life itself. Success in meeting this need is apparent in the demonstrated independence associated with having and managing money or other resources. The other point is related: an important defense against deterioration is the struggle to remain wholly or at least partially independent.

> Eighty-six-year-old Mrs. N, a widow, barricaded herself in her crumbling old house to which she had moved when her husband died the year before. It was to be bulldozed to make way for an extension of the airport, but Mrs. N refused to accept the money the court had awarded for the property, or to leave the house. For two weeks, she gave a former neighbor (the only person she would admit to the home) the money and marketing list to supply her needs; she endorsed her Social Security check to this woman so it could be cashed. Finally, Mrs. N was carried bodily from the house, her possessions placed outside. To the newspaper reporters who thought she surely must have had a long attachment to the house, she said "I'm not fighting for an old house; I'm an old woman fighting for my life. *I* know I can take pretty good care of myself, but who else knows?"

It is commonly questioned whether assistance payments can be appropriately handled by such recipients as the teen-age unmarried mother and the older unmarried mother of several children. Reference has been made to both in other, earlier chapters. It should be emphasized that it is not the unmarried state of the parent that determines capacity or motivation to manage money well, nor is age per se a disqualifying condition. There is no reason to believe that unmarried dependent mothers automatically are unplanful, impetuous, immature managers who should not be tempted by money made available to them on a regular basis for support. Should the individual unmarried mother have difficulty in money management, however, and seek money counseling, such help may lead her to develop orderly decision-making processes which she may apply to other areas of living in which she has difficulties to bring them under control, as well.

FREQUENCY OF PAYMENTS

The ability of a family to manage its income over the span of a month evidences the family's ability to plan, to postpone gratification, and to exercise self-discipline. The receipt of a once-a-month check often requires careful allocation to assure that there will be some money left for food when the end of the month is approaching. Similarly, if the income is received weekly or semimonthly, some families have difficulty in putting aside sums that will be needed to make any large once-a-month payments.

> When widowed Maureen R receives her monthly Social Security check for her three small children, more than half is paid at once for rent. The rest she divides into four equal parts to meet food and transportation costs. She receives a small supplement twice each month from the public welfare department (AFDC) and this is allocated to utilities, clothing, and school expenses for the children. However, the Social Security money is gone well before the month is, and she draws on the welfare supplement for food. No clothing has been replaced for a number of months, and one child is refusing to go to school without a "whole" dress.

On the surface, the management patterns of Mrs. R and Mr. M have some outcome similarities although the sources and periodicity of their incomes are different.

> Mr. M is working in the assembly line of a soft drink company. He is paid weekly. He has never had so much money before, he and his family having farmed on an Indian reservation, with very little profit, until a year ago. He keeps falling behind with rent, has been threatened for the third time with eviction and, for the second time, with disconnecting of utilities. The Indian agency worker despairs of persuading Mr. M to put aside enough out of each paycheck to enable him to meet the costs of rent and utilities when they fall due in the early part of the month. The agency has paid these bills as each emergency has arisen, but this will not be possible in the future.

Costs attendant on handling the sheer volume of checks is a compelling reason for many income maintenance organizations to issue checks only monthly. This is the pattern in federally funded Social Security and SSI payments. It is also a common pattern in public assistance agencies, although, in some, arrangements can be made for weekly or biweekly payments either routinely or on a showing of cause.

Unemployment insurance benefits, formerly paid weekly—both to conform to prevailing private industry practices and to permit closer monitoring of the unemployed person's "willingness" to work—increasingly are being paid by states on a biweekly basis. It is not unusual to hear the recipient of a transfer payment explain the failure to manage because of the timing of the check's arrival. Similarly, counselors frequently attribute to the periodicity of the payment some, if not all, of the family's problems in allocating their assistance money.

Some people find it hard to manage their limited income on the monthly basis: the newly arrived full payment often appears deceptively large and tempts unplanned uses that the total amount really cannot accommodate. Individuals who have little experience in planning because all their energies have been focused on meeting each day's survival needs may find allocation by future time blocks particularly difficult. The reasons differ, but the consequences may be the same for the person who is impulsive, neurotic, or self-gratifying, or who cannot perceive time properly. The hazard for any of these people, as well as for the family accustomed to weekly or biweekly paychecks that now must switch to monthly income, lies in the expenditure of a disproportionate amount of the allowance in the early part of the month. Or the common unawareness that dividing income for use in four weeks of a month fails to take into account the average balance of a one-third of a week in each month that, over a short few months, can create a sizable deficit. In the interest of helping the family use its funds effectively, especially a family whose dependence on public assistance is the result of temporary unemployment, it would be desirable if the assistance payments were issued to conform with the family's former income and spending patterns.

The complexity of statutorily mandated rules for computing the payment or benefit level is often a source of considerable anxiety and confusion for both the eligible person and the counselor or interviewer. The SSI program has introduced another dimension which presumes that eligible individuals or couples can plan on a longer basis than the traditional monthly period that has been characteristic of public assistance payments to adults. Although payments are made monthly, total amounts to be paid, when there is other income to be accounted for, are determined on the basis of a calendar quarter. The income received in a single month often is spent in that month; however, the deductible amount is distributed over the three months in the quarter. Consequently some persons have to manage on reduced funds for the months in the quarter that contains no outside income. For some this constitutes no problem. For those, however, who can manage only in the immediate present, special help may be required in learning to apportion the outside income so that it is also distributed evenly over the particular period.

Routinizing the mailing of benefit and assistance checks is reputedly an element in the increasing incidence of their being stolen while en route or at the place of their delivery. For individuals and families whose income is barely sufficient to manage until the next check is due, such loss can be devastating. Ordinarily, when they produce evidence of theft —which is often their testimony plus scrutiny of the endorsement on the check after it has cleared through the bank—some emergency assistance or a replacement check may be supplied. But this process is often time-consuming and, during the delay, anxiety and indebtedness can mount. If the intended recipient of the check does not manage well even if the replacement check arrives in good time, the management problem worsens in this waiting process. A device to reduce the theft of benefit checks has been inaugurated in some programs. Social Security and SSI payments, for example, can be mailed directly to a bank, credit union, or other financial institution of the recipient's choosing, and the money will be placed directly in the person's account, available for immediate use. It will be of interest to note how this arrangement affects the person's management pattern and under what circumstances possibly new attitudes will influence the way the individual draws out or saves the money thus banked.

MONEY MANAGEMENT AS A FAMILY RESPONSIBILITY

When a family suffers a substantial decrease in income with a consequent reduction in the standard of living, all family members are directly affected. Their ability to weather this storm depends on their personality structures. Most persons can mobilize themselves to take on new responsibilities, to compromise, and to face current and future realities. The counselor has a particular contribution to make in helping various family members set appropriate new goals.

Financial planning on a shared basis may be customary in a family that meets with economic reverses, but the cause of the economic reversal may also disturb family relationships and disrupt previous planning patterns. For example, if the father is dead or is away from home on a permanent or longtime basis (desertion, incarceration, or other reasons), the mother usually takes over the responsibility for managing the family's affairs. If the burden is too heavy, she may endeavor to lighten it by delegating certain duties and decisions to adolescent children. The adolescents, whose dependence-independence conflict is at its height, may react with anger, particularly if they work and are expected to turn their earnings over to the family. If the counselor does not include them in the family planning that involves their contributions, they may sabotage it, deliberately or unconsciously.

Too often the counselor discusses needs, budgetary allowances, and expenditures only with the mother, even when the father is at home. This occurs partly because women usually have taken responsibility for seeking aid, and partly because the woman is viewed as the manager of the household. It is important to engage other family members in counseling about money matters; the process of discussing their respective needs and responsibilities increases understanding among all members, and helps in establishing long-range plans. Counselors working under the pressure of heavy caseloads may rationalize that involving various family members is unnecessary or too time-consuming, but its values for the family are too great to ignore.

Social workers and other counseling personnel too often feel overwhelmed or frustrated by what appears to be a morass of procedures and requirements with which both the needy family and the worker too must conform to assure assistance. They sometimes deal with their own resistance to these requirements by encouraging resistance among the family members. A constant goal in working with any individual or family is to help them remain connected with reality so that they can cope with its demands as effectively as possible. Therefore, it is important for the counselor to acknowledge the family's anger and the reasonableness of being angry about some of the rules and regulations, particularly those that carry some components of invasion of personal or family privacy. But the counselor must be cautioned against reinforcing the family's hostility so that its effect is a self-defeating immobilization of their emotional energies. The objective should be to enable them to express anger and to redirect it into constructive action in overcoming the impeding or obnoxious requirement.

The family or its members may be unable to make headway alone, and may rely on the support and advocacy of the counselor. A particular member's unhealthy resistance may require the combined coping effort of all the family. The aggregate family hostility may be immobilizing for all unless the counselor can decide when and how a small piece of the problem may be tackled by one or more members, thereby giving them the courage to work on the next part. The rage and resistance felt by many recipients of public aid are often directed against the agency as well as inward and can reach to insurmountable heights unless the problem can be partialized, each small piece mastered in turn.

In large measure, it is the quality of the relationship that the counselor establishes with the family that enables the members, separately and together, to handle the constraints and implications of the financial assistance they receive. The relationship is one that can enable the family to express facts, attitudes, and feelings with a guaranty that the counselor's responses will be geared to the family's needs, not the counselor's. It must have elements of compassion, impartiality, respect, trust, and interest in the family's efforts to gain ascendency over its financial problems through adequate management of the available income. This involves ascertaining from the family what action they think can be taken to use the limited amount of assistance as effectively as possible, and what consequences they foresee in the contemplated actions. It involves stimulating the family members to explore the possibility of resources within themselves or in the environment, considering with them possible agency or community resources (for example, debt adjusters, counseling by a dietician, homemaker services, or community classes for learning how to improve management), encouraging the consideration of alternatives and their merits and demerits, and reaching a decision concerning next steps. This process assumes that the counselor will not take over the control or decision-making responsibility that is the family's. Rather, that the counselor recognizes the importance of regarding the family and its members as healthy and capable unless there is evidence to the contrary, and that the outcomes of intervention are more likely to be effective if the counselor's efforts are addressed not to weaknesses, but to the actual or potential strengths the family or individual members within it may possess.

NOTE

1. Adele M. Blong, Barbara Leyser, and Steven J. Cole, eds., *NWRO Supplemental Security Income Advocates Handbook* (New York Center on Social Welfare Policy and Law, 1975).

10
Paying One's Way

For the most part, in today's world, despite the broad dissemination of information about helping sources and processes, people simply do not want to be helped; they are often afraid to seek and use help. They believe that to do so, in a culture that continues to place a high premium on independence and self-help, reveals that something is or may be wrong, that the individual has lost or cannot gain control over whatever is amiss, and that a personal weakness exists—thereby, in a sense, giving another person some control over the seeker of help and lessening respect for the latter. To request help also is to imply a willingness to change which again is acknowledgement that weakness exists—else there would be no need to contemplate change. It is that fear of being thought weak or of losing status that may prompt these people to say "All I want is. . . ." Thus they are setting a limit on the scope of help that might be used; they are exercising some control by not giving over fully to the helping person. It is that fear that is evidenced in exorbitantly unrealistic demands, and in aggressive assertion of rights to particular kinds of assistance for which they may or may not be eligible. These persons may even appear to be grasping or greedy or overly dependent. By attempting to set the conditions under which they will accept help, they may actually be trying to shield themselves from their own reduced self-esteem from the helper's anticipated attitudes, and from the feeling that control might be transferred to someone else. Through borrowing rather than taking, and through paying fees, such individuals feel (for it is feeling rather than thinking) that they retain mastery over their own circumstances and destiny. This trait is desired and desirable in our society and instrumental in effective social functioning.

The key to successful counseling with many persons who are fearful about taking help is not what is given but how it is given. Points expounded previously, especially in Chapter 9, about the importance of the counselor's responsiveness to feelings are particularly relevant to the individuals and family groups who cannot take anything without paying or in some way reciprocating.

LOANS OR GRANTS?

During the depression of the 1930s when economic need was general throughout the country and clearly related to the universal economic situation, the individual asking financial aid of an agency frequently said, "This is just a loan." Doubtless, many applicants were trying to assure themselves that conditions would change—that they would soon have jobs and would again be self-supporting and self-respecting.

When the agency interviewer asked that these applicants for loans provide security by giving a lien on their property or an assignment on their insurance, they often reconsidered their requests. They of course knew that a loan required security and that if they had such security they could borrow at a bank or some other commercial lending facility. A request for "a loan" from an agency at that time had an unreal element; it was at once a way of saving face and of denying fear.

In recent years requests for financial aid have been more realistically presented, although the current recession has brought an increased number of applicants for welfare asking for loans much as was done in the 1930s. Today, people know much more about the multiplicity of public programs and about eligibility for assistance in various forms: money; food stamps; medical care; family planning counsel; public housing; veteran's benefits; and so forth. They also are more sophisticated about public and voluntary agency services: mental health; marital counseling; out-of-home placement of adults and children—well or ill; adoptions; and other counseling or social services. Nevertheless, some applicants continue to turn to public and private agencies asking for a loan. Often a loan is an appropriate and realistic solution, but sometimes the request for help couched in terms of a loan has the same quality as that expressed by Samuel Johnson when he said, "Boswell, *lend* me sixpence—*not to be repaid.*"

The request for a loan may be a denial of the individual's inability to handle financial and, perhaps, other affairs. It may contain fantasy elements—a belief in magic, that somehow, some force will intervene to cause an improvement in the unhappy situation.

The person's need for financial help stirs up a cluster of attitudes about money, many of which have been described in preceding chapters. When the person's wish to be independent and to "pay my own way" is frustrated, the reactions are likely to include resentment, depression, and a feeling of worthlessness. There may be an accompanying fear of loss of social prestige in being given something, whether money or other help, without reciprocating.

Social workers in earlier periods (as well as some today) tended to agree with the person who took the position that a loan was more respectable than a grant. Such requests were regarded as indicative of strength and adequacy on the part of the applicant. Newer psychological insights, however, have made it clear that a person's willingness and ability to use help are in themselves signs of maturity and strength. A request for a loan may be soundly based; but if it has no relationship to the individual's capacity to repay, it may represent an easy and evasive way to ask for help. Such evasion of facts can actually prolong a person's dependence and failure to deal realistically with the problems.

A request for a loan must be considered in relation to the person's motivation as well as the justification for incurring the debt. Justification exists only when there is sufficient margin in the current income to permit repayment of the debt, or there is a realistically based expectation that there will be such a margin in the future. The single mother without resources who is helped by loans to procure costly laboratory technician training is likely to have so many financial obligations after beginning to work that the debt for the training alone may be so heavy as to prevent her becoming self-supporting and her family's becoming self-sufficient.

Some voluntary agencies, particularly those that have served refugees not eligible for aid from public sources, have extended loans for education or for help in establishing businesses. Past patterns or experiences of the individual, as well as the person's potential for reestablishment at a better-than-minimal poverty level, are indexes to the validity of considering a loan rather than a grant. In making this decision, attention must also be given to the way the individual is likely to deal with the fiscal and psychological pressures of being obligated to repay money while trying to earn enough to meet current needs.

Because of legal or administrative policies, most public agencies do not extend loans. Many, however, do stipulate that proffered financial assistance or medical care may be reimbursable. This stipulation is implemented by a written agreement, or by the lien the agency holds on property or other assets, or by other forms of security for the funds or costs of services advanced. Ordinarily the counselor or application worker has no discretion in deciding whether the funds given are to be considered reimbursable. A county hospital, by ordinance or state statute, may exempt certain conditions from repayment but bill the patient or estate for others. Los Angeles County, California, and other jurisdictions, for example, for public health reasons do not require payment for hospital treatment of tuberculosis or infantile paralysis. Public welfare organizations that supplement SSI benefits or that extend general assistance through nonfederally aided programs may require liens on property or assignments of life insurance or other resources. The public agency then has first claim against the estate when it is distributed, if the aid has not been repaid prior to death of the recipient, and the balance goes to the designated heirs.

This procedure is designed to provide safeguards against the exploitation of public funds—and the taxpayers' "largesse"; and to assure, to the extent possible, the return of funds to the public coffers when a person's situation improves or death intervenes. In a number of states there is no requirement that adult children contribute to the support of their elderly dependent parents; instead, a lien on the property of the parents assures that the state will be repaid for aid given before the children, who did not carry "their" filial responsibility for parental support, receive any inheritance. For many elderly persons who strongly believe that something must be left of themselves to children or grandchildren, such lien laws appear primitive and constitute a hardship emotionally—and financially, as well, if the laws deter them from receiving economic help that they need and cannot procure through other sources, including their children.

Policies of demanding reimbursement for funds or services advanced are open to many challenges, among them issues of rights and responsibilities. Most families who receive public assistance or health care are not able to make full or, often, even partial restitution because their income tends to continue at a low level. Many are therefore unable to satisfy the lien on property or the assignment on insurance, and their dependent survivors may face consequent hardship at the time of the property owner's death. The policy is a legal device that may prevent some exploitation by the unscrupulous but it also may negate the principles of individualizing need and of helping people to make the best social use of their resources. It should be pointed out that the use of this device for reimbursements is not the equivalent of granting a loan. A loan implies an agreement to repay a specific amount at or by a particular time.

GUIDELINES FOR DECISION-MAKING
The counselor who has discretion about meeting financial need with a grant or loan should base the decision on a realistic assessment of the

financial factors involved. The actual and potential earning capacity of family members should be evaluated. Consideration should be given to the family's composition, its continuing expenses, and its ability to manage those expenses in order to meet such a future commitment. The amounts and the timing of the payments should be clearly understood by all concerned. Will the payments begin as soon as the health care, for example, is ended, or immediately after the family no longer requires or is no longer eligible for assistance? Or will the payments begin at a specified or approximate future date and continue periodically for a designated span of time? For instance, educational loans, whether they be government-insured loans extended by a financial institution or loans provided by a voluntary social agency, frequently are made on a delayed-payment basis, permitting the student time to complete the training and become an earner. Sometimes a loan is made to a family in order to consolidate debts, enabling the family to "make a fresh start" toward improved management in the future. Such loans may be an effective technique to help some immature persons who tend repeatedly to seek help with each in a series of small emergencies to handle their funds more realistically.

> The Ls, married for five years, with a 3-year-old child, lived in a comfortable suburban apartment from which Mr. L walked to work. Mrs. L repeatedly asked the local family service agency for funds, usually to help meet the rent payments, but sometimes for payment to a creditor for furniture purchased on a conditional sales contract, when she was threatened with repossession. She was disinclined to examine with the counselor the overall money management picture or to involve her husband in an interview that might be directed toward exploring the problem and alternative solutions.
>
> On two occasions, in the face of imminent eviction because of nonpayment of rent, she was given money to prevent actual eviction. Confronted with these real emergencies, Mrs. L reluctantly had brought her husband to the agency; they had discussed the fact that his take-home pay of more than $600 per month should have been adequate to meet the family's fixed payments and daily necessities. Mr. L left all household operation, including payment of bills, to his wife. "That's *her* job; things always finally work out okay." Mrs. L was a careless manager, unable to recall what had been done with money from month to month, and indifferent to the idea of planning ahead: "I don't like being tied to a rigid plan!"
>
> When Mrs. L came to the office with another final dispossess notice, obviously expecting that the agency again would come to her rescue, her request was rejected. She was appalled and disbelieving. She proposed that she be given a loan, promising to repay it in weekly installments as the first obligation on her husband's salary check. Following a careful budget discus-

sion with Mrs. L, the worker agreed to make the loan and Mrs. L agreed that both she and her husband would seriously examine and modify their financial planning and money-handling pattern, conferring with the worker on a time-limited systematic basis. Frightened by the "narrow escape," the Ls followed through on this plan—to the accompaniment of some self- and mutual criticism about assuming and abrogating responsibilities. The loan was repaid per the original agreement; thereafter, the couple put aside a designated sum each week to cover the rent and other fixed payments. No further requests were made for financial help.

In considering a request for a loan, the counselor should take into account the availability to the clients of the community's usual resources for meeting such requests—commercial banks, veteran loan plans, and other lending facilities. Inherent in the social work goal of helping people to accommodate realistically to living in today's money world is the expectation that people will selectively and thoughtfully seek out existing economic resources. Sometimes an individual requires the help of an agency in learning about the existence of specific facilities as well as in undertaking to use them with the maturity essential to move toward independence.

Jim K, 24, had supported his wife and three children as a truck driver until he fell on an icy street and sustained a spinal injury. The injury precluded his continuing to perform heavy work. During his hospitalization he was alternately deeply depressed, withdrawing into silence when the doctor or the physical therapist saw him, or loudly angry, berating the doctor and the therapist for not "getting me out of here." The hospital social worker, calling on Mr. K on referral from the doctor, was met with the same anger. It was dissipated when the worker volunteered that Mr. K had a right to feel angry! Because of his freak accident, he was now forced to alter his lifestyle, including his way of earning a living and supporting his family. Mr. K bitterly replied that his wife was now "stuck" with working and earning, and for how long? His disability insurance would not last much longer and what then?

Discussion of vocational plans with him revealed that Mr. K's longtime ambition had been to become a doctor. Brought up in a ghetto, as a black boy he had not felt he could see such a plan through, and his hardworking widowed mother could not help him and also support the four younger children. He had been a good high school student, had managed to complete two years of community college work in basic sciences while working. With an associate arts degree, however, what could he do?

During the long convalescence, with the encouragement of the medical social worker in the outpatient service (on referral from the hospital worker) and Mrs. K, he undertook a battery of vocational tests, which pointed to the practicality of a career as a pharmacist. The couple were enthusiastic about this prospect. However, although Mr. K was admitted to the local school of pharmacy, only limited tuition help could be supplied, and he was unable to obtain a government-insured student loan because of past poor credit performance. Mrs. K continued to work, but her earnings were low and not likely to be increased for she lacked marketable skills. The Ks believed, nevertheless, as did the social worker, that his earnings would be sufficient to enable him to repay a loan to cover the costs of the education. With the worker's intercession, the family agency agreed to lend Mr. K the needed funds from its scholarship fund for minorities, payments to begin a year after he had begun to earn.

Within two years after Mr. K had become a licensed pharmacist, he had repaid the educational loan. Shortly thereafter, he told the family agency worker he had been offered an opportunity to "buy into" the small pharmacy where he was employed; he would need $2,000 for the initial investment, which he did not have. By then his earning capacity had been demonstrated and his credit rating was excellent. Encouraged by the counselor, he was able to procure a commercial loan.

Subsequently, in a letter that accompanied a voluntary contribution to the agency's scholarships-for-minorities fund, he wrote: "When I was handed the check for that loan, I knew I was a man again!"

THE COLLECTION OF LOANS

Obviously, it is unrealistic to give a loan to a person who has no resources to repay it. Anxiety about the debt may hang over the family like a cloud and have depressing effects on all members. The anxiety itself may deter the person from continuing a needed counseling relationship with the agency.

It is equally unrealistic to make a loan and not support it with businesslike collection procedures. If a social agency fails to make efforts to secure payment of a validly made loan, this neglect has negative effects on the family and defeats any attempt of the agency to provide budget counseling. An artificial counseling atmosphere is created if the borrower is not expected to meet the obligations incurred and to accept responsibility for the resulting actions. Such evasions do not further the goal of helping families to live responsibly in our money world.

FEES FOR SERVICES

In our culture we are accustomed to paying fees for professional services. People are likely to select with greater care the services they must buy, and tend to value them more highly than those that are free. The relationship between the receiver and the giver of the service tends to be more reciprocal. But of special importance in the helping relationship is the fact that the individual or family that finds it painful or otherwise difficult to ask for help, interpreting such a request as a sign of weakness or transfer of control over one's affairs to a stranger, retains a sense of power by paying a fee. This fact implies, as was stated earlier, that the troubled individual or family makes the decision to pursue or discontinue the relationship, directs or dominates the interaction with the counselor, and determines the conditions under which advice will be heard and followed or rejected.

On the surface it may seem ironic for a social agency to charge a fee for providing counseling on money problems. But financial problems are myriad and diverse and are not restricted to families on marginal incomes. For low-income families, particularly those that require assistance to meet their survival needs, being charged a fee may not be just ironic, but inappropriate. However, if counseling or other service is being rendered for resolution of a problem with a money dimension—either as a symptom or a causal factor—a fee may be both appropriate and desirable regardless of the source or level of the family income. In keeping with this view, the 1975 Social Services Amendments to the Social Security Act (Title XX) authorize public agencies, either directly or indirectly providing services, to apply a fee schedule to any user of social services even when the family income is solely or mostly from public assistance sources.

Practices and attitudes with respect to fee charging in social agencies vary considerably. In some quarters there is a strong belief that community supported social agencies should provide services without charge. Others recognize that, while many community resources, such as hospitals and universities, are subsidized, payments to them cover only part of the actual cost of their services. Because social work has been identified traditionally with helping the economically or socially disadvantaged, the idea of charging fees sometimes seems incompatible with social work values and functions. In reality the charging of fees has been a means of encouraging often-neglected groups of troubled persons to use the counseling services of social agencies—a policy that has opened the door to nonpoor whose problems are susceptible to social work intervention but who were reluctant to request counseling service for fear they would be classified as inadequate or flawed (their perception of people who are poor). In like manner, many poor are more accepting of services for which they pay even a token fee, thus nourishing their self-respect by demonstratring a certain independence in "paying their way."

Paying One's Way

The use of fees is steadily growing, sometimes because of statutory stipulations, sometimes because of conviction in the agency about the benefits and values to the individual in paying a fee, and sometimes because both conditions exist.

The individual seeking help with a personal problem may not be aware that it contains an element of money as such. But when the fee policy is broached, the response is apt to reflect the individual's feelings about money as well as characteristic attitudes toward and ways of handling relationships. This person may argue about the fee—its imposition, amount, or timing—and may try to evade paying it or entering cooperatively into the plan. The pattern of payment may well be related to the problems precipitating the need for help. Discussion about the applicant's attitudes toward payment of the fee or about the payment pattern may in itself constitute an important tool for helping the individual understand the nature of the personal problem for which help is being sought. When the E family conferred with the counselor (chapter 8) and Mr. E realized that fees were charged for counseling service, he angrily announced that he did not

> "have money to throw away on words and advice that probably won't do me any good anyhow!" Mrs. E said, "The fee isn't *that* much" and if he took a greater interest in Carol, their only child, she "wouldn't be in such trouble with the law!" Carol and the counselor listened to the parents accusing each other of responsibility for the girl's "trouble." At the first lull, Carol looked at the worker and broke her silence to mutter, "You see? It's always the same: we're throwing away *his* money. *We* don't count."
>
> As he began to protest this accusation, the father paused, asking his wife, "Is that the way it looks to you? Money isn't *that* important," he added, and if paying a fee was a necessary way of "getting back on the track, I'm ready."

COUNSELING SERVICES

The establishment of a fee policy has become a fairly common practice among counseling agencies, notably family service agencies and mental health programs. For a considerably longer time it has been an integral part of the operation of health care agencies. In the latter, the fee generally has been for the medical care obtained rather than for the counseling by social work or psychologist personnel. The payment might be fixed by item of service (X ray of hand or skull, for example, or a specific laboratory test, or examination of a child by the pediatrician). It might be a flat membership fee for all, covering any service that is required of a particular clinic or medical facility. It might be on a sliding basis, adjusted in accordance with the family income.

In family or mental health counseling, where there are not likely to be laboratory procedures, medical examinations, or prescriptions, the fees are not related to a predetermined scale of values. The fee may be uniformly applicable to every user of service, regardless of income. Thus one agency with middle- and upper-income clients charged fixed fees of $17.50 for an individual interview and $25 for a joint or family interview.[1] More commonly, fees are set according to the family income and the capacity to pay. It might be on a sliding scale, based on steps in gross income, but with allowances for income tax, family size, and normal and unusual expenditures. It might be set for a specified period of service (a week, a month), or by family unit (individual as well as family interviews included in a single charge) rather than the actual number of interviews. The fee generally is discussed in the first interview, and the amount and conditions of payment are established at that time. An agency may decide to waive the fee for the first contact if the individual is unaware of one and unprepared to pay it.

Most persons accept the established fee as a natural expense attendant on receiving counseling services. Some, however, ask to have it waived or reduced even when they are able to pay. And sometimes persons with limited incomes express a wish to pay more than they can afford. When resistance to paying is displayed, the counselor must endeavor to understand its nature. Often it is a sign that the person does not really want to tackle the extant problems.

> Mr. G, 30, a junior executive, married with one child, came to the agency seeking help for rather vague "marital troubles," saying it might be necessary to place the child, that he had many problems about which he thought he needed counseling, and describing his wife as a grasping, hostile woman.
>
> Exploration with him and with his wife about the problem revealed that Mr. G seemed to gain negative satisfaction out of the marriage and to be carrying on a struggle with his wife for dominance and control. He abused his wife physically. He was constantly in debt, and his credit rating was seriously jeopardized because of late payment of bills. He had a bank loan outstanding on which he barely managed to meet monthly payments. Despite regular increases in salary, he had to arrange a renewal of the bank loan. He falsified his expense account. He was planning at this time to convert to cash his interest in his company's retirement plan in a manner that would bring him into disrepute with his employer.
>
> A fee was discussed in the initial interview. Mr. G said he could not pay the scheduled amount. The worker then asked him to submit a detailed statement of his income and family expenditures. His first account was slipshod. He was asked to prepare another, and the second was a thorough report of his financial situation. On the basis of this report, a temporary

reduction in fee was granted with the understanding that the fee would be reconsidered at the end of two months, when the couple and the worker would evaluate the effectiveness of the counseling series. If they agreed there was merit in continuing, Mr. G would be expected to submit another financial report.

During this period Mr. G participated in individual and joint sessions. He described his relationship with his mother, who had dominated him and managed the family finances during his childhood. He was helped to see that his dissatisfactions in his marriage were related to his feelings about his mother. He expressed fear that if he extricated himself from debt his wife would divorce him. As he was able to separate his old feelings from his present reality, he was able to work and handle his money better. He received an advancement in his firm. He liquidated his bank loan and paid off his debts. At the end of the two-month period he began to pay the full agency fee for a second goal-focused series of counseling sessions.

The marriage relationship did not improve, and the couple decided to separate. They made a property settlement and Mr. G arranged to pay suitable alimony to his wife, as well as support for the child.

In instances where the person wishes to pay more than the scheduled fee, or to pay a small token fee when the income is below the fee scale, it is important to understand the meaning of the desire to pay. Often it indicates a dependence-independence conflict which should be understood and handled appropriately. If the conflict is strong, the counselor may permit the person to overpay for a period, discussing the meaning of overpayment in the course of the ensuing counseling situations for the purpose of aiding the person to achieve insight into behavior that may be self-defeating.

The S family had left their native Samoa to live in Hawaii. Mr. S had earned enough to bring his parents to live with him and his wife and four children, and they now were totally dependent on him; neither parent had a marketable skill and neither qualified for Social Security benefits. The mother-in-law and wife fought incessantly; they alternated in their threats to leave—his mother to return to Samoa, his wife to "just take off" and leave the family to the mother-in-law's care. Feeling the strain of the high costs of living in Hawaii, Mr. S decided to move his family to the mainland. He withdrew their savings, bought the air tickets, and without discussion quit his job and announced the departure date. Mrs. S inferred that the parents were being left behind, so she raised no objection until all were on the plane and she realized that they had come along not just to say goodbye, but to travel with the family.

A friend who had preceded Mr. S had arranged for a small house in the vicinity of the church attended by many Samoans. Mr. S found work almost at once, earning at the same level as in Hawaii. Costs of living were slightly lower; nevertheless, he was unable to manage his income to remain out of debt. To ease the family situation, he rented a separate apartment for his parents, dividing between the two family units the income left after paying the rent for his parents and his immediate family. His wife threatened to leave, but he protested that "after all," how could he not be a good and dutiful son? His wife was "unreasonable." He could not permit his parents to turn to others for their care. He had now developed a serious colitis and the aggravation with his wife would cause him to get worse, and then how would either family manage?

The agency fee had been discussed with Mr. S in the first conference. Review of his obligations and income had indicated the appropriate level in the scale used by the agency, but Mr. S became angry when he saw that there were several higher fee levels on the fee-scale chart. He wasn't poor, he insisted, and could take care of his responsibilities, including "paying full freight." For the first three sessions, he gave the bookkeeper-cashier the maximum agency fee. By the fourth session, he could see that this insistence was part of a behavior pattern evidenced in his relationships with his parents and wife and might well affect the colitis, also. He could now move toward looking realistically at the relationships *and* his health condition. His insights were expressed in his request to reduce the fee to the level originally set for his income level.

Individual agencies determine the criteria that will govern the amount of the fee. There may be a statutory guideline, as in some state-aided community mental health clinics which fix eligible income below the income level that presumably can purchase private counseling service, then scale downward in specified gradations. Fees for public social services offered in accordance with federal statutes to persons whose income is not linked to public assistance are established according to median family income in the given state. Other agencies may begin with the determination of the administrative cost of providing services and use the resultant figure as a basis for developing a flat fee or a sliding scale correlating this figure, or a reasonable fraction of it, to the range of disposable (after taxes) incomes from which the families might be expected to pay for goods and services.

Formulas for fee-setting vary, but ordinarily the family's gross income is used as the first index. If the individual raises questions about the amount of the fee, a more detailed discussion of income and expenses follows. Often the individual's questioning of the amount stems from personal problems which are not related to income insufficiency. (This was true of Mr. G.) Fee-setting, then, becomes an integral part of the study and treatment process.

Experience has shown that most people who apply to family agencies or community mental health agencies for counseling are more accepting of the idea of fee payments than are social workers themselves. Many of the latter still feel some uneasiness about asking for fees, which may be related to their professional heritage. Voluntary social welfare agencies had their origins in philanthropy, and, for many years, were primarily concerned with the problems of poverty and related social ills. These concerns have not been abandoned, even though the voluntary agencies do not generally assume responsibility for meeting maintenance needs of families. Their clientele, however, includes economically depressed families, as well as those in comfortable circumstances. As a result, the social worker in these agencies must be able to identify appropriately with both groups; this dual role undoubtedly creates some discomfort and uncertainty in applying a fee schedule.

Agencies that provide homemaker service frequently find that fee-setting has additional complexity, particularly in the variations that may affect the agency's operating costs in providing such service: twenty-four-hour care or daily day-time hours, geographic location of the assignment (isolated or high-crime area, for example), the specific nature of tasks that will be required in a given instance (many children, mental disturbance, an absent parent, or other factors requiring particular skills or stamina), and others. In most voluntary agencies offering such service, the charge to a given individual or family may be geared to the actual cost or adjusted according to the family's capacity to pay. Fees may also be charged for the related counseling; or one or the other charge may be reduced or waived.

Handling the voluntary agency's fee for service to an economically independent elderly person may also require special consideration. The counseling may be focused on helping the elderly person's family to cope with their concerns, guilt, and realities in relation to their perception of someone else's need. At the same time, there may or may not be a realistic need for homemaker service for the subject of their concern. There may be special problems in a situation that arises if the elderly person lives apart from the family members and the latter are unable or unwilling to pay for the service.

Homemaker (or housekeeper) service provided under the auspices of a public social services agency may be extended on a basis much like that of the voluntary agency that either includes homemaker service as part of a larger service or counseling program, or focuses its total program on homemaker services. Many public agencies operate their own homemaker service, employing a wide range of skills to cope with an equally wide range of problem situations—from protective care of children or of elderly persons, to teaching or modeling housekeeping roles in a household with a parent of limited experience or capacity, to daily care in a one-parent family not yet emotionally ready to obtain commercial housekeeping help, to the provision of the care of a full-time attendant or an occasional housekeeper to clean and market for a housebound individual. Many public agencies, rather than administer such programs directly, purchase the needed service, at full cost, on a contract or case-by-case basis. The fee to those who need the service may be on the sliding scale previously mentioned, based on median family incomes, or there may be no charge at all if the income of the individual or family derives from public assistance payments.

Even if a family has heavy indebtedness, the counselor may decide to set a fee for budget counseling. This procedure may be a crucial step in helping the family members face the personal problems that have created the financial difficulties and in helping them achieve the goals of reducing their indebtedness and of learning to live within their income.

> For ten years the Bs, torn between their ingrained religious belief supporting the necessity of having children, and the population control movement, had practiced birth control. Now in her early thirties, Mrs. B had miscarried in the fifth month of pregnancy when the car in which she was riding was struck from the rear by a car on which the brakes had failed. Mrs. B irrationally held her husband responsible for the miscarriage; *he* had been driving their car. She went on an orgy of spending, buying furniture, clothes, and imported perfumes. A mixture of feelings—guilt, responsibility, identification with her unhappiness—led Mr. B to encourage her wild spending; he even bought her some extravagant gifts. Their savings exhausted, they ran up bills they could not pay.
>
> They applied to a family counseling agency, presenting their problem as need for marital counseling, for they now were quarreling constantly, each blaming the other for faults that placed them in their present childless, debt-ridden state. Their gross income, though heavily encumbered by debt, fell within the fee schedule, and the stipulated amount was set. The worker believed that the fee would symbolize the economic reality that they could manage on Mr. B's earnings. The couple agreed that their first goal must be to bring their financial situation under control, so that they could then look more clearly at other elements contributing to their unhappiness. They concurred that they *should* be able to manage the fee for counseling. They were referred to the local consumer credit counseling agency, where a plan was formalized for orderly payment of their debts and the service included distribution of prorated payments to creditors from sums supplied weekly by the Bs. For this service they also paid a fee. Counseling proceeded in the family

agency while the credit counselor concurrently implemented the repayment plan, maintaining contact with the family counselor along the way.

As the indebtedness became more manageable, the couple were able to devote their attention to the factors that had contributed to their behavior, with each taking appropriate responsibility for exacerbation of the tensions under which they had been living. The pattern they established of devoting fixed payments to debt repayment and for fees for counseling and credit adjustment was later converted into saving for Mrs. B's confinement, for she became pregnant again.

CHILD CARE SERVICES

Traditionally, parents have been expected, to the extent that their incomes have permitted, to pay for the care of their children placed in foster family homes, institutions, or day care centers. In agency-supervised foster home placements, the cost usually has been geared to the amount paid by the agency to the foster parents. In independent placements, of course, the cost has been negotiated directly by the parent with the foster parent and the former has been responsible for meeting the full designated cost. However, in agency-supervised foster home placements, the agency generally provides a comprehensive cluster of services to the child, the foster parents, and the natural parents for which a fee may be paid to the agency exclusive of any arrangement made for the placing parents to pay for the cost of the child's care.

For a long time, the payments by agencies to foster parents covered food, clothing, and minimal incidental costs; the agency generally carried the responsibility for medical and dental care. In effect, the cost covered the expense of maintaining the child, and included no payment for the time and physical and emotional energy devoted to the child's care: the idea of financial profit was not acceptable. Parents, depending on their circumstances and resources, might have been expected to reimburse the agency for part or all of this cost. In recent years, as knowledge has increased about the meaning of payment for both the parents and the foster parents, agencies have begun to change their basis of charging as well as of paying. The meaning of money to all persons involved in the placement has been discussed in an earlier chapter.

Agencies have come to recognize the importance of parents' paying a realistic amount, based on their income, for the care of their child. The determination of the amount and the handling of the parents' attitudes regarding payment are integral parts of the counseling process. It is important, however, that the parents understand clearly how much they are paying for the agency's service, and how much for the child's care.

If the payment arrangement calls for direct payment by the parents to the foster parents for the child's care, the counseling fee is paid directly to the agency. It also is of importance, as was stated in Chapter 5, that the placed child be aware that the natural parent is carrying financial responsibility for the foster care, thereby signifying to the child that the parent cares, no matter how tenuous the relationship may be.

In recent years, there has also been a trend among voluntary and public agencies toward including a charge for the foster parents' services in providing for the child's care. This concept has been accepted somewhat slowly, for the idea runs counter to the long-held assumption that persons who expect money for such services have no compassion or love for children. But the gradual acceptance of a service payment suggests that greater weight is being given to another deeply entrenched cultural assumption: work should be paid for in money.

The setting of a fee for counseling in connection with foster care—institutional as well as family home care—has heretofore been more common among voluntary child-care agencies. A high proportion of public agency foster placements nationwide have been court-ordered for any of many reasons, including child protection, or delinquency of the child or parent. In these cases, the payment for care often is worked out by the court or by an authorized representative such as a probation officer, and counseling fees are not taken into account. Placements may be made by other public organizations for mentally or physically handicapped children, as well as for emotionally disturbed, and special problem children. The placement may be precipitated by a need for continuous physical care which the parents cannot provide or for treatment of a particular problem that is better resolved outside the family home. Policies about payment vary among the agencies and the individual circumstances: parents may be expected to pay part or all of the cost of care, and this determination may or may not be related to the source and amount of family income; the parents may be expected to pay a separate fee for counseling, as they might to a voluntary agency. Again, there is statutory approval in the Social Security Act to assign fees to users of public social services, including child placement, if they are not economically dependent on assistance payments but are income-eligible—that is, their income falls at or below the median family income in the given state.

The expanding labor force of working mothers has created new demands for day care services, either in foster homes or child-care centers. These facilities are required not just by mothers who work (or wifeless fathers who work), but also for children in other circumstances. Day care, whether in a foster day care home or a child-care center, increases the probability that the child may be maintained in the parental home. Day care can obviate the working parent's need to find a substitute home for the child; the handicapped child may not have to be institutionalized; the family confronted with a crisis may be able to tolerate more readily the traumatic demands of the situation through the relief and support provided by day care.

In any of these situations, the public or voluntary agency may pay full cost of care, or require the parents to pay all or part of the care. And, as is true of twenty-four-hour foster care, the combination of family gross income, circumstances of the placement, and statutory or agency policy determine whether a counseling fee will be requested of the placing parent and, if so, how much it will be.

ADOPTION SERVICES

In both public and private adoption agencies, there is a growing trend to charge the adoptive parents a fee. In some states the basis for the fee, and its upper limits, are written into law. Ability to pay a fee is not a criterion in assessing the suitability of parents to adopt a child, although from time to time complaints are heard from prospective adoptive parents that they were rejected for this, rather than some other undisclosed reason. The fee is quite common among voluntary adoption agencies, but there are marked differences among public agencies that place children for adoption. Some believe that, as tax-supported agencies, their services should be available to everyone without charge. Conversely, there are those who protest that potential adoptive parents who can afford to pay for the adoption service should not be subsidized by the general tax-paying public.

In general, the amount charged covers such costs as the child's care prior to adoption, fees for the medical study, fees for legal adoption procedures, and the counseling service involved in the process of relinquishment, preplacement, and supervision. It is not uncommon for potential adoptive parents to pay a fee at the time of application for an adoptive study—with no refund if, as a result of the study, no child is placed with them.

Many applicants accept the idea of a fee to an adoption agency as a matter of course; they recognize the costs involved for the agency and realize that they would be under expense if they bore their own child. Other applicants object to the fee. Their objections may stem from unrecognized reluctance to take on the responsibility of adopting a child, or they may associate fee-charging with black market activities. The objections may be related to ethnic or cultural factors. For example, one public adoption agency has found that many black adoptive parents react in either of two ways to adoption fees. Some refuse to make a payment because the practice seems to them to be reminiscent of the buying and selling of slaves. Others, even with inadequate means, may insist on paying the maximum amount to affirm their equality with other adoptive parents.

Agencies do not expect a married or unmarried mother who is relinquishing her child for adoption to pay for the child's preadoption care. They believe such payments would serve to strengthen her tie to the child and thereby add to the separation difficulties. However, mothers are generally expected to pay, to the extent of their ability, for their obstetrical costs.

HEALTH CARE SERVICES

Despite the availability of Medicare, Medicaid, veteran's programs, and certain other health care services provided under federal statutes, provisions for medical care, both hospital and outpatient treatment as well as preventive health services, vary considerably throughout the country. Most communities have some provision for free or low-cost care under both public and voluntary auspices. In general, no special fee is charged for medical social services. Any charge for such service is included in the total fee that a clinic or hospital sets for outpatient or inpatient care.

When a fee for clinic and social services is charged, it is usually based on a sliding scale and is not designed to cover the actual costs. Such a scale generally takes into account current earnings and other income: savings; property owned; insurance; and other assets, as well as present debts and future obligations. It also takes into account the size of the family and its financial responsibility for relatives. Some scales allow for a reasonable standard of living and, in applying the scale, consideration is given to the cost of any needed medical treatment. In many communities, public and private clinics base their fee scale on a standard dependency budget. Consequently, many persons with moderate incomes are ineligible for either health care or medical social services in these clinics. They may be eligible, however, for various services provided by the federal government for veterans, or for special medical and rehabilitative services provided by public or private organizations for persons with specific illnesses and handicaps.

THE PSYCHOLOGICAL VALUE OF FEES

To be able to pay a fee for a service has a particular psychological meaning to people in our culture. There is a persistent belief that a service that costs something is better than a free service. The latter appears to hold "a joker," a potential for exploitation by obligating the users in ways inimical to their self-respect and ability to retain control over their own affairs. By paying their way, they feel their stature as adequate independent beings has not been impaired. The discussion of the fee conveys to them their right to ask questions and express fears and doubts about the service, for it is an accepted part of individual adequacy to examine what is about to be bought. One is supposed to avoid "buying a pig in a poke."

The individual or family response to the fee-setting process supplies the counselor with important clues to the nature of any psychological problems of the people involved. Furthermore, discussion regarding fees, both in setting them and in collecting them, provides a means to help people gain an awareness of their troubling attitudes and behavior, and to work toward resolving the practical and psychological problems.

For many counselors, the process of explaining, establishing, and collecting fees is uncomfortable. Their personal uneasiness about money affairs and management of money in their own lives, and perhaps their failure to come to terms with the personal meanings money holds for them, add to their reluctance to set and follow through on fees. Sometimes their resistance stems not from their personal money management feelings and experiences, but from a conviction that counseling is adequately compensated by the satisfaction derived from helping others, or that it can be effectively conducted only in an atmosphere uncontaminated by psychologically coercive financial considerations. For such counselors, advice is good but money is bad; tangible affairs and help are downgraded; "the love of money is the root of all evil" and distorts their focus on the basic reasons that bring troubled individuals to the agency for counsel. They unconsciously chafe at the constraints placed on them by the payment of a fee. For in many situations the presence of a fee is a dynamic in pressing the counselor to a responsible, maximized use of time (time is still equated with money) and skill in focusing on the problem at hand and how it is to be solved.

Once an agency has established a fee policy, and its application becomes part of the counselor's tasks, it is important that the fee that has been set be collected, for the same circumstances and consequences obtain as were described with regard to the collection of loans. Part of the individual's or family's functioning in the real world is the maturity with which accepted obligations are met; the counselor does a family a disservice in thoughtlessly helping them to avoid obligations realistically assumed, including the payment of fees.

NOTE

1. Ruth Fizdale, *Social Agency Structure and Accountability* (Fair Lawn, N.J.: R.E. Burdick, 1974), p. 62.

PART 4
APPLICATIONS—VALUES, NEEDS, RESOURCES

11
Human Needs and Values

Low levels or standards of living are not necessarily related to low or lagging income. Judged by United States standards, for example, a primitive tribe may have a "low" standard of living but this does not always mean that the tribe lacks resources. The tribe's material possessions may be few, yet the members may not consider the standard low, for their needs are satisfied either more readily or differently than are those of persons living in a complex industrial society. They do not consider the level low if it is the norm for the group and compatible with the aspirations of the group members. An income that is on the poverty line in one country may represent riches in another. Poverty, in one sense, can be viewed as the discrepancy between recognized needs or desires and the opportunity for satisfying them.

Living standards rise as the level of an economy rises. Goods that were once luxuries become comforts, and later these comforts become necessities. In the United States such changes in values have been rapid because of high productivity, the susceptibility of people to the new and novel, mass communication, beguiling advertisements, and the accessibility of consumer credit.

Standards change as new equipment such as telephones, cars, radios, television sets, and air conditioners are improved upon and made available. Other standards change as scientific knowledge about human relationships increases and as concepts of family and individual lifestyles alter. For example, the social work goal of keeping children in their own home instead of placing them when certain family crises occur demonstrates that homemaker services have become a recognized community need for which provision should be made. The movement of women into the labor force means that there must be recognition of the economic cost of child care and that domestic help and convenience foods must be considered in family budgets. In the same way, awareness of the needs of the adolescent has altered ideas about educational needs, and brought acceptance of the costs involved. Public assistance and Social Security regulations in many instances now enable adolescents to complete a program of higher education or special training, instead of routinely giving them no alternative to supporting themselves at the age of eighteen.

Needs, desires, values, and aspirations are not static. It behooves the money counselor to understand the many social and cultural changes that take place, and the pressures families and individuals feel to obtain the multitude of goods and services generally viewed as essential to a good quality of life. Instalment buying is now a part of our culture and can be used creatively or destructively. Indebtedness in itself no longer can be viewed as poor management or as a sign of excessive need for personal gratification. Indeed, as suggested earlier, it is almost inevitable in our present economy that families will have some unpaid bills: for mortgages, automobile loans, credit card and other charge accounts, or medical or dental services. To some extent, this state of indebtedness is offset by the assets reflected in the increasing equity in home, car, and other instalment-purchase durables, and by credits being accumulated in Social Security insurance or pension funds—credits that sometimes lessen the urge to save for the future. As guaranteed-income plans become more prevalent, it is not unlikely that credit buying will increase. This assumption is predicated on the fact that persons with relatively secure incomes, such as civil service employees, are considered to be fairly good credit risks and therefore use credit more than some other groups.

Furthermore, other conditions in our society push many people to the utilization of credit for the sake of convenience. The reluctance of some gasoline service stations to accept cash instead of a credit card during certain hours encourages customers to obtain and use the cards. The outpacing of income by living costs leads many to use credit devices for everyday transactions in lieu of maintaining ready cash for such purposes. The newly instituted system of mailing Social Security benefit checks to banks is likely to lead the beneficiary, when regarded as creditworthy, to obtain the bank's credit card and simply charge to the account the daily purchases for which cash heretofore had been paid. These remain devices of convenience as long as the user pays the bill promptly on receipt; failure to do so in effect adds to the cost of the transactions. Hence changing conditions and systems more or less subtly influence our values and daily patterns for coping with need.

Needs and values are also influenced by the attitudes of a specific cultural group. Insurance, for instance, may be purchased for different reasons. To some groups it represents protection from costs associated with death; to others, savings for the future. Parents of first- or second-generation Mexican background and other nationality groups frequently purchase a small policy for each child at his birth. The policy is an expression of their affection and their acceptance of the child into the family. Failure to buy a policy connotes rejection. The counselor must be alert to the significance of expenditures such as these, evaluating them in relation to cultural attitudes. "Unusual" expenditures are not necessarily signs of waste or of pathology.

The psychological as well as the physical needs and values of a family must be understood. For instance, a family, in adjusting to a downward shift in resources, may elect to pay a disproportionate amount of its income for housing in order to live in a "good neighborhood," compensatingly reducing the amount spent on food or clothing. Or an unemployed father may forego a haircut, much needed in keeping with hair and grooming styles suitable for approaching a prospective employer, in order to buy a toy to celebrate his child's birthday. The budget counselor must be sensitive to the psychological need of people to maintain their dignity and self-respect, and their place in the family and in the community. People who are forced by outside pressure to give up the means for satisfying their psychological needs are in danger of developing feelings of helplessness, hopelessness, worthlessness, and dependency.

The counselor, therefore, has two tasks: one is to learn to accept and evaluate the variations in spending patterns as well as the constant changes that take place in these patterns; the other is to develop skill in helping individuals and families learn to utilize the resources available to them in the changing economic scene, as realistically and creatively as possible. Adequate fulfillment of these tasks combines understanding of the economic milieu in which the family lives, and sensitivity to the significance of individual behavior with regard to the receipt, possession, and utilization of money.

NEEDS ASSESSMENT

What constitutes a need? Can need be differentiated from desire? Clearly, the line between the two cannot be sharply drawn. Although, in general, needs may be defined as those elements essential for survival, the concept of these essentials is not the same in middle-income and lower-income families. Desires, on the other hand, are all the things people might like to have. Because resources for gratifying desires are usually limited, people must make choices within the reality of their economic resources.

Desires, however, change as the person's values alter; and certain desired objects, once acquired, come to be considered necessities. A father may have been content with a safety razor but his son demands an electric shaver. In the modern household a washing machine, a vacuum cleaner, and often a car and a television set are on the list of necessities.

In spite of the trend toward standardization in many areas of life, no standard package of necessities has been developed. There are, however, certain basic items that must be included in every household budget. Their inclusion is predicated on the fact that certain items are fundamental to survival (food, shelter, clothing) and that certain additional items satisfy the compelling need to be healthy, productive, and mobile members of our society (health care, transportation, education, personal care, recreation, and others).

The three standards of living described in chapter 2 allow for differences in kind, quantity, and quality of budget components that express those personal and familial aspirations that can be met at varying levels of income. These standards of living are geared to expenditure patterns, and are adjusted for regional differences and changing costs of living. They have been developed around hypothetical families, but nonetheless offer a useful set of guidelines as to what is generally perceived to be need in our society. However, the expenditure patterns do not and cannot take into account the wide variations in personal and environmental circumstances, perceptions of need, capacity to plan and execute the plan, family interactions, and numerous other elements that have different or even unique dimensions and effects on particular families. Against the standard selected as the most pertinent to a given family's composition and income, the money counselor must assess with the individual or family their needs and wishes, and their financial circumstances and goals. The following pages offer some questions and guidelines that one needs to consider (or consciously eliminate from consideration) in working with a specific family or individual.

Food

Food is the human being's most basic need. It is the first priority in a family budget because of its direct bearing on the physical health, productivity, and emotional growth and development of all family members, and because the expenditure for food tends to absorb the highest proportion of the annual family incomes under $20,000.

Differences between poor and rich families in the level and pattern of food and other consumption have drawn the attention of social reformers for nearly two centuries.[1] In recent years, however, food sources and resources, knowledge about nutrition, and food habits themselves have changed drastically, and have affected food patterns in many similar ways for both poor and rich in the United States. But still there are income- and culture-related differences. The nineteenth-century Prussian economist, Christian Engel, formulated a much-quoted law ("Engel's Law") holding that as income increases, the proportion spent on food and other necessities decreases. Subsequently, an early United States Commissioner of Labor, Carrol Wright, modified that law to state that as income increased, the proportion devoted to food decreased, the part allocated for shelter, fuel, and clothing invariably remained the same, and the proportion for "sundries" (all other categories of consumption) increased. Subsequent studies have confirmed the first and last of Wright's assertions, but not the second. Nevertheless, there is a similarity in food expenditure patterns of American households at different income levels: as income increases and standards of living rise, the relative expenditure patterns of the several income groups become more comparable.

The expenditure for food does not increase proportionately with income. In a low-income family, food costs may take 35 to 45 percent of the budget, but in a middle-income family, they take only about 25 to 30 percent, and even less in wealthier groups. Inflated food prices of course may change these proportions for a family that has not had a concomitant rise in income. Other factors, too, may alter these proportions. Usually the ratio will be higher if an undue number of meals are eaten in restaurants, if illness requires additional expenditures for certain kinds of food, and if expenditure for food is based on social, rather than nutritive values. The food dollars may buy much or little, depending upon the choices made. Because a food is expensive does not necessarily mean that it provides high nutritive value. Food needs and costs vary with individuals, with lifestyles, with the life cycle, and with external circumstances.

Modern medical science stresses the importance of an adequate well-balanced diet for all members of the family, from the infant to the elderly person. Food is important not only for physical growth and well-being, but for fostering emotional well-being. The infant's first sense of love and security is gained from the early feeding experience with the mother, definitely affecting the child's personality development, particularly the ability to withstand frustration. The continuing interrelationship between nutrition and mental health is cited by the Group for the Advancement of Psychiatry:[2] children's ability to respond appropriately to significant stimuli in their environment is reduced during the period of chronic malnutrition, and continued malnutrition is accompanied by progressive behavioral regression. It is also a common observation that many anxious and distressed persons throughout life turn to food for solace. Although it is evident that families whose income is low are more susceptible to malnutrition with its physical and emotional consequences, vulnerability to poor nutrition is not related to income alone.

Food also has social values. It is used to express affection, goodwill, and sympathy. In many cultures in this country as well as elsewhere, a gift of food welcomes a new family to a neighborhood or community, or offers comfort to a bereaved family member.

In helping a person determine the amount that might reasonably be spent on food, the counselor must take into account not only nutritive standards, but other factors as well. Cognizance should be taken of the social, cultural, and psychological needs that are expressed in food habits and, also, certain considerations that affect the cost, selection, and preparation of food. What homemaking skills are present in the family? Are shopping facilities accessible? Are there facilities for food storage? What members of the household are employed outside the home? What work patterns affect the household's food planning and patterns?

Nutritional research has made available extensive knowledge about the food needs of persons of different ages, sex, and activity. This knowledge is made accessible through literature, radio, television, and many other means. Numerous pamphlets designed for lay readership are issued by the Consumer and Food Economics Institute of the United States Department of Agriculture and by many extension services supported by departments of agriculture within individual states. Many of the pamphlets are also issued in Spanish or other translations in accordance with the size of the foreign-language populations in the area served. These pamphlets contain practical suggestions for the selection of foods and offer guides to the quantity of food needed at various ages.

Food costs are substantially influenced by the nature of the choices made. A sirloin steak costs more than chuck steak; chicken is likely to cost less than beef or pork; apples out of season may prove far more expensive than exotic fruits in season; an initially higher-priced cut of meat may be more economical than a cheaper one if the latter contains nonedible portions that effectively reduce what is left for serving. The family with limited income has to use greater care in choosing the foods that are at once cheaper, nutritious, and satisfying. And some people are restricted by their limited income in their ability to make the appropriate choices; indeed, they are additionally disadvantaged because the food share of the income has less margin for error.

Individuals who consciously seek to make the best use of the available food money generally can effect some savings, although undoubtedly the amount is sharply affected by their skill, intellectual capacity, time, and patience. There are some common guidelines, however, among which every household manager, from the most to the least sophisticated and able, can find some that are compatible with the individual family's interests, needs, and capacities.

Food costs can be kept at a minimum by planning meals and purchases ahead of time instead of relying on haphazard day-to-day marketing. The use of a shopping list can reduce unnecessary spending and can be an aid in avoiding impulsive purchasing. Prices in store advertisements should be compared when possible as the shopping list is being made up—with due caution to the fact that the added cost of transportation to a shop featuring certain bargains may consume the amount that can be saved on the purchase itself. There should be sufficient flexibility in planning meals and marketing to substitute especially good buys when they are discovered.

The shopper who possesses some rudimentary knowledge about nutritional values and in what alternative foods they are to be found, can take advantage of items that offer the same nutrients for less money. More and more products are labeled with information about nutritive content, the percentage per serving of minimum daily requirements of various vitamins, protein, calcium, iron, and so forth, as well as the caloric content. Different brands of the same product can vary widely in price, yet be approximately the same in quality and nutritional value. At different times, various protein foods display sharp differences in price. Substitutions of one for another among them may lead to effective conservation of food money: for example, poultry instead of red meats; eggs, cheese, or beans instead of meat. And comparison of the different forms of the same food may result in savings: fresh, dried, canned, frozen.

Consumer protests and a growing number of protective laws have reduced some of the hard work shoppers formerly had to invest in deciding which of several packages was the most economical. Accordingly, in many states and cities the costs of similar products of various sizes must be shown for comparison by weight, volume, or count. Larger quantities usually are more economical than smaller, but the size or shape of the packaging alone does not provide accurate information and is often deceptive. However, it is not always economical to invest in the larger quantity even though the unit cost is less, for if all that is purchased would not ordinarily be used (even as left-overs) the additional quantity represents waste. This suggests the importance of knowing what the cost of a food item is per portion, which can be found by dividing the price of the amount to be purchased by the number of portions this amount will supply. Of course, there is no waste involved in purchasing breads, cereals, or other bulk items like sugar and flour. More weight for the identical or a lesser price represents saving—and when such merchandise is in bags rather than boxes, the savings may average as much as 20 percent.

Cheapness in itself may be expensive, even if the posted nutrient contents are adequate. Freshness and condition of the food items should be considered. It is now fairly general practice that perishable foods show the last date on which the product can remain on the shelf in the store. This is not actually the date by which the items would be spoiled, however; it is generally anticipated (with the exception of some dairy products) that they should retain flavor and edibility for a week beyond that date and sometimes longer. If the shopper does not expect the item to be eaten by the family right away, it is provident to select from the shelf the item stamped with the most distant date. Similarly, if the stamped "pull" date has arrived and the item is on special sale, it may be a bargain that should not be overlooked—if it is to be consumed without further delay.

In the same vein, while many markets place on "special" shopworn cans or packages, these should be examined with particular care: frozen foods covered with deep frost or dented cans should be bought with discretion. Bulging cans should be avoided without hesitance, for their contents may cause disastrous consequences, including costs of medical attention, painful discomfort, or even death (as in well-publicized cases of botulism). Such foods are a particular hazard for some old people or poor residents in certain urban neighborhoods.

> Mrs. P was brought into the emergency clinic with food poisoning. Although frail and malnourished, to the amazement of the hospital staff she survived several days of intensive care and was then placed in a nursing home to fully recover. She was unduly anxious during this time. Would she lose her rented room because she was not there? Would someone arrange to pay the next month's rent when her Social Security check came if she were still in the nursing home?
>
> The medical social work consultant to the nursing home talked with Mrs. P and learned that since her husband's death three years ago, she had been completely alone. Twice she had been robbed of her money when her monthly checks were cashed, and now she was afraid to open her door to anyone. She left her room only to go daily to the market in the neighborhood. Because she was bent and wrinkled (she was 83), the children would taunt

her as she hurried to and from her rooming house, calling her "witch!" Most of her Social Security benefits (she received the minimum amount, for her husband had been in low-paying work) went for room rent. She was paying $5 per month for her small television (now in the third year of payments), and had an average of $25 left each month for food and staple household items. She bought mainly food items that were in the discard bin; damaged cans were a special bargain on which she relied.

If the family has adequate storage facilities, quantity purchases may yield savings, but only if they will keep safely until they can be used. Meats, fruit, and vegetables purchased in season generally are cheaper and at their best. If they can be properly stored until needed, they may really be bargains. The grade of food to be bought is determined by menus and available funds: nonfat dry milk commonly costs about half as much as liquid milk and can be used for drinking or cooking; grade B eggs or grade C tomatoes for cooking will reduce costs.

While it may seem gratuitous to suggest to the mother of several small children that she should not take them with her to the market, surveys disclose that those who shop after meals and without the accompaniment of children spend up to 17 percent less than hungry shoppers with children or others. Similarly, persons who shop when they are angry are apt to buy items they do not need.

The question of where to shop, while presenting no problem for most people, does make a considerable difference for others. The family may have access to several shopping facilities, or be limited by restricted mobility to one or two in the immediate neighborhood. Food items in the independent neighborhood store are usually priced higher than in a chain store. Transportation costs, however, must be taken into account if the chain store is some distance away. The question of credit, too, sometimes enters into the choice of market. The family whose income is irregular or low may feel more secure in shopping at the neighborhood grocery where credit is extended. Sometimes, because of their indebtedness to the local store, families continue to purchase there out of a sense of obligation or of fear. Or the family dependent on public assistance or other transfer payments may rely on the neighborhood grocer to cash the checks. Sometimes this check-cashing process carries the stipulated or understood expectation that the payee will spend some of the money with the check-casher. If the family does not have access to other check-cashing resources, they may indeed have no alternative as to where their marketing is done.

The poor family living in an inner city ghetto has often been faced with another problem in maximizing the use of the food money. Examination into the factors that caused residents of the Los Angeles community of Watts to riot, burn, and pillage revealed a common belief that the neighborhood chain and independent markets put on display inferior or deteriorating merchandise on the days that residents dependent on public assistance received their benefit payments. The residents were further convinced that such merchandise was often moved in from stores in better neighborhoods and sold to the "captive" market at higher prices than they could possibly command in the other stores.

The subsequent establishment, in several states and communities, of consumer advocates to protect the public has been one source of control. Residents of ghetto or inner-city enclaves and counselors who have an advocacy function should be alert to possible exploitation of food shoppers and be prepared to report such practices to appropriate authorities.

Working members of the family may eat meals out, children may have lunch at school, or the family may eat in restaurants on special occasions. Lunches packed at home are often thought of as more economical than meals purchased, but this assumption bears scrutiny. If special foods are purchased for the lunch boxes, there may be no saving. The social and psychological meaning should also be considered. Children whose companions buy lunch in the school cafeteria may feel set apart by having to carry a home-packed lunch. In the same way, it may be desirable for the father to go out to lunch with his co-workers. In these days of "coffee breaks," an allowance for such expenditures should be computed in the food costs.

If the mother is employed outside the home, the careful planning of food expenditures should take into account the cost of her outside meals. In addition, it should be borne in mind that because of her limited time and depleted energy, perhaps she cannot buy and prepare food as economically as the full-time housewife. The family may need to use food that can be prepared quickly.

Many busy consumers, such as the working mother and the single person who lives alone, like the convenience of frozen-plate dinners and skillet main-dish mixes, but think they are more costly than similar foods prepared from "scratch" at home. The commercial and homemade products were studied in the foods laboratory of the Consumer and Food Economics Institute, and the findings were reported in *Family Economics Review*.[3] If time or cooking skills are limited, partially prepared dinners such as the skillet mixes may be a good buy. They do not save as much time as the frozen-plate dinners when compared with homemade counterparts, but they are convenient because all of the ingredients are assembled in one package; some of them also are money-savers. The frozen-plate dinner does not offer as much saving in money, but because the time spent in heating such a dinner is less than that required for other preparations, for many working mothers the convenience is worth the added cost. Before embarking on a pattern of utilizing such convenience foods, however, two suggestions are offered by the reporters. One is that some assessment should be made as to whether the quality and amount of the product suit the family palate. The other is that if the home-prepared food has been counted on to provide a specific nutritional component for the day (a serving of meat and two vegetables, for example), the convenience item replacing it should also meet this need.[4]

Involving the family members as a group in these determinations may be a valuable way of engaging their interest and participation in food budgeting and management. The reasonably intelligent and organized working mother can operate her household efficiently, and sometimes the family cooperates with great *esprit de corps,* but costs may be higher. Some households suffer, however, both economically and nutritionally if the mother works.

In many families, whether the mother is employed, the husband and children help with the marketing. In some, the cultural pattern places the responsibility on the husband for paying the grocer, though the selection of items may be done by the wife or by both. In other families, the marketing and food management tasks are regarded entirely as those of the woman, and the husband takes no part in the process until the food has been converted into a meal—or it appears to him that an undue portion of the family money is being used for food.

> Mr. McK, husband and father in a family of six, brings home about $21,000 annually as an electronics engineer. He is always in debt—not to a great degree, but enough to make him constantly anxious and irritable. He cannot understand the reason for never quite having enough money to last through the month. His mortgage payment, his utilities, and taxes take about 58 percent, his transportation expenses, including payments on the family car seem reasonable; there are no large medical bills or other special demands on his earnings; the family, he states, does not live in luxury. Nor is he putting anything aside for the future, except for keeping up payments on term insurance that he has carried for a number of years.
>
> Yet before each payday (twice a month), for several days the family charges its purchases at the neighborhood grocery; there is no ready cash to meet the costs.
>
> Why? When Mr. McK asked his wife this question, she merely shrugged. His mother, who makes her home with the McKs and their three children (two teen-age girls and a 10-year-old boy), tells her son that his wife is

wasteful and lazy, that she buys only the most expensive cuts of meat, prepared and frozen foods. Furthermore, if Mr. McK turned the grocery money over to his mother, he would find the picture quite different.

Mrs. McK states that if her mother-in-law didn't live in the home, Mrs. McK could save enough to support the mother-in-law in an apartment of her own! Exploration disclosed that the two women had been feuding since the couple's marriage, to which the mother had openly objected, and from which time she had lived with the couple. She constantly criticized the younger woman's home management, supervision of the children, and cooking, always maintaining she could cook better and more economical food. Mrs. McK insisted that they could not afford to keep the older woman in the home (indeed, the mother-in-law had ample resources of her own for meeting her needs but was unwilling to use them because she was saving them to leave to her children when she died).

Mrs. McK was demonstrating that she didn't have enough to get by, that therefore the older woman should leave. She could make her point most effectively by not having enough money for food. She estimated that groceries, milk, meals out (all three children ate lunches out daily, and Mrs. McK went out for lunch three or four times per week) accounted for more than $190 weekly.

When the problems in this family began to be worked through—the mother-in-law actually moving to her own apartment, which she was going to share with a widowed sister—the McK's money problems suddenly cleared up. Mrs. McK and the two girls took pride in planning and preparing meals, seeing what could be done about saving for the education of the children. They figured, on the basis of some three weeks' experience, that they could manage comfortably on a budget nearly 60 percent less than before.

Mrs. McK certainly had engaged in planning, but toward using the food money as a lever for ejecting her unwanted mother-in-law from the household. Even though she succeeded in this objective, the neurotic behavior produced other problems: Mrs. McK and the girls had allied themselves against the father, depreciating his role and feelings. He began to go to his mother's for dinner almost every night; as a result, his wife became angry and his mother gleeful.

The counseling now had to be refocused, moving from budget counseling and intergenerational problems to the marital discord expressed in the sharing of meals with Mr. McK's mother. The financial counselor whose help had been sought by Mr. McK originally to bring the budget expenditures under control now referred the family to the family service agency. In the referral, the financial counselor remarked that perhaps he had identified too much with Mrs. McK's wish to have her mother-in-law move; he too had a mother-in-law in his home whom he did not believe he could afford to continue to support.

It is always important for counselors to be aware of their own feelings and attitudes, and to guard against their becoming impediments to objectivity in helping family members to examine and tackle their problems in a healthy and realistic fashion.

Certain health conditions may require special diets that add to the cost of the food budget. Some special diets simply replace common foods with others at no additional cost, but this is not always the case. And some health conditions make additional demands on the food budget because considerable food intake is required. In such instances, if income is low and there is no assistance from outside sources to cover their food costs, the family may need the help of a nutritionist to determine the kinds and consumption frequency of foods that are likely to be most effective in meeting this dietary need. Special food is also required at various stages in the individual's life cycle, such as infancy and adolescence.

Food costs vary too with the stages of the family cycle. The new bride or any housewife under twenty-five is usually not a shrewd buyer. She tends to buy widely advertised products, and these are often the most costly. She is also inclined to experiment, and food costs may mirror this adventuresome spirit. Because younger housewives usually have limited money to spend, they are not likely to purchase more than enough to meet their immediate requirements. Although they do not take advantage of quantity buying, they are quick to redeem coupons and to accept free-trial offers and other money-saving devices.[5] Single persons living alone also ordinarily purchase food in small quantities unless they have adequate food storage facilities, including a freezer. There is a recent trend to package frozen and other foods in quantities small enough to accommodate the needs of single persons; but such packaging adds to the cost of the food, as does the waste when the individual has to buy more than can be used.

The food costs of the expanding family also merit special attention. Market research studies disclose that first-born babies are fed an average of 50 percent more processed baby food than are subsequent children at the same age. The child in latency is likely to create budget problems by responding to cereal advertisements that feature prizes sponsored by the child's "heroes"—a factor to be reckoned with in planning food expenditures. And everyone is familiar with the stereotype of adolescents, whose appetite is exceeded only by the energy they expend in opening and closing the refrigerator door.

According to one market research study, housewives forty-five years old and over are the most efficient food shoppers.[6] Their efficiency may be the result of experience but they also have more time to shop. Besides, they probably have sufficient funds to take advantage of large-order economies.

The food habits of elderly persons may be affected by both physical and emotional problems. Either anorexia or an insatiable appetite is sometimes a means of expressing emotional disturbances. Elderly persons should have a nutritious, well-balanced diet; since they are not as active physically as younger persons, they do not need to consume as many calories.

Those engaged in counseling should bear in mind that a person's expenditures for food may reflect neurotic as well as realistic attitudes about money and its use in procuring food.

SHELTER

Benjamin Disraeli remarked that "the best security for civilization is the dwelling; and upon adequate and attractive dwellings depends more than anything else the improvement of mankind. Such dwellings are the nursery of all domestic virtues, and without an adequate and attractive home the exercise of those virtues is impossible."[7] Perceptions of the place and form of "domestic virtues" have undergone considerable change since Disraeli's time, but the continuing impact of inadequate housing on people has been well documented. Many problems of physical and mental health, as well as those of family relationships, can be traced to unsatisfactory housing. When family members have little opportunity for privacy, for social and recreational activities, and for rest, emotional disturbances and tensions are likely to develop. The emotional damage may be more far-reaching and difficult to correct than the damage to physical health.

A family may choose from any number of ways to provide for its housing needs. It may rent space in an apartment, an apartment hotel, a one-family or two-family house, or buy an apartment or condominium, a mobile home or trailer, a used house, a new ready-built house, or a custom-built house. Cost, of course, influences a particular family's choice. And wide choice, even within a liberal price range, is not always possible. It is limited by geography, by transportation, by family size, and most important of all, by what the family can afford or is willing to sacrifice in order to have suitable housing. Housing shortages, an intermittent problem since World War II, became particularly evident in some localities during the 1970s for reasons discussed earlier. Costs for rentals or purchase of dwellings have reached new highs and show little prospect, in the face of general inflation, of moving downward. Long a major single component of a family's consumption and a good indication of its economic well-being, the proportion of family income diverted to shelter costs has moved steadily upward: next to food, it is the largest expenditure by families with incomes below $20,000 and the largest for incomes around that figure. For physical, emotional, and economic reasons, therefore, special attention must be addressed by families—and by individuals counseling them—to the matter of shelter.

A first consideration in selecting living quarters is the amount of space required. The beginning family usually requires few rooms and the young couple often think of their first home as a temporary one. The expanding family requires space for preschool children to play indoors and, if possible, outdoors, and to sleep. Also, the homemaker needs adequate space to carry on the usual household tasks and to permit some temporary escape into quiet. For a number of years in this family stage, the house or apartment is filled with children and adolescents, and both children and adults need some provision for privacy. The contracting family, consisting usually of two adults, often moves back to a small dwelling, but many remain in the longtime home.

A second consideration in selecting living quarters—and for many families this may be the controlling factor—is the amount of income that can be expended. Setting the figure is difficult since the decision is based on many factors. Housing may require 20 to 40 percent of the annual household budget. Environmental factors or personal needs or wishes may lead some families to invest a still higher proportion of income in housing. Even the lower percentage may call for some sacrifice of other items; the larger one may cause actual distress. And at the opposite end of the scale, there is a point below which no reduction in housing costs can be made.

Housing costs of course should be examined in relation to rental or ownership of the dwelling. But consideration of costs should not stop with the monthly amount to be devoted to mortgage or rental payments, or the down payment or deposits required. Location is an important factor, not just in terms of appreciation or depreciation of the neighborhood, but because of its accessibility to services such as schooling, shopping, and recreation, and also its proximity and accessibility to place of work. Lower-income families without automobiles or adequate public transportation may find themselves unable to reach jobs, restricting their employment opportunities. Single-parent families may be faced with constraints related to availability or quality of child care facilities if the parent is employed. Moreover, the relationship of home location to both work place and child care facility may add a burden of extra time to the parent's pressures—time that means added payment for longer hours of care, and drain on the physical and emotional energies of parent and children.

If the family elects to rent, the matter of computing costs is relatively simple. The tenant knows in advance what the cost will be, at least for the present. But there is no assurance the rent will remain stable unless the tenant has a lease, and even then the assurance is only for the duration of the leasing period. A lease may provide the tenant with protection, but it is not always a requirement for rental. Before signing a lease, the tenant should exercise caution, reading it carefully to ascertain the obligations placed on both tenant and landlord. What appliances (stove, refrigerator, heating unit, for example) are included in the rent? What utilities? Is a garage provided and, if so, is it included in the rental? Who is responsible for what repairs? What deposits are required, and under what circumstances are they returned or forfeited? If the lease is too technical for the tenant to understand, an attorney's help should be obtained to interpret it. The tenant (and, for that matter, the landlord) should avoid verbal promises, being sure that whatever arrangements have been made with the landlord are incorporated into the lease. Conditions of cancellation or renewal of the lease should be clear, as well as any limitations regarding who and how many persons and under what circumstances, may reside in the leased quarters. The person counseling the renting family should be aware of the resources (including any protective ordinances or statutes) available in the given community to uphold the rights of tenants. For example, for three months Mrs. R's landlord failed to repair a leak near the chimney, and with every rain, the family was inconvenienced, a fact regularly brought to his attention with the request for repair. The housing codes permitted a person in such a situation to pay for the repairs, deducting the cost from rent, which Mrs. R did.

Dwelling rentals in some public or private housing projects may have certain requirements to be met by the tenant, and the conditions set forth in the leases should be carefully perused. Some leases, for instance, specify minimum items of furniture that the tenant must provide, or stipulate the kind of plantings and care required for areas immediately adjacent to the living unit. A tenant may be disconcerted to discover too late that a commitment has been made for purchases or labor whose costs work a hardship on the lessee.

A common rule of thumb for deciding the proportion of the family's income that should be available for rented shelter suggests that total shelter costs (including utilities) should range from 25 to 35 percent. The larger the income, the greater the expenditure is likely to be for shelter. Economically dependent families, however, more often find themselves faced with the almost impossible task of trying to rent shelter according to an amount specified by the agency for rent. It is not uncommon that these families divert a larger portion of the assistance grant to housing costs, so that the portion for shelter costs consumes 40 to 60 percent of the income from assistance sources.

Homeownership is a goal toward which many families aspire. To them a home connotes security, independence, social status, financial investment and achievement, and freedom. To others a home means only unwanted added responsibilities like putting up storm windows, repairing leaky faucets, and weeding and mowing the lawn.

If the family decides to buy a house, consideration should be given to the following points: homeownership is a commitment to settling down in one place, usually while children grow up, employment is stable, and income is rising until retirement age. Equity in owned housing is a major form of saving; in reality, it is the major form for most American families; for many, it is the only form. If possible, the house should be in a neighborhood that is likely to improve; the improvement serves to increase the value of the property. Effort should be made to select a house that fits the family's current needs and can be adapted to meet future needs. The property should be appraised by a reliable expert prior to purchase, as to the suitability of the purchase price, and to take into account any defects that might require correction and further costs.

The financial obligation assumed should not be larger than can be comfortably handled from current dependable or realistically anticipated income. There is general agreement that the purchase price of a home should not be in excess of two and a half times the annual dependable income. For the person with a potentially higher income, however, it is practical to invest more than this; similarly, the family with large savings or other resources for a down payment or to supplement monthly income for mortgage payments may decide it can afford a larger investment. But the contrary is also true: the family with income not likely to increase, and with heavy expenditures for food, clothing, medical care, or other necessities, may find it desirable to buy a less expensive dwelling.

The real costs of homeownership should be estimated with care. These include down payment, total yearly payments on capital and interest (amortization), taxes, special assessments, water fees and taxes on other utilities where these exist, insurance, upkeep and repairs. If financing is through amortization, it is wise to seek a reducing mortgage

—one that permits making additional payments on principal without penalty, thereby reducing interest costs. The tax benefits extended to homeowners also should be taken into account: deduction of mortgage interest payments and property tax payments, for example. Offsetting the savings components, tax benefits, and investment growth potential are the real costs of tying up savings (if any) and the rate of interest on savings that is not available because the resources are invested in the home.

Many people enjoy gardening, making repairs, and performing other tasks essential to keeping the house and grounds in good condition. Potential homeowners, however, should ask themselves whether they are temperamentally endowed for these tasks. If not, the estimate of the cost of homeownership should be computed on the basis of hiring gardeners, painters, and plumbers. When the house is in a suburban area, additional transportation costs should be estimated.

Two other kinds of homeownership warrant brief mention, for they have become increasingly common. One is the condominium. As with a single-family house, the purchase involves signing a sales contract and arranging a mortgage loan. With the condominium, however, exclusive ownership generally stops with the interior walls, and only sometimes includes exterior areas such as a patio or balcony. Costs of operation, maintenance, and replacement of all shared facilities are the joint responsibility of all the co-owners, for which a periodic fee usually is levied. In addition, the individual owners must adhere to a set of rules over which no individual options may be possible. Some states have enacted legislation to provide certain protections which the prospective buyer should be urged to study before an irrevocable contract is assumed.

The mobile home is the other nontraditional kind of housing. It may be modest or lavish in construction, size, and appointments. It may be truly mobile, readily moved from one location to another, or it may be transportable only with the help of large tow trucks, if at all. Unless intending that the mobile home be stationary, the potential buyer should examine its mobility and safety of construction carefully. Originally, trailers or mobile homes were financed through the use of relatively costly chattel mortgages; now loans may be obtained for them through commercial banks or savings and loan associations. Unless a parking space is owned by the mobile-home buyer, space must be rented. The rents may be low in relation to apartment rents, but when added to monthly mortgage payments, the total monthly cost may be nearly as high as for a conventional house. On the other hand, property taxes on mobile homes tend to be minimal, whether they are included in land rental fees or are paid directly as assessed.

Decisions about renting or buying housing—and the kind—ideally should be derived from assessment of current needs and future desires, the fiscal realities, and social and psychological factors unique to the individual or family. Often, however, such an assessment is a luxury that the family is unable to afford because of housing shortages, inability to find a lessor who will accept children, or inadequate financial resources that constrain the exercise of options. Or there may be unexpected changes in circumstances that alter the needs but limit the possibilities of making more suitable housing arrangements. A divorce, for example, may leave a mother and children in a house she cannot maintain comfortably on her reduced financial resources; but she cannot relinquish it because she cannot afford to move or she thinks that the children should not be "uprooted." Or when a job change or transfer necessitates the family's obtaining shelter without delay in another community, a home may be purchased impulsively in a neighborhood or in a condition or at a price that is quickly regretted. In such circumstances, families may not be able to keep up mortgage payments or may meet them at the expense of other family needs. The consequent stress may be expressed in recriminations and quarrels that appear to threaten family relationships. The counselor should be able to look objectively with such people at the strains imposed on them because of their housing situation, and help them to consider any available housing alternatives—or how best to cope with their present predicament.

CLOTHING

Clothing is generally the third largest family expenditure. Unlike costs for food and shelter, which can be estimated with some degree of accuracy, clothing expenditures tend to be erratic and are much more difficult to fit into a budget plan. The reasons for fluctuations are fairly obvious. Types and styles of clothing worn are socially determined, and the fact that clothing generally must be changed with the seasons compounds the budgeting problem. Because clothing is a relatively flexible item in the family budget, it is usually the first to be curtailed if the family has a downward shift in income.

The basic purpose of clothing, of course, is to provide protection against the elements. However, it has important secondary values. Clothing plays a significant role in the socialization process which leads to the development of self-esteem and healthy identity, and it is not uncommon that parents will forego meeting other needs to assure that children have certain clothing. Similarly, adults may sacrifice in less visible areas in order to have clothing to maintain the kind of appearance that they believe necessary to advance vocationally or socially, or that adds to their sense of well-being and enables them to cope with other, harsher elements in their emotional or physical environment.

For the sixteen-year-old girl who has begun to "date," clothes are a means of furthering her success in her social group. The wrong clothes can create embarrassment for anyone, but young persons are particularly sensitive to the disapproval of their peers. A growing boy hates to wear woolen trousers when other boys wear denims, or whatever else is de rigueur at the moment. Even the young child is not satisfied with a good new outfit if it is offered as a substitute for the uniform of one of his peer-group's current heroes.

Fashions change with relative frequency, and failure, particularly on the part of young people, to conform to the modern mode can result in social ostracism. For a family to keep up with these changing fashions is not easy, particularly when there are family members of different ages. A skilful mother or daughter may make or remodel clothing for the family and reduce costs. Inability to do a workmanlike job, however, can actually add to clothing costs and create unhappiness for the sensitive wearer.

Occupations influence clothing costs. Special kinds of clothing may be required for the manual laborer, the junior executive, the secretary, or the school teacher, as well as for persons who wear uniforms. When the mother is employed outside the home, it is not uncommon for her to require more changes of clothing for children because her working hours do not give her the flexibility to launder and iron their clothing as frequently as they may need them. Additionally, if the family lives in a locality where weather conditions may prevent easy drying of clothes —even precluding getting to a laundromat—an extra supply may have to be on hand, affecting the clothes budget. Poor quality, which cannot always be measured by cost, may require frequent replacement of clothing items. Mistakes in buying, made because of inexperience, also add to the yearly cost.

As income rises, the proportion spent for clothing may or may not rise. Clothing expenditures usually account for 10 to 15 percent of the total family expenditures. Social workers counseling families are frequently confronted with the problem of finding adequate leeway in the income to budget clothing. This problem occurs both with families receiving assistance and with those who are self-supporting; they often resolve the dilemma by buying clothing on an instalment plan. Although instalment buying spreads the costs over a period of time, the plan often works to their disadvantage. Credit purchases generally cost more than cash purchases, and limit the shopping range to charge-account stores.

Instalment buying may also encourage the family to buy clothing on the basis of desire rather than of need. A self-disciplined family, however, may use a charge account constructively for planned purchases if reliable stores are selected.

Careful management is usually necessary if the entire family is to have adequate clothing. A first step is to inventory the amount and condition of clothing on hand. Clothing that can be repaired or remodeled should be checked off. New clothing needed in the next year—or even in the next two or three years—should be listed in order of urgency. The parents should estimate the amount of money available for clothing by the week, month, or other specified period, and should set priorities for purchases.

Before purchases are made, it is advisable to shop for values and prices. Information about quality, workmanship, shrinkage, fastness of color, care, and upkeep should be secured and considered. Requirements imposed on manufacturers to show such information on the labels of clothing are a protection for the thoughtful consumer, and directions on labels should be read and followed carefully. The employed mother or any parent whose time or energy is limited may find it economical to weigh the value of easily cleaned and maintained synthetic fabrics, even if the cost is greater, in order to save labor. Children should be taught to take good care of their clothing. Adolescents should be helped to budget for their own clothes and to make appropriate choices and purchases. This experience is invaluable in preparation for their own adult money management.

TAXES

Every tax affects the consumer and the budget. Taxes may be levied by federal, state, and local jurisdictions. Some apply throughout the United States; others in certain geographical areas.

The federal income tax places earners on a pay-as-you-go basis. This device has reduced the budgeting problem for most families by enabling them to better plan for the use of their disposable or "after-tax" income. The withholding tax plan, however, is an overall collecting device, so that while some people overpay during a calendar year, a great many more underpay. When the annual adjustment is made, many taxpayers who have underpaid are not prepared to meet the additional amount due. Often the realization that more money is due comes as a shock to the family.

Some states and a few cities also require payment of an income tax. The rates and base of calculation vary in different states or localities. The tax is paid either on a particular date or at specified intervals throughout the year, or, like the federal income tax, is on a payroll withholding basis, with the same positive and negative consequences.

Most local units of government—cities or counties—apply a general property tax on real or personal property, or both, to cover costs of government operations and services. They may also levy special assessments on real property, usually to cover the cost of street, school, or other improvements. Although the taxpayer cannot always estimate the precise amount of local taxes that will have to be paid in a given period, a fair approximation can be made. Failure to pay property taxes or assessments can lead to the government acquisition and public sale of the property. All states have provisions, which are not uniform, for redemption of property if certain terms are met by the individual. When the family seeks help from the counselor about questions regarding taxes or redemption of property, legal consultation should be sought.

A sales tax may be imposed by any unit of government, raising the cost of the commodity or utility purchased. Consequently, in computing expenditures for taxable items, a family should include an appropriate amount for the sales tax. Other forms of taxation may allow for reductions on the basis of the payee's age, dependents, veteran status, or certain handicaps (blindness, for example) but no special provisions apply to the payment of sales taxes. In some states, however, sales tax does not apply to groceries. Such taxation is regarded as imposing an unreasonably heavy burden on low-income families and the general purpose of this exemption is income redistribution. But taxes on other consumer items—gasoline, alcoholic beverages, cigarettes—levied by the federal, state, or local government are not subject to exemption.

Nearly everyone, self-employed or working for an employer, also pays Social Security taxes (shared equally with the employer or adjusted upward for the self-employed) to provide some financial and health care protection on retirement because of age or disability, or to supply income to the widowed dependents and children who meet the age qualifications. Counselors working with individuals about to start on a first job should remind them that deductions for withholding and Social Security taxes (and, in a few states, state disability insurance taxes) should be taken into account as they contemplate use of their earnings.

Household Furnishings

Like clothing, household furnishings can be costly or inexpensive. Some of the factors that govern the selection of clothing or the kind of dwelling may operate in furnishing a home. A pretentious or a modest home may reflect not only the family's economic needs and level but also its status aspirations and emotional needs.

The amount of money available determines which items a family can buy at a given time and whether the purchase is a luxury or an economy. For the beginning family, for example, the purchase of an automatic dishwasher may be sheer luxury; for the expanding family, especially if the mother is employed, it may be an economy. The same may be true of other modern equipment. If the homemaker is not working outside the home, it may be more economical to do certain work manually than to depend upon expensive automatic equipment. An important consideration is whether the investment in such equipment releases time and energy that the homemaker should devote to children or to other important activities including self-fulfillment.

Certain equipment, however, is now fairly standard and consequently may be considered a need. Automatic refrigeration, not necessarily with a deep-freeze unit, is essential for economical, safe, and efficient storage of food, particularly if there are children and a relatively heavy consumption of perishable products. Refrigerators and other equipment usually can be purchased more economically on a cash basis than on the instalment plan, but not all families believe (realistically or not) that they really have a choice about using cash or credit for such purchases.

In planning the purchase of household furnishings, the family with limited income should weigh the merits and demerits of procuring used furniture. Required furnishings should be listed in order of both their urgency and the length of time they are to be used. A bassinet, for example, is quickly replaced by a crib. Purchase of a crib with padded guards might eliminate the need for a bassinet. The required items should be related to the amount of income available as well as the intensity and duration of their expected use. Cheaper quality or second-handedness may prove to be uneconomical over time. Combined instalment purchases should not exceed 10 to 12 percent of available dependable income. There is general agreement that the total initial cost of house furnishings should not exceed 30 percent of the cost of the house itself and annual replacements should remain under 3 percent of the general budget.

HOUSEHOLD OPERATION

The operating expenses of a household, as distinguished from maintenance expenses, include the regular payments for such items as electricity, gas, water, telephone, rubbish disposal (if not a tax-paid service), laundry and dry cleaning, household supplies, replacement of small equipment, and wages for service in the home. The cost of household operation usually averages more than 10 percent of the annual budget, depending upon the amount of outside help required. For the beginning family, the proportion is relatively small. It increases steadily with family size and may rise sharply—well above the 10 percent—if child supervision must be provided to free the mother to work outside the home (see "Household services" below). The proportion of the budget devoted to payment for services in the home is likely to decline when the parents are again alone. However, as was indicated in chapter 6, as persons become elderly their expenses for services may increase because of their waning ability to take care of themselves.

In our culture many labor-saving devices and services are considered necessities. As was noted before, the washing machine is a desirable piece of equipment for the family with small children. Sometimes such facilities as a self-service laundry or a diaper service can serve the same purpose at less cost. The cost for the latter service, including the diapers and their laundering, varies with the area. For many mothers, as well as their youngsters, this service has particular value since it helps reduce the tension involved in toilet training. The cost of using self-service laundries should be compared with the cost of purchasing and operating one's own washing machine. All electrical appliances require not only an initial outlay of funds but also payments for operation and repairs. The cost of gas or electricity varies considerably from community to community. Recent developments in the arena of energy conservation indicate that costs for fuel in all forms will continue to mount throughout the nation, becoming a budget item of increasing size and importance, and suggesting new scrutiny of alternatives to home appliances that utilize gas, electricity, coal, or oil products.

Economies may be made in household operation expenditures if families give attention to details. For example, the gas bill may be reduced by having the mixture regulated to give a blue flame or, if a water heater is used, by keeping the electricity or gas turned off except when hot water is needed. The cost of electricity can also be lowered by the use of bulbs of proper size for various purposes, such as low-watt bulbs for halls where bright light is not needed. Cooling food before it is placed in the refrigerator also reduces operating costs. Such economies are not necessarily convenient, but they can be effective in conserving both energy and money in the budget of the family straining to make ends meet.

Standard budgets in social agencies usually include the cost of electricity for lighting, but not always for operating considerable electric equipment. The electrical equipment in a modern household may include refrigerator, freezer, air conditioner(s), vacuum cleaner, iron, toaster, waffle iron, coffee pot, stove, washing and drying machines, radio and television set. There may also be an electric garbage disposal unit, a dishwasher, and even a rubbish compactor. Expenditures for operating such equipment vary greatly; but it is clear that the marginal-income family likely cannot afford to operate such an array of equipment on its limited resources. This problem may especially trouble the family whose breadwinner has unexpectedly lost his job after longtime attachment to a particular employer or industry.

The quantity of fuel required for heating purposes varies with the type of equipment, number and arrangement of rooms, condition of the building, insulation, climate, and season. For many low-income families the purchase of ice must also be planned.

Household supplies, such as soap, scouring powder, and other cleaning agents, also have a place in the budget, as does replenishment of small equipment, such as china, utensils, bedding, and towels.

For many persons, a telephone is a necessity. It may be required for business purposes, for social and family contacts, and for medical or other emergencies. It is a protection for the elderly person, ill or well, who lives alone, and for mothers who are at home alone with small children. A telephone has great psychological significance to the modern adolescent who has a need to be in constant communication with peers. The types of telephone service available should be looked into and the appropriate one selected. Economies in its use, even by adolescents, can be practiced.

TRANSPORTATION

Because of the trend of families' moving to the suburbs, transportation often calls for sizable expenditures. Not many people can live near their work and not all can use public transportation. Even shopping centers and schools frequently are not within walking distance.

An automobile, therefore, is often a real necessity. The operational costs as well as the cost of upkeep must be budgeted. Costs must be calculated not only for fuel but for repairs, replacement of parts, licenses, insurance (generally at very high levels if one or more younger drivers are in the family), parking and garage fees (if any), service, depreciation, and replacement of the automobile itself. When families own two cars, the cost is likely to double except for insurance; many companies offer a reduced rate for coverage of more than one family car. The usual transportation costs to a family with one working member and with one car constitute from 9 to 12 percent of the family's expenditures.

HEALTH AND DENTAL CARE

Costs of illness usually are not predictable, but a family may be unable to allocate sufficient funds in advance to cover even anticipated health care expenses that will not be met through some form of prepaid health insurance. Every budget should make some provision for medical costs. Preventive care can be anticipated. The cost of prenatal and postnatal care, delivery, infant care, and immunization can be planned in advance. A high proportion of families have at least some hospital and medical care insurance coverage, purchased directly by them or as part of employment fringe benefits for which payment may be made by the employer, employee, or both. For families whose income is linked to public assistance, there is likely to be the resource of Medicaid, and for the older person or one disabled in the context of the federal social insurances, there is Medicare. The budget counselor should be alert to the likelihood that the family with health insurance of some kind, including Medicare or Medicaid, probably still has to pay for some portion or some kinds of medical care not covered by the insurance plan. Elderly people, for example, must pay a monthly fee (usually on a quarterly basis) for the medical care phase of Medicare (the hospital provisions were paid for in their Social Security payroll deductions); there is an initial amount each year they must pay before Medicare payments begin, and the latter do not pay full cost of care even then, nor do they cover prescriptions—a considerable drain on the incomes of most elderly persons on fixed low incomes. Similar limitations exist in most other health plans, too. The consequence is that it is the rare and ever-healthy family that is not faced with expenditures for health care. It behooves the counselor to be alert to such unavoidable expenditures rather than assuming that the existence of a health plan precludes outlay on the family's part.

As Chapter 2 noted, families of comparable size tend to spend similar dollar amounts for health care, but the proportions of these expenditures in relation to family income vary decidedly, from 10 percent in the lowest standard to just above 5 percent in the highest of the three standards. In actuality, families ordinarily have to allocate about 10 percent of their expenditures to payment for health insurance and health care, including dental and eye care, which rarely are included in health plan coverage but are of particular importance to the growing child and the aging person. The experiences of an expanding family and of an elderly couple may, in fact, suggest that even more than 10 percent needs to be allocated for health care. Because many elderly are not insurable, they may have to depend on savings to meet the cost differences between the sums covered by existing government plans and the actual bill for hospital and health services.

HOUSEHOLD SERVICES

All families at some time need to pay for services related to the maintenance and operation of the household. In families where the mother works outside the home, a regular budget item for such services may have to be included, possibly for special child care services, such as nursery school or foster day care, or for domestic services. In all families with young children, some service within the home may be needed. The employment of baby-sitters enables the parents to pursue adult interests and to have some recreation. Full- or part-time domestic help may be required by some families because of a parent's ill-health, or simply because they can afford some relief from household tasks. Some families find it expedient and financially manageable to employ a household cleaning service on an occasional or periodic basis to eliminate the heaviest cleaning chores. This enables the family—especially an elderly couple with physical limitations—to keep abreast of the other household tasks without undue taxing of their time, energies, or patience. For some this can also be advantageous financially because it may be possible to save the Social Security tax that the employer of household help must pay quarterly for each person earning at least $50 in a given household during that period.

Other household services might also be needed. If the family members are unable or unwilling to do necessary work on the grounds, a gardener's service may be engaged on occasion. In budget counseling these services should be considered and the budget item computed in relation to prevailing costs.

OTHER FAMILY COSTS

A term still found commonly in budgets developed by home economists is "advancement." This catch-all (a step removed from the "miscellany" category) usually is applied to many items of a social and cultural nature and therefore could represent large or small expenditures. Except for life insurance premiums, which generally vary relatively little for long periods of time, the items in this group are diverse in kind as well as in costs. Educational expenses, for example, may be high for the expanding family in certain years, but are likely to be reduced in the contracting phase of the life cycle along with such other expenses as for reading matter, recreation, contributions to church and community organizations, and gifts to children and grandchildren. Yet educational expenses may be elevated because the wife, freed from child and family care responsibilities, may elect to complete interrupted education; and other costs may rise sporadically because of the nature of the recreation (a long trip, for example). Gifts, contributions, recreation, newspapers—these may vacillate repeatedly from high or low from the outset of the family life cycle to its close. And personal needs (haircuts, hairdressers, other supplies and services) change from time to time.

If the income is limited, some of these items are simply crowded out of the budget (or, as in education, outside resources may be utilized), or they are paid for by "bootlegging," or by foregoing something covered in another area of designated expenditure. Family expenditures for this comprehensive group of items may range at any time from 3 to 12 percent of the family income.

SAVINGS AND INVESTMENTS

Samuel Johnson's comment that "A man who both spends and saves money is the happiest man, because he has both enjoyments"[8] captures the dilemma in which men and women find themselves in today's money world. Observance of the virtue of thrift—that persistent measure of an individual's adequacy and independence—is evidenced by saving and serves to reduce anxiety about economic security in the future. But the spending signifies to the observer that one has successfully acquired the means for spending, thereby enhancing the image of adequacy and independence. Some persons believe that everyone should follow a savings plan, and for many this conviction is actually an obsession. Others believe that thrift is an old-fashioned custom, that money is for present use. Their belief may stem from their idea that it is best to "live a day at a time" or—perhaps, and—that government will step in to meet future needs that the individual personally will not be able to supply. The attitude that prevails in a given individual or family derives, of course, from a lifetime of developmental and environmental experiences combined.

The key to deciding whether to save and, if so, how much, lies in the realistic purposes to which the savings would be put. As was discussed earlier, there are many neurotic reasons for saving, and many neurotic ways in which savings are used. Aside from the long-term goal that an individual or couple may have for accumulating an estate for their children or other legatees, there are some practical reasons for saving that every family needs to bear in mind. These reasons are predicated on the understanding that the central purpose of saving is to accumulate reserves to be spent for specific items or objectives, including emergencies that may arise. This reasoning also assumes that the amount available for savings is the balance of income after all payments have been made for meeting present needs, that this balance will differ with age and earnings of the family members and with their changing needs and aspirations, and that different people have different capacity and motivation for the planning and self-discipline ordinarily necessary for saving.

A major reason for saving is to build a protection against the difficulty in meeting survival needs from continuing or reduced recurring income—to provide for costs of illness or accident, or of daily needs in a period of unemployment or during retirement. To be sure, in any of these situations, income may be or is available from prepaid commercial or social insurances, but such coverages rarely meet full costs of care or of daily life, especially over a sustained period of time. The need for such savings protection may center not so much on the average individual or that person's immediate family as on elderly parents or other dependent persons.

Another major reason for saving, especially in the beginning and expanding stages of the family life cycle, is for education—one's own or the children's. The kind and cost of education will vary with the family and person to be educated determining the amount to be put aside. If education beyond the high school level is expected, advance planning is required to assure some financial support even when financial aid might be procured from an educational institution or a government program.

A third reason for saving is to facilitate a purchase to satisfy needs or desires at the least ultimate cost—to permit making a larger down payment on the item to be purchased, or to eliminate the use of credit with high-interest carrying charges. And the fourth reason is simply to be prepared for the unexpected, whatever it may be. Unanticipated expenses can often be met by the use of credit, but there are many times when time and urgency demand immediate access to cash.

Earlier chapters commented on the patterns of saving in our society. Just about everyone who works does some involuntary saving through the taxing mechanisms for social insurances that will yield a deferred wage when its need arises. The heaviest savers are the middle-age groups, at peak income and without dependent children. The dissavers are the young people, whose earnings or other income do not keep pace with needs; and the older persons who draw on savings to supplement the OASDHI and other possible pension and dividend incomes that may barely support them.

For families with incomes under $10,000 per year, the savings goal may be as high as 10 percent of annual income, but 3 to 5 percent is perhaps more usual and realistic. The savings may take many forms: cash in a bank or other savings institution, life insurance, equity in a home or other real estate, stocks and bonds, or, sometimes, credit—that is, making payments on items, such as a car, in which equity is being accumulated.

Whatever the form of savings, a reasonable early goal for every family should be a fund equivalent to a year's income; for many families it should be larger. In times of recession, it may take this long for a family to become reestablished after a job loss or change, and unemployment benefits have been exhausted. But for ordinary purposes, most families can manage to meet emergencies or to keep to a minimum the costs of using credit if a sum equivalent to at least six months' normal income has been saved.

NOTES

1. See, for example, D. Davies, *The Case of Laborers in Husbandry* (Bath, 1795); Sir Frederick Morton Eden, *The State of the Poor* (London: n.p., 1797); and Ralph and Muriel Pumphrey, eds., *The Heritage of American Social Work* (New York: Columbia University Press, 1961).
2. Group for the Advancement of Psychiatry, *The Welfare System and Mental Health*, vol. 8, Committee on Psychiatry Report no. 85 (New York: Group for the Advancement of Psychiatry, 1973), pp. 348–49.
3. U.S., Department of Agriculture, *Family Economics Review*, Summer 1974 (Washington, D.C.: Consumer and Food Economics Institute, Agricultural Research Service), pp. 10–13.
4. Ibid.
5. S. G. Barton, "The Life Cycle and Consumer Behavior," *Consumer Behavior*, vol. 2 (New York: New York University Press, 1955), p. 54.
6. Ibid., p. 56.
7. From Benjamin Disraeli's speech at the opening of Shaftesbury Park Estate, July 18, 1874. Quoted in anonymously edited *Wit and Wisdom of Benjamin Disraeli: Earl of Beaconsfield*, new ed. (London: Longmans, Green and Co., 1886), p. 48.
8. Quoted in James Boswell's *Life of Samuel Johnson*, April 25, 1778 (New York: New American Library, 1963).

12
Family Resources

The term "family resources" usually suggests earnings, real estate, stocks, bonds, or money in the bank. In a money world, these material resources are certainly important. But just as vital are the nonmaterial resources—the human strengths—that can be utilized to make life satisfying. The aggregate of these tangible and intangible resources represents the family's total assets. Its liabilities are its monetary problems and its human frailties. The financial counselor should study both sides of the ledger and endeavor to understand the relation of the assets to the liabilities. The knowledge and skill brought to this counseling task can help the family obtain the maximum value from its assets. Effort should be directed not only toward using the available economic and environmental human resources constructively, but, insofar as possible, toward converting liabilities into assets. This goal is generally facilitated by concentrating especially on the strengths, exploiting them as a foundation for building enough new strengths for mastery of the problem, and by remaining alert to weaknesses that might require some intervention to prevent their obstructing progress.

TANGIBLE RESOURCES

The problems for which counseling is sought may have their origin in external or internal factors, or both. The counselor should have certain basic information about the family's tangible resources in order to evaluate the nature and extent of the economic problem and to develop an effective plan for its correction.

The family's financial resources consist of its earnings, together with its reserve funds and its capital assets. Reserve funds and capital assets should be built up as soon as possible so that they can serve the family during times of peak expense, such as when children are born or when they enter college. These funds and assets may be in various forms: family home, other real estate, investment securities (stocks, bonds), cash value of insurance, household capital goods (equipment, furnishings, furniture), automobile, investment in business or business equipment, savings, and pension plans. Some of these tangible resources will be addressed here in the context of their function as resources to be utilized or protected by the family, to guide the counselor in the necessary assessment of the family's various financial assets and their current and potential value, both economic and psychological. If some assets must be liquidated, consideration should be given to the need in each individual family for a particular asset, the cost of replacing it, and the relative merits of liquidating it or using it as security for a loan.

Many alternatives are available to families when they need additional funds. The family home may serve as collateral for a mortgage loan. If a first mortgage exists, a second can sometimes be obtained. Under certain conditions, automobiles, home furnishings, appliances, business equipment, stocks, bonds, and insurance may serve as collateral for loans from banks and consumer finance companies.

Because of the volume of inquiries they receive about the value and use of various assets, some social agencies employ specialists who offer consultation to the social worker or advise the client directly. Sometimes an agency may arrange for such consultation with bankers, realtors, or attorneys who are members of a committee or of the board, or who are on a panel from which the agency draws expert consultation; on other occasions, the family may need to be referred to a legal aid society or other organization for the indicated expertise.

Earnings

Some of the factors that affect earnings have been mentioned previously. It has been noted that while in our society the earnings of the male head of the family constitute the major source of family income, in a substantial proportion of families it is the wife or mother who is the primary (perhaps only) breadwinner. Earnings generally are received on a periodic basis, and the earner knows in advance the amount of the gross income and intervals of payment. Because deductions for income tax, Social Security, and other mandatory (disability taxes, for example), and voluntary (union dues, group health insurance) items are fixed, the earner generally knows the amount of the net, or take-home pay—at least after receipt of the first paycheck. Some persons are engaged in seasonal occupations and may know what they will earn for certain months, but not for the balance of the year. Salespeople may earn only commissions, or commissions plus base pay. The amounts of these commissions vary from month to month, but an annual review will indicate the pattern—the peaks and valleys—of such earnings. In a household with both parents, the earnings of the wife or other employed family members should also be computed as part of the family income even though the earnings may not be regular or the primary source of the family's income. The sum of the earnings (not counting earnings an adolescent or other child may not put into the family pot) may be used entirely or in part for meeting current obligations, or it may constitute a resource for meeting future needs and desires. All earnings are a resource not only because they can be used to defray current and future expenses but because they serve as evidence that the earner is a good credit risk.

Failure of the earner to meet certain financial obligations may result in legal proceedings such as attachment, garnishment, or assignment of wages. *Attachment* is a proceeding auxiliary to a legal action designed to secure the property of a debtor to answer a judgment that may be obtained by the creditor. *Garnishment* is a legal procedure by which a creditor seeks to secure payment of a debt by means of applying to the debt the property, wages, money, or credits of a debtor which are in the possession of another. Garnishment means "warning" and the person in whose hands the effects are attached is the garnishee because of having been garnisheed or warned not to pay the money or deliver the property to the debtor. The purposes and function of attachment or garnishment are twofold: it seizes property of an alleged debtor in advance of final judgment and holds it subject to appropriation in satisfaction of such judgment, if finally obtained, thereby preventing the loss or dissipation of the property by fraud or otherwise. State statutes are the basis of attachment and garnishment; they provide for certain exceptions.

Assignment of wages is an agreement by the wage earner, frequently included in instalment or conditional sales contracts, to permit demand upon the employer to divert a part of the debtor's wages to defray the financial obligations of the contract. Statutes in many states place limitations on wage assignments and provide the bases for such actions. The creditor, executing a simple document, may apply directly to the debtor's employer for periodic payments.

Since 1970, the Federal Truth-in-Lending Act has limited to 75 percent the wages that may be garnisheed, and has prohibited garnishment out of a weekly paycheck of $48 or less, after deductions. (States that permit a relatively high percentage of wages to be garnisheed tend to have more bankruptcies because debtors declare bankruptcy to cancel the debts that impelled garnishment or to prevent garnishment.) The exemption statutes of most states are designed to protect the welfare of the debtor and the debtor's family and to enable the earner to remain employed. In most jurisdictions the exemption statutes exclude from attachment or garnishment some wages, work tools, insurance benefits, and so forth. When legal proceedings have been directed against an agency client because of indebtedness, the social worker should refer the person for legal counsel. If legal proceedings have not yet been instituted, but the creditor has brought to the employee's or employer's or even, on a rare occasion, the counselor's attention that this action is contemplated, an alternative to legal counsel may be the local consumer credit counseling agency, if one exists in the community.

Employers often frown on requests for wage garnishments, tending both to object to the bother and cost attached to compliance with the request, and to regard the offending worker as a poor manager of his or her own affairs and, therefore, a poor worker. Some companies dismiss such an employee on the first occasion; the policies of others allow for two or even three garnishments before the employee becomes subject to dismissal. In times when there is a scarcity of skills that the indebted employee possesses, the dismissal policy tends to be waived, in contrast to times of recession when even the highly skilled employee can be replaced by someone more stable.

SMALL BUSINESSES
The source of a family's income may be a business operated by the husband, or by the wife, or by both. Income may be regular and predictable, uncertain, or seasonal. The family sometimes draws a stipulated weekly or monthly amount from the business and turns the balance back into the business. Even a relatively unprofitable business may represent a resource in equipment, merchandise, skills, or goodwill, and in self-employed Social Security taxes that constitute an investment and a protection for the family when they are faced with one of the common hazards of loss of earnings because of retirement, disability, or death. The 1974 Federal Pension Reform Act not only may be the channel for building at least some pension from even modest business earnings, but also for qualifying those in the business for certain income tax deferments that may provide a considerable saving in the years when the family may find it harder to draw enough from its income to pay these taxes.

The failure of a person to realize a profit from a business may indicate poor business management, inappropriateness of the business for that individual, a poor location, or a poor investment. Sometimes a business with good potential is not fully developed. Or a normal balance of debts and assets may exist but the businessperson may have undue anxiety. In recent years, especially since there has been great emphasis on helping economically disadvantaged individuals (and particularly members of ethnic minority groups) to realize their aspirations and potentials through self-employment, a number of organizations, both government- and privately-sponsored, have emerged to provide counseling or more tangible help in making the undertaking successful. If there is no such channel in the community or in the agency itself for providing expert counseling to the troubled small-businessperson the social worker may find it advisable to arrange for consultation with a member of the agency's board or, in some instances, with a legal counselor.

SAVINGS

A family may place its reserves in banks, savings and loan associations, credit unions, government savings bonds, or mutual savings accounts. Or they may be stored in the proverbial sugar bowl or piggy bank or under the mattress. The reserves placed in the first group of facilities are regarded as "savings" rather than investments because of their safety features. The sugar bowl, piggy bank, and mattress are not safe devices because of their vulnerability to access and easy dissipation. The first two can be useful when confined to accumulating small sums for short-term objectives, including later placement in a savings or other account, or a learn-how-to-save goal. The mattress system is more likely to suggest hoarding, secretiveness, or other neurotic and distrusting behavior. But none of these informal arrangements, though liquid (that is, readily accessible for immediate use—if not impeded by a psychological barrier), produces any earnings. Making the money work to produce additional income while in the safety of the financial institution or arrangement is an important feature of the first group of savings methods.

Savings may be either temporary or permanent. Temporary savings are designed to achieve a fairly immediate goal, such as purchasing a household appliance or planning for an impending vacation. Permanent savings are set aside for future security and financial protection. The funds are easily available and are usually the first resource used by the family to meet an emergency. The money can be either withdrawn directly or pledged for a loan. The withdrawal of savings however is usually less expensive than contracting for a loan, for the interest on a savings account or bonds generally is less than interest charged on loans. Under some circumstances, however, a loan may be preferable to withdrawing savings. The time the money is needed should be considered in relation to the time of interest payments. For example, if interest is credited quarterly or semiannually, the entire interest on the savings may be lost for that period if the savings are withdrawn before the last day of the interest period. Also, some savings plans preclude withdrawal of funds until after a designated period has elapsed.

The *checking account* is a common, safe, and convenient tool for accumulating small or large sums from which bills can be quickly paid, about which accurate records can be maintained (at least by the banking facility), and that can be withdrawn for investment elsewhere when the size of the account suggests the wisdom of so doing. The kind of checking account selected for use should be related to the individual family's financial patterns and needs. Some regular checking accounts have minimum balance requirements, various service or activity fee charges, and may impose fees for checks and deposits. Some banks charge a flat monthly service charge for which a designated number of transactions may be made with no additional cost. Others require a monthly maintenance charge and a fee for each check paid and each one deposited. Often, depending on the average balance maintained in the accounts there may be a minimum activity charge for the month.

Charges vary from bank to bank, one kind of checking account to another, and from city to city. If only a few checks are written each month, a *special checking account* is usually cheaper; if ten or more are regularly written each month, a *regular checking account* may be more economical. To arrive at a decision as to the most suitable and economical checking-account arrangement for an individual or family to have requires not only knowing the average number of checks that might be written each month, but how much money is likely to be kept in the account over and above that needed to cover the checks to be written. Some people, by design or because the size of their income gives them no option, have only enough in the checking account to cover the checks issued. Others feel more secure, and have the financial resources, maintaining a margin of several hundred dollars or more in the event unforeseen expenses arise.

The checking account system selected and the cash balance maintained in it should be reviewed by the depositor to decide if the charges for serving and maintaining it as well as interest not paid by the banking institution on the unused balance constitute an effective loss in family income. Competition among banking institutions and consumer demands has lately led to the development (where banking regulations permit) of "free" checking accounts that are actually "checkable" savings accounts paying depositors interest on the unused balances in the checking accounts. Shopping for a checking account should be a careful process. Guidelines to take into account are periodically updated and reported in various consumer publications issued commercially and under government auspices.

There are several kinds of savings institutions in which the customer's money is protected and interest is paid to the customer from the earnings received by the institution through investment of a portion of the customer's funds: commercial banks, mutual savings banks (mainly to be found in the Northeast), and savings and loan associations (also now commonly known as "thrifts" and formerly as "building and loan associations"). Until recently only the commercial banks offered checking accounts; and savings and loan organizations paid higher interest to investors. (The government allowed this to encourage people to save in such organizations as a reward to these institutions for financing home purchases.) Now these differences are blending—savings and loan associations often provide checking accounts, and commercial banks no longer disdain home loans. As a consequence, when a family is contemplating opening a *savings account* in a bank, the major differences and similarities of the several bank arrangements should be examined in the light of the financial needs and practices of the particular family.

Passbook savings accounts (cash or its equivalent is exchanged for an entry in a passbook at a bank or savings institution) provide maximum liquidity, meaning that the money is readily available and can be drawn out at any time. Because of this greater liquidity, regular savings accounts pay the lowest rate of interest among the different types of savings deposits. A statutory provision authorizes institutions to require up to 60 days' notice before funds are withdrawn, but this provision is not often invoked. *Time deposits,* however—also known as certificates of deposit, savings certificates, and investment certificates, or high-interest passbooks—must be left in the institution for a specified period. The longer the time period, the higher the interest rate. A penalty is imposed in accordance with federal statute if the funds are withdrawn before the period specified: the interest rate is reduced to that paid on regular passbook savings accounts. Both the latter and the time deposits are protected by federal insurance purchased (with rare exceptions) by the banking facility, covering each individual account up to $40,000.

The maximum interest rates the different banking facilities are allowed to pay on various kinds of savings deposits are set by federal or state authorities, or both. Individual savings institutions, however, may calculate differently the interest on the accounts, and the potential saver who wishes the greatest possible return should plan to shop around for the most favorable method in use and accessible. There are three main variables: the interest rate; the frequency of computing and compounding interest; and the bookkeeping method. The interest rate is stated as a per annum rate (such as 5 percent per annum). Interest may be computed quarterly or semiannually, or as is becoming more common, monthly, daily, and even "continuously." An appropriate fraction of the per annum rate is used (1.25 percent quarter or 2.5 percent semi-annually, if the per annum rate is 5 percent). The shorter the time span for computation of the interest, the earlier the interest itself begins earning interest. The bookkeeping method determines what portion of the funds in the savings account is eligible to earn interest. There are five basic bookkeeping methods. The depositor should learn which is used in a particular institution, for it will make a difference as to withdrawal or deposit times if interest is paid on funds in the account for the entire interest period; or on the number of whole months the money is in the account and whether withdrawals are deducted from money in the account at the beginning or end of the interest period; or on whatever funds are in the account on the day of withdrawal. Many institutions advertise their interest rate and the frequency with which they compute and compound interest, but they do not advertise their bookkeeping method.

Credit unions are nonprofit saving-and-borrowing organizations, owned and operated by their depositors, who generally have a common tie, such as a professional association or other formal or informal organization, or an employer with 500 or more employees. An individual joins by purchasing one or more "shares," usually $5 each. The earnings of this cooperative organization are divided among its shareholders on a share-for-share basis. About two-thirds of the credit unions are federally insured for up to $40,000 per account, and some other credit union accounts are protected by state insurance. Federal law sets the limit on both the interest that may be paid to depositors and the interest that may be paid by borrowers. Some credit unions pay no interest at all. Some provide life insurance to their members equivalent to a specified maximum amount of deposit (usually $2,000) before a specified age (usually fifty-five years, with a decreasing fraction deposited thereafter on the basis of age, until the maximum base is reached).

United States savings bonds (not to be confused with other Treasury bonds) are a good savings resource for many families. The Series E and Series H bonds both yield 6 percent. However, the interest on the former accrues as semiannual increases in the redemption value over five years. These appreciation bonds can be sold back at successively higher prices, but the full value can be realized only if the bond is held to maturity. One advantage is that this bond comes in small denominations ($18.75 will buy a $25 bond), and is in easier reach of most families than the current-income Series H bond. These bonds cost $1,000; interest is paid each six months over a 10-year period. There is a wide spread belief that the interest rates are extremely low, considering the time period required for obtaining full interest income.[1] However, for the insecure individual —especially older persons or uneasy widows with children—this form of saving has a psychological benefit that compensates for the differences in earnings ratio.

The counselor should be cognizant of the psychological meaning that savings per se have for the individual, as well as of the individual's feeling of trust in the institution where the savings may be deposited. The elderly person, for example, may be fearful of drawing upon savings because there is little likelihood that the funds can be replaced. At the same time, if this individual recalls vividly personal or others' experiences with bank failures there may be a reluctance to deposit savings with a banking facility. Such a person may seek irrational and expensive ways of keeping the savings intact. Similarly, people sometimes ask an agency for help in an emergency, such as illness requiring a temporary homemaker, and are reluctant to use their savings to defray all or part of the cost. Their savings are set aside for a "rainy day"—but somehow this is never that day! It is incumbent on the counselor to be sensitive to feelings about the meaning of savings and their locus, and to be able to refer the individual to sources that will facilitate the person's coming to a soundly based decision as to the arrangement that will meet his or her realistic needs for protected and liquid savings without threatening the personal feelings about how and where the reserves will be maintained.

SECURITIES AND INVESTMENTS

Government securities is a broad category of savings outlet into which families often put unspent funds with the expectation that a reasonably good rate of return will be received for this investment. Particularly in periods like the mid-seventies, when the stock market's fluctuations were frequently attributed to recession or concurrent inflation or both, persons who in other times might have risked investing in stocks turned instead to the purchase of Treasury notes and other government securities. Such notes, bills, and bonds, regularly sold by the government to raise cash, hold considerable appeal because their safety is backed by the "full faith and credit" of the federal government, their relatively high rate of return, and their exemption from state and local income taxes. Currently the minimum purchase requirement for Treasury bills is $10,000. They are sold on a "discount" basis, which means that they are sold at less than face value and redeemed at face value on their maturity dates, which vary from three to twelve months. Treasury notes mature in one to seven years; and bonds mature in seven or more years. Both pay interest semiannually, and the purchase denominations for these range from $1,000 to $10,000. The family with such government securities and in need of cash should be alert to the possibility of losing money if the securities are sold before they mature. Other types of securities, issued by many governmental units at federal, state, or local levels should also be appraised in relation to the risk of loss if the individual or family is in unexpected need of substantial sums of cash.

During the past several decades, many families with modest or moderate incomes have invested in *common stocks*. The reasons vary: a hope of realizing earnings higher than those in conventional savings accounts; a response to "tips" from friends or to promotional activities of brokerage firms; or sheer risk-taking on which the gambler thrives (psychologically only, perhaps). Many of these families already have accumulated funds in a savings institution, or as equity in their home and its furnishings, or in insurance protection. They may already have a modicum of financial security and can afford to risk investing in stocks. Ordinarily it is expected that prospective investors in stocks and securities, in addition to their regular and dependable source of income, have more assets than debts and liabilities; have some of their funds in the form of cash or its equivalent; and have few if any pending financial obligations that might necessitate selling off holdings to an unfavorable market.

Clearly, the less a family has to invest, the less risk they can afford. The stocks and bonds that are listed on the regulated exchanges are liquid in that they may be converted into cash at any time. Yet, fluctuations in the selling price may mean selling the stocks or bonds at a loss at the time the owner's need for cash is urgent.

If a family owns stocks and bonds and contemplates selling these as a way of meeting a financial problem, a reputable specialist in this field should be consulted in order to help make a decision. Whether they should be utilized as a resource depends on the nature of the securities, the interest and dividends they realize, and their potential future value. A weighing of these factors may lead to the alternative plan of arranging a loan, using these stocks and bonds as security.

COMMMERCIAL LIFE INSURANCE

Although statistics disclose that most people in our society survive the perils of childhood and early and middle adulthood, and live long enough to reach the retirement years, the risk of death by illness or accident exists, and the financial impact of death on dependent survivors can be disastrous. To be sure, some of the edge of such financial impact is dulled by the availability of the social insurances delineated in the Social Security Act (see below); but these are not likely to be much more than minimal. Consequently, the purchase of life insurance represents a major way in which American families endeavor to cope with the financial needs that arise on death of a family member. If the breadwinner—father or mother—dies, life insurance may be the resource for meeting final expenses (medical care, funeral arrangements, settlement of an estate); for providing money to live on while the family readjusts itself to the new conditions with the breadwinner gone; for providing family income while the children are growing up; and for assuring an income for the surviving parent after the children have left home.

If the mother dies, whether or not she worked outside the home, the proceeds from life insurance additionally may be needed to purchase housekeeping services for the family as long as the children require such care—services the mother had provided directly or had purchased with her earnings. The financial drain associated with the death of another family member—a child, for example—may be met in part or entirely from insurance.

Life insurance may be purchased directly by an individual or family. It may be provided by an employer as part of an employee fringe benefit package (or through union membership). It may be part of an employer-employee joint payment program. It may be purchased through a group plan available in the place of employment or through an organization to which a member of the family belongs. The purchase arrangements, the kinds of insurance plans available, and the kinds of companies that sell insurance plans comprise a subject that is too complex to be considered here in great detail. Much helpful information for counselors is to be found in the materials published by the Institute of Life Insurance. A few specific points about life insurance as a family resource, however, merit consideration here.

Irrespective of the cultural, emotional, and economic meaning of insurance to particular persons and families, the primary purpose of life insurance is to provide protection against financial hardship caused by death. Some forms of life insurance also provide a means of saving as an incidental feature. Some are a resource for borrowing against invested funds at a comparatively low rate of interest; but the family purpose in buying life insurance rarely is to have it serve as a resource of this kind.

The insurance needs of families vary because of differences in responsibilities, income goals, and standards. They also vary over time and the cycle of family life: income protection takes on additional dimensions with each member added to the family; it alters with the departure of children from the household and as the life expectancy of the parents grows shorter. Hence there is value to the family in reexamination of its insurance program whenever any important change occurs in the family's composition or lifestyle. The decision that the mother will enter the work force, for example, is a factor that bears on the overall insurance picture of the family.

In addition to the purposes already noted, these are among the factors to be considered in the purchase of insurance when the father is the primary breadwinner: How many children in the family? (This consideration should take into account not just children from the present marriage, but any from a prior marriage for whom he has some financial responsibility.) What are their ages? How long are they likely to be wholly dependent? How old is the breadwinner? Are his earnings stabilized? Will they continue to rise, have they peaked, will they decrease? What financial resources are available to the family—in savings, property, investments? How much cash will the survivors need to have readily available to manage until the estate is settled? to pay any taxes that are likely to be imposed on the estate? What Social Security or private pension payments or job-connected fringe benefits will accrue to the survivors? What amount of supplemental income will be required to enable the family to maintain its customary standard of living when the earnings no longer are forthcoming?

The questions to be considered when the mother is the primary or a secondary breadwinner are similar—with the even more crucial question of the kind and cost of child care that may have to be met after the mother's death. The survivors of the wife who is working are likely to have to replace not only her income but also find funds to pay for the household services she performed or paid someone else to perform.

The single woman, on the other hand, like the single man, must look to replacement of her own income in the event of disability or retirement. If there are no dependents, the single person may not wish to buy insurance. Yet the situation could change in several respects. The parents of the single person may become the latter's dependents and need some financial protection in the event of the adult child's death. The single person may marry or have children as a single parent. Or the health of the individual may change, precluding later purchase of insurance when there are dependents.

If an individual or a family is contemplating using equity in life insurance as a resource, an analysis of the insurance holdings and the individual's or family's current and future needs for this protection is essential. Sometimes a reduction in amount of coverage or a conversion from one type to another can serve to release sufficient cash to meet a current need and still leave adequate insurance coverage in force. The counselor whose own agency does not employ an insurance consultant or have such a service available among its volunteers may obtain an analysis and advice about possible adjustment from the insurance company, or may consult the Institute of Life Insurance.

The life insurance plans of private insurers possess distinctive features and include "ordinary" life insurance, group life insurance, industrial insurance, credit life, or mortgage life insurance. From a functional viewpoint there are only three kinds of life insurance: term, whole-life, and endowments. Everything else is a modification of one or a combination of more than one of these forms.

Term insurance provides protection only for as long as the premium is paid. The lowest-cost plan when premium alone is considered, term insurance offers the same basic protection as any other policy—namely, a predetermined sum for the beneficiary of the insured person who dies while the contract is in force. But the insurance is in force only for a limited period: it may be for one year or five or ten years—to meet temporary rather than lifetime needs. The premiums for such policies generally go up every year over every five years, reflecting the rising probability of death as age advances. Rarely does a term policy pay dividends. It provides maximum protection at minimum cost. It costs a young parent comparatively little to buy term insurance. As the children grow older, the cost increases in direct relationship to the insured's increasing age. By that time, however, children generally are well along the way to economic independence and the parent can begin to reduce the premium costs by reducing the amount of insurance carried to protect the family.

A term policy is "renewable" if the coverage can be continued at the end of each period simply by paying the increased premium, without a need for a new medical examination. Many of these policies provide for renewal without further examination until the insured reaches the age of sixty-five or seventy. Needless to say, with advancing years, it becomes increasingly important that changes in health not affect insurability of the policy holder. A term policy is "convertible" if it can be converted into a whole life policy without a new medical examination.

Whole-life insurance, which is *"ordinary-life"* or "straight-life," carries the level-premium concept of term insurance (level for each new or renewed period) a step further: the policy holder pays more than is necessary to cover the insurance company's risk in the early years and less than would be necessary to cover the company's risk in the later years. This higher cost in the early years creates a special reserve fund, the cash value, which is somewhat similar to a savings account. An outstanding feature of whole-life is its permanence: the coverage can be kept in force for a lifetime without any increase in premiums. The second outstanding characteristic is its flexibility. The cash value can be used as security for a loan or converted into a smaller amount of insurance that will stay in force for life without any further payment in premiums. At the time of retirement, the cash value can be taken either as a lump sum or in instalments.

There are several variations of whole-life insurance, including *straight-life and limited-payment-life.* The latter differs from the former because, although protection is for life, premium payments are compressed into a shorter period—usually twenty or thirty years or until a specified age, like sixty-five, is reached. The earlier buildup of reserves calls for a higher premium, which also results in more rapid accumulation of cash reserves.

The *endowment plan* is really a savings plan, with a term protection feature. Premiums are thus higher than is true in either of the life plans. Premiums are paid for a stated number of years and the face value of the policy is payable to the insured at the end of this period. If the insured were to place annually in a savings account the same amount as the premiums, a higher rate of interest could be obtained and more funds would be accumulated over the time the policy would have matured. But the protection received through the insurance would not have been available; moreover, it takes a fairly high degree of self-discipline in tandem with sufficient income for an individual to maintain this routine without the presence of the compelling obligation to and reminders from an external source.

Endowment policies enable the insured to accumulate a given sum of money by a given age. If the policy "matures," the insured is paid; if the insured person dies before the policy matures, the beneficiary collects in full. In effect, this is a savings plan with a decreasing-term insurance component. The amount of the coverage is calculated so that the amount of the term coverage combined with the accumulated savings always equals the face amount of the policy. The premiums are the highest of any type of policy and generally therefore are not regarded as advisable for the family whose basic family protection requirements have not been met. There are several kinds of endowment policies, including *straight endowment* (usually featuring a fixed payment period of ten to thirty years to meet such special goals as college funds or a daughter's wedding expenses) and *retirement-income endowment* (which can be taken in a lump sum at a specified age, or in stipulated monthly payments for life with a minimum number of years of payments guaranteed).

Family-protection policies, special combination plans, have been developed in recent years to meet the needs of the head of a family with minor children and to accommodate to some extent to the fact that needs for protection alter as the family moves through the cycle of family life. The *family-income policy* combines a decreasing-term component, which runs for ten or fifteen or twenty years from date of purchase, with a straight-life policy. A $10,000 policy would provide the family with an income of $100 a month on the death of the insured family head for the balance of the protection period in addition to a lump sum of $10,000 from the permanent portion of the policy (or, optionally, this can be used to provide income). If the insured outlives the period protected by the term insurance, a life policy for $10,000 remains, probably with a reduced premium. The *family plan policy* also combines straight-life and term insurance on the family head, but typically includes $5,000 of whole-life on the breadwinner (generally the father), term coverage of $1,000 or so to age sixty-five on the mother, and a similar amount on each dependent child, including those born after the insurance policy was written. The cost is not much more than the parents would pay for similar protection individually.

Other special insurance plans are worth noting here. One is based on the idea that a young wage earner needs a lower premium rate for the first three to ten years, then the rates become somewhat higher, but the amount of the whole-life policy thus being purchased remains the same throughout life. This is a *modified* or *grade-premium policy.* The other is a *guaranteed-insurability option* which, for a small extra charge, guarantees the right to purchase additional insurance at standard rates regardless of the insured person's insurability. Alternatively, a number of term policies can be purchased and gradually converted as income increases. Generally these policies are available to persons under age forty for the purchase of whole-life or endowment policies, and are a protection against medical handicaps or occupational hazards that can either increase insurance costs or make insurance unobtainable.

The counselor and family examining the insurance aspects of the family's financial plan and resources should be aware of the difference between *participating* and *nonparticipating policies.* Participating policies pay dividends to the policyholder; nonparticipating policies do not. A dividend is an annual payment to the policyholder made at the company's discretion. Although the premiums for policies that pay dividends are generally higher than for those that do not, the true cost of the former may be lower over time. To know whether there is really a benefit requires comparing costs for the same coverage by a participating or a nonparticipating policy, then estimating the amount of dividends (these will vary with how well the insurance company does with its investments). The family contemplating a change in its insurance program should inquire of the agent or the company about any accumulated dividends that may be either withdrawn or applied to future premiums.

Families often do not know the difference between one plan of insurance and another, and consequently may purchase the most expensive. A policy should be read carefully and understood clearly before it is purchased. Each policy contains provisions that bind both the insured and the company. In other words, the policy is the contract between the insurance purchaser and the company. If a family's income is low, it is wiser to purchase term insurance with options to convert to other types without medical examination. For young families whose income is at a low or moderate level, this may be the primary device for assuring adequate protection to the family during the years such protection is most needed. Families should be reminded to check periodically to make sure that the beneficiary is properly stated in each policy the family carries.

Group life insurance is term insurance written under a blanket or master policy issued to an employer or sponsoring organization which extends it to all members of a group. Because it is issued at a quantity rate, the premium is lower than the rate for ordinary insurance. It usually is advantageous to join such a group. The insurance coverage often is fixed at one to two years' salary or earnings. The employer and employees usually share the cost of group insurance (sometimes a union shares the cost), with the employees' share deducted from their salary or wages. Some employers bear the entire cost. The employee who leaves the employer usually loses the group insurance but has the right to buy an individual policy for the same coverage (the cost varying with age) without medical examination. There generally is a time limit for the exercise of this right.

Various plans of group permanent life insurance have been developed during the last few years. Costs are higher for these plans, but the employee who leaves the employer retains some part of the group protection as fully paid permanent insurance, and also has the right to buy an individual policy without evidence of insurability. In some situations, employers continue to carry group life insurance for employees who have retired. The amounts may be nominal, and a reduction in its scope may be made immediately on retirement or gradually over a period of years.

If the employee (or a recent employee) dies, the employer should be consulted to ascertain what insurance benefits may accrue to the survivors.

Industrial life insurance for many years was an important—usually the only—insurance protection purchased by many industrial workers. For policies, often under $500 but sometimes as large as $1,000, the family paid a weekly premium of 5, 10, or 25 cents directly to the insurance agent who called in the home to collect. The family might have one or more policies on the breadwinner and one on each family member, a new policy purchased for each child as it was born. These small weekly sums often were as much as the family could afford—and perhaps more. The average life of these policies was short, many being allowed to lapse. Also, they could be purchased without medical examinations, especially of children. The cash surrender and loan values of these policies were small. A significant feature was the fact that the insurance agent frequently became the family adviser; his regular visits to collect the premiums made him a familiar and not unwelcome figure, trusted to counsel on a variety of family matters.

Today, with the rapid rise of workers' incomes, industrial life insurance sales have not been maintained at the former level. But many people still pay the small periodic premiums for such insurance because they are unable or unwilling to pay larger premiums less often. The collection expense of course increases the cost of this insurance, and most holders of such policies pay nearly double the usual rate for the small policies they carry.

Credit life insurance is used to repay a personal debt were the borrower to die before the payments have been completed. The dual purpose is to assure repayment to the lender without placing the burden of the debt on the survivors. It was introduced during World War I (1917) in the United States in connection with instalment financing and purchasing. Banks, savings and loan associations, the federal housing organizations, instalment sales finance companies, consumer finance companies, credit unions, and other organizations concerned with consumer credit arranged with the debtor for insurance to cover the amount of the credit. The debtors purchased the insurance themselves, sometimes voluntarily, sometimes as a condition of advance of credit. The cost was nominal, as low as 50 cents per annum for each $100 of the credit. As is the case today with airplane travel insurance, no physical examination was required to obtain this protection. Now most of the coverage is by group insurance purchased under a master contract issued either to a bank or other type of lending agency, or to a retail store selling goods on credit; generally it is an integral part of the charge the user pays for credit.

Mortgage life insurance, like credit life insurance, has been developed for the purpose of retiring the debt on property in the event of the wage earner's death, without the burden of meeting mortgage payments falling to the survivors. Unlike credit life insurance, however, mortgage life insurance requires a physical examination. It is sold as a separate declining-term insurance policy, the amount of the insurance purchased corresponding to the balance owed on the mortgage. The sum carried in the policy diminishes in each succeeding year by approximately the sum that has been retired on the mortgage, and the policy can be obtained either at a relatively low constant rate or at a low and declining rate. Some policies make provision for conversion to other forms of ordinary life insurance at a given age and without further medical examination. If conversion is elected, the insured will have acquired savings as well as having protected the family from a substantial financial crisis that might have resulted from the wage earner's death.

GOVERNMENT LIFE INSURANCE

During World War I, servicemen were able to purchase government life insurance to a limit of $10,000. These policies were issued as five-year term, straight-life, 20-payment life, 30-payment life, 20-year endowment, 30-year endowment, and endowment at age sixty-five. Although these would have matured long before now, it is not unusual today for a veteran or veteran's widow or children to be unaware that the resource exists; many have gone unclaimed.

World War II servicemen and women also could purchase government insurance to the extent of $10,000. These policies were issued as term insurance and could be renewed every five years or converted to any of several ordinary life, payment life, or endowment plans. Some of these policies have matured and many have some loan value. Generally the government pays annual dividends to holders of National Service Life Insurance.

Legislation effective in 1951 provides that no further government insurance be issued on the participating plan (dividends payable). Instead, government indemnity is provided to all persons while in service and for a specified period after honorable discharge. The ex-serviceman or woman may then elect to purchase nonparticipating (no dividends payable) term insurance. Disabled veterans have the privilege of converting from term to a life or endowment plan.

The Department of Veterans Benefits of the Veterans Administration should be consulted regarding the availability and use of such government insurance as a resource for the family in need.

ANNUITIES

Rates for life insurance and for *annuities* are based on actuarial calculations, but there the resemblance ends. Life insurance is purchased to provide some financial protection to the beneficiaries of a person who dies. An annuity helps to provide security in the form of income payments the individual cannot outlive, and whose prolonged life will not be at the possible expense of heirs. Annuities, though not based on the principle of life insurance—that is, with payment due at the time of the insured's death—are sold by life insurance companies.

Two kinds of annuities, *straight-life* and *refund,* guarantee an income for life. Payments stop when the owner of a straight-life annuity dies. Refund annuity payments, however, are made to a beneficiary if the owner dies before receiving the amount paid into the annuity; the refund, as instalments or a single lump sum, together with the payments that had been paid the annuitant (the insured person) equals the purchase price. The straight-life annuity costs less than a comparable refund annuity, but pays a larger income because it is on the life of one person only. Some people buy their annuities through regular payments on an instalment basis, over a period of years. Others use accumulated funds to purchase an annuity with one lump sum. The income can begin at once or be deferred to a later date.

The *retirement annuity,* to which is given various names, is written to meet the needs of people who want to save regularly for a life income and who need no insurance protection. Most individual retirement plans —the deferred annuities—are closely related to life insurance. They build up cash values more rapidly than the usual life insurance policy, for the same need for protection usually is not present. Indeed, annuities are a safe way of saving money. Prior to the maturity date, the policy has a cash surrender value and also a loan privilege. After the annuity payments begin, however, the policy has no cash surrender value.

Annuities may not be a good investment for everyone; for example, individuals from short-lived families and those in poor health may not find them feasible. Nor should annuities be the sole source of retirement income: they do not provide a resource for obtaining money for emergencies. Because companies are highly competitive on rates, the person contemplating an annuity would be well advised to shop around. If two people—husband and wife or two brothers or sisters, for example—need supplementary retirement income, the annuity plan may be less than perfect. One person could outlive the other well beyond the refund period or guaranteed number of instalments. If a *joint-and-survivor annuity* is developed, however, income could be provided both living annuitants, and if one dies, instalments continue at the same or a reduced level to the survivor. Because women generally live longer than men, they pay lower life insurance rates. But the greater life expectancy also means that the yield they receive on annuities is lower. In determining the amount to be paid, women are usually considered to be four or five years younger than men of the same age. Some legal challenges are in process that such sex-age elements are discriminatory, but these challenges have not been resolved at this time.

Two recent developments have become available in the arena of annuities. One is the *tax-sheltered annuity*, available to employees in certain charitable, educational, and religious organizations approved for this arrangement by the Internal Revenue Service. A portion of the individual's salary, to a specified level, is not taxable as current income. The effect is to lower income taxes during the earning years. The other is the *variable annuity*. Like the other annuity forms, this is designed to pay a regular monthly income for life. However, the purchaser's money is put wholly or partially into common stocks and retirement income may vary from month to month but not fall below a stipulated amount. The risk, therefore, is shifted to the annuitant.

The decision as to whether an annuity—and what kind—should be purchased should take into account how much income the individual will need or want after retirement in which there is no recurring income from current work; what income will be available from Social Security sources, pensions, investments, contributions from children or others; and what the costs would be of the annuity—in dollars as well as in satisfactions or anxieties about managing one's own investments in order to obtain income that is at least equivalent to the annuity income. For many elderly people, though they may chafe at having transferred responsibility for managing investments to someone else (the insurance company), the relief from such management responsibility is a strongly positive factor.

In recent years a number of *group annuities*, issued to employees under a master contract held by an employer, have been developed. The employer and employee frequently share the cost, the employee's portion being deducted from salary or wages. Some employers, however, pay the entire cost.

PENSIONS

Significant legislation was enacted in 1974 by Congress to open membership in pension plans to many more employees and to protect employee rights to a future pension. The same federal statute also covers the broadened conditions for self-employment pensions mentioned previously in connection with small businesses. In accordance with the pension reform act, by 1976 full-time employees must be allowed into an existing pension plan by age twenty-five if there has been a year of service with the company. The service component may be lengthened if the plan provides full rights to earned pension benefits even if the employee leaves the company before retirement. Certain tax-exempt education organizations can use age thirty and a year of service as the maximum waiting conditions. Older employees, previously often excluded from pension plans because of the higher costs associated with age, now too will have some protections with regard to annuities or benefit plans. The statutes also contain rules on *vesting* (guarantee of a future pension because some pension rights have been accumulated), *accrued benefits* (the balance of funds in the individual's account and the life insurance or annuity purchasable with that balance), and *portability* (the transfer of payments from an Individual Retirement Account into a pension plan and from one pension plan directly to another).

Most of the provisions of the new pension reform law do not apply to persons who already have retired. The major exception involves employees who are receiving pensions or have vested rights to future pensions from a former employer who is terminating a pension plan. The rights of these retirees can be clarified by contacting the company itself as well as the Pension Benefit Guaranty Corporation, Washington, D.C. 20044.

Pensions usually are established by purchasing an annuity for the employee (see preceding section), and a pension plan may offer several choices. One option that must be offered a retiring employee who was married one or more years before annuity payments are scheduled to start is a *husband-wife pension* (the *joint-and-survivor annuity* described earlier). Electing this option means that the surviving wife or husband of a retiree who dies is not entirely cut off from pension income but, instead, receives a lifetime income which must be at least 50 percent of the retiree's benefit. Again, as was pointed out in the section on annuities, because the payments have to span two lifetimes instead of one, the joint-and-survivor annuity provides a smaller monthly pension income than the straight-life annuity which is payable only as long as the pensioner lives.

This law does not require that employers institute a pension plan, so it is conceivable that many workers will still have as their primary retirement income the benefits available under the Old-Age, Survivors, Disability, and Health Insurance (OASDHI) of the Social Security Act, and such resources as they have independently and privately developed. However, it is of importance that counselors be aware of the provisions of the pension reform measures and their implications for the situation of the individual or family being counseled.

OLD-AGE, SURVIVORS, DISABILITY, AND HEALTH INSURANCE BENEFITS

OASDHI (especially the first four letters) refers to the cluster of programs under the Social Security Act that provide for replacement of earnings by payments to persons who are retired or disabled, or to the dependents or survivors of retired or disabled workers. The standard retirement age within the framework of this act is sixty-five years, but men or women may retire at age sixty-two and draw a reduced level of Social Security benefits. Widows or widowers are eligible at age sixty. (From time to time proposals are considered to reduce these ages to fifty-five or fifty years.) In addition to the monthly benefit for the retiree or dependents and survivors, a *maximum* $255 payment toward funeral costs is available.

The act's definition of dependents includes not just spouse and own children, but dependent parents, certain divorced women, adopted children and dependent grandchildren, an adult disabled before age twenty-two, and others. Families troubled with financial pressures related to their own needs in later years or because of the death or disability of the family wage earner or by the needs of elderly parents or other dependent relatives, should explore the prospect that there is eligibility for some benefits under the OASDHI program. Current and detailed information about eligibility and payments can be obtained from the local or regional offices of the United States Department of Health, Education, and Welfare.

UNEMPLOYMENT AND TEMPORARY DISABILITY INSURANCE

Every state now has a program of unemployment insurance benefits, established in accordance with the Social Security Act (and the Internal

Revenue Act) and administered by the state. The data presented in Chapter 1 stressed the paradox of high unemployment and concomitant high inflation. Not since the depression have so many Americans been out of work. But today, in contrast to that earlier depression period, the unemployment insurance program exists to replace some of the wages lost by unemployment. The majority of those not covered under regular programs of Unemployment Insurance Benefits (UIB) are domestics, farm workers, and state and local government employees. In all states, the benefits are keyed to previous earnings in order to enable beneficiaries to have at least a semblance of their former standard of living. The goal usually has been to provide 50 percent of previous earnings, to a maximum of two-thirds of the average wage in each state. Some jurisdictions have achieved this; others have not.

Eligibility factors are generally similar among the states, primarily centering around availability for and ability to work. The persistent high unemployment rate led the federal government to enact emergency legislation for which benefits became available to the continuing unemployed, as well as to create public service jobs in areas of high unemployment for people who had been out of work for a specified period. The Supplemental Security Income (SSI) program has augmented the benefits, providing that unemployment benefits may be paid for up to 26 weeks to otherwise uncovered persons such as domestics and farm workers, state and local employees. Public service employment has been provided by the Emergency Jobs and Unemployment Assistance Act of 1974, and the Comprehensive Employment and Training Act (CETA).

Five states recognize the need of persons whose unemployment stems from temporary disability. The disability renders them ineligible for unemployment insurance benefits and not infrequently requires hospital care. The Temporary Disability Insurance (TDI) benefits replace some of the lost wages in much the same way as is true of UIB and, in addition, pay something toward the cost of hospitalization. The states that have this program finance it by a tax on the employees' pay, in contrast to the UIB, which is financed by a payroll tax paid by the employer.

Either the TDI benefits or the UIB may constitute an important resource for an individual or family being counseled. Information about these social insurances can be secured from the state employment service of the respective state.

WORKER'S COMPENSATION
Every state now has worker's compensation laws (still entitled workmen's compensation in most jurisdictions), although all occupations in

each state are not covered. The employer pays for this nonfederally aided social insurance. The permanence of the injury and the degree to which it incapacitates the worker in relation to the latter's normal occupation are the chief factors that determine the amount of compensation to be paid. Medical and surgical services are provided, as are payments to certain dependents in the event of the death of the worker. Worker's compensation payments usually cannot be assigned or attached. The waiting period for adjudication of the claim and the amounts of compensation vary from state to state.

HEALTH INSURANCE

A fifth of all persons under age sixty-five in the United States have no insurance to help them defray the costs of medical care.[1] This includes many low-income families and individuals, to whom cost is a major deterrent to obtaining adequate health insurance protection. Also without coverage are persons regarded as health risks by private insurers. Although Medicaid has benefited many low-income persons, millions still are not covered.

Among persons with health insurance, many do not have complete coverage of all costs of medical care. Even though Medicare pays for a large protection of the medical costs incurred by its enrolled population, these elderly persons still must bear large costs if they become ill. About half of those over age sixty-five have private hospitalization insurance and slightly less than half pay for surgical insurance to supplement their Medicare coverage. And only about half of the United States population has major medical insurance protection against bills resulting from serious and prolonged illness.[2]

What is *health insurance?* Ordinarily this type of insurance is bought not to protect health but to alleviate the impact of the hospital, surgical, and other medical expenses related to the regaining of health when injury or illness occurs. It is a relatively high-priced form of indemnification not against a crisis that is an extraordinary occurrence, but against the bills incurred by events that nearly everyone will experience one or more times. There are different classes of health insurance policies that pay hospital bills, doctors' fees, and other medical expenses. Some policies are designed to replace income during disability. Some policies are addressed only to meeting certain costs in connection with certain illnesses or diseases (*catastrophic insurance* coverage for cancer or infantile paralysis, for example). Others exclude certain illnesses that may arise (mental illness, for instance) or predate the issuance of the policy. Certain health histories may preclude coverage in a health insurance plan, whether individual or group. Prior treatment for cancer often leads to exclusion from coverage even when there is apparently complete remission and, medically, the recovered patient is fully employable.

The basic purpose of health insurance is to provide protection against disastrous bills. The goal of the family should be to procure insurance that pays the bulk of anticipated and unanticipated hospital, surgical, and medical bills, and provides this coverage at the lowest cost in premium payments. It is generally more economical in the long run to budget for less expensive items if the family's health care needs are fairly typical, leaving the larger costs to be covered by health insurance or a health plan. The larger the "deductible" (the first $100 or $200 or $500 of the bill before the insurer begins to pay), the smaller the premiums are likely to be. The share (normally 20 to 25 percent) of the whole medical bill that is paid by the insured—the "co-insurance" feature— also influences the cost of the total health insurance package.

The individual's or family's health plan may be a group plan selected by the employer or the union rather than by the insured. It may omit certain forms of protection (such as maternity benefits) or be very comprehensive. The family should examine the extent and conditions of protection the plan offers—remembering that worker's compensation assures possible additional protection for people who become ill or injured as a consequence of or in connection with their job—and decide which form and amount of additional protection is suitable to meet the family's particular needs. There are several basic elements of coverage that should be taken into account.

Hospital/medical/surgical coverage pays for the hospital room (usually semiprivate or a maximum dollar amount) and other hospital services, and the doctors and surgeons for services during the hospitalization. It also pays for most accidents or illnesses that led to the hospitalization; other hospital services (laboratory tests, X-rays, operating room fees, and so forth) may also be covered. Some policies pay nearly the full cost of this care; others pay only part. Some limit the number of days per illness (from 28 to 365 days). In fact, hospital and surgical care may be in separate plans.

Major medical coverage purports to cover the individual or family against the really serious accidents or drawn-out illnesses. Generally it is designed to pick up costs where the basic hospital/surgical plan ends, with the insured paying a deductible and then fixed percentage (usually 75 to 80 percent) for those items specifically covered.

Disability income provides money to live on if the wage earner is sick or disabled for a prolonged period. Such income can be supplied by insurance (including the several state temporary disability programs referred to earlier), by the employer's sick leave plan, or by a combination of the two.

Medicare supplements cover part or all of the hospital and doctor bills not covered for participants in the Social Security Act's Medicare program.

The individual seeking to purchase health insurance protection for the family should watch for broad coverage with as few limitations and exclusions as possible. Policies should be avoided that insure against only specified diseases. Care should be taken that all members of the family are covered. It also should be ascertained that the policy is noncancelable and guaranteed to be renewable even if one spouse reaches age sixty-five and becomes eligible for Medicare. Group protection usually is cheaper and superior to coverage that can be bought by an individual; the risks and costs are spread over the whole group and, in balance, each participant is thus benefitted. Having more than one health care policy rarely serves a valid purpose, for most insurers coordinate their policies and make adjustments to the benefits each pays. Rather than saving, the owner of more than one policy is likely to expend more for premiums without compensating benefits unless it can be determined in advance that the policies are truly complementary.

Even though the benefits from such prepaid medical plans may not cover the full cost of medical or hospital care, they offer considerable protection to most families. When illness is a factor in a family's economic distress, the social worker should explore carefully the family's eligibility for benefits. Sometimes wage earners are covered in plans through their companies or through their unions without being aware of the benefits, particularly if the payment is fully covered by the employer or the union, or the employee is not clear about the meaning of codes that appear on the paycheck that indicate a deduction is being made for health care.

Accident and health insurance policies generally have no cash or loan value.

VETERANS' BENEFITS

A broad spectrum of benefits and services are available for veterans or their surviving dependents, those eligible ranging from as far back as the Spanish-American War to those presently being separated from military service in domestic or foreign bases. These benefits and services may include income support, health care, educational and vocational training, home loans, legal protection for the incompetent, and the previously mentioned life insurance. All of these are provided through a federal service delivery system under the direction of the Veterans Administration. Many similar benefits also are available in state-authorized programs, especially assistance in purchase of homes or starting farms or small businesses. Information about these resources can be obtained from the Veterans Administration directly, or the United States Veterans Assistance Centers (usually located in major cities near high-density population areas), or from state agencies established to address such varied matters as home loans, property tax exemptions, civil service preference, and scholarship and other loans.

LOANS OR MORTGAGES

The majority of persons wishing to become homeowners make a down payment on the desired property and borrow from a lending agency whatever additional funds are necessary, giving a mortgage on the property as security. The down payment and the subsequent payments constitute an investment and may be viewed as savings. Each payment increases the value of the equity in the property. Sometimes a loan, secured by a second mortgage, can be obtained on the property, the amount of the loan depending on the owner's equity. Loans made on real estate are insured by the mortgage, which is the legal credit instrument, the potential conveyance of the property serving as security for the payment of the debt.

The size of the loan (whether a first or a second mortgage) is determined largely by the value of the property in question, but capacity to repay is also a factor. Until recently, neither value of the property nor size of the proposed loan nor ability to repay were given much credence when the borrower was female, regardless of her financial or social status. Recent federal legislation prohibits denial of mortgage loans to women on the basis of sex rather than ability to fulfill the terms of the obligation.

Mortgage loans generally are *amortized* on a constant-payment basis. This calls for fixed monthly payments which include both the interest due and a portion of the principal. As the payments progress, the amount allocated for interest decreases correspondingly as the amount applied to principal increases. The amortization plan is the soundest for the average family, since the terms are definitely established in advance to fit the family's financial status and mode of living, facilitating an orderly retirement of the debt.

A *straight* or *fixed mortgage* is a loan made at a given interest rate for a definite period, with the borrower promising to pay the full amount on a specific date. Should the borrower (mortgagee) be unable to meet the obligation when it falls due, it may be possible to renew the mortgage or it may be necessary to borrow the money elsewhere to pay off the mortgage. This kind of mortgage is no longer common, but still is to be found on occasion.

A third kind of mortgage loan has recently appeared—the *flexible mortgage*. A product of inflation, this arrangement has two possible variations. One is a variable interest rate, wherein the interest rate charged on a loan can be changed when conditions in the money market change: if interest rates in general rise, so does the rate charged on the mortgage loan. This resembles the escalator clauses that for a while found their way into some mortgages and still exist in some areas. While the variable interest rate may be advantageous for the lender, it can create an inflexible burden on the homeowner who is more likely to face rising rather than decreasing costs.

The *flexible payment plan,* the other variation on the flexible mortgage, allows the borrower and lender to negotiate a payment schedule tailored to the borrower's financial needs and the anticipated changes in capacity to make future payments. This can be costly over time, and has the added disadvantage of precluding the family's planning its housing expenditures with some certainty, even though the family would be party to deciding if payments would be higher or lower for the first few or last few years of the mortgage period.

There are three primary sources of mortgage loans: the Veterans Administration (or a state veterans program) for qualified veterans; FHA loans, which are insured by the Federal Housing Administration; and the loans from private organizations or lenders that involve no government underwriting. The interest rates on VA and FHA loans are regulated by the government, and rates on conventional loans are determined by the conditions in the economy and vary from place to place and time to time. All three types are arranged through private lenders: commercial banks, mortgage companies, brokers and bankers, mutual savings banks, savings and loan associations, and life insurance companies.

In any type of mortgage, failure to meet payments for interest, principal, taxes, or required insurance may result in foreclosure proceedings. The surrender of the title to the mortgage holder or to another party does not necessarily cancel the mortgagee's obligation. Many ex-service people, for instance, who resold homes they had purchased under special provisions for veterans, found that they were still obligated to pay on their original contracts. Persons confronted with possible foreclosure of a mortgage on their property should be referred to legal counsel to ascertain the extent and nature of this continuing obligation, as well as to protect any equity they may still hold in the property.

COMMUNITY RESOURCES

Certain resources to help the troubled family are available in every community, and some communities have particular programs that are not found everywhere. The federally aided welfare programs—AFDC, SSI, Medicaid, food stamps, rent supplements, and others—usually are available to economically or medically needy families. Mental health resources, medical clinics of various kinds, special vocational or educational programs, and many others under public or private auspices can be called on by the family or the counselor to complement the tangible or counseling services being extended by the organization to which the family already has turned. If no welfare information and referral service is located within a given community, information about possible resources for family use may be obtained from the local chamber of commerce, public welfare organization, council of churches, or federated financing organization (such as a United Way, Jewish Welfare Fund, Catholic Charities organization), or others.

PERSONAL RESOURCES

Families often are confronted with the necessity of accommodating to living on a reduced budget because of lowered earnings, expansion of the family, or other changes in the family's make-up, situation, or goals. The purchasing power of the dollar may decline and the insidious and subtle effects of inflation may not be fully apparent until the family finds itself in debt.

Personal resources must be marshaled if the family is to adjust to a lowered income. Such adjustment calls for intelligence, skill, imagination, and courage. The counselor can often render constructive service in helping family members to mobilize their strengths and to find ways of managing their shrunken funds.

Whether these human resources can be effectively mobilized depends to a great extent on the attitudes that the family members have toward each other and toward a common family goal. The counselor's task lies in understanding the nature of these attitudes and the potential for modifying them if they are negative, hostile, and overcompetitive. Thus, an adolescent girl may be helped to overcome her resentment because her father is unable to give her money for a new party dress: she may be helped to acquire sufficient skill to make the desired dress and other needed clothing; the help given her may enable her to seek babysitting or other work to earn money to purchase the dress. Or, a father and son, with the help of public night school instruction, may undertake to build needed items of furniture. Or, a family vegetable garden may produce enough vegetables for current use as well as for canning.

Family members may also be helped to reexamine their attitudes toward the use of free or part-pay community resources. Can the public library be used as a substitute for a book rental service or the purchasing of periodicals and comic books? Does the family make use of such free or low-cost public recreational facilities as playgrounds, concerts, swimming pools, and parks? Can neighborhood community centers be utilized for recreational and cultural activities? Would any of the family members enjoy developing skills in sewing, carpentering, or auto, electrical, and plumbing repairs through courses offered by the public schools? Do family members take advantage of the resources provided by utility companies and other groups for learning about nutrition and economical food planning and preparation?

The counselor can often stimulate families to rethink their goals and living patterns.

> Mr. N's gross earnings were $18,000 a year and his wife earned $4,080, after taxes. A housekeeper provided supervision for their five-year-old child. Mrs. N's mother developed a serious illness and Mr. N undertook to meet the hospital and medical bills. Soon the Ns found themselves sinking into debt and Mrs. N turned to a social agency for advice. In the discussion with the social worker, Mrs. N disclosed that she resented working and would prefer to stay at home. However, she said that she felt she could not give up her employment at this time. Mrs. N and the social worker reviewed the costs involved in Mrs. N's work, such as transportation, meals eaten out, and the housekeeper's wages. Also, her earnings moved the family into a higher income tax bracket. The additional taxes plus the items mentioned totaled $3,200 a year. In addition, there were other costs related to her employment, such as higher expenditures because of hurried shopping, food for the housekeeper, personal grooming and added laundry expenses. The total cost of Mrs. N's job was estimated at $4,730, which represented an annual net loss of $650.
>
> Mrs. N and her husband decided that the family would be better off financially if she stopped her outside work and devoted her full attention instead to managing the household and the family's financial affairs. After operating the household on a new basis for several months, Mrs. N reported that the family was again solvent and, for the first time in several years, able to save.

In this instance, the financial costs of the wife's work, coupled with her dislike of outside employment, indicated the inadvisability of her continuing that arrangement indefinitely. In contrast is the situation of the Bs, who also found themselves deeply in debt.

Mr. B, a bookkeeper for the same firm for fourteen years, suffered a heart attack. He had no prior history of illness, his hospital and medical expenses for this incident were largely covered by the group hospital and medical insurance supplied by the employer, and for two of the three months of his sick leave he was on full pay. However, by the time he returned to full-time work, the Bs were behind with the mortgage payment and instalment payments for purchases made over the previous year. Mrs. B had worked before their marriage but not since the two children, now 9 and 11, were born. She had wanted to resume work when both children had started school, but Mr. B had carefully computed the total costs of her employment and she had agreed that there would be a financial loss.

Now, with the children requiring less constant supervision and the intense financial pressures felt by the parents, they agreed that she should work until they were out of debt. Mr. B thought that the income reductions resulting from his being on disability pay for a while plus the heavy medical expenses would bring the income tax to a low enough level, even with Mrs. B's earnings, to produce a net gain instead of a financial loss.

Mrs. B quickly found work as a receptionist in a large chemical plant. While her take-home pay was not high, she discovered several factors about the job that were pleasing to her. One was the enjoyment she experienced in being in the bustling office with fairly congenial people. The other was that the fringe benefits, while not materially affecting her take-home pay, nevertheless added considerable security to the family's total financial situation. The health benefits package was better than that in Mr. B's company and required no payment on her part; Mr. B's did. Moreover, the latter's employer had requested that Mr. B waive future medical care reimbursement connected with the coronary ailment, because this boosted the premium that other employees had to pay. Although he had some question about the legality of this request, Mr. B felt that he could not challenge it and jeopardize his job. Mrs. B's company also provided for discount purchases, had a credit union from which loans as needed could be made more cheaply than from the other sources to which the Bs had turned, and both life insurance and a pension plan were made available to her.

Instead of working temporarily, the Bs decided that there were many long-range benefits, financial and emotional, to be gained by the mother's continuing on this job. The immediate net financial improvement in their situation was minimal, but the protections against the financial drains by possible future crises, and the satisfactions Mrs. B derived from working, were characterized by her husband as "worthwhile."

The problems faced by the Bs and the Ns were similar—and not very different from those confronting many families in this country. The immediate family solutions also were similar. But the personalities, the aspirations, the internal and external resources on which these families could draw for sustained planning for and coping with problems that might easily recur, differed markedly. These two families, by their differences, illustrate the necessity for individualization, for examining the family needs, wants, goals, and resources, and for tailoring compatible and appropriate solutions to those measurements. Such tailoring compels careful consideration and selection of the consumer devices that may be used effectively in the family's immediate and long-range interests. Chapter 13 describes available consumer credit arrangements and offers some guidelines for their constructive use or thoughtful elimination.

NOTES

1. Marjorie Smith Mueller, "Private Health Insurance in 1972: Health Care Services, Enrollment, and Finances," *Social Security Bulletin* 37 (February 1974): 20-40.
2. Ibid.

13
Consumer Credit

If you would know the value of money, go and try to borrow some.

These words, penned more than two centuries ago by Benjamin Franklin's Poor Richard capture the essence of credit in today's world: borrowing implies debt, cost, and trust. In today's money world, not many people pay cash for everything, and nearly everyone owes a few debts. Moreover, it is considered "good business" to establish that one is trustworthy, that the trust displayed in advancing money, goods, or services is merited. To thus establish one's credit is difficult if all purchases are made with cash and no record exists about how financial obligations have been met. Hence, it is common practice for a family moving to a new community to establish credit at one or more local stores—to assume some debt and pay the charges for it, in order to demonstrate trustworthiness or creditworthiness. If the family meets its obligations when they are due, a good credit rating is established. Subsequently the family finds it much easier to arrange credit for other or larger purchases, to secure a loan, or even to rent a dwelling.

Credit increases purchasing power for the moment, but simultaneously, credit purchases create a debt. The family's purchasing power, therefore, decreases as obligations increase. In other words, the use of credit restricts subsequent buying power. On the other hand, the family that refrains from using credit, but saves for future buying, also restricts its purchasing power during the saving period. Credit in any form costs money, the rates varying with general economic conditions. They may range from 6 to 36 percent for the use of cash or instalment credit.

People's attitudes about the use of credit vary greatly and to a considerable extent are determined by the attitudes of their parents and the buying patterns of their families as well as peers. Some persons have an abhorrence of debt. To them, paying cash is almost a matter of morality. This attitude may stem from an overly rigid conscience that permits no indulgence. Or it may be an expression of a cultural pattern or a reflection of deep personal insecurity. Other people, however, use credit for practically all purchases, manage to pay their bills when they are due, and are not abnormally bothered by having a debt to pay. These are the "normal" users of consumer credit.

Some persons, however, use credit carelessly. They buy impulsively without planning, and when they find that they cannot meet their obligations they become anxious and panicky. Sometimes they become anxious only when they are under pressure to pay. Among those who use credit destructively are persons who meet neurotic needs with it and those who have little control of impulse. Their buying is not related to the practical management of their income.

The use of consumer credit can be constructive for the family if the members are fully aware of the attendant costs and of the fact that consumer credit may create a false sense of the size and elasticity of income. The family should also recognize that the necessity to meet current and future payments will limit their purchasing power for a specified period of time. The use of consumer credit can be destructive for the family when members treat it as if it actually were income, failing to relate such spending realistically to income, and failing to keep the debts in proper relation to liquid assets.

Persons in the latter group frequently are in financial trouble and seek the help of social agencies. Their many money troubles may be the result of attempting to compensate for lack of love and attention, of attempting to attain prestige, or of "getting even" or punishing someone. By always having a debt to pay, some people punish themselves to allay feelings of guilt.

Social work intervention often is needed to help individuals with such personality problems. The L case (Chapter 10) is illustrative of such help, and so is the case of the Os.

> Mrs. O, the mother of three children under three years of age, applied to a family agency saying that she was physically exhausted and "at the end of my rope." Mr. O earned only a modest salary as a shipping clerk, and Mrs. O had managed to meet their living expenses out of this income. She now declared that she was leaving Mr. O because of his "stinginess." He had refused to buy her an automatic washing machine and other labor-saving devices. When Mr. O was interviewed, he recalled his experiences as a child. His family had been evicted following a foreclosure of the mortgage on their house; his father had not been able to keep up the payments after he had lost his job during the depression years. With the social worker's help, Mr. O was able to see that his fear of debt was excessive. He realized that his wife needed a washing machine and subsequently made arrangements for an instalment purchase. When this debt was cleared up Mr. O unhesitatingly agreed to

provide his wife with an automatic dryer. Mrs. O's health improved, as did the marital relationship.

To be of maximum help in money counseling, the counselor should understand not only the psychodynamics affecting individuals and families, but also the economic arrangements that can be instrumental in easing family tensions. It is not enough to seek ways to increase income. It also is necessary to find ways to stretch current income realistically in order to secure optimal benefit from it. This entails knowing something about what is involved in establishing credit, about the range of resources that might be available for particular consumer credit purposes, and about the protections and resources that can be called on if the credit user has been rash or has been exploited.

THE NATURE OF CONSUMER CREDIT

Individuals and families use credit, whether for cash loans, goods, or services to be paid for later, when the usefulness or the personal gratification from having the cash or the commodity is greater than the cost of the credit. Either the utility or the personal gratification (or both) may be of a high order if there is an emergency; if enjoyment from the goods and services endures over a longer period of time than the period of payment, and the enjoyment derived is more important than the period of payment, and the enjoyment derived is more important than the payments; if the convenience of the credit is important; if the instalment payments substitute for savings that would not have been accumulated or that for consciously identified reasons should not be drawn on; and if the commodities obtained on credit actually are used for a period of time without charge (the interest-free period in a charge account, for example).

Lending institutions—or credit grantors—act primarily on the basis of the amount and stability of the potential borrower's income; the individual's social and psychological stability as demonstrated by such factors as occupation, duration of residence, marriage, or employment, and past credit record. Consumer credit-granting organizations tend to group these items into three broad criteria for determining whether credit for merchandise or a cash loan should be made. Commonly called the "3 Cs" of consumer credit, with some minor variations on the major themes, they are: capacity, capital, and character (credit experience). Capacity to repay is found in any grouping of "3 Cs." Capital also is general, and means ownership (house, life insurance, savings, stocks, other assets). Sometimes, however, what the capital represents is the guiding criterion: frugality? habit of saving? carefulness? a sense of the value of family or personal security? The third "C," character, is also sometimes expressed as credit experience. It centers around trustworthiness and past record of paying other loans and regular bills (utilities, rent, and so forth).

Many credit grantors utilize scoring systems in which the various attributes are rated; a credit applicant has to have a score at a specified level to be granted credit. The information on which the score is based may come from credit applications, from personal interviews with the applicant, or from files of credit-reporting organizations which furnish credit histories to subscribers for a fee. Such histories are likely to include past indebtedness patterns and payments, present financial burdens and resources, and promptness in paying for rent, utilities, and other obligations. An individual now has the right to learn (for a small fee) the nature of the information that such an organization may have on file. Moreover, the Equal Credit Opportunity Act prohibits credit grantors from regarding married persons per se as more creditworthy than unmarried persons or those who are separated.

Different kinds of credit serve different purposes. The circumstances under which these resources are available and the costs and other conditions that are pertinent to their utilization also may differ.

Charge Accounts

Charge accounts are carried not only by retail stores, but by doctors, dentists, garages, plumbers, and other providers of goods or services. Purchasing on charge accounts provides an immediate increase in buying power, for cash need not be at hand to make a purchase. Generally it is expected that payments will be made on charge accounts once each month. This expectation probably derives from the idea that payment will come from income (earnings, usually) received in the same month in which the purchases were made. In some rural areas, payments may be expected at less frequent intervals and are related to seasonal work activity customary in those areas. Hence, some Eskimo villagers can expect to settle their bills when the summer fishing is over and the catch has been sold or the work in the canneries ended until the next season; farmers in some sections of the "lower 48" pay their accounts when the crops or livestock are sold.

There are several types of charge accounts. One is the *open charge account*. In this form of credit, the consumer is expected to pay the full amount due at the end of the month or in approximately thirty days. This also is known as the *thirty-day charge account.* This type of account is not as common as it was in the past, but still is available in "carriage trade" department and other retail stores. If the account is not paid in the thirty-day period, it may be carried over to the next month without a carrying charge. More customarily today, however, the failure of the consumer to pay the bill within the thirty-day period results in a credit service charge. Such arrangements constitute the "optional" revolving account discussed below which is common in department store and oil company credit policies.

In the open charge account system, the customer presumably makes purchases at various times during the thirty-day month; the agreement to pay for the purchases when the bill is received is supported by the customer's signature on each charge purchase sales slip. The modern cyclical billing system, commonly used by department stores and other providers of goods or services, spreads the mailing of these bills over the month, usually alphabetically, and the consumer is notified about when to expect the bills. They may not arrive on or close to the first of the month, and the customer is expected to pay the bill well before the next billing cycle ends. The purchase and billing sequence often provides less than a thirty-day credit period to the customer; occasionally the period may be a few days longer.

The goods purchased on such accounts become the consumer's property immediately on delivery; they do not become subject to repossession should the customer fail to fulfill the legal and moral obligation to make payment. Such accounts are also called *convenience accounts.* The consumer is able to pay in one check for all purchases made in the thirty-day period. This charge account permits the person to make unforeseen purchases, which may be both a convenience and economically advantageous at times of special sales or a sudden need. Other advantages lie in the fact that a charge account saves shopping time, for credit purchases —in person, or by mail or telephone—usually can be handled more rapidly than cash transactions. Charge account customers often have the benefit of advance notices of sales, of announcements of items offered at special prices, and of greater ease than cash customers in returning merchandise. Some people also think it an advantage to pay for all their major purchases at one time in the month.

But often charge accounts have disadvantages. The added cost of doing business on a charge basis may add to the cost of merchandise for all customers. Purchasing food on charge accounts, for example, usually increases the cost of this basic budget item, which is large for families on marginal incomes. Careless buying is sometimes encouraged by the delayed payment option and the greater ease in returning merchandise. Open charge accounts are conducive to overbuying and, as a result, the buyer may need to sacrifice making more important purchases. Their greatest disadvantage lies in the fact that they permit some customers to incur obligations beyond their capacity to pay. Since pay periods rarely coincide with cyclical billing dates, some people tend to overlook them, and the family may be confronted with an overwhelming accumulation of past-due and current bills. Such an accumulation of bills may well require the development of a repayment plan. When this occurs, payments are extended for some time into the future, thereby decreasing purchasing power. The advantages of the use of open charge accounts are chiefly those of convenience, not of economy. For many individuals, however, convenience is economy.

An "open line" of credit may be arranged (generally with a top dollar limit) against which purchases are charged as in the open charge account, but with monthly payments to which are added credit service fees. This is the *revolving account*. It has two major forms: one known simply as "revolving," the other alluded to earlier, the *optional revolving account*. In this latter form, the customer requests the option whereby the whole balance may be paid within fifteen or twenty days of receipt of the bill (for which there is no service charge) or a portion may be paid if that is convenient. The subsequent bill then includes a *service* charge for the unpaid balance of the prior month's bill. Legal title to the items purchased passes to the buyer at the time of purchase unless it is specifically stipulated (usually when the item is furniture, an electrical appliance, or other costly merchandise) that the title is to remain with the store until the purchase price has been paid in full.

The revolving account introduces the principle of two more payments, as in instalment credit, and also retains important features of the thirty-day charge account. The consumer signs a contract at the outset. This may be a conditional sales contract, a chattel mortgage, or a bailment lease. New purchases may be made at any time but the total obligation may not exceed the original top dollar limit.

Credit cards, as was pointed out in Part One, have become a common device for charging merchandise or services to be paid at a later time, either on the thirty-day or the revolving account basis. Many merchants and most oil companies encourage their customers to use these identification cards, permitting the holders to charge quickly almost any product or service. Until recently, such cards were usable only for purchasing from the issuing vendor; the cards thus have been known as *limited-purpose credit cards.*

General-purpose credit cards are issued by national firms for use in their own branches, or in stores, hotels, transportation companies, or other establishments that are willing to bill and be paid by the card issuer, who in turn bills and receives payment from the customer. The cards of the now well-known specializing credit card companies represent agreements between the issuers and a multitude of retail and service businesses where the card holders may charge purchases on signature and presentation of the cards. Often known as "travel and entertainment" cards, they encompass many purchases beyond classification within these two subject areas.

The credit card system is financed in several ways. Primarily, the card holder agrees to pay the issuing company each month on being billed for the items charged to that point. In many instances—sometimes because the card user does not have enough money on hand to pay the full bill, but often because of the way the bill is set forth (emphasis on the "minimum payment," for example)—the customer pays only part of the bill and becomes liable for payment of finance charges added to the unpaid portion of the preceding month's bill (the revolving credit feature). Although single company cards usually are issued free, with the expectation that the card holder will reciprocate by patronizing the issuer, many of the issuing firms take in money in another way. They may charge the retailers and the service establishments in which the customer has used the card a percentage against all sales slips as they are delivered to the issuing company for payment. They may also make an annual charge to each card holder for the privilege of carrying the card.

Credit cards issued by banks are similarly financed: through the "discounts" from merchants who permit customers to buy goods or services with the cards, and the monthly finance charges from the consumers who elect not to pay their bills in full by the due date, and, in some instances, an annual charge to the holder. Banks augment these customary methods of handling credit-card transactions with several others that are designed both to facilitate the use of the bank's credit cards by its customers and to increase the revenue to the banks.

These devices are known by various names, depending on the sponsoring bank's creativity, including "redi-checks," "charge account banking," "privilege checking," or "checking plus." The first reflects a blank-check system, whereby the bank issues blank "checks" that can be used by the consumer to make as many purchases as the consumer may desire up to a total that has been established in advance as the top amount of credit for the person or family. Each month the customer receives a statement which records all of the checks that have "cleared" the bank. A service charge may be added, but if the customer has deposited enough money to cover the charges in the statement (usually within ten, fifteen, or twenty days), there is likely to be no service charge except a sum (perhaps 25 cents) to cover the bookkeeping necessary for handling each check. It is not uncommon for a bank to stress the versatility of these checks to pay doctors or others who may not accept credit cards. Sometimes, however, the customer is unaware that there is a finance charge involved.

The "charge account banking" (or other titles used) provides consumers a line of prearranged credit. Customers can overdraw their checking account up to that amount without the checks' being returned or charged for "insufficient funds." The overdraft is treated as a loan, and interest is charged on it. Such overdraft checking arrangements may be advantageous when used selectively and infrequently to protect against unforeseen expenses which otherwise might cause a check to be returned for insufficient funds. The overdraft account may then cost less than handling the returned check. However, the service fees that may accumulate for maintaining a balance in such an account should be weighed against the insufficient-funds charges.

Credit cards have now come to be used to cover costs associated with a wide range of daily life activities—for groceries, gasoline, medical bills, concerts, even for church collections. The convenience of not negotiating for each separate transaction, of having the bank or a credit-card company pay all the individual bills while the consumer focuses on the single transaction with the card issuer, may entail different costs. It is of cardinal importance that the card holder know what these costs are and be alert to some practices that may increase them. For example, many customers are lured by slow billing (which may permit postponement of payment for weeks or months), or the focus of attention in the monthly bill on payment of the minimum due rather than the total owed. In either instance, a finance charge may have to be paid. The Fair Credit Billing Act, effective in late 1975, attempts to protect the unwary credit-user against some of these practicies. Thus, creditors must mail statements at least fourteen days before the due date, and inquiries regarding billing must be acknowledged within thirty days and complaints settled within ninety days. Moreover, creditors are prohibited from sending dunning letters until such questions have been resolved. In this connection and worth noting is the prohibition against issuing unfavorable credit reports on disputed accounts until customers are notified and collection agencies are informed that the bills are in dispute. Another important section of the act gives the cardholder the right to withhold payment for items that prove defective, without being held liable for the entire amount owed.

Consumer Credit 329

The actual amount of interest required on balances in these "charge-it" arrangements (charge accounts or credit cards) varies in accordance with state laws, and should be taken into consideration when a charging plan is being contemplated. For the consumer, the cheapest of the accounting systems is the *adjusted balance method,* sometimes called the *closing balance method.* Here the finance charge is calculated on the unpaid balance of the previous month, less credits and payments made in the current month. More costly to the consumer is the *previous balance method.* The finance charges are calculated on the amount owed on the final billing date of the previous month. The calculation does not take into account any payments made to reduce the balance or any credits for returned merchandise. It is estimated that the interest cost of this method is approximately 16 percent higher than under the adjusted balance method.[1] Also about 16 percent higher than the adjusted balance method is the *average daily balance method* used by most banks. The finance charges are calculated by dividing the sum of the balances outstanding for each day of the billing period by the number of days in the period, then multiplying by the daily rate of interest. The longer the payment is deferred, the higher are the resulting finance costs.

The individuals and families who utilize the open-end credit systems can benefit from them as long as it is clearly understood that failure to pay the full bill promptly and to exercise the self-discipline incumbent in keeping purchases within the limits of income result in additional costs.

> The Ds, for example, replaced some needed household items and clothing with the help of the general-purpose credit card issued by a national credit-card company. They paid on this account, but continued to make additional purchases so that the average daily balance was $500 in merchandise purchases outstanding on their credit card. Their failure to pay regularly and in full on the due date subjected them to a finance charge equivalent to an annual percentage rate of 18 percent. Over a year, this amounted to at least $90 for the $500 worth of credit.

In the preceding chapter, reference was made to the fact that banks will compound interest, or pay interest on interest for savings on deposit. Similarly, banks charge interest on interest for unpaid balances. The interest assessed on the unpaid balance each month becomes part of the balance against which interest is charged the following month.

> Accordingly, when Mr. R was unexpectedly laid off in April by the aircraft company that lost a sizable contract, he had an unpaid balance of $200 in his credit-card account. He was unable to make any payments in May and

June from his unemployment insurance benefits, his sole income during those months. The monthly interest charge of 1.5 percent added $3 in May. The interest charge for June was imposed on $203, adding another $3.45. The accumulated interest charges for these two months ($6.45) was the equivalent of the amount in the family's new "unemployed" budget for "recreation" for the two children.

Failure to pay the minimum due each month may also lead to late charges. These generally come to 5 percent of the minimum monthly payment required, up to a maximum of $5.00. When these charges are also added to the unpaid balance, they become part of the base on which the interest is figured in subsequent months.

INSTALMENT CREDIT

Instalment credit is distinguishable from other forms of personal credit by the fact that it is amortized; that is, it is gradually liquidated by stipulated weekly or monthly payments, each of which includes interest and retirement of some of the remaining principal. This is the means by which most Americans finance the purchase of automobiles and other durables. The consumer may be able to purchase a major item at a discount-for-cash price and believe that the discounted price justifies the cost of the loan.

The *instalment sales account* and the *instalment loan account* have many similarities. The periodicity of payments (monthly, biweekly, or weekly instalments) and the duration (usually from four to twenty-four months but may be written for longer or shorter periods) are much the same. The instalment sales account is initiated by a written contract in which *title to the articles purchased remains with the seller until the last payment is made,* when it passes to the customer. Instalment loans may be made on signature of the borrower alone, but collateral or security that may be required is specified in the note, which is the loan contract. The title to this collateral is technically transferred to the lender, usually by a separate document, until the final payment is made. Then the note, collateral, and the title instrument are returned, the full title reverting to the original owner (usually, the borrower).

The increase in instalment credit buying, which has been noted in earlier chapters, is a source of considerable anxiety to many people. Instalment payment plans, however, provide many advantages for the well-integrated, reasonably disciplined person. They enable the buyer to have immediate use of an article upon making a down payment or the initial payment which generally represents a small fraction of the total cost. The customer has the convenience of spreading payments over a period of time. In a sense, instalment buying promotes thrift by providing the reward for savings in advance of their accumulation. Inherent in instalment buying is a strong incentive to save, since failure to make the ongoing payments may result not only in loss of the merchandise but also in loss of the money already paid. Many purchases made on the instalment plan are self-liquidating; for example, the use of sewing machines, washing machines, or refrigerators may save more than the cost price.

The necessity to channel money into instalment payments promotes economy. For many persons, the necessity to earmark a known amount for a given purpose facilitates the planning of other expenditures and of total income. This represents in many instances a means of enforced saving.

Instalment buying also has disadvantages. It may create a burden of debt that is difficult for the buyer to carry. It may encourage overbuying and extravagance. The carrying or finance charges may run high whereas accumulation of savings in the amount needed to make a specific large purchase may simultaneously reduce the purchase price by eliminating carrying charges, and make more money available for use in the form of interest that is applied to the savings for the time the purchase is deferred.

A major problem in instalment buying lies in the fact that it places a lien on the income of the buyer, with no allowance for unfavorable contingencies. When these occur, the necessity to meet payments may compel family members to make drastic economies, sometimes to the extent of denying themselves necessities.

The seller of goods under an instalment plan almost invariably requires the purchaser to sign one or more legal documents which set forth the terms of the transaction. Some states have passed protective legislation setting limits on these terms. Protective legislation, however, does not prevent individuals from buying beyond their real or imagined ability to pay. Thus, a large proportion of people who seek help with money problems are having difficulty because they have overcommitted their incomes to instalment payments. The legal documents hold them accountable for payment within a specified time period. In order to meet the most pressing of these obligations, the family may engage in considerable maneuvering and manipulation of income, which often only increase their indebtedness. Or the family may suddenly avoid creditors, and thus provoke creditors into exercising their legal right to repossession.

In advising families about instalment buying, the financial counselor should consider the following points. How much of the family's income has already been mortgaged? In many families, instalment payments up to 10 percent of the disposable income may signal danger. Some families, however, depending on income and responsibilities, may safely allow their instalment payments to amount to as much as 20 percent of the income. How necessary is the item under consideration? How does the family expect to manage payment or repayment? What social and economic purpose will be achieved by buying it? Value judgments must be made about the social usefulness of the purchase as well as about the soundness of the financial transaction—that is, will the funds be invested or squandered? The financial counselor should also be familiar with the various kinds of contracts that are involved in credit or instalment buying, as well as the expectations of many lenders that the purchaser will pay for credit life insurance to insure liquidation of the debt in the event that the debtor dies before the final payment has been made (see Chapter 12).

The customer who pays cash receives some kind of sales receipt or sales agreement. This may be the legal basis for transferring the title of the purchased item—especially durable goods; usually it includes the vendor's warranty of quality. If the customer pays by check, that fact is entered on the sales receipt; the vendor has several legal recourses available should the check not be good. When a purchase involves the use of credit, the buyer cannot renounce the sale but takes possession of the merchandise, paying taxes on it and holding it without title until all the payments have been completed.

The seller's risk may be high because the customers' purchases contain little owner equity: a low down payment or low trade-in allowance, plus low monthly payments may cause the buyer to feel indifferent about continuing to make payments for merchandise that has depreciated in value or usefulness for the consumer; and the seller may regard as too costly the process of repossessing an item with little or no resale value. A *conditional sales contract* permits the seller to retain title to the merchandise until the last of the stipulated payments has been made. If these payments are made on the dates they are due, title passes to the buyer when the full obligation to pay has been met. (Some leniency is generally shown about the exact date of payment.) However, if the buyer is unable to make payments when they are due, the contract gives the seller the right to repossess the merchandise. But merely giving up the merchandise does not free the buyer from paying the unpaid balance; if the seller does not receive enough from the resale to cover the unpaid balance, the buyer may be sued for the difference. Moreover, the seller does not have to repossess. Upon default, the whole unpaid balance may be declared to be due and the customer sued for this sum. Often, however, buyers are protected by a state law that requires the return to them of the excess of the merchandise's resale value over legal fees and reasonable financing costs, to the extent of the debtor's previous payments. Only when the whole unpaid balance has been liquidated is the buyer free from the contract. Some contracts are drawn so that the sellers, even if the resale gave them more than the unpaid balance, are not required to return the excess to the original instalment buyer.

Some contracts permit new items to be added to the contract before final payment is made on the original purchase; this is known as an *add-on purchase.* Failure then to meet payments on this accordion-like arrangement jeopardizes all merchandise included in the contract, past as well as current, and repossession of all of the items mentioned in the contract may result. Even if all the goods have been repossessed, the family may still not be relieved of the obligation to pay the bill. It is often advisable for the counselor to refer a family for legal counsel in order to secure a clarification of its rights and obligations in a particular transaction.

A *bailment lease* is a contract that provides that the goods shall be merely rented to the buyer, the "rent" being the stipulated series of instalment payments. Hence, title is held by the seller during the period of credit extension. When the rent payments have been completed, however, the seller agrees to turn the title over to the buyer for a nominal payment, such as one dollar. This form of contract is commonly used in the purchase of television sets.

A *chattel mortgage* is a contract used mainly as security for a cash loan, and always applies to movable goods such as furniture or automobiles. The contract must be recorded with the proper public authority. When a chattel mortgage is employed in a purchase, the seller gives the buyer title to the goods and takes the mortgage as security. Repossession becomes possible if the buyer fails to fulfil any part of the contract, the most usual default being on the payments due to the seller. As with the conditional sales contract, if the repossessed property cannot be sold for a sum sufficient to liquidate the unpaid balance, the seller has the right of further legal action against the buyer to collect the balance due.

A *general credit contract* is an instalment buying contract, and is called variously a budget plan, a three-payment plan, a six-payment plan, a revolving credit plan, an easy payment plan, a flexible account, and so forth. In contrast to the other three types of instalment contracts that have been discussed, *general credit contracts do not give the seller the right to repossess.* In fact, if the buyer defaults on payments, the recourse of the seller is the same as that under charge account credit—he has the right to sue.

Under the three-payment plan, which is used by a number of merchandising stores, the goods and the title to the goods are turned over to the buyer as soon as the sale is made. The total purchase price is divided into three equal parts, with each part payable on specified dates in three subsequent months. No written contract is signed; the oral contract is binding. Frequently no carrying charge is added; stores usually assess 1½ percent per month on the entire amount or on the unpaid balance. The six-payment plan operates the same way, but nearly always with a carrying charge because of the time extension.

Under revolving credit plans, a maximum credit figure is established for the customer. Typically, this figure is divided by six or by nine or by twelve, to give the amount the customer must pay monthly. Any time the balance drops below the maximum, the customer may make additional purchases within the limit set. A charge of 6 to 12 percent per year on the maximum amount, which comes to 12 to 24 percent annual interest on the unpaid balance, is customarily charged. A service charge for opening the account is also charged in some cases.

The implications of all these budget plans are ironic. The family is relieved of the chore of budgeting; the retailer does it instead. This was graphically shown in a recent cartoon in which the wife, sitting with her husband at the car salesman's desk, suggests, "Maybe we'd better buy the car, dear, if only to get the fine budget plan he's worked out for us!"

BORROWING

In making comparisons between buying on the instalment plan and taking out a loan to pay cash for the desired purchase, it is essential to know not only the dollar cost of the goods but the dollar and percentage cost of credit. For example, Mrs. J wishes to buy a rug which is marked at $100 cash or $106 on the budget plan. The dealer tells her he will deduct $5 from the cash price if she will pay him the $95 immediately. The budget terms are $5 down and the balance of $101 in twelve equal monthly instalments. Therefore she would be paying $11 (the difference between the budget plan price and the actual cash price) to use this type of credit for twelve months instead of using the alternative plan of borrowing $90 to complete the cash payment. In reality, then, she would be paying $11 for $101 credit. However, because the debt would be gradually decreased by payments, she would be receiving credit that would be roughly about one-half of the starting balance. Dividing $11 by that half gives an interest rate of nearly 22 percent.

Contrastingly, Mrs. J can go to a credit-granting agency—for example, a credit union—where she can borrow $90 at an interest rate of 1 percent per month on each month's unpaid balance. Because interest is computed on the actual unpaid balance, this would mean an annual interest rate of slightly more than one-half of what she would have to pay in interest if she bought the rug on the time-payment plan.

How can Mrs. J know she is using her limited money to her best advantage? How can she know if an instalment credit plan is cheaper for her, or whether she would have more money for use if she were to withdraw cash from the bank to pay for the rug? It is important that she shop for credit, and that she ascertain not only the percentage per year (which the credit grantor must stipulate under federal law), but the dollar cost for the loan for a specified number of months. How does this seller's price compare with the cash prices of other sellers? with the carrying charges of other sellers? What monthly payments (or weekly or biweekly) are required? What penalties would be imposed if some unforeseen emergency requires that Mrs. J request an extension? fines? repossession? collection from endorsers?

Money is borrowed for many purposes. Usually it is to pay for some large extraordinary expense that was not budgeted for, planned for, or insured against, such as household repairs or taxes, illness, or accidents. Sometimes money is borrowed to pay off instalment contracts or to consolidate debts. Or cash loans may be obtained for education, vacation, acquisition of cars or property, starting a business, paying alimony, or helping relatives. Nearly all states have enacted legislation regulating the practices of the various kinds of lending organizations and specifying maximum interest rates.

Social agencies, as a rule, do not act as resources for borrowing. Their helping role is of a different nature, although at times an agency may grant a loan, as was discussed in Chapter 10. If a loan is indicated, the counselor may be able to help the person find a commercial lending resource. The advisability of suggesting such a step and evaluating the use the person may make of the resource require that the counselor have some basic information about the various types of lending organizations, as well as the advantages and disadvantages for the person becoming encumbered with a loan.

Organizations that lend money fall into two distinct categories—commercial and noncommercial. The latter type includes various cooperative and philanthropic organizations. The former, by far the most encompassing, includes commercial banks, finance companies (both consumer and sales finance companies), credit unions, retail credit outlets, industrial banks, remedial loan societies, and pawnbrokers. In addition, there are unlicensed lenders (employers, family members, personal friends).

Commercial organizations are subject to federal regulation with respect to many of their consumer instalment credit activities, and each state also has enacted statutes governing their operations, although state statutes are not uniform. (See Consumer Protection later in this chapter.) This is not always true of noncommercial organizations, which generally require lower—if any—charges on loans.

In exploring the feasibility of applying for cash any loan, the methods of stating the loan charges should be scrutinized carefully. The interest rate charged on a loan is affected by a number of considerations, not the least of which is the credit standing or creditworthiness of the borrower. The amount of money borrowed and the type of loan also influence the interest rate. The larger the loan, the lower the rate. And new-car loans are more favorable than used-car loans and unsecured personal loans because they are backed by collateral (the more valuable the collateral, the lower the interest rate on the note is apt to be). There also are specialized loans to finance such matters as home improvement or tuition. The most economical approach to obtaining an instalment loan is to borrow against accumulated assets, which may be in the form of stocks, bonds, or funds in a savings account. Lower annual percentage rates usually apply to loans backed by such assets in contrast to unsecured loans. All lenders are required to quote loan costs in terms of the annual percentage rate (APR), but they can use different methods to calculate the finance charges, then convert these charges into the equivalent annual percentage rates.

The three methods generally used to state the finance charge on instalment credit are add-on, discount, and interest on the unpaid balance. In recent years, many states have adopted a form of rate quotation similar to that frequently used by commercial banks when they make consumer instalment loans.[2] This is the *add-on method*. The charge is calculated as if the borrower had the use of the total amount of the loan for the full period, and this charge is added to the amount of the loan. When interest is computed by the add-on method and payments are completed in a shorter period, the actual amount of interest paid is slightly less. Similarly, when payments are late, a late charge may be assessed, the effect then being a higher cost for the loan.

The *discount method* is sometimes used for cash loans. The finance charge is calculated (as in the add-on method) as if the borrower were to have the use of the face amount of the note for the full period. In this method, however, the dollar finance charge is deducted from the face amount of the note to determine how much the borrower receives. This means that on a note for $1,500, discounted at 7 percent per year, the interest for 15 months would amount to $131.25. The borrower receives only $1,368.75, for the 7 percent is taken off at the outset. (If the borrower had needed the full $1,500, it would have been necessary to borrow enough more to allow for the discounting.) Were the borrower to have the full use of the $1,368.75 for the 15 months and repay this sum at the end of that period, the true interest rate would slightly exceed 7 percent. However, when the note is repaid in instalments, the true interest rate is slightly more than twice the discount rate of 7 percent, for over the entire 15-month period, the debtor had the use of only about half of the discounted value of the note. Had the loan been for a longer period, the rate would be a little higher, just as it would be under the add-on method.

When interest is charged on the unpaid balance, the length of the loan period does not affect the true annual interest rate. The most favorable method for most consumers is the *simple interest method* in which the lender charges interest only on the exact amount borrowed for the exact amount of time it is loaned.[3] This method has a built-in reward for early payment and a penalty for tardiness in paying. Under this approach, a regular repayment schedule with equal monthly payments is set up, with a final "equalizer" payment at the end. If the repayment schedule is followed precisely, the final payment would be approximately the same size as all previous ones. If the debtor were regularly late, the final payment would be a little larger, for the money would have been available to the debtor for use for a longer period. (Late charges may also be imposed.) Similarly, the final payment would be somewhat smaller than the others if the payment schedule was consistently accelerated. In some states, creditors who use the add-on or discount method to figure the finance charges are required to return interest to the borrower who has repaid the loan early.

Credit granting organizations about which the counselor should have some knowledge are described briefly below. Some of these organizations have been considered in the preceding chapter from the standpoint of their constituting a resource to the family for saving and investing. Here the focus is on their opposite role, as a resource for borrowing. (Sources for obtaining fuller information are shown in the bibliography for this chapter.)

Commercial banks extend both commercial and personal loans. The former are short-term loans, usually for sixty or ninety days, for which the rate of interest fluctuates with the general economic situation, and usually ranges between 6 and 10 percent. These loans are secured by negotiable collateral or on the promise (note) of the businessperson seeking the loan. Preferred customers (that is, those with good business and credit standing and experience) may expect to pay interest in the lower ranges.

Personal loans are secured by a pledge of an automobile, or by a note signed by one or more responsible comakers or endorsers. Most commercial banks use the advance discount rate method of charging interest, and many require credit life insurance. There may also be a fee for investigation of creditworthiness and sometimes a minimum service charge.

The comaker or cosigner who endorses a note is liable for the full unpaid balance of the loan, including principal and charges, if the borrower defaults. There is no legal obligation upon the lender to try to enforce collection from the borrower before proceeding against the endorsers if the borrower is delinquent in meeting payments. Some banks may charge 5 percent a month penalty on the delinquent payment due. Many state laws prohibit interest on this penalty payment.

By and large, the borrowing rate is relatively low, for the commercial bank selects its risks and ordinarily there are no extra or hidden fees or charges. For some families, however, this is not a viable resource because they may be unable to meet the more rigid requirements of commercial banks.

Industrial banks, also known as industrial loan companies or consumer banks, operate in some ways like commercial banks; in other ways they resemble consumer finance companies. They were organized originally to lend money to persons earning wages in industry, generally members of low-income groups. When Arthur Morris in 1910 began a new type of institution (known then and now as Morris Plan banks) for low-income borrowers, it was his idea to encourage the accumulation of savings; these banks insisted on the borrowers' purchase of savings certificates to demonstrate their commitment to a continuing savings program. Some industrial banks still operate on this principle, paying the saver interest on deposited sums.

Under the Morris Plan, the borrower is required to sign a dual contract with an industrial bank, embracing a loan agreement that contains a flat percentage rate for the period of the loan, plus the agreement to make regular payments on a savings certificate that will be worth enough at maturity to retire the sum owed to the bank. Morris Plan banks, like other industrial banks, operate in many states under the banking statutes; in others, under general business statutes. Like commercial banks, the industrial banks generally use the advance discount method of charging interest. They usually are also permitted to make an investigation charge, or to require the borrower to pay a small premium for credit life insurance.

Savings and loan associations (also known as *building and loan associations*), lend chiefly to finance the purchase or construction of homes, farms, or other real estate, or to remodel, repair, or improve property. In most states they restrict themselves to mortgage loans, but in some they also lend money for general purposes, the loan secured by the savings balance in the institution.

Consumer finance companies or *small-loan companies* are governed by state licensing, and by legal limits on interest rates and size of loans. Rates for cash loans vary from 36 percent annually on the smallest to 12 percent on larger, well-secured loans. While the average is about 21 percent, interest in some states can go as high as 42 percent. The variations in rates set by the states take account of the fact that the consumer applies for a loan or financing without verified evidence regarding assets that reduce and liabilities that add to the risk of making the loan. This is in contrast to the practice in commercial banks and other sources that require a verified statement of net worth to support the application for a loan. The loans are usually repaid in regular instalments within twenty months. Although small-loan companies use the various methods for determining interest that were previously noted, in recent years many states have adopted the add-on method for consumer instalment loans, as is common in commercial banks.

If the borrower is able to repay the loan in full before it is due, the small-loan company accepts payment without penalties or extra charges. If a payment to a small-loan company is overdue, the laws usually permit interest to be charged only on the true balance outstanding.

Small-loan companies usually make loans on the basis of the borrower's signature; some loans, however, are secured by chattel mortgages. Because most of the loans are based on the character of the borrower, the companies are usually willing to readjust the payment plan if the borrower is unemployed or has unforeseen expenses. They offer assistance in budgeting the payments at the time the loan is made and also if readjusted.

For many families, borrowing from a consumer finance company has disadvantages in that the interest rates are higher than those of commercial banks, and the maximum amount of money that may be borrowed sometimes is less than from banks. But for many individuals and families, there are advantages to be weighed: the small-loan company will take greater risks than a commercial bank and very often the financially troubled family has little but risk to offer! Moreover, a smaller loan can be obtained from such a company—even just a few dollars if that is all that is needed. As the charge is based on the unpaid balance of the loan, payment is only for the credit actually being used. A grievance against a small-loan company may be taken to the state supervisory agency, where advice and help can be supplied without expense.

Credit unions, consumer cooperative lending-agencies chartered by the state or federal government to make loans to members of the cooperative at a low annual percentage rate, handle not only small loans; they also engage in financing of automobiles, durable goods, house trailers, boats, and so forth. Most of the credit unions are conducted by employees of large business firms or governmental organizations, or by churches. The person borrowing must either be employed by the organization or be a member of the church to buy shares in the union. The credit union has the disadvantage of being unable to be selective in its risks; consequently some have gone out of business, to the loss of members who bought shares. However, some corporations and governmental bodies have encouraged these unions, sometimes providing partial financial backing. This underwriting has served to stabilize many of these organizations, as has the fact that credit unions enjoy tax exemption.

Credit unions usually charge a legal maximum rate of 1 percent per month on the unpaid balance, although in a few places the rate is .8 percent. The maximum loan period generally is two years. On loans up to $50 no security is required. On loans between $50 and the usual maximum of $500 the endorsement of comakers is required, unless the borrower can pledge shares equal in value. Collateral is usually required for loans above this amount unless the member has sufficient shares to cover the cost of the requested loan. Many credit unions insist on wage assignments. These allow a credit union to deduct loan payments from salaries of delinquent borrowers without court hearings.[4]

It is interesting to note that most loans made from consumer finance companies are to consolidate overdue bills; the second largest group is for medical, hospital, dental, and funeral bills. The same holds true for personal loans from banks. But the largest number of loans from credit unions is for automobile expense and purchase of cars; the consolidating of overdue bills is second; and medical expenses third.

Aside from the obvious advantage of the low cost of the credit union loan, for many members there is a disadvantage in using this source. The pattern most of the credit unions follow, requiring assessment of the validity of the loan request and approval by a committee of members, is distressing to the individuals who are reluctant to reveal borrowing and financial problems to fellow workers.

The *pawnbroker* is almost the only source of credit for the nearly destitute person whose creditworthiness has not or cannot be established. Additionally, the pawnbroker often is the credit source chosen by persons whose incomes may at times be very high but who are temporarily in need of credit. The sharp inflation of the 1970s and the concurrent recession led many wealthy residents of Beverly Hills and Long Island, for example, to bring items of value to the pawnbroker, to be redeemed when "conditions" had straightened out again. Similarly, over the years, many in the theatrical profession, for example, pawn their diamonds to secure a quick loan during seasonal lulls. Some foreign-born persons turn more readily to the pawnbroker than to other resources. It is not uncommon for persons prior to having to move from their native country to use their savings to buy jewelry which, if need arises, can be used as security for cash.

Pawnbrokers are licensed, state regulated, and usually required to execute and file a bond. Although they charge a high interest rate, they provide the quickest form of loan service. Loans are made only on pledges—usually personal goods, tools, jewelry, musical instruments, and sometimes clothing. There is no note for the loan. The pawnbroker is subject to special taxes and must generally keep records of his pledges. Permissible interest rates in some states may be up to 3½ percent per month and in others up to 5 percent per month for certain amounts, the interest decreasing on loans for greater amounts. In some states a service charge is allowed. In effect, pawnbroker rates range, per regulations of the individual states, from 24 percent to 120 percent a year.

Ordinarily pawnbrokers will lend only from 60 percent to 90 percent of the auction value of the asset that has been pledged against the loan, and the asset must be left with the pawnbroker for the life of the loan. The borrower is given a pawn ticket showing the date, the amount of the loan, description of the property pledged, and sometimes the monthly interest rate and maturity of the loan. The pledge usually can be redeemed within a year by payment of the loan and the interest due. The loan must be repaid in a lump sum.

If the loan is not repaid within the specified period, the lender has the right to sell the pledge, ordinarily at public auction. The borrower has a right to any surplus from the sale, after the loan and interest have been paid. This practice, however, tends to be nonexistent because the lender himself usually bids on the property and offers no more than the amount owed, and is rarely outbid. If the property is sold to someone other than the lender for less than the amount owed, the pawnbroker has no legal claim against the borrower for the deficit. If the items offered the pawnbroker as a pledge have value for the borrower, care should be exercised that enough time is provided during which the pledge may be redeemed by repayment of the loan.

Remedial loan societies are semicharitable organizations, formed in the late 1800s and the early 1900s to provide loans to small borrowers at rates lower than those customarily charged by pawnbrokers and loan sharks. Only a few remain in the United States, all of them in large cities. They grant loans on the same kind of security as pawnshops: watches, clothing, tools, and so forth. Some also grant loans secured by chattel mortgages on automobiles and household goods.

Interest rates are usually 2 percent a month for chattel loans (24 percent per year) and less for pledge loans—generally 1 percent a month on the unpaid balance. The average amount of the loan is $50, with duration of the loan usually one year. The loan may be paid off in monthly instalments or in a lump sum at the end of the year. The interest is usually computed on the unpaid balance. When the loan is made against a chattel mortgage, the borrower must also sign a note, and usually a comaker's signature is required. If the loan is not paid at maturity, and the mortgaged property brings less than the amount owed, the borrower may have his other property or his wages attached for the balance still owed. In actuality fewer families today need to turn to such an organization for a loan. Unemployment insurance benefits and other arrangements in our modern society have tended to displace the need for remedial loan society help. But pledging an asset against a loan from a remedial loan society is preferable to an ordinary pawnbroker.

Insurance policies, while providing protection against the financial impacts of death, often also can serve as a resource for borrowing funds. A whole-life policy (not term), after two or three years of premium payments, may be a cash asset, the policyholder being entitled to borrow most or all of the accumulated cash value at a guaranteed rate of interest. The cash value also can be used as security for a loan from another lender —or the insurance company itself may lend the insured the cash surrender value for a fee. The total that can be borrowed is determined by the policy's guaranteed cash value, which increases with each year that premiums are paid. Because insurance interest rates are limited by law in the various states, they tend to be comparatively inexpensive, the interest rate generally falling well below that of any other lender. Moreover, technically the loan does not have to be repaid, for it is the borrower's own asset that is being used.

Even though a loan on insurance is obtained relatively easily and is relatively cheap, it must be remembered that borrowing against a life insurance policy reduces the financial protection for the family, and financial protection is the only valid reason for possession of most life insurance. There is another disadvantage for many people: there is no specified time for repayment of such a loan (which may also be an advantage for some financially troubled families). Interest may therefore be continued indefinitely, thereby decidedly increasing the cost of the insurance and decreasing the face value of the insurance. Most individuals and families are better off if they are compelled to repay their loan in instalments, liquidating it rather than carrying the burden of the debt for an unnecessarily long period.

A few *philanthropic societies* operate loan programs or are established as lending societies to help needy people who can pay no interest but would benefit by a loan. These organizations generally employ a trained advisor and they often work closely with, and sometimes only with, social agencies. Each loan is handled on an individual basis in terms of its purpose and the manner of its repayment. If it is to be used in relation to a new, an established, or a contemplated business, the society usually provides business analysis and consultation services through its board or other interested persons.

There are other sources for borrowing, some alluded to in other contexts in previous chapters. *Veterans' loans* are available to veterans with honorable discharges after at least ninety days of active service (or fewer if there is a service-connected disability). Such veterans may be eligible for loans from state as well as federal sources for a variety of purposes: to purchase, construct, or improve a home or farm, or to buy a business or undertake to expand a legitimate business undertaking. Sometimes loans can be obtained to liquidate delinquent indebtedness incurred in connection with these enterprises. *Second-mortgage loans* may be procured from specialized second-mortgage loan brokers who arrange to lend money on the security of a second mortgage. The costs of such loans often involve exhorbitant fees for handling the loan application, title searches, appraisal fees, and placing the second mortgage with a customer interested in investing money in a second mortgage. Interest on a second mortgage may be as high as 15 percent for the money loaned, aside from the other fees and costs. Many states in the last several years have been examining the arena of second mortgages with the view of increasing regulatory measures to protect the homeowner.

Many *employee loan funds* exist, the condition of borrowing and repaying being determined by the individual organization. *Educational loans* are available through institutions of higher education directly, or may be obtained from commercial banks when the loan is insured by the federal government under various statutes. Information about these generally should be obtained from the educational institution directly, or from commercial banks that grant such federally insured educational loans.

CONSUMER PROTECTION

Until recent years, most of the laws affecting instalment selling and lending of money were state laws. The role of the federal government in enacting and implementing legislation and providing mechanisms to regulate credit-granting organizations, to protect the consumer from exploitation, and to define the rights of consumers has been increasingly aggressive. Some impetus was supplied by the Economic Opportunity Act of 1964 which assisted in the establishment of neighborhood legal aid services. Many of these legal aid services included among their programs protection of consumers and prosecution in exploitive situations, and many of these legal aid functions continue to be maintained today in various parts of the nation. The establishment of an office of consumer affairs in the office of the President directed special attention to the plight of Americans who are victimized in the course of their efforts to raise their standards of living or to cope with financial problems that have moved beyond their control. There long had been federal statutes with regard to bankruptcy, but with the enactment in 1969 of the Truth-in-Lending Act, a new era of federal monitoring in the interests of consumers was initiated.

Only brief reference can be made here to the far-reaching aims of the 1970s' legislation, and in previous chapters certain specifics have been noted. (Fuller particulars can be obtained from the several federal agencies that have responsibility for carrying out the intent of these laws: the Bureau of Consumer Protection unit of the Federal Trade Commission, the Federal Reserve Board, the Department of Labor, and others.) The Fair Credit Reporting Act (1971), the Fair Credit Billing Act (1974), and the earlier Truth-in-Lending Act seek to guard against exploitation by mandating the disclosure of rates and other information important to the consumer, and by specifying time frames for billing, acknowledging complaints, and so on. Other legislation aims to reduce discrimination and inequity. Examples are the Equal Credit Opportunity Act (effective 1975) which amends the Truth-in-Lending Act to prohibit discrimination in granting credit because of sex or marital status; the 1974 Pension

Reform Act, which purports both to protect the rights of employees to pensions and to enable the self-employed person to establish a tax-shelter pension arrangement from which retirement benefits can be drawn when the retirement age has been achieved; and the limits which become effective in early 1975 with regard to garnishment of wages. The counselor who is uncertain which federal unit should be consulted with regard to a particular or general situation will find it expedient to contact the Office of Consumer Affairs, Department of Health, Education, and Welfare, Washington, D.C., or the Bureau of Consumer Protection of the Federal Trade Commission, which has many regional offices.

Some states have a long history in the enactment of protective legislation; others have entered this area relatively recently. Aside now from the federal requirements that take precedence, laws vary from state to state with regard to credit policies and procedures. Some states require that the instalment dealer be licensed; other states have such legislation under consideration. Among other things, the laws usually stipulate the form of the contract and the items that must be included in the contract. Some laws stipulate that the seller must give the buyer a written instrument evidencing the sale, and the document must include the cash price, the amount of the down payment (either in cash or trade-in value), the unpaid balance, the cost of insurance, the dollar as well as the per annum amount of the finance charges, the time for paying the indebtedness, and the manner of payment. Finance charges and service charges are limited and the "kickback" to the dealer is rigidly regulated. The laws frequently contain a penalty for violation. Instalment dealers have done considerable self-regulation; however, legal regulation has been necessary to protect the careless or unsophisticated buyer from certain abuses by a few unscrupulous sellers—particularly where language barriers have prevented full understanding of contract stipulations.

In order to protect the borrower of money, state laws set a legal or lawful rate of interest that may be charged on ordinary small loans to wage earners. A contract providing for an interest rate greater than the lawful rate (maximum fixed by law) is considered usurious. However, usury laws vary from state to state, and the statutes frequently make exceptions for certain types of lenders and borrowers. The majority of states now have such laws, based for the most part on the Uniform Small Loan Law originally developed before World War II by the Russell Sage Foundation.[5] The best small loan laws place a statutory limit on the amount of the loan and regulate charges; the companies are under state supervision. In more recent years, many commercial lending organizations—commercial banks, savings and loan associations, mutual savings banks—have entered the arena of large personal loans and sales finance operations. The Uniform Consumer Credit Code (UCCC), which applies to credit sales and loans for consumer purposes, is the model proposed in 1969 and revised in 1974 for use by states to regulate credit to individuals up to $25,000 (larger amounts when real estate is involved). This proposed overall regulatory law to replace all existing state consumer credit laws has been adopted by seven states. It specifies maximum rates for various levels of loans and instalment sales; it contains significant regulatory provisions as to disclosure of contract terms, collection remedies, and other conditions; and it includes heavy civil and criminal penalties specified for violation of the UCCC.[6]

The laws affecting the borrower and the instalment purchaser are complex, as well as different in the various states. The social worker or other counselor should be alert to the protective legislation and arrangements that exist and where the troubled family (alone, or with the advocacy assistance of the counselor) can consult as the occasion arises. Many states, as well as a number of large and small counties and cities, have not only a tax-supported consumer affairs consultant, but also voluntary organizations that concentrate their efforts in the field of consumer interests. Such offices or groups may be good sources of information or counsel. When questions arise about the legality of a loan, the interest rate charged, or the terms of a credit contract, the troubled family should be helped to obtain legal advice.

DEBT CONSULTATION

The nonpayment of obligations may lead the creditor to take legal action against the debtor. It is often at the point of threatened or actual action that the distressed individual seeks the help of a social agency. The reason for the person's or family's failure to meet the obligation must, of course, be evaluated. If income has been suddenly and unexpectedly curtailed or there are extraordinary expenses, the counselor should advise the debtor to approach the creditor, laying the facts "on the table." These facts include not only the reasons for not keeping up the payments, but also future prospects for repayment. Sometimes an adjustment satisfactory to both the debtor and the creditor can be effected; it then becomes the debtor's obligation to make every effort to carry out the temporary or permanent revision of terms that may have resulted from the conference. If the individual is unsuccessful in working out an adjustment—or it appears that the person's life experiences or personality development would jeopardize the effort—the counselor may decide with the debtor to assume the role of advocate and intercede in the debtor's behalf. Such measures not infrequently lead to a suitable settlement.

Should the creditor be unwilling or unable to negotiate the payment plan with the indebted individual or family, three courses of action should be weighed. First, an intercession on the debtor's behalf by a debt counseling organization; second, an invoking of the "wage earner plan" per Chapter XIII of the Bankruptcy Act; and third, a plan to declare bankruptcy. These are not mutually exclusive measures for consideration. Rather, the logical beginning is to approach the debt counseling service, following this, if the effort has been unsuccessful, with "Chapter XIII," and then, if necessary, bankruptcy.

DEBT COUNSELING PROGRAMS

The social worker counseling with a family toward resolving its social-psychological-economic problems may conclude that the family's insolvency requires the expert assistance of a specialist in handling problems of indebtedness (see Chapter 8). The resource may exist within the social worker's own agency (whatever its setting and auspices) or a local voluntary family service agency. Debt counseling may be a program operated by a *labor union, credit union,* or *legal aid service.* It may be available in the wage earner's place of employment (the personnel office or a special employee counseling unit) or church. Various branches of the armed services offer such counseling to military personnel and their families. In some communities, the local bank gives more or less informal guidance to overburdened customers.

An increasing number of *family service agencies* in recent years have established special programs or units to offer financial counseling. Many that do not provide this as a direct service work closely with credit counseling agencies established especially to serve the overly indebted individual and family. The latter offer the technical financial guidance, while the former direct their attention to helping the family member solve the psychosocial problems that led to or stem from the financial difficulties. Information about the location of a family agency with special interest and focus on financial counseling and related services can be obtained from the Family Service Association of America, 44 East 23rd Street, New York, New York, 10010.

The *credit counseling agency* is a free-standing nonprofit organization, generally titled Consumer Credit Counseling of _____, with membership in the National Foundation for Consumer Credit, Inc. Such local organizations pay a membership fee to the National Foundation and subscribe to operational standards enunciated by the organization. These operational principles include a fee limit for service, and governance by a board of directors with 60 percent of its membership drawn from community organizations (family agency, legal aid, Red Cross, and others), and the other 40 percent from credit-granting organizations. A directory of Consumer Credit Counseling agencies can be obtained from the National Foundation for Consumer Credit, Inc., 1819 H Street N.W., Washington, D.C. 20006.

The problem confronting the family may have its origin not so much in overall indebtedness as in a particular instance that reflects a serious difference between the consumer and a provider of service about what is owed, by whom and for what. This situation may have reached the point where the credit standing of the consumer has been negatively affected. There is a growing tendency to submit such disagreements to *arbitration*,[7] available in more and more cities under the auspices of the Better Business Bureaus. This is cheaper and faster than appealing to the courts. Under this system, a customer and a businessperson who have been unable to negotiate their differences agree to submit the dispute to arbitration by a member of a panel of volunteer lawyers. The lawyer selected from the panel examines the situation and renders a decision which both parties consented in advance to accept.

The problem brought by the family to the debt consultant may be complicated by the fact that there are several creditors. The family may be helped to develop a plan for consolidating its debts, obtaining a single manageable loan with which the various creditors are paid and arranging an orderly system for repaying this larger loan from recurring budgeted income. Or a prorating plan may be developed by the family and the credit counselor to apportion the available income among creditors each month, according to an advance agreement negotiated by the family and the creditors (usually after the intercession of the counselor). Or the whole process may be conducted solely by the credit counselor, the family and counselor only working together to develop a manageable budget: the family member may then deliver the income check (from wages, child care, or other sources) to the counselor when it is received, receive back the sum agreed upon for living purposes, and empower the counselor to distribute the balance among the creditors in keeping with the prearranged formula. As was stated earlier, a fee may be charged for this debt or credit counseling service.

The social worker or other counselor who plans to refer a family for credit counseling service that may involve prorating should be cautioned against commercial "debt consolidators" or "proraters." Although such commercial proraters are banned in more than half the states and in some cities, and regulated in some other states, they frequently have been profitmakers at the decided expense of the debtor whom they have not really helped to bring the indebtedness problem under control.

The avowed purpose of these businesses is to prorate the income of a debtor to the creditors for a fee or service charge. In principle, the plan works as follows: A definite amount of the debtor's income is allocated to the adjustor for debt retirement purposes and for payment of the adjustor's fees. The latter then prepares a plan for distributing the available income at specified times to the various creditors on a prorata basis (similar to the arrangement of the nonprofit credit counseling service). The adjustor makes arrangements with the creditors, receives the money from the debtor, and disburses the funds in accordance with the formula that has been worked out. The service charge is usually high, ranging from 15 percent to 50 percent of the total indebtedness.[8] Some proraters pay the specified amounts to the creditors first, collecting their own service charges only after the debtor's obligations are well along the way toward liquidation; most others are not so altruistic and some have been accused of not paying any of the money received from debtors. This plan often merely results in further debt and in the acquisition of a new creditor.

THE WAGE EARNER PLAN

The counselor may be led by assessment of the individual situation to think that the solution to the family's indebtedness requires more drastic action than debt consolidation or proration. Legal advice from a voluntary legal aid society, public defender, or other source would be in order. The Great Depression-born Chapter XIII amending the 1898 Bankruptcy Act is a court-supervised plan for paying off debts—often called *the wage earner plan.* It is *not* bankruptcy despite its relationship to the Bankruptcy Act. With an attorney's help, a budget plan for repayment (usually over a 36-month period) is filed with the bankruptcy court, along with a petition for immediate relief from creditor harassment and collection pressures. Once the plan is approved by the court and creditors (not necessarily all of them), the court appoints a trustee who receives the payments from the debtor and distributes the money to the creditors. The trustee is paid 5 percent of the amount thus distributed. Court costs and attorney's fees usually total several hundred dollars.

It is estimated that invoking Chapter XIII is successful in about half the cases that are filed for this relief.[9] If a family emergency keeps the debtor from making the agreed-on payments, the court may set aside the plan and the creditors then can obtain garnishments, start collection efforts, and repossess property. The successful completion of Chapter XIII action is regarded as a positive sign—for it is evidence that the indebted individual or family is willing to make sacrifices to pay honest obligations, and to demonstrate trustworthiness and, hence, creditworthiness.

BANKRUPTCY

The debtor who elects the Chapter XIII process over bankruptcy proceedings often does so because *bankruptcy* seems to signify failure to manage one's financial affairs and, consequently, immorality, inadequacy, and unworthiness as a human being. In reality, the wage earner plan may merely prolong the agony of liquidating debts. Bankruptcy, moreover, does not preclude later payment of debts should the individual desire to pay them. But bankruptcy per se is the only legal way that debts can be canceled without payment; it is a way of making a fresh start. To file a bankruptcy petition in a United States District Court, debts do not have to exceed assets by any specified amount. It should be emphasized that bankruptcy does not wipe out all debts. Six classes of debts are excluded from bankruptcy relief, and must be taken into account before considering bankruptcy as a device for becoming debt-free: (1) state and federal taxes due within the last three years; (2) fines and penalties arising out of criminal violations and traffic offenses; (3) child support and alimony; (4) debts arising from willful and malicious acts; (5) debts incurred by fraud or by false pretense; and (6) debts for which others have cosigned and may now become liable.

After filing for bankruptcy, the petitioner in effect gives the court nearly all personal possessions. A trustee is named to check on assets (either cash or property) available for distribution to the creditors. Certain items are exempt generally, and some are more explicitly defined in state laws. Tools, a car, and other items when necessary to earn a living, as well as food, clothing, and basic furniture are exempt. Usually the home is also. In some instances and in some states, however, the creditor may seek security in the form of property—such as a mortgage on a house or an encumbrance on a car.

Bankruptcy generally affects the creditworthiness of an individual—although it is not uncommon for a person, barely out of bankruptcy hearings, again to be granted credit and to fail to pay the new debts. It also is not unusual for the individual to be further obligated for the bankruptcy court costs and lawyer's fees, which tend to be $400 or more. It is possible to file for bankruptcy again in six years.

In the *Rubaiyat* of Omar Khayyam appears a comment that is ironically used in many circles today: "Take the cash and let the credit go." In today's money world, this is not easy to do, for we place considerable emphasis not only on the use of credit to stretch the cash available for maintaining a comfortable standard of living. We also rely on the utilization of credit as one important ingredient in maintaining our national economy at a healthy level. To assure that consumer credit is used appropriately rather than abused, and that it serves individuals and families as a constructive tool for achieving a healthy family and national economy, requires careful management of family income. Once one falls deep into debt, getting out is more difficult than would have been the devising of a design for remaining solvent. The ingredients for developing a design or blueprint for living—solvent—in today's money world are described in the next and last chapter.

NOTES

1. "How to Shop for Credit," *Consumer Reports,* 40 (March 1975): 172.
2. S. Lees Booth, *1975 Finance Facts Yearbook* (Washington, D.C.: National Consumer Finance Association, 1975), p. 62.
3. *Consumer Reports* 40 (March 1975): 176.
4. Ibid., p. 178.
5. Walter Stern Hilborn, *Philosophy of the Uniform Small Loan Law* (New York: Division of Remedial Loans, Russell Sage Foundation, 1923).
6. Booth, *1975 Finance Facts Yearbook,* pp. 58–60.
7. The *Wall Street Journal,* April 21, 1975, p. 1, reported that since the program was initiated in 1972, 92 of the nation's Better Business Bureaus have established arbitration boards.
8. "Getting Out of Debt Without Going Broke," *Changing Times* 25 (July 1971): 28.
9. Ibid.

14
Design for Living in Today's Money World

*I don't want to be pinned down. A budget takes the joy out of life!
I don't have enough income to budget!
It's just too much work!*

These comments by individuals so mired in debt that they sought professional help in extricating themselves, not only express common attitudes about "budgeting" but also are clues to personality traits that influence the pattern of an individual's management or mismanagement of money. They have to be understood by the financial counselor (and, at some point, by the individual or family) if the troubling problems are to be not only brought under sufficient control for the present, but successfully avoided in the future. Previous chapters have been addressed to understanding factors in the economic and social milieu of the family that interact with the developmental and relationship elements to determine the quality of family functioning in a money world, at different stages in the cycle of family life or in the life cycle of nonfamily individuals or household units. Earlier chapters also have considered goals and techniques of counseling where a money element is encompassed in the problem, and have discussed needs, values, and resources relevant to understanding and working with families and individuals toward resolution of such problems.

This final chapter concentrates on the principles and measures that must be taken into consideration in helping a family to develop a design for living in a modern money world. The design may be a written or a mentally constructed blueprint. But it always is flexibly tailored to the needs, wishes, and resources of the individual or family at a given time and for a set of personal and environmental circumstances.

Whether they like it or not, every family is benefited by consciously formulating some kind of blueprint to follow, regardless of whether it is committed to written form or is strictly or haphazardly followed. The process itself of considering what should go into constructing and implementing the blueprint—even if the process is superficial or aborted—

generally means that a decision to spend or not to spend has been deliberately (even if not satisfactorily) reached. Perhaps the universal benefit was best stated by Robert Benchley when he remarked that "The advantage of keeping family accounts is clear. If you do not keep them you are uneasily aware of the fact that you are spending more than you are earning. If you do keep them, you *know* it."

FREEDOMS AND FRUSTRATIONS

The term "budget," when associated with individual or family financial management, often is an emotion-laden word. Few people would dream of operating a business without maintaining and evaluating a record of how its resources will be apportioned, making adjustments in the allocations to minimize losses and to maximize profits. It is expected that there will be fiscal planning, and success is measured by the business profit and loss statement. In the arena of management and deployment of a family's resources, however, success is measured differently. The equivalents of "profit" vary with the aspirations and lifestyles of individual families, and the validity and actuality of recordkeeping evoke myriad feelings that are inextricably tied in with individual attitudes and perceptions about money.

> The Cs fought constantly during their first two years of marriage over his indulging his hobby of photography (adding to his equipment the constant stream of new or improved products appearing on the market) and her desire to invest these funds in "nice furniture or a trip *somewhere.*" Both resisted developing a budget, for it would be a "straitjacket." They had to be helped to see a budget not as a device for the control of one spouse by the other, but as a means for realistically deciding how much of their income they could free to meet their wishes, and how they could compromise their differences in spending patterns and goals by planning priorities and systematically allocating "spare" income to fulfill their individual and joint desires.

> The Ps, whose income (unlike that of the Cs) seemed barely enough to cover their shelter, food costs, and expenses of getting to and from their jobs, had decided that "two cannot live as cheaply as one," especially when the husband was having to pay tuition for the evening extension courses he hoped would equip him for better-paying work. Neither Hal nor Ruth P got along with their respective in-laws. Now they were faced with deciding whether to accept the invitation made by both sets of parents "to move home until you can get on your feet." Their quarreling over solutions led them to the marriage counseling service.

What kind of financial planning did the couple undertake in order to decide what alternatives were available to them? They were surprised at the counselor's asking this question. *They* did not have enough income to budget; it all had to go for bare necessities, so budgeting was "pointless." In their desperation to avoid moving to either parental home (they did not want to be constantly reminded that they were "too immature, too young to have married") they decided to "try" a budget. The beginning process provoked rancorous attacks on each other; each found the other was less than "careful." As they looked at their own and each other's spending habits they found sufficient leaks to enable them to maintain their independent living pattern as well as a new and more satisfying marital equilibrium.

Mrs. G's doctor thought her stomach pains were emotionally induced, that perhaps the aggregate of her responsibilities as a divorced working mother with two small children caused her frequent gastric distress. But Mrs. G protested to the family service caseworker that the doctor probably was wrong. She earned "good money" despite being absent from work several days each month (without pay, for she had insufficient "sick leave" to cover these absences). The exploratory session disclosed that the cause of the illnesses probably could be pinpointed to two circumstances. One was the occasional failure of the children's father to forward child support, which Mrs. G needed to "manage." The other was the mid-month period when cyclical billing by department stores and other vendors brought the bills that Mrs. G would now be faced with paying from her next paycheck. She always was sure there would not be enough to cover these obligations, and she would incur charges for delinquency. Did she use a budget? No, she had never been good with figures and she was sure she was not up to managing the "work" required to fill in "all those lines and columns."

The Cs, Ps, and Gs have numerous counterparts who, for similar and different reasons, avoid budgets as devices that constrain, frustrate, control, require unaccustomed facility with figures, and impose more self-discipline than they wish or feel able to exercise. Some even declare that they are "just not *naturally* economical" or offer other explanations as to why they should not expect or be expected to perform a task they may feel will cast the stern light of day on inadequate or idiosyncratic management of their income.

Certainly many persons find the need for and the process of budgeting baffling and frustrating. Others who handle this task with ease nevertheless chafe at the necessity for it. And many people who recognize the importance of developing and following a financial plan to achieve a particular goal find the process a source of anxiety or anger because they follow a complex budgeting scheme not shaped to their needs, interests, and capabilities. Or they unhappily feel caught up in a plan that is inflexible, or is executed by a budgeting partner who is compulsive about including even the most minute details or about adhering rigidly and literally to every budget line.

The fact is that there is no single right way to develop and keep a budget. Certain principles can be identified, and certain steps can be elucidated; but the principles should be drawn on selectively, and even the order of the steps can be rearranged to meet the needs, inclinations, and talents of each family. If the principles and the steps are applied in keeping with the goals and circumstances of the individual or family unit, there is enhanced probability that the family will be noticeably less troubled by money problems and will more likely be able to achieve short-term as well as long-term money goals. There will be reduced frustration and increased freedom to use available and potential income for purposes satisfying to the family and important in its effective social functioning.

SELECTED PRINCIPLES

A design that a family or an individual can construct for living in a money world generally consists of two parts. The first is essentially a plan for deciding how income shall be used over a period of time, how it shall be divided among different kinds of goods and services, how the income will be balanced (or budgeted) to meet present and future needs and wants. It is a proposal for spending, built up from the family's past experiences (from written records, or verbally recalled, or no longer in conscious memory). Or it may be based on current experiences if the individual or family has no personal history of having and spending income—as so often is true among newlyweds or young couples setting up nonmarital households. The second part of the design for living is a periodic review of how the family was able or unable to carry out the proposed plan, then modifying the plan to incorporate learnings from the experience.

The design should not be expected to solve all of a family's financial problems. It will not increase the level or regularity of a family's income, although it may point to a need for change. It will not eliminate all emergency needs for funds, but it may enable a family to be prepared for emergencies. It will not necessarily lead a family to accumulate savings, yet it may point the way to reordering priorities so that saving, if a family goal, takes precedence over other less desired items. Nor will the design, by its creation or by adherence to it, automatically result in increased (or in some) trust among family members, or enhanced self-esteem in those charged within a family to manage its income. Of itself, the design cannot render healthier the marital or family equilibrium that has been skewed by conflicting or inadequate attitudes and behavior regarding receiving, controlling, and using money.

Nor, once the design has been formulated, should it be viewed as static. Many circumstances will dictate the advisability of reviewing the plan. Has there been a change in the resources available to the family? Has the composition of the family changed? How have the family goals, or those of individual members in the household, been modified? What altered conditions in the wider community affect family income or income management?

Over time, it normally can be expected that a family's income will rise, that some resources will be acquired, that yesterday's wants will become today's necessities. As the family moves through the cycle of family life, the goals and needs of the beginning family will give way to those of the expanding family. Priority then tends to be given to the needs of children rather than those of the marital couple, and other needs may be sacrificed to assure that the children will receive adequate food, shelter, medical care, recreation, and education. There is a compelling need for reserve funds or resources to meet anticipated or unforeseen emergencies. In the middle years, expenditures and savings objectives change, the expenses tending to decrease without a corresponding decrease in income; planning for the next stage is accelerated. In old age, because of such factors as medical care, expenses rise again, but income drops with little prospect of being replaced. Single persons who have not been living in family groups often have different spending priorities and objectives, their lifestyles and family responsibilities differing from those of married households. If they enter a legal or a social (nonmarital) union, a shift in goals and priorities in spending may also occur.

It is not unusual for a family to complain that it has followed most conscientiously its carefully developed budget, yet outgo exceeds income, or some items that have been budgeted on paper fall by the wayside. Although the income may be unchanged, steady inflation has the effect of reducing it. Consequently, as prices for goods and services rise, client and counselor must be sure that the spending design takes the additional costs into account. Changing costs of living may be as or more important in updating the spending plan than changes in family composition, life-cycle stage, or family goals.

IMMEDIATE AND LONG-TERM GOALS

Because of fluctuations in both income and expenses, individuals and families have to view their economic life in a broad time perspective. Their design for living should include not only the needs of the present, but the needs of the future, the needs set against a backdrop of the family's short-term and long-term goals. The conceptions of individual family members about the nature and relative value of these needs determine to a large degree the manner in which families use or conserve their available resources and how they endeavor to maintain or increase them.

But people have different capacities (or, sometimes, opportunities) for thinking about immediate or long-range goals, as was discussed in an earlier chapter. Families with very low incomes may be able to do nothing more than take care of their immediate needs: this month's or last month's rent, this week's or today's food supply, or clothing for school now. For them the long-term goal of getting children through high school may loom larger and take more planning than aiming for a college education requires of families with higher incomes. They may feel too hopeless or helpless to identify any goals beyond immediate survival, preferably in a solvent state. They may need special help in seeing and doing something about leakages. Or the planning process may help them to come to terms with the fact that, at least for the time being, they really do not have enough income and need the help of a community resource.

> Mr. J, idled by a lengthy factory strike, and despondent over his inability to find more than an occasional short-time job, accused his wife of being wasteful, buying unnecessary "frills" for the two young children, and squandering their small savings by running up grocery and other bills unnecessarily. She reacted by "going home" to her mother, with the children. Two weeks later, Mr. J attempted suicide, leaving a note that he was a "failure" and Mrs. J could manage better without him "in the way." To the mental health counselor he later explained that the family would at least have received Social Security benefits—more money than he was earning or had received in the form of unemployment insurance benefits. When the Js reviewed with the counselor their income and financial needs, the husband was able to see that he had been expecting Mrs. J to manage the household on irregular income supplemented by the credit to which he had objected. He had been unwilling to acknowledge their financial need, refusing to discuss with his wife "*her* budget," and becoming increasingly angry about the mounting bills. He accepted the idea of applying for public assistance (which he regarded as utterly demeaning), planning carefully with his wife how this money would be spent. When later in the year he returned to full-time work, they planned together the apportionment of the income, budgeting not only for the present needs, but for possible recurrence of involuntary unemployment.

It really does not matter whether a family's planning begins with immediate goals, long-range goals, or intermediate goals. They may be able and wish to describe their goals in terms of their children's finishing high school or college, or of their having enough in old age to manage comfortably. They may center their planning around a goal five years (or another suitable time period) hence: making a down payment on a house, or reducing a mortgage; adding on a room; purchasing or replacing a car; scheduling orthodontia for a child or a trip for parents; planning for child-care arrangements that will free the mother to work part- or full-time outside the home. They may be able to decide on objectives for only a year at a time: buying a household appliance, or reducing overindebtedness, or finishing an educational program.

Most families and individuals are able to plan beyond the immediate week or month, to look at their expectations or wishes for one year, five years, or more. Indeed, having a long-term goal is often a stimulus to adequate management and economic functioning in the present. However, the long-term goals should be realistic, which means that there must be recognition of changes that may and often do affect such goals, and that the family's changing capacities and aspirations should be incorporated in a changed design for meeting its current and future needs and wants.

In any event, a family may not need to review its overall financial planning each year but, rather, only as a change in need or circumstances arises. Occasional deliberate examination should be undertaken—even if income and needs ostensibly have not changed—to decide if the goals are the same and if, in a changing world, the same plan will serve to achieve them.

PLANNING FAMILY PARTICIPATION
AND SHARING RESPONSIBILITIES

The chapters on money and counseling addressed the importance of involving parents and children in understanding and coping with the problems needing resolution, recognizing that not all family members will always be involved to the same degree in this process. So it is, too, with developing and following a financial plan: the extent to which each of the family members will be engaged in the design and execution of the plan must depend on circumstances and qualities relevant to that family. In two-parent families, it is important that both partners participate equally in the planning—although this may not be practical if one partner is incapacitated or some other special situation obtains. In ordinary circumstances, however, each parent probably has some special knowledge to contribute (the wife may know more about household linens needing replacement; the husband, about car or roof repairs). They should decide together not only on what they hope their plan will achieve, but what items it should include and how income should be apportioned to them. And both should decide who will carry what responsibility for carrying out the plan. Is the husband more comfortable with writing checks and keeping track of bills due and paid? Is this a chore he deplores and that the wife might therefore better assume? Is one more comfortable than the other with decision-making about specific items in the spending plan? In most families one or the other marital partner may do the buying for everyday purposes, pay the bills, keep the records. Which one does these tasks is not as important as their both being involved in the planning, conferring when a change is indicated or contemplated in the spending plan, and agreeing on the division of responsibility for carrying out the plan.

Parents often are reluctant to involve the children in discussions of family income and income distribution: what their children may reveal to neighbors or others often is unpredictable and may be a sensitive area. Nevertheless, it is desirable that children participate in the designing and implementing the financial plan as early and as fully as their understanding and maturity will permit. This will vary not only with the stage and nature of the children's development, but also with how comfortable the parents feel about sharing family income and outgo matters with the children, about giving the children personal allowances for which they do not have to account, and about the children's participation in other aspects of household operation by virtue of being members of the family. The benefit to the children in learning about financial responsibility and management through participation cannot be underestimated. It is also an important device for helping children to understand and trust their role and importance as sharing family members.

BUDGET STANDARDS AND GUIDES

The central task of the financial counselor is to assist the family to evaluate the soundness of its spending plan with the objective of balancing income and outgo while meeting current needs and wishes and progressing toward reasonable short- and long-term goals. The counselor may need to help the family begin at the beginning—that is, to develop a design for money management. What models does the counselor or family have to draw from? When is a particular expenditure reasonable for this family?

Obviously, there are no absolute criteria that can be applied to all families, but budget standards that have been developed in various quarters are useful guides. Some social agencies construct a budget guide for the use of their own staff, revising it periodically to conform with shifts in prices. Other agencies use, or adapt for their own use, standard budgets developed by other sources. For example, the Budget Standard Service of the Community Council of Greater New York periodically releases costs schedules that social agencies in that city can use to plan budgets. Some state welfare agencies not only develop budgets for economically dependent families of varying size and composition, but often also make these budgets available for use by voluntary and other agencies serving the same area. The three standards of living developed by the Bureau of Labor Statistics (see Chapters 2 and 8); the price changes measured for farm families by the Statistical Reporting Service of the United States Department of Agriculture in the "Index of Prices Paid by Farmers"; the budget standards published by extension services of various states and counties, taking into consideration regional conditions and populations—all of these are important contributions to the data base the financial counselor should have at hand.

But such budget standards are geared to average needs and average costs prevailing at a given time; they represent statistical norms rather than people. The Bureau of Labor Statistics budget standards, for example, purport to reflect expenditures: dollars and proportions of income already spent for specified items. (The exception is the budget standard developed by public—and some private—income maintenance agencies which base the amount of the assistance payment on the pricing of the components included in the individual's or family's budget; they expect but do not necessarily require the recipient to spend money per these guidelines: so much for rent, food, transportation, and so forth.) Because no family is truly an average family with average needs and expenditures, these statistical norms cannot be simply and literally adopted for use by a family. Individual differences in family values, standards, needs, and desires, which derive from cultural, psychological, intellectual, and economic factors, make it necessary to particularize each item in the budget and to weigh its relative importance in the aggregate expenditures. Every spending plan or budget must be highly individualized—and averages reflect both good and poor management.

The usefulness of these standards for the family and for the financial counselor, then, lies largely in having a benchmark for testing the family's needs, for seeing how far and in what way the individual budget departs from the standard. The discernment of any considerable disparity suggests exploration as to its cause and validity. The deviations from the norms are expressed in many ways and must be considered from many angles. Should the Rs be encouraged to maintain high-cost living quarters at the expense of stringent economies in food and clothing? Or can Mrs. H, a divorced woman with young children, who works full-time as a clerk, be expected to manage on a minimal food and clothing budget? Can Mrs. S, who has limited intellectual capacity, improve her haphazard manner of managing her household and thereby reduce household management costs?

Because of his wife's illness or death, the father in some instances may be not only the breadwinner but the family manager. He, therefore, must assume responsibility for marketing, for household planning, and possibly for providing the children with outside recreation. His double burden doubtless will increase expenditures for food and other household items, and possibly for household service and for recreation.

Personal factors may affect a decision that a given family for a time-limited period will deviate from the norm, then swing back to it when a particular objective has been accomplished. Accordingly, three families may wish to buy a major household appliance on credit. In Household A, the father is compulsively careful about management of the family budget, weighing each expenditure against the merits of saving, watching each penny that enters and leaves the household; his wife is skillful in effecting small economies. Household B has only ordinary management skills; the income and the outgo remain in moderately good balance, with bills generally paid with reasonable promptness, but with no particular stress on postponing gratification now for future comfort. Household C, with the same income level and family size and composition as Households A and B, is less concerned with how an item is to be paid for than with having it on hand; more than 30 percent of their income is already committed to instalment payments. Obviously, Households A and B are in a safer position to contract additional debt than Household C.

The financial counselor should be aware not only of the individual factors affecting expenditures but also of patterns of spending as family incomes increase. When income is limited, people tend to place emphasis on securing a satisfactory *quantity* of basic goods and services. As income increases, the factor of *variety* enters into their consuming patterns. When income is more than sufficient to provide quantity and variety, people then direct effort toward securing goods and services of progressively higher *quality*. In some families, quality may precede variety.

The importance of individualizing the family and its spending plan cannot be overemphasized. When an agency that provides income maintenance utilizes a standard budget, the family should have maximum opportunity to apply it as flexibly as possible to meet their priorities. (See Chapter 9 for the rationale.) The process of budgeting should be viewed as a means of managing the income, not as a controlling or monitoring device to curtail expenditures or impose conformity. In working on budget problems with self-supporting families, the counselor should be able to help them construct budgets that meet their particular situations as they see them.

What guidelines can serve to help the family know that their spending plan is within reasonable parameters? Table 6 offers such guidelines, permitting fundamental flexibility while suggesting the outside limits that spell danger. The acceptable variations are presented for the traditional hypothetical family of four: employed father, mother at home, thirteen-year-old boy, and eight-year-old girl. However, the parameters suggested are equally applicable to smaller or larger family units, for they are geared to needs and standards that vary from family to family. The variations are built not on prescription of certain kinds and quantities of food, for example, but on sums of money the particular family may utilize to provide its unique needs (whatever they are) and remain solvent.

The incomes shown are gross incomes (before taxes). The variations take into account the fact that if a family elects to pay a higher proportion of its income for shelter, it may have to adjust for this by spending a lower proportion for some other item: food, clothing, household help, or another—or some combination of items. But in no event should the total spending equal more than 100 percent.

If both parents are employed, certain adjustments pertinent to the individual family should regularly be given attention. Is additional child care purchased to free the mother to work? If this is care at home, has adjustment been made in the tax bracket for the Social Security tax that the parents are now obligated to pay as employers? What effect does the wife's earnings have on total taxes paid? The proportion to the increased income may be nominal, or it may be considerable. Any upward adjustment, then, to the household care and tax items must be reflected in a downward adjustment in some other item, so that the total budget remains in balance. The single mother, working to support her children, may also have to devote a larger proportion of income to child care (and perhaps taxes).

The key to the application of the acceptable variations guide is, of

TABLE 6. RANGE OF ACCEPTABLE BUDGET VARIATIONS FOR A
FOUR-PERSON FAMILY

Annual income	$5,500	$8,000	$12,500	$18,000
Item	Percent range	Percent range	Percent range	Percent range
Food	35–45	30–40	30–40	20–30
Housing	25–35	25–35	25–35	25–35
Clothing	8–12	9–13	9–15	9–15
Transportation	6–9	8–12	8–12	7–15
Taxes	6–16	6–16	6–20	15–30
Health and insurance	7–10	7–10	7–12	7–15
Savings	0–10	0–10	0–10	5–15
Instalment payments	5–12	5–12	5–15	5–15
Household help	0–5	5–10	5–12	5–15
Other consumption	3–12	4–12	5–10	5–15

INCOME is gross (before taxes) from all sources, in family.
FOOD includes all meals eaten in and out of the home.
HOUSING is rented or owned shelter, and includes real estate taxes, maintenance, fire insurance, household operations, utilities, and household furnishings. (Household appliances, or other furnishings or repairs being purchased on a credit plan should be included in "Instalment payments"—and not in this item.)
CLOTHING includes expenses for all members of the family; it covers not only costs for new purchases but also dry cleaning, pressing, and repairs.
TRANSPORTATION includes public carrier fares, automobile payments and insurance, repairs, tires, fuel, and other maintenance costs; it covers transportation for work, school, recreation, or other purposes.
TAXES include federal and other income taxes (whether or not these are withheld by the employer), Social Security and other taxes mandated by a state or local jurisdiction except real estate).
HEALTH AND INSURANCE include current medical costs and payments for prepaid health plans, health insurance, life insurance, and disability insurance (group or individual plans for many).
SAVINGS comprise stocks, bonds, investments, bank or other accounts; payments to pension plan.
INSTALMENT PAYMENTS include all credit purchases other than 30-day accounts.
HOUSEHOLD HELP includes sitters, housekeepers, cleaning personnel; and gardeners, plumbers, other maintenance help.
OTHER CONSUMPTION includes costs for recreation, charity contributions, education, personal needs, gifts, and personal allowances.
NOTE: It should be observed that the low and high columns for each range, except in one instance (and that, by chance only), do not total 100%. In application, of course, allocation percentages for each item line must be adjusted so that the column total does not exceed 100%.

course, judgment: thoughtful assessment of what is needed and desired by the specific family and how they propose to meet these needs within their income limits. In effect, the application of the acceptable variations guidelines has but two purposes: to serve as a reminder about what is usually a reasonable upper-limit expenditure; and to increase conscious examination of the interrelationships of the various items for which money basically must be spent in most households regardless of the amount of income, or normal or neurotic behavior, or needs, aspirations, and values.

BUILDING THE FINANCIAL DESIGN

There is no single "best" system for developing a financial plan for the use of all families. Probably as many people have no formal system as do; and the variations among the latter are numerous. Some people also have less need for a formal system, at least on a continuous basis. For example, the couple whose income has varied little over the years, whose expenses shift only in response to higher food and clothing prices, may have an adequately clear idea of how much of the recurring income can be spent for what purpose without setting this information down on paper every month, or even every year. If their income provides a reasonably comfortable cushion after expenditures, there may be no pressure on them to examine their spending pattern for leaks or for rearrangement of priorities. Only as they develop a specific goal that requires scrutiny of their spending are they likely to construct a budget—for example, to buy an extraordinary item or service, or to systematically increase investments in retirement planning.

There are individuals who claim to have an "intuitive feel" for how their funds should be apportioned and spent; they too do not transfer this feeling to paper to be visible to the eye. The likelihood is that, like the couple noted above, they either have sufficient leeway between income and outgo to make errors or indulge wishes, or over time, they have incorporated into their thinking an operational pattern that has become "intuitive."

Many people who do not have a budget system would benefit from one. Equally as many others have budget systems which do not benefit them. The reasons for the latter are many, but common ones are these: the system is complex, more detailed than can be tolerated within the family's level of patience, capability, or interest; the items contained in the budget system are not totally relevant to the needs of the family and, therefore, the pertinent ones are lost in the morass; the self-discipline that tends to be nurtured by necessity or strong desire is at too low a level for coping with the essential periodic examination (often *self*-examination, for which tolerance also is low) of income, goals, and expenditures.

The development of a design for living in our modern money world may embody one or more of these family objectives: to preserve a balance between income and expenditures (or restore a balance in the face of overindebtedness); to save ahead for needed purchases or activities (durable goods, education, future financial security, a trip); to locate and stop leaks (controlling expenditures in lieu of impulsive or aimless spending); to use the planning and implementing process to establish or maintain communication and cooperation among family members. Whether the family's approach to the construction of a financial plan is reluctant or eager, impatient, or painstaking, it must include four basic components: income, fixed obligations, day-to-day needs, and discretionary balance (if any).

The format and the minuteness of detail will vary with the needs, capabilities, and interests of the family. But the design should be written. There are many advantages, in addition to the fact that we usually analyze better what we see and that we think more precisely when working within a pattern which is set down on paper. A written plan is more likely to be comprehensive, detailed, and accurate than a verbal or "in-the-head" plan can be: decisions are not relegated to uneven or selective memory; its omissions are more noticeable; corrections can be made as needed; estimates of future income and expenditures can be better anticipated; lining up the items permits easier weighing and ranking by order of importance to the family. Family members can participate more readily when they are constructing and looking at the same material. Their recorded decisions (how much is to be spent for what, when) stiffen resolve to adhere to the plan, and help to reduce haphazard or impulsive spending. The written plan also provides a baseline that can be reexamined at later times to discover exclusions or unrealistic inclusions and to make adjustments consistent with changes in the family, the income or needs, or the external economic realities, without having to start from scratch with a new plan.

Many models of written plans exist. A number of banks, some insurance companies, consumer-interest periodicals, and others make them available from time to time. (Some sample sources appear in the references in the bibliography.) Many families find models useful. Many do not, for the priorities offered may not be that family's priorities, or the details may be overwhelming or irrelevant. Moreover, most of these budget plans assume a rather high level of sophistication, if not education, which the financially troubled family may lack. Many families are better served by being invited to simply rule off (or use already ruled) sheets of paper on which they can enter the pertinent headings and details regarding items, times, and money. In its simplest form, the financial plan will have only four sets of figures and a summary. To start, therefore, several 8½" × 11" sheets of paper can suffice.

THE PRELIMINARIES

Certain agreements should be reached by the counselor and the family: the kind of financial counseling desired; the desirability of developing a financial plan; the nature of the family's long- and short-range goals; who will participate in the counseling and who in the design construction. Then the beginning step in helping the family to tailor a budget design to their needs is to analyze actual expenditures against the background of income received. Past spending patterns for as long as a year provide a basis for recalling the unexpected demands that arose; the temptations that were wisely or improvidently met (a bargain?); the peak periods of certain kinds of expenditures (fall clothing purchases in anticipation of school); the intermittent payments that had to be made (quarterly or semiannual insurance premiums, annual automobile license). It is useful for the family to examine its records, such as receipts or canceled checks, to find out as closely as possible how past income has been spent individually and jointly.

If the family is a new unit with no combined spending history, the members will find it practical to study current expenditures, keeping a detailed account of family expenditures for one month. Sometimes, because of the urgency of the situation, the counselor and the family may agree that the survey must be based on the client's memory. The items studied should include those in the preceding table and any other expenditures, such as alimony, child support, and loans or payments to relatives or friends.

This opening experience with the family in record keeping and assessment will offer the financial counselor important clues about the way the family members think about and invest themselves in coping with the task at hand. Should the plan for the family be sketchy and, while generally covering all uses of its funds, leave day-to-day details to be filled in as they go along? Have they already developed a spending pattern that appears to need only minor changes in practice? Will this suffice? Do they need help in filling in the details in only one part of the spending design (for example, expenditures related to various aspects of the transportation item, like automobiles)? Is the uneasiness of the family such that they should have help in considering not only the general framework of the spending plan but also component details? Or will this only serve to deepen their anxiety? The intent of this gathering of data should not be for purposes of criticizing what was or was not done; rather, it is to learn something about where money has gone and why, for the insights such information holds as to what might be expected, and what should be encouraged or discouraged in the course of tailoring and following a proposed budget plan.

Another preliminary is in order but, unlike the expenditure information which should be developed for all clients, some selectivity should be exercised as to which families are ready and able to take this written step: to record the intermediate and long-range financial goals of the family. These would be more than "get out of debt" or "come out even every month" goals. They generally are the short-range goals, and many families are so beset by them that they are not ready to think beyond them. The more distant goals would include major purchases the family would like to make (a freezer? a second car? a new roof?); the size of the financial reserve they hope to have on hand in a stipulated number of years for a child's education; a family trip; resources to guard against financial emergencies; or investments for future income.

DETERMINING INCOME

The next step is to determine whether the current income is sufficient to cover needs. In the period covered by the analysis of past or present expenditures, did the family supplement its income by borrowing? How much was bought on credit? Were payments skipped on some items? Was there dissaving? Was the spending—or borrowing—realistic in relation to the available income? What income does the family have now? And what income can realistically be anticipated?

Before dollar amounts or percentages of income can be allocated to various needs, the family must be clear about how much money they will have for spending, and when it will be on hand. This information is best projected, if possible, for the period of a year in order to deal with both the irregularity or seasonal character of some income and the periodicity of some payments that will fall due. Three dimensions should be charted for consideration: the sources of the income, the amounts received, and the time they become available. A sheet of paper (separate or fastened into a notebook) marked "Income" can quickly frame the needed picture by (1) marking off columns for the months of the year, the headings spaced horizontally across the top of the sheet, with an extra column for the yearly totals; (2) listing on the left side of the sheet all sources of income received in this family with a separate line for each source (husband's work, wife's work, work of another member of the household, child support, alimony, year-end bonus, dividends, interest, rental income, gifts, or others); (3) entering in the appropriate month the amount of money expected from the designated source; and (4) totaling in the far right column the yearly sums to be received from each source, and totaling at the bottom of each monthly column the amount of money expected.

Families who receive a fairly regular wage or pension, or have a business from which they draw a definite amount each month, ordinarily would have little difficulty in preparing this income sheet. Families with income from a business, farm, or profession, or whose earnings derive from sales commissions, may have to estimate their income, subject to change during the coming year. If the family in such a situation is uncertain about what its income is likely to be, it is advisable to estimate the largest and the smallest amounts of spendable income likely to be available, and to use the lower amount for planned spending. If the yearly income is paid in, for example, ten pay periods (as with many teachers), the family has the option of showing money for the actual months in which these payments are received, leaving the spaces blank in the nonpayment months. Or the annual salary may be divided into twelve equal sums, entering these on the chart for each month, reminding the individual to set aside enough of the money received in each month to provide money for the months without paychecks.

Sometimes a family is not clear about the amount actually earned. Budgeting should be done on gross income rather than on take-home pay to accommodate to the frequent confusion about payroll deductions that are mandatory or actually are voluntary. All deductions made at the source of the income should then be allocated to the appropriate item. Involuntary deductions usually include Social Security payments (often designated as FICA) and income taxes; frequently there are mandatory deductions for retirement, disability, group health, or life insurance plans, or for union dues. Voluntary deductions may include purchase of savings bonds, contributions to charitable organizations, or payments for some form of optional group insurance. It is important to distinguish the voluntary from the involuntary contributions in order to be able to decide, should this become necessary, when the wages diverted to voluntary items would be better used for some other purpose.

If income from an absent parent, though awarded by the court, is received sporadically, there should be an assessment as to whether the pattern in the given situation justifies counting the income as received in each month, in certain months only, or not as a regular reliable sum available for spending. All income, including earnings of each adult and the amounts contributed by working children, should be shown—estimated or provisionally noted if not fixed. Certain costs related to work, such as union dues, work tools, and contributions for gifts to fellow workers, reduce the amount of real income. (Such items should be recorded in the pertinent categories included in the third chart, "Day-to-Day Needs by Week and by Month.")

Earnings of employed children cannot be included in full, but should be represented by a figure which is proportioned to their earnings and personal needs, and to the monetary value of their living costs and services provided in the household. The decision about the reasonableness of the contributions of working children should be based on an objective appraisal of these items along with the feelings of the young workers about their earnings and their role in the family.

A family may also derive income from renting space in the family home or in other property. The cost of producing such income should be taken into account, much as it would be in preparing estimates for income tax reports. Accordingly, the extra cost of utilities, linens, cleaning supplies, and upkeep should be deducted from the gross payments received. Such computations, as for any business expense, should be shown in a separate reckoning and the net transferred to the income chart for inclusion in the income picture.

The basic income could be shown as in Chart 1.

If, as the year progresses, income is increased, the family may decide to proceed for the balance of the year on the originally projected plan, or to revise many items accordingly. A beneficial alternative is to acknowledge the fact of the additional income, but put it regularly into reserve, proceeding with the rest of the plan as originally developed. It should be borne in mind that expectations about the increase often are higher than the actual net increase because of the automatic increase in taxes and other percentage-of-income mandatory withholdings. It is therefore essential that the increase not be committed for spending until it actually is in hand and the amount truly available is certain.

Retired couples or families who anticipate a year or partial year without earned income may have another matter to consider before completing the income chart. The recurring income (pension, Social Security benefits, unemployment insurance, disability, or other) may need to be augmented by savings or income from investments previously planned for such an exigency. They may have to complete the computations for fixed obligations and day-to-day needs prior to deciding the minimum amount of savings or other assets to make available each month to supplement any recurring income. Or, depending on the amount and kind of resources they have in reserve, and the duration of

CHART 1. INCOME

Sources:	JAN	FEB	MAR	APR	MAY	JUN	JUL	AUG	SEP	OCT	NOV	DEC	TOTAL
Wages or salary of:													
A Gross*	$	$	$	$	$	$	$	$	$	$	$	$	$
Social Security taxes*	$	$	$	$	$	$	$	$	$	$	$	$	$
Income taxes*	$	$	$	$	$	$	$	$	$	$	$	$	$
Other mandatory (list)*													$
Net**	$	$	$	$	$	$	$	$	$	$	$	$	$
B (same details)													$
Contributions from:													
C (working child)							$	$					$
D other													$
Child support	$	$	$	$	$	$			$	$	$	$	$
Rental													$
Dividends	$				$			$		$			$
Bonus												$	$
Etc.													$
Etc.													$
Totals	$	$	$	$	$	$	$	$	$	$	$	$	$

*If paid/withheld weekly, multiply by 4.33 weeks to find monthly earnings; if biweekly, by 2.16 weeks; if semimonthly, by 2.
**Add only net (gross minus withholdings above) in total.

the period for which they will be required (a few months? the lifetimes of one or two persons?), they must distribute among the months the expected dollar income, and bring their fixed-obligations and day-to-day needs expenditures into conformity with it.

With the income from various sources and the timing of its receipt spread over the year, the family or individual is now ready to see whether peak spending periods and peak income periods are or can be coordinated, and whether funds received at certain times must be set aside to meet specific due dates for payments on outstanding obligations.

FIXED OBLIGATIONS
Every individual and family has certain expenses that are unavoidable: some may be fixed by a contract or agreement (insurance premiums, mortgage payments, instalment debts); others may have to be estimated (income taxes, automobile licenses, property taxes). Examination of the

preliminary listing of expenditures in the preceding year should disclose the pattern of due dates and sums due. Are the times to be the same next year? the amounts? Have some obligations been liquidated, like completing the contract on the purchase of a television set, or a loan? Are new obligations expected (college tuition, payments on a car to be purchased)? The carryovers and the anticipated inescapable obligations should be entered on a chart constructed similarly to the income chart: listing in the left-hand column all expected unavoidable expenses; placing in the column for the specific month the amount then due; entering the yearly total due for each item in the final column at the right; and in a row along the bottom, showing the total that must be paid out in each month. (See Chart 2, Fixed obligations.)

The "must" items that fall due each month (housing, child care,

CHART 2. FIXED OBLIGATIONS

Obligations	JAN	FEB	MAR	APR	MAY	JUN	JUL	AUG	SEP	OCT	NOV	DEC	TOTAL
Taxes*													
federal				$									$
state				$									$
real estate			$			$							$
other (list)													
automobile	$												$
Mortgage** (or rent)	$	$	$	$	$	$	$	$	$	$	$	$	$
Insurance													
(list) A	$							$					$
B	$		$					$		$			$
health	$	$	$	$	$	$	$	$	$	$	$	$	$
other—													
property	$												$
fire/theft	$												$
automobile			$										$
Alimony	$	$	$	$	$	$	$	$	$	$	$	$	$
Loan payments to—***	$	$	$	$	$	$							$
Credit payments													
(list) A	$	$	$	$	$	$	$	$	$	$	$	$	$
B	$	$	$	$	$								$
Totals	$	$	$	$	$	$	$	$	$	$	$	$	$

*Enter in accordance with month(s) due and/or withheld.
**Enter real estate tax above if included in periodic mortgage payments; enter mortgage-related insurance payments below.
***Enter in accordance with month(s) interest and/or principal payments fall due.

instalment debt payments, others) should be entered. Include those payments made by payroll deduction: group health insurance, group automobile or homeowner's insurance, pension plans, Social Security (OASDHI), taxes, union dues, and others. This is important because not only is take-home pay reduced by these amounts but the family should have a clear picture of where its earnings are going. It is important also because the deduction system may alter (the employer may decide to discontinue handling auto insurance deductions, for example), or the deduction exceeds or is less than the obligation, and the family must be prepared either to claim reimbursement at the appropriate time or to complete the payment at a given time. For example, more federal or state income taxes may be withheld than the family ultimately is obligated to pay, or a moonlighting family member may have additional Social Security deductions from one or both employers' paychecks. These overpayments would be claimed and shown on the income chart as income to be received in the following year. It is more likely, however, that income taxes actually due will exceed the year's tax withholdings, and provision for payment of the balance must be made.

Families often are caught unawares by the arrival of a once-a-year bill. Annual business or automotive licenses and fees, for example, tend to be forgotten. Quarterly, semiannual, or annual premiums for insurance often create consternation. While some insurances may call for monthly premiums, this usually is more expensive than the less frequent payments. Entering the amount due under the month the premium should be paid is a reminder that either a sum must be set aside each month to be ready for the payment, or the due date should be coordinated with the coincident receipt of extra or intermittent income.

The spread of payments due for loans or instalment purchases, itemized separately, offers a clear picture of payments that will span the whole year and those that might come to an end during the year. It is thus possible to decide by which months a certain proportion of income will be freed either to handle other obligations or for savings.

Chart 2, with its picture of fixed obligations, brings to sharp attention the need to have more dollars available in certain months than others. It encourages finding ways to save from the income of some months for use in these high-obligation months—or points to the necessity to borrow needed dollars by dissaving or through normal credit arrangements.

> The Ls were faced with paying in February a life insurance premium of $120, an instalment of $320 on their local property tax, and an instalment of $50 on their son's college tuition. In the prior October, when they had developed

the chart for the first time, they became aware that their income for the months of November, December, and January was fully committed, that there would be no savings in these months to prepare for the February needs —which could not be met, either, from the February income. They decided to use $190 from their small savings toward these February obligations. They would take a loan of $300 for the balance and show the payments on the fixed-obligations chart, beginning with the first one in March. They looked ahead at the total of the fixed expenses to which they were committed for the year, including the new loan. By dividing all of the year's fixed expenses by twelve, they could decide how much of the total burden should therefore be borne by each month's income so they could put aside the required sum on a systematic basis.

The use of twelve pay periods is the most common, for these are usual income and obligation periods. However, a similar money management plan can be developed on quarterly, semimonthly, or weekly time intervals if the family so chooses, although it is less efficacious as a rule.

A variation on this recommended simple method for this phase of the financial design is to divide each month's column into two vertical parts, the first to show what is planned, the second to enter what actually was expended. This refinement offers the family a quick assessment of shortages or surpluses in each month and helps the money manager to be prepared for developing trouble (if expenses were higher than planned) or to detect unexpected savings (if the expenses were lower than planned).

The essence of a good design for money management is spreading the fixed obligations so that each month carries a share of them, and the needed resources are thereby available at the time each payment must be made.

Day-to-day needs

When the expenses in Chart 2 are totaled and subtracted from the income in Chart 1, the amount of money available in each income period (or month) for meeting daily needs plus other objectives (see next section) is placed in sharp focus. All the expenses the individual or family has that are variable should be listed. The family members have more immediate control over these variable or flexible items, in contrast to the fixed obligations which must be paid either as originally assumed, or on a revised arrangement agreed to by the overburdened family and creditors. It is generally through juggling, paring, or selectively eliminating costs for some of these items that the family too deep in debt, struggling unsuccessfully to make ends meet, or seeking ways to commit some of its income to savings can solve its money management problem.

Unlike Charts 1 and 2, which spread the pictures of income and fixed obligations over a year, the plan for daily living expenses should be set up for only a month or two ahead. Whether one- or two-month periods are used, or whether weekly intervals are preferable to months should be related to the time frame that is more readily handled by a given family or individual. Some people find it easiest to plan their day-to-day spending on the basis of a month, then divide this into weeks, remembering that there are 4.33 weeks in a month. Others are more comfortable computing their daily needs for a week, then multiplying the total by 4.33 to find the costs for the month, placing them against the backdrop of the income available after fixed obligations have been covered.

The preliminary examination of expenditures is an important source for knowing what items need to be included in the day-to-day list, and what sums should be allocated. The family and the financial counselor will quickly be aware that there is less solid information available for inclusion in this part of the plan, and that items on which money will have been spent are often forgotten until the need reappears. Filling in the "Day-to-Day Needs" chart is best accomplished by involving as many family members as possible. Each will recall some individual spending and stimulate other family members to remember such items as lunch money, a new magazine subscription, movies, television repair, and a child's weekly or monthly allowance. Review of the plan after it has been applied for one or two months helps the family to see what was bought or spent that should be avoided or modified, applying this learning as soon as possible to subsequent months. Such alterations (up or down) will keep a spending plan viable. While the family will find it important to list for the months ahead the items that unavoidably reappear (utilities, lunch money, gasoline, and others), affixing a projected cost to each usually is not necessary for many months in advance.

Chart 3 is offered here only as a model for form, with some reminders about common needs. However, the specific needs of any individual or family may not correspond in all or any ways with this model.

Many families find it useful to adopt the same kind of variation proposed in relation to Chart 2, inserting a column next to the one for planned expenditures, to list actual expenditures for the items shown in the plan and for items that come up but that had not been included during the planning. This comparison of how the plan was carried out quickly points out to the family the oversights, over- or underspending, and reasons for unexpected deficits or welcome surpluses. Planning for

Chart 3. Day-to-Day Needs by Week and by Month

Needs	per week	April	May
Food	$	$	$
at home			
meals eaten out			
A's lunches, snacks			
B's lunches, snacks			
Utilities			
gas (oil, coal, etc.)			
electricity			
water			
phone			
Household operation			
improvements			
repairs			
replacements			
Automobile			
fuel			
repairs, maintenance			
Public transportation			
to school			
to work			
other			
Clothing			
father			
mother			
child a			
child b			
cleaning, repair			
Personal allowances			
father			
mother			
child a			
child b			
Personal care			
Medical, dental			
Education			
school			
newspapers, etc.			
Recreation, entertainment, vacation			
Gifts, contributions			
Miscellaneous			
Total	$	$	$

NOTE: Some items, such as Food, are most easily computed first on a weekly basis, to be multiplied by 4.33 to reach the monthly total. Others, such as utilities which are commonly billed monthly, should be entered first in the monthly columns, to be divided by 4.33 to reach the weekly total. Where large variations between months may occur (during school vacation periods, for example), it may prove helpful to insert a second "per week" column before the second month.

subsequent months should be based on this comparison of expectations and experiences.

Some bills recur on a regular basis—either monthly or every other month: utilities, rubbish collection, home-delivered milk, newspapers. In the not too distant past, it was thought that families could plan with some accuracy and ease what these kinds of items would cost and how they would fluctuate from season to season (heating costs, for example, that rise in certain months, fall in others). In fact, it commonly was recommended that certain inclusive categories always be used in planning: household operation, transportation, and so forth. Today, however, the family troubled with financial stress—or seeking to avoid it is well advised to examine and plan for the components separately. Household energy bills, for example, have been shooting up; new costs and new utilities taxes consume dollars in ways for which families often are unprepared. Assessing each household expense independently will not halt the price increase, but may enable the family to devise ways for reducing use and therefore costs. Similarly, the surge in costs associated with operating automobiles (fuel, repair) may suggest that children should not be driven, but should take public transportation to school, or that curtailment of other use of automobiles may result in effective savings.

When accounting for day-to-day needs special attention should be devoted to noting certain recurring costs associated with the work or community roles of family members. Such costs can quickly erode income available for daily use. This is not to say that these are expenditures to be avoided. Some might, perhaps, be pared down; many, however, are necessary to fulfillment of the respective roles and each item should be conscientiously examined on its own merits. Mr. C sends alimony and child support to his former wife and their two children. The children spend every other weekend with him and his present family. In addition to the usual "outing" and its attendant costs, Mr. C gives the children "a little something extra to put in their pockets" until he sees them again. Mr. B volunteers his services to his church for repairing the electrical system in lieu of his making a cash contribution, which the family feel they cannot afford. But he is reluctant to ask for certain materials he needs to do the work, and so he buys them. Johnny J, with the encouragement of his parents, is running for president of his high school class. His campaign calls for "treating" his campaign workers to refreshments while they work on the planning and executing of the campaign. Mrs. W finds that at least twice each week she is asked for a "sympathy" or "hospitality" contribution, or to attend a shower, lunch, or "coffee" because of illness, engagements, or weddings of fellow employees in the company where she works. Mr. M, lunching with his fellow workers, finds that he "picks up their lunch checks" more often than they pick up his in their almost daily "toss" for the check.

How should such expenditures be handled? How much are they a part of the expected behavior of people generally, or these people especially? When does emotional gratification justify defining an item as a need rather than a want? In all of the above examples, the expenditures reflect recurring costs (identical or similar) that the respective families mention casually, or with surprise that they might need to be taken into account since they do represent regular demands on income. The financial counselor would be well advised to consider the implications for the individual and the family if such items are or are not accepted as needs or wants to be regularly provided for in the budget.

Because leaks from income are more likely to be in the area of day-to-day expenditures rather than in the larger fixed obligations, it becomes especially important for the family to look honestly and openly at the listing and perceptions of this group of needs and expenses. The development of a really effective spending plan rests on the careful delineation by each family member of personal needs, spending patterns, and understanding of how that individual's role may affect the total family spending plan.

Does the outside work of the mother not only affect performance of her usual family tasks, but also deplete her physical energy as well as the quality and quantity of the emotional energy needed for mothering tasks? This may mean that more money should be planned for convenience foods, outside laundry service, day-a-week cleaning help, child care center fees, or larger expenditures for school clothing—to lessen the pressure on her to perform certain tasks (like washing and ironing) more frequently than energy, time, and temperament suggest is advisable. Does the fact of the mother's working outside the home mean that more income should be allocated for pediatricians, medicines, or sitters because the mother who is not at home anxiously utilizes such resources for preventing a suspected illness that another mother's presence at home permits her "to nip in the bud," or because the child care centers often exclude children with "sniffles"? Open family consideration of such costs, often not identified with precipitating reasons, not only leads to more realistic planning for what become normal expenditures, but also helps the family members think through possible values not previously identified by them. Are the children healthier because the added watchfulness by the mother (even if stimulated by anxiety or guilt) supplies them with medical attention? Do these expenditures bring other rewards:

less strain in marital and parent-child relationships? personal gratifications? fringe job benefits that provide some protections for the present (health or disability insurance) or the future (retirement income)?

If the husband dislikes performing certain household chores, how much should be budgeted for outside help to do the necessary tasks? If he travels in connection with his work and is inclined to bring each child a gift on his return from another city or state, how and where should such expenditures be noted?

From the above it should be eminently clear that Chart 3 not only must be tailored to the individual family's emotional and physical needs, but must also serve as a vehicle for communication among family members, for insights and understandings to be attained by joint focus on the components, rationale, and carrying out of a spending plan. It also should be clear that all identifiable items should be noted. It is important, however, that items not be excluded or "cut down on paper" because either they "look" large or the family members have not come to terms with the necessity for the expenditure. If they occur, they should be shown!

BALANCING PRESENT AND FUTURE NEEDS

When the total needed for day-to-day expenses is subtracted from the sum remaining after deducting fixed obligations from income, is the outcome a plus or minus? Is there a balance sufficient to finance the short- and long-term goals previously identified? How much of the available balance can be put into savings or other liquid assets to meet emergencies that might be anticipated or totally unexpected? How much can be put aside for future necessities—savings to purchase a durable item or to go toward education, insurance and investments that increases the family's financial security if certain common hazards were to strike? How much can be saved from this positive balance for future fulfillment of dreams or wishes, for assuring economic comfort in later years or indulging a special desire?

A negative balance (not enough money left in each month to permit the creation of at least an emergency reserve) demands special scrutiny to discern reasons for discrepancies between expenditures and income. It is impractical for the counselor to propose cutting any item beyond the family's capabilities or desires if the deletion would rob them of motivation to adhere to any plan developed.

How can family members "tighten their belts"? Or when should the belts be let out a notch? If curtailment is indicated, what item(s) should be affected? One would expect to make the larger savings in the larger

Design for Living in Today's Money World

items of expenditure, but some of these large items, like rent or payments on the mortgage, are inflexible. Food also is a large item; if it is possible within nutritive standards to reduce costs by 10 percent, the savings may be substantial. Ten dollars would be freed on a $100.00 food budget, while the same percentage of saving on a $20.00 clothing budget would free only $2.00. Families in the lower-income brackets usually cannot afford to reduce the food and clothing items without jeopardizing health and well-being. Yet it is in these items that poorer families make adjustments when already low income declines further (evidenced either in dollar amounts or rising prices), or emergencies arise.

For many families, postponement of a single purchase (a new winter coat when the old one is still serviceable, for example) until budget revisions or additional income permit its purchase may make an immediate difference. But decisions such as these about what to eliminate or defer are highly personal and must rest with the individual or family.

If there is not enough money to cover day-to-day expenses, or not enough to assure some basic savings for emergencies, consideration might be given to some common alternatives. These can include spreading the time allowed to cover debts, as shown in the fixed-obligations Chart 2; changing the kinds of insurance to those that will provide protection at less cost; deciding whether less expensive housing would be possible and feasible; examining food bills and shopping patterns to see where valid economies can be effected. The insufficiency of money may result not from actual insufficiency of income but from the way it is managed—or not managed. Has the responsibility for money management been lodged with a family member who has less aptitude or tolerance for such a task than another member? Again, it is advisable for the counselor to involve—or encourage the family heads to involve—all of the members possible to participate in considering the nature and amount of economies that can be planned (planning they would help to carry out) and the nature and extent of money management responsibility that should be assigned to each family member.

Although rigid adherence to a family-developed plan to bring income and outgo into positive balance is a necessary ingredient for ultimate success, there should not be an expectation that once a plan has been devised it is unalterable. Experience with the plan may suggest better ways of dealing with the budget problems. Moreover, continuing experience may bring its own successes, which may point to the timeliness and efficacy of revisions. Accordingly, periodic review of the efforts to bring the expenditures under control and to develop a viable spending plan is necessary. Improvements in the situation should be acknowledged and appropriate adjustments incorporated.

ASSETS AND DEBTS

In formulating a design for living in today's money world, families and individuals need to deploy their income so that their fixed obligations and day-to-day needs are met, and so that they are setting aside a reserve for future spending for emergencies, desired purchases, or future economic security. They also have to know what assets and liabilities they have, and, especially, how to cope with any pressing debts. A periodic (annual, biennial, five-year) inventory of assets has several purposes. It discloses evidence as to whether financial actions have been sound, and whether both future and current daily management of income are being protected. It offers some guidelines as to whether to buy on credit, to use assets to secure a loan, or to incur additional liabilities. It can encourage or warn the family with respect to need for more insurance, and the advisability of purchasing a home or a new car, and of making a vocational change. Knowledge of the family's net worth can support or depreciate the validity of some proposals they might consider for coping with problems resulting from too heavy a load of debts.

Earlier chapters have considered reasons for overindebtedness and pointed to resources available to families for resolving it. The family's financial planning, however, should also include a systematic approach to debt liquidation if Chart 2 shows the debts to be out of proportion to family income, and if Chart 3 discloses too small a positive (or too large a negative) balance after totaling the costs.

Many families, despite careful planning, sometimes get beyond their depth in the use of credit or loans as the result of unemployment, illness, death of a family member, or other reasons. If a family suffers several exigencies, it may overuse credit and then the day inevitably comes when debts are piled high and the family is under pressure to pay them. Whether the individual or family might or might not have been able to prevent or control the indebtedness, the solution is predicated on establishing a margin of income above actual living expenses to be set aside for debt retirement.

Chart 2 will reveal whether certain obligations will be satisfied before others. Is it feasible to ascertain whether smaller payments to these creditors (whose accounts will terminate sooner) over a longer period of time will reduce the credit payments to a manageable sum each month? Does the spacing of several instalment obligations along the twelve-month chart suggest the feasibility of requesting deferment of one or more to a specified future date while others are being paid off, with the creditor being assured that new debts will not be assumed before the amount due him is paid?

Sometimes it is advisable and possible to pay off the most pressing debts first, and then move to the less pressing obligations. An alternative plan may be to prorate the money available for debt repayment among the creditors, assigning proportionately larger sums to meet the larger debts. Whichever plan is followed, it is wise for the family to talk with creditors and explain the nature of the proposed plan. If the plan is practicable and the attitude of the debtor is sincere, creditors often are willing to make adjustments. In most instances, the family can make the arrangements directly with the creditors. Sometimes the plan can be effected only through the intercession of the financial counselor (see Chapter 13).

Another method of handling debt problems, particularly if legal action is threatened, is to obtain a loan with which to clear up all debts at once. This plan is sound only if the family is able to meet the new payments as they become due. The family in reality is assuming another debt, a debt that carries interest charges. The loan should be obtained at the most reasonable rate of interest possible; liberal repayment terms also are usually an advantage. The advantages of a loan for debt payment lie in the fact that the family will owe one creditor instead of a dozen and that monthly debt repayments can be reduced by spreading them over a ten- or twelve-month, or even longer period. It is important that all debts be included in such a plan of debt clearance because one overlooked creditor can garnishee wages, negating the entire plan. The individual or family whose indebtedness has reached proportions not amenable to adjustment simply by fiscal planning—alone or with a counselor—should consult with an expert in financial counseling, perhaps considering some of the legal remedies described in Chapter 13.

ANTICIPATING CHANGES IN THE FINANCIAL DESIGN

It is impossible to overemphasize how important it is that every spending design be reviewed and evaluated from time to time. Fluctuations in prices, changes in the make-up of families, and unusual expenses can throw the projected spending plan off balance. If prices rise, more money is needed to maintain the former level of purchasing. Incomes usually rise with a rise in prices, but only rarely at about the same time. If a family keeps records of its expenditures, it will be alert to inflationary signs and be better able to guard against inflation's insidious effect on the budget.

As has been discussed earlier, the needs of families change as families change in size and composition and move from one phase of the life cycle to the next. For example, children's clothes become more expensive, school expenses increase steadily, and children gradually want larger sums for activities outside the home. These changes in expenditure are small and may not be noted for several years. Suddenly, probably as the children begin to enter the teen-age stage, the family budget seems strained. These shifts in needs of particular family members should be reviewed periodically and provided for in budget planning. Costs of clothes, food, and recreation increase as children reach adolescence. Medical costs increase as people become middle-aged and elderly. Family incomes, too, may shift considerably over the years. Sound financial planning implies that these life-cycle fluctuations will be anticipated realistically, and that economic changes that impinge on the family's financial situation and planning will be accorded appropriate attention.

FOLLOWING THE FINANCIAL DESIGN

It is far easier to work out on paper a design for money management than it is to translate the design into practice. Although various mechanical devices can be helpful, the essence of successful money management is the capacity of individuals and families to discipline themselves in following such a plan.

Many people prefer a joint-checking account method. This system calls for the establishment of a checking account (usually at a neighborhood bank) in the names of both the husband and wife. All earnings go into that account and each may write checks against that account to meet their expenses. They may divide responsibility for checkwriting, one person perhaps paying the fixed obligations, the other the day-to-day needs and putting aside the agreed-on sums for savings. Or one person may be delegated all checkwriting except for personal items. Which spouse carries responsibility for all or part of this method is less important than that they agree on this delegation of responsibility and on the fiscal plan itself. This system, which mingles the earnings and income of the marital partners, may be devised so that basic expenses (fixed and day-to-day) are drawn indiscriminately from these commingled funds. The plan may provide that the family will live on one salary, having the other income in reserve to meet special purposes, including savings and investments. Such *planned* arrangements, using a joint checking account, ordinarily work well for families where the parents are married to each other and the legal as well as social, economic, and emotional

Design for Living in Today's Money World 383

commitment is clear. Problems may well arise in the social union, as we observed earlier.

Some families with moderate to high incomes find it satisfactory for each marital partner to have a separate checking account. (Some low-income families also prefer it.) This system generally involves depositing the husband's earnings in the account in his name, and he draws checks to the second account, which is in the wife's name. If the wife also is employed, her earnings may be placed in his account, or kept separately in hers—with or without contributions from his earnings paid into her account. The division of responsibility for checkwriting may be that the husband pays the fixed obligations, the wife the day-to-day expenses; or either one may do all the checkwriting for family expenses, fixed or variable. This system requires quite careful control of accounts so that some requisite payments are not overlooked and the level of the bank balances remains good. If the couple's fiscal design calls for all family bills to be paid from one salary, or some other apportionment as was mentioned above, the segregation of incomes by separate accounts may make for easier fixing of responsibility. Unless the family income is fairly large, however, this system of two accounts may be impractical—and a larger danger may lie in its implication for how responsible the respective marital partners feel for their joint and separate undertakings and the impact of these on the marital equilibrium.

If the family will not have many checks to write, they may find that placing their income in a savings account and drawing out the amounts as they are needed is advantageous. Monthly allowances to each family member may be handled this way, with one member responsible for paying certain expenses from this allowance. If there is likely to be a small bank balance in a checking account, the savings account method is beneficial: there are no charges for writing checks, and some interest may accrue to the savings that are held in the bank.

A combination of savings and checking account systems works well for many families. The checking account is used for payment of all regular and recurring expenditures, and the savings account holds the cash being accumulated for major expenses that arise only occasionally during the year as well as for savings. Funds thus held in a savings account accumulate some interest and are available for emergencies. Moreover, there is usually greater reluctance to draw money out of savings than checking accounts, and this psychological element works to the advantage of many families.

Some people plan best if they keep account books and check income against expenditures at regular periods. Some persons like to manage household funds with cash, placing the money for particular items in labeled containers, such as envelopes or jars. Some persons write checks as bills are received, deducting the amount immediately from the bank balance but not mailing or delivering the check until the due date. (Mrs. T places the date the check should be mailed or delivered in the spot on the envelope ordinarily occupied by a stamp. As the date arrives, the envelope is stamped and mailed.)

Whatever device is used, the person should be sure to allocate income to (1) past unpaid expenses or debts, (2) current expense, and (3) future spending and saving. Special attention must be given to future spending and saving if a family is to develop control over its fiscal operations and avoid serious money problems.

Any plan designed to maintain or regain solvency of the family involves the cooperation of all members. Keeping solvent is not an easy task. Often current satisfactions must be given up for future gains. The financial counselor must help the family realize that a budget is solely a guide—a device to be used flexibly but which sets certain limits. The counselor should always endeavor to help the family construct a spending plan according to its particular needs, taking into account the characteristics that distinguish this family from all others. This concept of financial planning imposes on the counselor the responsibility for understanding people and the cultural, social, economic, and psychological factors that make them what they are.

The individual growing from child to grandparent passes through a series of personal relationships. From each relationship and from each experience certain standards and values are absorbed. Included among the values are some that pertain to economic status and economic strivings, and these values are connected in complex ways with the quality of feeling and the degree of security the individual experiences in relationships with family members and with the wider community. The individual's success in filling various roles throughout life and the satisfactions gained from these roles, are inextricably interwoven with the individual's feelings about money. Money not only is part and parcel of the social and economic life of individuals and families, but it also is a major determinant of the quality of their emotional health in today's money world.

Bibliography

I. TODAY'S MONEY WORLD

Booth, S. Lees, *1975 Finance Facts Yearbook.* Washington, D.C.: National Consumer Finance Association, 1975.

Caplovitz, David. *Consumers in Trouble.* New York: The Free Press, 1974.

Chandler, Robert. *Public Opinion: Changing Attitudes on Contemporary Political and Social Issues.* New York: R.R. Bowker Co., 1972.

Colcord, Joanna C. *Cash Relief.* New York: Russell Sage Foundation, 1936.

Economic Report of the President, 1975. Washington, D.C.: U.S. Government Printing Office, 1975.

Feldman, Frances Lomas. *Human Services in Rural Alaska: Highlights from the Evaluation of the Rural Areas Service Project.* Los Angeles: University of Southern California, 1972.

Feldman, Laurence P., and Star, Alvin D. *Racial Factors in Shopping Behavior.* Summer 1968 Proceedings of the American Marketing Association. Chicago: American Marketing Association, 1968.

Fromm, Erich. *Escape from Freedom.* New York: Farrar & Rinehart, 1941.

Galbraith, John K. *The Affluent Society.* Boston: Houghton Mifflin, 1958.

General Mills, Inc. *The General Mills American Family Report 1974–75: A Study of the American Family and Money.* Minneapolis: General Mills, 1975.

Goode, William J. *After Divorce.* Glencoe, Ill.: Free Press, 1956.

Groom, Phyllis. "Prices in Poor Neighborhoods." *Monthly Labor Review* 89 (October 1966):1085–90.

Hendricks, Gary, and Youmans, Kenwood C., *Consumer Durables and Installment Debt: A Study of American Households.* Ann Arbor: Survey Research Center, Institute for Social Research, University of Michigan, 1973.

Katona, George. *The Powerful Consumer: Psychological Studies of the American Economy.* New York: McGraw-Hill, 1960.

Krassa, Lucie G. "Women and Homeownership." *Family Economics Review* (Fall 1973):16–17. Publication ARS 62–5. Washington, D.C.: Consumer and Food Economics Institute, Agricultural Research Service, U.S., Department of Agriculture.

Liu, Ben-Chieh. "Variations in the Quality of Life in the United States by State, 1970." *Review of Social Economy* 32 (October 1974):131–47.
Mandell, Lewis; Katona, George; Morgan, James N.; and Schmiedeskamp, Jay. Survey of Consumers 1971–72: *Contributions to Behavioral Economics.* Ann Arbor: University of Michigan, 1973.
Miller, Herman P., ed. *Poverty: American Style.* Belmont, Calif.: Wadsworth Publishing Co., 1966.
———. *Rich Man, Poor Man.* New York: Thomas Y. Crowell, 1971.
Miller, S.M., and Roby, Pamela. *The Future of Inequality.* New York: Basic Books, 1970.
Morgan, James N; Dickinson, Katherine; Dickinson, Jonathan; Benus, Jacob; and Duncan, Greg. *Five Thousand American Families: Patterns of Economic Progress.* 2 vols. Ann Arbor: Survey Research Center, Institute for Social Research, University of Michigan, 1974.
"Mortgage, Construction, and Real Estate Markets." *Federal Reserve Bulletin* 59 (July 1973):481–92.
"The Pattern of Growth in Consumer Credit." *Federal Reserve Bulletin* 60 (March 1974):175–88.
Patton, Arch. *Men, Money and Motivation.* New York: McGraw-Hill, 1961.
Rich, Margaret E. *A Belief in People: A History of Family Social Work.* New York: Family Service Association of America, 1956.
Rudd, Nancy. "Employment and Earnings of Women." *Family Economics Review* (Fall 1973):3–8. Publication ARS 62–5. Washington, D.C.: Consumer and Food Economics Institute, Agriculture Research Service, U.S., Department of Agriculture.
Schumacher, E.F. *Small Is Beautiful: Economics as if People Mattered.* New York: Harper & Row, 1973.
U.S., Congress, Joint Economic Committee. *Achieving Price Stability Through Economic Growth.* H. Rep. 93–1653, 93rd Cong., 2d Sess. Washington, D.C.: U.S. Government Printing Office, 1974.
U.S., Department of Commerce, Bureau of the Census. *Statistical Abstract of the United States 1974: National Data Book and Guide to Sources.* 95th ed. Washington, D.C.: U.S. Government Printing Office, 1974.
U.S., Department of Labor, Bureau of Labor Statistics. *Urban Family Budgets and Comparative Indexes for Selected Urban Areas, Autumn 1974.* Washington, D.C.: Bureau of Labor Statistics, 1975.
Veblen, Thorstein. *The Theory of the Leisure Class.* New York: H.B. Huebsch, 1922.
Whyte, W.F. *Money and Motivation.* New York: Harper & Row, 1955.

II. THE CYCLE OF FAMILY LIFE

Birren, James E. *Handbook of Aging and the Individual: Psychological and Biological Aspects.* Chicago: University of Chicago Press, 1959.

BIBLIOGRAPHY

Current Population Reports, Washington, D.C.: U.S., Department of Commerce, Bureau of the Census: "Birth Expectations and Fertility," series P-20, no. 248, 1973. "Households and Families, by Type: March, 1973," series P-20. no. 251, June 1973.

Cutright, Phillips. "Illegitimacy: Myths, Causes and Cures." *Family Planning Perspectives* 3 (January 1971):25–48.

DeJesus, Carolina. *Child of the Dark.* New York: E.P. Dutton, 1962.

Desmonde, William. *Magic, Myth, and Money: The Origin of Money in Religious Ritual.* New York: The Free Press of Glencoe, 1962.

Dostoevsky, Fyodor. *The Gambler.* New York: Macmillan, 1931.

Epstein, Cynthia Fuchs. *Woman's Place: Options and Limits in Professional Careers.* Berkeley: University of California Press, 1971.

Epstein, Joseph. *Divorced in America: Marriage in an Age of Possibility.* New York: E.P. Dutton, 1974.

Feldman, Frances Lomas, and Frances H. Scherz. *Family Social Welfare: Helping Troubled Families.* New York: Atherton Press, 1967.

Gruenberg, Sidonie M., and Gruenberg, Benjamin. *Parents, Children, and Money.* New York: Viking Press, 1933.

Hansberry, Lorraine. *Raisin in the Sun.* New York: Random House, 1959.

Hemingway, Ernest. *The Old Man and the Sea.* New York: Scribner's, 1952.

Herzog, Elizabeth. "Perspectives on Poverty: 3—Facts and Fictions About the Poor." *Monthly Labor Review* 92 (February 1969):42–49.

Kaplan, Saul. *Support from Absent Fathers of Children Receiving ADC: 1955.* Public Assistance Report no. 41. Washington, D.C.: U.S. Government Printing Office, 1960.

Katona, George. *Psychological Analysis of Economic Behavior.* New York: McGraw-Hill, 1951.

Katz, Sanford N. *When Parents Fail: The Law's Response to Family Breakdown.* Boston: Beacon Press, 1971.

Krause, Harry D. *Illegitimacy: Law and Social Policy.* New York: Bobbs-Merrill, 1971.

Levenson, Sam. *Everything but Money.* New York: Simon and Schuster, 1966.

Lynes, Russell. *Cadwallader: A Diversion.* New York: Harper & Bros., 1959.

Mallan, Lucy B. "Young Widows and Their Children: A Comparative Report." *Social Security Bulletin* 38 (May 1975):3–21.

Mandell, Lewis; Katona, George; Morgan, James N.; and Schmiedeskamp, Jay. *Survey of Consumers 1971–72: Contributions to Behavioral Economics.* Ann Arbor: University of Michigan, 1973.

Mossly, Carmen, and Woener, Ralph. *Sex, Living Together, and the Law: A Legal Guide for Unmarried Couples (and Groups).* Berkeley, Calif.: Nolo Press, 1974.

O'Neill, Eugene. *Long Day's Journey Into Night.* New Haven, Conn.: Yale University Press, 1964.

Rainwater, Lee, and Yancey, William L. *The Moynihan Report and the Politics of Controversy.* Cambridge: The M.I.T. Press, 1967.

Ruderman, Florence A. *Child Care and Working Mothers.* New York: Child Welfare League of America, 1968.
Scherz, Frances H. "Strengthening Family Life Through Social Security." *Social Casework* 36 (October 1955):352-59.
Schorr, Alvin. *Filial Responsibility in America.* Washington, D.C.: U.S. Government Printing Office, 1960.
Simon, Ann W. *Stepchild in the Family.* New York: Odyssey Press, 1964.
Smuts, Robert W. *Women and Work in America.* New York: Schocken Books, 1971.
Towle, Charlotte. *Common Human Needs.* Rev. ed. New York: National Association of Social Workers, 1965.
U.S., Congress. Joint Economic Committee. *The Family, Poverty and Welfare Programs: Factors Influencing Family Stability.* Studies in Public Welfare Paper 12, Part I, 93rd Cong., 1st sess. Washington, D.C.: U.S. Government Printing Office, 1973.
U.S., Department of Health, Education, and Welfare. *Health in the Later Years of Life: Selected Data from the National Center for Health Statistics.* Washington, D.C.: U.S. Government Printing Office, 1971.
U.S., Department of Health, Education, and Welfare, Welfare Administration. *Growing Up Poor,* by Catherine S. Chilman. Publication no. 13, May 1966.
Walshok, Mary Lindenstein. "The Emergence of Middle-Class Deviant Subcultures: The Case of Swingers." *Social Problems* 18 (Spring 1971):488-95.
Weller, Jack E. *Yesterday's People.* Lexington: University of Kentucky Press, 1965.
Zeegers, Machiel. "The Swindler as a Player." In *Motivations in Play, Games, and Sports.* Edited by Ralph Slovenko and James A. Knight, pp. 219-31. Springfield, Ill.: Charles C. Thomas, 1967.

III. MONEY AND COUNSELING

Beck, Dorothy Fahs, and Jones, Mary Ann. *Progress on Family Problems: A Nationwide Study of Clients' and Counselors' Views on Family Agency Services.* New York: Family Service Association of America, 1973.
Brown, June H. "Social Services and Third World Communities," *Social Work Papers,* 12. Los Angeles: University of Southern California School of Social Work (January 1974):23-36.
Carter, Genevieve W.; Fifield, Lillene H.; and Shields, Hannah. *Public Attitudes Toward Welfare—An Opinion Poll.* Los Angeles: Regional Research Institute in Social Welfare, University of Southern California, 1973.
Changing Times, including: "Financial Retirement," 27 (September 1973):28. "If You're Hurt on the Job, 'Workmen's Comp' Pays," 28 (May 1974):21. "Set up a Retirement Timetable," 27 (February 1973):40. "When Folks Get Too Old or Too Ill to Manage Their Money," 26 (April 1972):31.

BIBLIOGRAPHY

Consumer Facts Leaflets, those listed. Madison, Wis.: Everybody's Money (Cuna, Inc.)
    Money Management for Young Couples, no. CCI-10.
    Student Loans for Your High Education, no. CCI-15.
    Veterans' Benefits, no. CCI-14.
    Your Will: A Plan for the Future, no. CCI-7.
Cutright, Phillips. "AFDC, Family Allowances and Illegitimacy." *Family Planning Perspectives* 2 (October 1970):4–9.
deCamp, Catherine Crook. *Teach Your Child to Manage Money: A Financial Guide for Toddlers through Teen-agers.* New York: Simon & Schuster, 1975.
Dong, Clarene N. "Clinical Social Work Practice." *Social Work Papers,* 12. Los Angeles: University of Southern California School of Social Work, 1974.
Feldman, Frances Lomas, and Scherz, Frances H. *Family Social Welfare: Helping Troubled Families.* New York: Atherton Press, 1967.
Freud, Anna. *The Ego and the Mechanisms of Defense.* Translated by Cecil Baines. New York: International Universities Press, 1946.
Garrett, Annette. *Interviewing: Its Principles and Methods,* 2d ed. New York: Family Service Association of America, 1972.
Hamilton, Gordon. *Theory and Practice of Social Casework.* New York: Columbia University Press, 1959.
Laughlin, John L., and Bressler, Robert. "A Family Agency Program for Heavily Indebted Families." *Social Casework* 52 (December 1971):617–26.
Roberts, Robert W., and Nee, Robert H. *Theories of Social Casework.* Chicago: University of Chicago Press, 1971.
Rubin, Theodore Isaac. *Sweet Daddy.* New York: Ballantine Books, 1963.
Scherz, Frances H. "Family Treatment Concepts." *Social Casework* 47 (April 1966):234–40.
―――. "Multiple Client Interviewing: Treatment Implications." *Social Casework* 43 (March 1962):120–25.
Taittonen, Edith. *Guide for Family Financial Counseling.* New York: Community Service Society of New York, 1972.
Towle, Charlotte. *Common Human Needs,* rev. ed. New York: National Association of Social Workers, 1965.
U.S., Department of Health, Education, and Welfare, Social Security Administration. *Disabled? Find Out About Social Security Disability Benefits.* Washington, D.C.: U.S. Government Printing Office, 1973.
U.S., Department of Health, Education, and Welfare, Welfare Administration, Children's Bureau. *Moving Into Adolescence: Your Child in His Preteens.* Pub. no. 431–1966. Washington, D.C.: U.S. Government Printing Office, 1965.
U.S. News & World Report (Joseph Newman, directing editor). *Teach Your Wife How to Be a Widow.* Washington, D.C.: U.S. News & World Report, 1973.
Weisberg, Miriam. "Joint Interviewing with Marital Partners." *Social Casework* 45 (April 1964):221–29.

IV. APPLICATIONS—VALUES, NEEDS, RESOURCES

Blong, Adele M.; Leyser, Barbara; and Cole, Steven, eds. *NWRO Supplemental Security Income Advocates Handbook.* New York: Center on Social Welfare Policy and the Law, 1975.
Booth, S. Lees. *1975 Finance Facts Yearbook.* Washington, D.C.: National Consumer Finance Association, 1975.
Caplovitz, David. *Consumers in Trouble.* New York: Free Press, 1974.
Changing Times reprints, including those listed. Washington, D.C.: Reprint Service.
  The Kiplinger Magazine, dates as shown. "Five-Year Plan for Managing Your Money," October 1973.
  "Getting Out of Debt Without Going Broke," July 1971.
  "Guidelines for Updating the Family Budget," November 1974.
  "Make a New Budget for Times Like These," May 1975.
  "Maybe Your New Budget Needs a Checkup," February 1972.
  "That Always Broke Feeling—and What to Do About It," March 1966.
  "Try a Different Way of Budgeting," May 1973.
Denenberg, Herbert S. *A Consumer's Guide to Bankruptcy or Going Broke in Order to Become Solvent: The Federal Bankruptcy Law in Brief.* Harrisburg, Pa.: Office of Special Advisor to the Governor on Consumer Affairs, State of Pennsylvania, 1975.
Group for the Advancement of Psychiatry. *The Community Worker: A Response to Human Need.* New York, 1974.
"The Half-a-Loaf Life of the Working Wife." *Money* 1 (October 1972):52–59.
Hawver, Carl F. *Basic Principles in Family Money and Credit Management.* Rev. ed. Washington, D.C.: Educational Services Division, National Consumer Finance Association, 1974.
Hawver, Carl F. *One-Week Advanced Teaching Unit on Consumer Credit.* Rev. ed. Washington, D.C.: National Consumer Finance Association, 1972.
Household Finance Corporation Money Management Booklets, including those listed. Chicago: Household Finance Corporation, n.d.
  Reaching Your Financial Goals
  It's Your Credit: Manage It Wisely
  Children's Spending
  Your Food Dollar
  Your Clothing Dollar
  Your Housing Dollar
  Your Home Furnishings Dollar
  Your Equipment Dollar
  Your Shopping Dollar
  Your Automobile Dollar

Your Health and Recreation Dollar
Your Savings and Investment Dollar
Institute of Life Insurance. *Making the Most of Your Money.* New York: Institute of Life Insurance, 1974.
──────. *Money in Your Life: A Woman's Guide to Financial Planning.* New York: Institute of Life Insurance, 1973.
Mueller, Marjorie Smith. "Private Health Insurance in 1972: Health Care Services, Enrollment, and Finances." *Social Security Bulletin* 37 (1974):20–40.
Porter, Sylvia. *Sylvia Porter's Money Book: How to Earn It, Spend It, Save It, Borrow It—and Use It to Better Your Life.* New York: Doubleday & Co., 1975.
Tippett, Katherine S. "Women and Credit." *Family Economics Review* (Fall 1973):17–19. Publication ARS 62–5. Washington, D.C.: Consumer and Food Economics Institute, Agricultural Research Service, U.S., Department of Agriculture.
Troelstrup, Arch W. *The Consumer in American Society.* 5th ed. New York: McGraw-Hill, 1974.
U.S., Department of Agriculture, Consumer and Food Economics Research Division. *Helping Families Manage Their Finances.* Home Economics Research Report no. 21 (June 1968). Washington, D.C.: Agricultural Research Service, U.S., Department of Agriculture.
U.S., Department of Health, Education, and Welfare, Social Security Administration. *If You're Self-Employed . . . Reporting Your Income for Social Security.* Washington, D.C.: U.S. Government Printing Office, 1971.
──────. *Improvements in Your Social Security Cash Benefits.* Washington, D.C.: U.S. Government Printing Office, 1972.
──────. *Your Social Security Rights and Responsibilities: Retirement and Survivors Benefits.* Washington, D.C.: U.S. Government Printing Office, 1975.

SHELTER AND HOUSEHOLD OPERATION

Changing Times, including:
"Facts to Know About Condominiums," 27 (October 1973):37. "How to Buy a House in Five Easy Steps," 27 (February 1973):6.
Institute of Life Insurance. *Our Family's Life Insurance.* New York: Institute of Life Insurance, 1970.
──────. *Understanding Your Life Insurance.* New York: Institute of Life Insurance, 1972.
U.S., Department of Agriculture, Farmers Home Administration Program Aid publications, including those listed. Washington, D.C.: U.S. Government Printing Office, dates as shown.
Home Ownership, no. PA-977, rev., August 1974.
Rural Housing Repair Loans, no. PA-1058, August 1973.
Rural Rental Housing, no. PA-1039, July 1973.

Food

U.S., Department of Agriculture publications, including those listed. Washington, D.C.: U.S. Government Printing Office, n.d.

Beef and Veal in Family Meals. Home and Garden Bulletin no. 118.
Composition of Foods: Raw, Processed, Prepared. Agricultural Handbook no. 8
Conserving the Nutritive Values in Foods. Home and Garden Booklet no. 90.
Family Food Buying: A Guide for Calculating Amounts to Buy and Comparing Costs. Home Economics Research Report no. 37.
Family Fare: A Guide to Good Nutrition. House and Garden Bulletin no. 1.
The Food We Eat. Miscellaneous Publication no. 870.
Toward the New, A Report on Better Foods and Nutrition from Agricultural Research. Agricultural Information Bulletin no. 341.
Your Money's Worth in Foods. Home and Garden Bulletin no. 183.

Health and Dental Care

Denenberg, Herbert S. *A Shopper's Guide to Health Insurance.* Chicago: Blue Cross Association, n.d.

Health Insurance Institute. *Our Family's Health Insurance: Do We Know the Answers?* New York: Health Insurance Institute, 1970.

"Meet the HMO—A New Way to Buy Health Care," *Changing Times* 26 (February 1972):1–9.

U.S., Department of Health, Education, and Welfare, Social Security Administration. *A Brief Explanation of Medicare.* Washington, D.C.: U.S. Government Printing Office, April 1973.

Life Insurance

Changing Times, including:

"Is It Smart to Borrow on Your Life Insurance?" December 1972.
"Look at What's New in Insurance," January 1973.

Consumer's Union. *A Guide to Life Insurance.* Mt. Vernon, N.Y., January 1974.

Credit

Black, Hillel. *Buy Now, Pay Later.* New York: Morrow, 1961.

Changing Times, including:

"Are You Using All Your Truth-in-Lending Rights?" November 1973.
"Bankers Like Credit Cards," August 1972.
"Before You Borrow or Say 'Charge It' . . . ," January 1972.
"Before You Sign That Appliance Service Contract . . . ," October 1972.
"Do You Owe Too Much?" June 1974.
"Does Consumer Arbitration Really Work?" July 1973.
"Don't Just Pay That Charge Account Bill. Read It!" February 1973.
"Ever Use A Pawnshop?" February 1972.

"Getting Out of Debt Without Going Broke," July 1971.
"How to Keep from Drowning in Debt," February 1969.
"If You're Dunned to Pay a Bill . . . ," March 1974.
"Should You Borrow from a Small-Loan Company?" November 1972.
Cobak Corporation. *Accepting Credit Responsibility: Teacher Guide.* Family Financial Education Program. Chicago, 1972.
Consumer Facts Leaflet. *Chapter 13—An Alternative to Bankruptcy.* Madison, Wis., n.d.
Consumer's Union. *How to Shop for Credit.* Mt. Vernon, N.Y., March 1975.
Laughlin, John L., and Bressler, Robert, "A Family Agency Program for Heavily Indebted Families," *Social Casework* 52 (December 1971):617–26.
Mandell, Lewis. "Consumer Knowledge and Understanding of Consumer Credit," *The Journal of Consumer Affairs* 7 (September 1973):23–36.
National Foundation for Consumer Credit. *Using our Credit Intelligently.* Washington, D.C., 1970.
U.S., Department of Agriculture, Division of Home Economics, Federal Extension Service publications, including:
Do's and Don'ts of Credit, no. PA-869, April 1968.
Should You Use Credit? no. PA-865, April 1968.
What is Credit? no. PA-864, April 1968.
Where to Get Credit, no. PA-866, April 1968.
Your Credit Contract, no. PA-868, April 1968.

SAVINGS

Changing Times, including:
"Best Place to Put Your Savings," February 1972.
"Checking Accounts That Draw Interest," January 1974.
"Credit Unions: Easier to Join, More Useful, Too," May 1973.
"Managing Your Savings for the Highest Return," December 1973.
"Save Money on Your Savings Account," August 1974.
Consumer Reports, including:
"A Guide to Banking Services," January 1975.
"Shaking Up the Banks," May 1975.
Rudd, Nancy. "Factors to Consider in Selecting a Savings Account," *Family Economics Review* (Summer 1973):17–19.

PENSIONS AND RETIREMENT INCOME

Changing Times, including:
"Annuities Can Stretch Retirement Money," September 1972.
"New Pension Law Could Be Good News for You," December 1974.
"Know Your Pension Plan," *Family Economics Review* (Summer 1974), p. 22.

Index

Abandonment, 201
Abortion, 145
Abused children, 200
Accident and health insurance; *see* Insurance
Accounts; *see* Charge accounts; Credit
Adaptive capacities, 181
Add-on purchase, *see* Conditional sales contract
Addiction; *see* Alcoholism; Drug abuse; Gambling
Adequacy and inadequacy, xii, xvii, 6, 62, 64, 65, 81, 82, 117, 123, 135, 136, 166–167, 189, 200, 201, 205, 207, 211–221, 228, 239, 255, 285, 350; *see also* Family; Morality
Adolescence, 62, 95, 102–106, 150, 161–162; *see also* Money
Adolescents, 66, 153, 235, 259, 260, 279
  Allowances for, 112–113, 153
  Earnings, 115–116, 291; *see also* Earners, earnings
  Use of money by, 102–106, 219
Adoptions, 58, 140, 147, 149, 238, 253–254
Advancement, 285–286; *see also* Recreation; Education; Gifts
Affirmative Action, 15, 71, 146
Aged; *see* Older Persons; Older Years
Agreements, counseling, 189, 202–204, 208

Aid to Families with Dependent Children (AFDC), 99, 144, 153, 218, 221, 317; *see also* Public Assistance
Alcoholism, 159, 220
Alimony, 154, 169, 170–171, 208, 366, 376; *see also* Child support; Divorce; Single parents
Allowances, 25, 62, 80, 100, 109–113, 175, 200, 383
Alternate household arrangements, 59, 71; *see also* Lifestyles; Living arrangements, variations in
American Indians; *see* Indians; Ethnic factors
Anger, 79, 82, 84, 88, 100, 123, 131, 135, 169, 190, 228, 235, 236
Annual consumption budgets, 24, 29–30
Annuities; *see* Insurance
Anshen, Ruth N., xx
Anxiety, 79, 96–97, 102, 121, 124, 131, 135, 143, 156, 161, 164, 169, 186, 195, 204, 205, 215, 216, 243, 322
Application, worker, 212–216, 238–239; *see also* Intake; Presenting problem
Arbitration, 348
Asian American, 127, 130; *see also* Ethnic factors
Aspirations, 5, 29, 55, 74, 259, 262, 287, 293, 320, 353, 358, 364

395

INDEX

Assets, capital, 121, 129, 130, 186, 259, 289–290, 369, 380
Assignments, 238, 240, 291, 312; *see also* Attachment; Garnishment
Attachment, 291, 292, 312; *see also* Assignments; Garnishment
Attitudes, development of, 8, 85–86, 94–95, 146; *see also* Counselor's Attitudes; Cultural attitudes; Money, attitudes about; Societal attitudes
Authority, 205
Automobiles; *see* Motor Vehicles; Transportation
Awareness, 182; *see also* Conscious

Bailment lease, 333
Bank credit cards, 92, 129, 260
Bank loans; *see* Loans
Bankruptcy, 45, 46, 127, 184, 208, 292, 347, 349, 350–351; *see also* Wage earner's plan
Bankruptcy Act, 46, 347, 349
Banks, 234, 238, 242, 293, 294, 347, 365; *see also* Commercial banks; Industrial banks; Savings banks; Savings and loan
Barton, S.G., 288
Beck, Dorothy Fahs, 388
Beginning family; *see* Family life cycle
Benchley, Robert, 353
Beneficial Management Corporation, xiv
Benus, Jacob, 386
Beresford, J.C., 138
Better Business Bureaus, 348
Biological needs, 96
Birren, James, 386
Black, Hillel, 392
Blacks, 10–13, 18, 33, 58, 66, 76, 126, 146, 150, 254; *see also* Ethnic factors
Blue-collar workers, 78
Blong, Adele M., 236, 390
Bonds; *see* Savings and investments
Booth, S. Lees, 351, 385, 390
Borrowing, 77, 182, 237, 334–344, 367; *see also* Credit; Loans
Bressler, Robert, 389, 393

Brief counseling; *see* Counseling; Goals; Social Workers
Broken family; *see* Family
Brotman, H.B., 138
Brown, June H., 388
Budget(s), 23, 88, 352–353, 354–380
  Acceptable variations, 363–364, 373
  Goals, 357–358, 364, 366–367, 378
  Guides, 359–364, 366–380
  Models; *see* Budget systems
  Planning, 357, 358–359
  Reviewing, 378–380, 381–384
  Standards, 221–226, 359–364
  Steps, 366–384
  Systems, 364–380, 382–384
Budget counseling; *see also* Budgets; Counseling; Counselor's Attitudes; Social Workers
  Agency practice, 250–251
  Fees for, 240–249
  Goals, 185–209
  As a tool in treatment, 189, 193, 198
"Budget plans," 334; *see also* Instalment purchasing
Budgeting, 270; *see also* Budget; Expenditure patterns
Building and loan associations; *see* Savings and loan associations
Bureau of the Census, 17, 57
Bureau of Consumer Protection, 344
Bureau of Labor Statistics, 18, 23, 24, 25, 36, 360
Business; *see* Small business

Calvinism, 64
Camp, Catherine Cook, 289
Caplovitz, David, 51, 385, 390
Carey, Matthew, 24
Carter, Genevieve W., 388
Cash, 321; *see also* Assets, capital; Resources, tangible
  Assets, 93
  Relief, 226
Catholic Charities, 317
Chandler, Robert, 51, 385
Charge accounts, 260, 279, 324–330; *see also* Credit
  Open charge, 324–325
  Thirty-day charge, 325

Charity Organization Societies, xi–xiii
Chattel mortgage, 276, 333
Checking accounts, 294, 295, 382, 383; see also Banks; Savings banks
Chicano; see Mexican American
Child care, 90, 92, 151, 158, 162, 171, 212, 251–253, 259, 273–274, 285, 300, 362; see also Budgets
Child support, 107, 153, 154, 163–165, 170–177, 192, 201, 240, 366, 368, 376; see also Alimony; Parent-child relationship; Legal aspects
Children
  Adult, relationship to parents, 63, 70, 81, 94–109, 123–124, 126–128, 201, 219, 240, 353, 378
  Allowances, 100, 109–113
  And money; see Money
  Developing attitudes toward money, 56, 63, 109, 162, 165
  Earnings, 102, 113–116, 368–369; see also Earners, earnings
  Effect on family budget, 61
  Illegitimate; see Nonmarital child
  In foster care, 106–109, 199–200, 251–253; see also Foster care
  Neglect and dependence, 145; see also Legal aspects
  Out-of-wedlock child; see Nonmarital child
  Participation in planning, 358–359
  Relationships with parents, 94–119, 160–161, 198–200
  Siblings, 95, 99, 158, 167
  Stages in family life cycle; see Family life cycle
  Stepchildren, 59
Chilman, Catherine S., 388
Civil rights, 152
Clothing, 121, 171, 222, 227–279, 350
  Budgeting for, 277, 278; see also Budgets
  Cost of, 279
  Expenditures for, 22–27, 277, 278
  Factors determining, 277, 278, 279
  Needs, 277, 279
  Social aspects, 277, 278

Colcord, Joanna C., 385
Cole, Steven J., 236, 390
Collaborative services, 208–209, 347
Collections, 242, 243, 255, 350; see also Liens; Security
Commercial banks, 238, 242, 295, 337
Commercial insurance; see Insurance
Commission on National Goals, 49
Commission to Study the Los Angeles Riots of 1965, 18
Communal households; see Lifestyles
Communal marriages; see Marriage
Communication, 89, 121, 164, 190–191, 198, 205–207, 214; see also Marital Problems
Community Council of Greater New York, 360
Community influences; see Environmental factors
Community resources, 236, 242, 244
Complementarity in marriage, 69, 71, 79; see also Marriage
Complementary counseling services; see Collaborative services
Comprehensive Employment and Training Act (CETA), 311
Conditional sales contract, 291, 332–333
Condominiums, 276
Conjoint counseling, 207
Conscious, 69, 77, 80, 182; see also Awareness
Conspicuous consumption, 47–49
Consumer and Food Economics Institute, 264, 268
Consumer affairs consultants, 346; see also Consumer protection
Consumer behavior, 76, 90
Consumer credit; see Credit
Consumer credit counselors, 44, 66, 188
Consumer Credit Counselors of Los Angeles, xii, 44
Consumer credit counseling, 66, 206, 208, 292, 347, 348
Consumer finance companies, 339–340

INDEX

Consumer instalment credit, 41–43, 77, 91–92, 121, 129
Consumer Price Index (CPI), 12, 18, 19, 25; *see also* Cost of living
Consumer prices, 8
Consumer protection, 66, 274, 276, 344–346; *see also* Protective legislation; Legal protections and statutes
Consumer unit, 10–11, 22, 69, 352
Consumption patterns, 23–46; *see also* Expenditure patterns; Spending patterns
Contracts for counseling; *see* Agreements
Contracts, instalment; *see* Loans; Mortgage; Protective Legislation
Contracting family; *see* Family life cycle
Contributions; see Gifts; Giving
Coping abilities, xvii, 62, 137, 160, 358
Cost of living, 18–20, 21–51, 262, 356; *see also* Consumer Price Index
Counseling, 66–67, 156, 176, 182, 213–214, 227–228, 235–236, 245–254, 261–262, 347; *see also* Counselor's Attitudes; Fees; Legal Aid; Money; Social Workers
  Agreements, 203–204, 208
  Budget, 193–198, 250–251, 352, 359, 361–362, 366, 381, 384
  Goals and techniques, 185–209
  Place of fees in, 243–256
Counselor's attitudes, xiv-xviii, 4, 202–208, 212–213, 217, 219, 261, 271; *see also* Counseling; Social Workers
Credit, 39–41, 48, 61, 66, 72, 77, 92, 121, 124, 191, 267, 278, 287, 288, 321–351, 361, 367, 372, 380; *see also* Borrowing; Budgets; Loans
  Establishment of, 323–324
  Open account, 324–325
  Purchases, 230, 260, 278, 279
  Risk factor, 159, 260, 291, 323–324, 350
  Use of, 77
  Women and, 142, 159

Credit cards, 41, 78, 92, 118, 121, 129, 130, 142, 260, 327–330
Credit life insurance, 338; *see also* Insurance
Credit rating, 159, 324, 350; *see also* Credit, risk factor
Credit union, 186, 236, 296, 335, 340–341, 347
Creditworthy; *see* Credit rating
Crisis, 89, 183–184, 185, 191, 228
Cultural attitudes, 5, 66, 80, 81, 93, 94, 97–98, 131, 132–133, 155, 207, 261, 321; *see also* Environment
  Differences, 97–98, 263, 264, 269
  Environment, xvii, 188, 189
  Expectations; *see* Societal expectations
  Factors, xvii, 47, 160, 185, 189, 229, 254, 260, 384
  Patterns, 155, 321
Culture, 66, 68–69, 73, 182
Cutright, Phillips, 387, 389

Davies, D., 288
Davis, Allison, 96, 119
Day care, 92, 251, 253
Day-to-day needs, 369, 373–378, 379, 380, 382; *see also* Budgets
Death, 127, 137–138, 140, 154–157, 160–162, 193, 299
Debt, 30, 49, 91, 157, 158, 184, 188, 191, 193, 194, 196, 208, 239, 250, 260, 267, 290, 292, 321
Debt consolidation, 186, 348
Debt counseling, 346–349; *see also* Credit counseling; Money
Debt repayment, 44–46, 346–347, 349, 350, 380–381; *see also* Budgets
Deferred payment, 349–350
DeJesus, Carolina, 387
Denenberg, Herbert S., 390, 392
Dependence and independence, 64, 80, 81, 95, 102, 105, 107, 124, 128, 132, 133, 135, 136, 143, 169, 190, 192, 210–236, 239, 261
Dependency, economic, xi-xii, 211, 227, 237, 244
Depression, 66, 121, 131, 133, 135, 143, 187, 198, 239

Index

Depression, economic, xiii, 13–14, 46, 69, 71, 238, 311
Deprivation, 61, 95–97, 104, 134, 137, 149, 162
Desertion, 154–159, 162–165; *see also* Broken family
Desmonde, William, 387
Developmental factors, 55, 60–61, 63, 160–162, 262–263
  Ingredients, psychological, 210
  Problems, 146
  Stages, 100–109, 162
Deviant life styles; *see* Family
Dickinson, Jonathan, 386
Dickinson, Katherine, 386
Disability, 290, 310, 311, 313
Disability Insurance benefits, 280, 310–311, 369
Displacement, 79, 80, 190
Disraeli, Benjamin, 288
Dissaving, 13, 75, 111, 367, 372–373; *see also* Saving
Distrust, 167–168, 205, 212; *see also* Trust
Divorce, 58, 122, 154–160, 165–172, 201, 277
Dong, Clarene N., 389
Dostoevsky, Fyodor, 387
Draper, Anne, 20, 50
Drug abuse, 230
Duncan, Greg, 286
Durable goods, 26, 39, 41, 44, 48, 76, 91, 121, 129

Earners, earnings, 7, 8, 25, 26, 74–75, 76, 77, 94, 127, 192, 268, 290–292, 368, 383, 389; *see also* Income
  Adolescents, 192
  Children, 113–116, 192
  Families, 10–13, 192
  Husbands, 24, 73
  Marginal, 13, 192
  Minorities, 10–13; *see also* Ethnic factors
  Mothers; *see* Mothers, working; Women
  Multiple, 71, 362, 383
  Overtime, 8–9
  Women; *see* Women; Work
Economic; *see also* Financial Assistance; Income Maintenance; Poverty
  Assistance, xi, 144, 192
  Behavior, 78
  Climate, xvii, 22, 29, 63, 96, 181, 188, 189, 261, 352
  Dependence, xi-xii, 73, 192, 210–226
  Factors, 68, 160, 191, 384
  Functioning, 63, 163, 182, 189
  Functions, 59–61, 62, 87
  Need, 170–171, 192, 238, 262
Economic deprivation; *see also* Economic Assistance
  Effect on children, 95–99
  And marital relationships, 162–163
Economic Opportunity Act (EOA), 6, 14, 344
Economic Stabilization Act, 34
Economics, xvii-xviii, 3–20
  And subjective aspects of money, 3
Eden, Sir Frederick Morton, 288
Education, 35–37, 66, 70, 71, 73, 120, 172, 259, 260, 285, 287
  Expenditure for, 19, 35–39, 92, 189
  Loans, 239, 241, 343–344
  Veterans' benefits; *see* Veterans
Elderly; *see* Older Persons; Older Years
Eligibility workers; *see* Application, worker
Emancipation, 143, 190
Emergency Jobs and Unemployment Assistance Act, 311
Emotional attitudes, 65; *see also* Illness, mental
  Development, 95–97, 162
  Factors, 63, 189
  Functioning, 68, 217
  Maturity; *see* Maturity
Employee loan funds, 343
Employment, 10–15, 71; *see also* Unemployment
"Engel's Law," 263
Environmental factors, 160, 183, 184–185, 217; *see also* Cultural environment; Economic climate; Psychological factors; Social factors
Epstein, Cynthia Fuchs, 387

INDEX

Epstein, Joseph, 387
Equal Credit Opportunity Act, 142, 324, 344
Equilibrium; *see* Family equilibrium; Marital equilibrium
Equity, 275, 287, 301
Eskimos, 18, 132, 207, 324; *see also* Ethnic factors
Estate, 156, 160, 240, 286
Ethnic factors, xviii, 5, 6, 10–13, 15, 33, 47, 55–56, 65, 66, 71, 74, 83, 97, 103, 126, 142, 147, 216, 243, 254, 274
Expanding family; *see* Family life cycle
Expectations, 69, 70, 72–75, 94, 126–129; *see also* Societal attitude and expectation
Expenditure behavior, 29–51, 70, 75–82, 90–91, 93, 129, 142–143, 144, 157, 158, 185, 261, 360; *see also* Consumption patterns; Family spending

Fair Credit Billing Act, 344
Fair Credit Reporting Act, 344
Family; *see also* Family life cycle; Nonbeginnings; Parenthood; Unmarried father; Unmarried mother; Unmarried parenthood
 Breakdown of, 145
 Broken, 154–172
 Cycle of family life; *see* Family life cycle
 Disorganized, or disorganization of, 181, 189, 190
 Equilibrium, 89, 95, 184, 188, 356; *see also* Marital equilibrium
 Expanding; *see* Family life cycle
 Functioning, 64, 352; *see also* Social functioning
 Functions, 68
 Goals, 68, 70, 72, 77, 81
 Idealized image of, 21, 55
 Multigenerational, 127
 One-parent; *see* Single parents
 Planning, 238
 Provider; *see* Roles
 Resources, 160, 289
 Separated; *see* Single Parents
 Spending, 23–49, 56; *see also* Consumption patterns; Expenditure patterns; Budgets
 Tasks, 68, 98
Family agencies; *see* Counseling; Social agencies
Family budget(s); *see* Budget(s)
Family counseling; *see also* Budget counseling; Counseling; Social agencies; Social workers
Family income, 181, 292, 355, 367, 368–370
Family life cycle, xvii, 55–56, 173, 263, 271, 286, 287, 300, 352, 356, 382; *see also* Living patterns, variations in
 Beginning, 66–68, 78–79, 88, 136, 196–198, 356
 Contracting, 62, 120–124
 Different stages of, 59–62
 Expanding, 56, 62, 87–117, 356
 And money, 55, 61, 64
 Nonbeginnings, 82–85, 141
Family resources, 289–320; *see also* Resources
Family service agencies, xiv, 245, 248, 270, 347
Fathering, 174–175; *see also* Roles
Federal Emergency Relief Administration, 226
Federal Old-age and Survivors, Disability, and Health Insurance (OASDHI), 136, 287, 310, 372
Federal Reserve Board, 344
Federal Trade Commission, 344
Fees, xv-xvi, 237, 243–256, 276, 294, 338, 348, 349
Feldman, Frances Lomas, xx, 20, 86, 209, 385, 387, 389
Feldman, Laurence P., 385
Fifield, Lillene H., 388
Financial; *see also* Income maintenance; Money; Public assistance; Resources
 Levels and standards, 217
 Needs, 62, 183, 192, 212, 216–221, 259
 Plan; *see* Budget
Financial institutions; *see* Banks; Consumer loan companies; Credit union; Savings and loan

Index

Fixed obligations, 370–373, 378, 379, 380, 382; *see also* Budget(s)
Fizdale, Ruth, 256
Flower children, 97
Food, 25–26, 27, 38, 61, 76, 92, 130, 141, 171, 222, 223, 238, 262–272, 350
  Costs, 22–31, and 262–263, 265–272
  Cultural factors, 263, 264, 269
  Expenditures, 263
  And family life cycle, 263, 271
  Planning, 263, 264–265
  Plans, 269; *see also* Budget(s)
  Psychological meanings, 264, 268, 270
  Social meanings, 264, 268
Food stamps, 73, 192, 211, 226, 238
Foreclosure; *see* Mortgage
Foster care, 92, 106, 107, 251–253; *see also* Single parents
Franklin, Benjamin, 40
Freeman, David, ix
Freud, Anna, 389
Freud, Sigmund, 16
Friendly visitors, xii
Fromm, Erich, 385
Fuel, 23, 35, 78, 129, 132, 280
Furnishings and equipment, 350; *see also* Budget(s); Credit; Expenditures

Galbraith, John K., 385
Gallup Poll, 31, 50
Gambling, 159, 230
Garnishment, 194, 204, 208, 291, 292, 350, 381; *see also* Assignments; Attachment
Garrett, Annette, 389
Gasoline; *see* Fuel
General assistance or relief; *see* Public assistance
General credit contract, 333–334
Gifts, giving, 100, 130, 134, 141, 167, 200, 285, 359, 368; *see also* Budget(s)
Goals, 68, 72, 74, 79, 98, 104, 187–209, 235, 242, 320; *see also* Budget(s)
  Attainment of, xviii, 189
  Counseling, 185–209

Long-term, 186–187, 189–191, 192–193
Short-term, 186–191
And techniques of counseling, 189–191
Goode, William J., 385
Government bonds, securities; *see* Savings
Government life insurance; *see* Insurance
Grants, 214, 221–226, 238–243; *see also* Financial assistance, levels of; Loans
Griffith, John, ix
Groom, Phyllis, 285
Group for the Advancement of Psychiatry, 263
Grow, Barbara, ix
Gruenberg, Benjamin, 109, 119, 387
Gruenberg, Sidonie, 109, 119, 387
Guilt, 98, 107, 124, 133, 149, 150, 156, 164, 201

Hamilton, Gordon, 389
Hansberry, Lorraine, 387
Hare Krishna movement, 97
Hause, John, 50
Hawver, Carl F., 390
Hazlett, William, 139
Health, 90, 95, 271, 284; *see also* Budget(s); Insurance
  Expenditures, 95, 189, 284
  Medical and dental, 22, 37, 90, 92, 95, 124, 130, 156, 157, 162, 183, 195, 223, 238, 240, 245, 254, 261, 284
  Mental and emotional, xv, 124, 156, 157, 181, 191, 195, 238, 263
Help and helping, 237, 244; *see also* Counseling; Counselors; Social workers
Hemingway, Ernest, 387
Hendricks, Gary, 51, 77, 86, 385
Herzog, Elizabeth, 387
Hilborn, Walter Stern, 351
Hoarders, 101, 105
Hollingshead, August, 70, 86
Home loans, 276; *see also* Loans; Mortgage
Home ownership, 75, 90–91, 120–

121, 129, 202, 315; see also Budget(s); Housing
Homemakers, 192, 214, 249-250, 259
Hospitalization; see Health; Insurance
Hostility, 70, 79, 80, 82, 104, 105, 107, 133, 134, 164, 187, 205, 216, 225, 235
Household
  Assistance, 62
  Costs, 282-283
  Management, 87, 163
  Operation, 22, 28, 39, 41, 75, 171, 276, 281-283
  Services, 276, 282, 285; see also Budget(s)
  Units; see Consumer units
Housekeeping services; see Homemakers
Housing, 48, 75-76, 81, 90-91, 129, 227, 238, 272; see also Budget(s); Condominiums; Expenditure patterns; Mortgage
  Costs, 22-27, 272, 273, 274-275
  Expenditures, 22-23, 75, 273-277; see also Shelter; Home ownership
  Factors determining, 33, 128, 129, 273
  And family life cycle, 273
  Mobile, 31-32, 44, 276
  Needs, 272-275, 277
  Ownership, 31-32, 44, 275
  Rental, 274-275

Identity, 68, 95, 146, 153, 190, 199, 213, 226, 277
Illegitimacy; see Nonmarital child; Unmarried parenthood
Illness; see Health
Immaturity; see Maturity
Imprisonment, 156
Income; see also Budget(s); Families; Earners, earnings; Lower-income families; Middle-income families; Upper-income families
  Amounts, xviii, 6-13, 24-28, 31, 32, 34, 35, 39, 89, 92, 125-126, 129, 142, 154-155, 181, 192, 193, 231
  Annual, 8, 10

Attitudes about, xi-xviii
Expectations; see Expectations
Expenditure of, 31, 129, 142, 186
Insufficiency, 59-61, 181, 183, 191-193
Lagging, 16-18, 33, 65, 67, 154, 191, 259
Maintenance, 210-236, 260
Managing family, 181, 352-384
Marginal, 151, 192
National, 6-7
Patterns, 72-73
Sources, 6-18, 14-15, 125, 147, 192, 193, 210, 231, 291
Income maintenance programs, xii-xv, 192, 360, 362
Income supplementation, 182
Income management; see Budget(s)
Indebtedness; see Debt
Indebtedness counseling agencies; see Consumer credit counseling
Independence; see Dependence
Indian, American, 188; see also Ethnic factors
Individual Retirement Account, 309
Industrial banks, 337
Inflation and recession, xviii, 9, 13, 21-22, 44, 48, 93, 137, 141, 227, 273, 316, 356
Initial interview; see Application; Intake
In-kind assistance, 192, 226, 230
Instalment buying, 77, 260
  Contracts, 291, 332, 333
  Credit, 91, 92, 330-334
  Purchases, 93, 121, 363, 370-373; see also Fixed obligations
Institute of Life Insurance, 299, 301
Insurance, commercial, 27, 30, 35, 38, 62, 260, 275, 299-309, 342-343, 365; see also Budget(s); Social insurances; Veterans
  Annuities, 125, 307-309
  Automobile, 223, 283
  Credit life, 305
  Endowment, 301, 302
  Family income, 303
  Family plan, 303
  Family protection, 303
  Group life, 304

Index

Health/hospital/accident, 19, 37–38, 45, 92, 130, 172, 284, 290, 312–314
Industrial life, 305
Life, 62, 77, 92, 129, 172, 287, 299–307
  Limited pay, 302
  Mortgage life, 301, 306
  Straight-life, 302
  Term, 301
  Whole-life, 301
Intake, 216, 221
Interest and dividends, 130, 192, 300
Intellectual factors, 89, 184–185, 187, 189, 361
Intergeneration factors, 158, 185, 200–201
Internal Revenue Act, 310, 311
Interpersonal problems, 190, 193–198
Interpersonal relations, 63, 68, 89, 183, 190
Investments, 125, 364; *see also* Interest; Savings
Isolation, 66; *see also* Loneliness

Jewish Welfare Fund, 317
Johnson, Samuel, 288
Jones, Mary Ann, 388

Kaplan, Saul, 177, 387
Katona, George, 20, 74, 86, 385, 386, 387
Katz, Sanford N., 86, 177, 387
Krassa, Lucie G., 385
Krause, Harry D., 176, 387

Latency; *see* Children
Laughlin, John L., 389, 393
Legal aid, 182, 208, 209, 290, 347, 349
Legal aspects, 84–85, 152, 169–170, 176–177, 240, 252–253, 381
  Inheritance, 147
  Legal problems, 84, 280, 291, 292, 293, 317, 333, 344, 346, 349, 350
  Legal protection, 82, 84–85, 138, 146–147
  Neglect, 145–146
  Paternity; *see* Paternity

Sanctions, 147
Statutes, 144, 145, 176
Leisure, 136
Levels of living; *see* Standard of living
Levenson, Sam, 387
Leyser, Barbara, 236, 390
Liens, 238, 239, 331
Life cycle; *see* Family life cycle
Lifestyles, xv, 23, 55–57, 70–71, 150, 227, 263, 353
Life tasks, 68, 72, 78–79, 87–89
Linton, Ralph, xvii
Liu, Ben-Chieh, 51, 386
Living arrangements, 150, 202
  Boarding homes, 150, 202
  Foster homes, 150; *see also* Foster care
  Group homes, 150, 202
  Life-care, 202
  Nursing homes, 202
Living patterns, variations in, 40, 59, 66, 140–177
Loans, 30, 181, 238–243, 260, 276, 315–317, 321, 335, 336, 366, 380–381; *see also* Banks; Budget(s); Credit union; Insurance; Mortgage; Pawnbrokers; Philanthropic societies; Remedial loan societies; Small-loan companies; Veterans
Loneliness, 124, 143, 201
Love, 68–69, 79, 82, 91, 95, 98, 99, 103, 107, 110, 116–117, 142, 165
Lower-income families, 39, 77, 96, 98, 137, 145, 150–154, 170, 244, 263, 267, 271, 273, 283, 338, 357, 383
Lynes, Russell, 387

Mallan, Lucy B., 177, 387
Man Assuming Role of Spouse (MARS); *see* AFDC
Mandell, Lewis, 50, 86, 119, 385, 387, 393
Marital
  Balance, 121, 196
  Conflict, 78–82, 99, 121, 123, 187, 190–191, 196, 229
  Equilibrium, 85, 88, 95, 121–122, 163, 186, 188, 356, 363

Problems, xvi, 89, 122, 206, 245, 246–247, 353, 378
Role, 55–59, 68–71
Marriage
 Complementarity of need; *see* Complementarity in marriage
 Common law; *see* Social union
 Marital counseling, 194; *see also* Counseling; Social Workers
 Non-legal, 71, 72, 83–85, 122, 138; *see also* Legal aspects; Single parent; Social union
 Tasks, 63, 68, 79, 82, 88, 95
 Maturity, 65, 78, 79, 80, 82, 94, 163, 188, 190, 191, 218, 239
Means test, 16; *see also* Public assistance; Social services
Medical and dental care; *see also* Health; Insurance
 Costs, 157
 Hospitalization, 156
 Medicaid, 192, 193, 211, 223, 254, 284, 312, 317
 Medicare, 129, 183, 254, 284, 312, 314
 Services, 226
Mexican Americans, 18, 150, 261; *see also* Ethnic factors
Middle class, 5, 49, 153, 246
 Culture, 98
 Families, 153
 -Income families, 5, 32, 39, 73, 77, 98, 137, 150, 155, 191, 250, 263, 383
Middle years, 103, 120–124, 125, 136, 287, 356
Miller, Herman P., 386
Miller, S.M., 17, 386
Miserliness, 101, 134–135, 162
Mistrust; *see* Trust
Mobile Homes; *see* Housing
Money
 And the adolescent, 62, 63, 102–106
 Attitudes about, xv, 4, 79, 148, 193, 238–239
 And the broken family, 159, 160
 And children, 94–102, 198–200; *see also* Children; Foster care
 Climate of a family, 160, 358–359
 And later years, 62; *see also* Older persons
 Management, 55, 68, 72, 78, 87–89, 100, 137, 143, 156, 182, 189, 229, 232, 234–236, 352–353, 360–384; *see also* Budget(s)
 And marital conflict, 187, 190–191, 245, 246–247
 And marriage, 196–198
 Meanings, xi, xvii, 60, 63–66, 68, 96, 97–99, 126–128, 146–148
 Needs of families, 59, 60, 192
 And parent-child relationships, 198–206, 240
 Problems and social agencies, 182, 186; *see also* Counseling; Social Workers
 As a symbol, 79, 80, 143, 149, 159, 198
 Values, 60, 63–64, 259–288
Money Payment Principle; *see* Unrestricted money payment
Moonlighting, 21, 186, 188, 372
Morality, 136, 162, 212, 226, 228, 236, 321, 350; *see also* Adequacy
Morgan, James N., 20, 386, 387
Morris Plan banks, 338
Mortgage, 22, 32, 33, 44, 77, 90, 120, 129, 142, 260, 273, 275–277, 290, 315–317, 350; *see also* Chattel mortgage
 Amortized, 277, 315
 Flexible, 316
 Second, 290, 315, 343
 Sources, 316
 Straight, 277, 315
Mortgage insurance; *see* Insurance
Mossly, Carmen, 387
Mothers; *see also* Earners, earnings; Women, working; Work
Single; *see* Single mothers
Working, 12, 51, 66, 92, 98, 151, 154, 158, 171, 187, 188, 191, 196, 223–224, 252, 268–269, 274, 276, 300, 362, 377, 383
Motor vehicles, 25–27, 34–35, 44, 45, 48, 51, 75, 76, 91, 121, 129–130, 350; *see also* Transportation
Mourning, 156
Mueller, Marjorie Smith, 320, 391

Index

Multiple families, 173–174; *see also* Children; Marriage; Parent-child relationships
Mutual savings banks, 295

Nash, Ogden, 63, 67
National Foundation for Consumer Credit, Inc., 347
National Service Life Insurance, 306
Native Americans; *see* Eskimos; Indians
Nee, Robert H., 389
Neglect, 61, 199, 230
Negro; *see* Blacks
Neurotic behavior, 184, 204, 270, 364
Needs, 184, 230, 322
Nickel, George D., ix
Nonbeginnings, 82–85
Nondurables, 37–38; *see also* Budget(s); Durables
Nonmarital child, 143–144, 146–147; *see also* Legal aspects; Unmarried parenthood
Nonspender, 162
Nonwhite families, 8, 10, 89, 90, 91, 150; *see also* Ethnic factors

Obatala, J.K., 119
Old-Age, Survivor's, Health, and Disability Insurance Benefits (OASDHI), 132, 136
Older persons, 43, 62, 76, 90, 103, 230–231, 240, 250, 272, 280, 282, 284, 285, 287, 310–311, 356, 369
  Dependency conflicts, 133–134
  And their children, 133–134, 135
Older years, 7, 125–139, 201–202
O'Neill, Eugene, 162, 387
One-parent families; *see* Families
Open-account credit; *see* Charge accounts
Out-of-wedlock children; *see* Nonmarital child; Unmarried parenthood
Ownership; *see* Home ownership
Overtime; *see* Earnings

Pacific peoples, 91–92, 224–225, 247–248; *see also* Ethnic factors

Parent-child relationships; *see* Children; Family; Parenting
Parent Locator Service, 153
Parental role; *see also* Parenthood; Parenting
  Tasks, 62–63, 95–100, 104, 114, 144–145, 155, 175–176
Parenthood, 103–113
Parenting, 88, 98, 99, 155, 160, 163
Parents; *see also* Living patterns; Marriage; Single fathers; Single mothers; Single parents
  Foster, 107–109
  Stepparents, 59, 99–100, 173–176
  Unmarried, 58
  Widowed, 154–162
Passbook savings; *see* Savings
Paternity, 147; *see also* Legal aspects
Patton, Arch, 386
Pawnbrokers, 341–342
Payroll deductions, 368, 372
Pension Benefit Guaranty Corporation, 309
Pension Reform Act, 292, 344, 345
Pensions, 77, 125, 130, 131, 132, 154, 155, 192, 287, 300, 309–310, 368, 369
Personal
  Care, 261
  Endowment, 189
  Problems, 193–198
Personal finance companies; *see* Consumer finance companies
Personal loans, 43–44
Personality factors, 64, 89, 160, 163, 184–185, 189–190, 320, 352, 361, 384
Personality development, 78, 89, 189
Philanthropic societies, 343
Pilferers, 105–106
Placement; *see* Children; Foster care; Older persons
Pollard, Spencer, ix
Porter, Sylvia, 391
Poverty, 13, 16–18, 65, 95, 97, 137, 146, 226; *see also* Income, lagging
Preadolescence; *see* Children; Developmental Stages
Premarital counseling, 154
Presenting problem, 186, 190, 216,

221; *see also* Application; Intake
Principal; *see* Loans
Property, 82–85, 125, 169
Prorating, 188, 206, 208, 348–349
Protective legislation, 274, 276, 331; *see also* Consumer protection; Legal aspects
Protective services, 250
Proxmire, William, 42
Psychological aging; *see* Older persons, Older years
Psychological problems, 190, 347
Psychosocial problems, 190
Public assistance, 94, 99, 117, 144, 149, 153, 162, 163, 164, 218, 228, 240, 250, 252, 268, 275; *see also* Public welfare; Social services; Social agencies
  Agency, 192, 193
  Historical development, xii-xv, 213
  Income maintenance programs, 192
  Repayment of loans, 239–240
Public welfare, xiii-xvii, 213; *see also* Public assistance; Social services
Puerto Ricans; *see* Ethnic factors
Pumphrey, Muriel W., 50, 288
Pumphrey, Ralph E., 50, 288
Purchase of services, 208, 250

Quality of life, 36, 46–49

Race; *see* Ethnic factors
Rainwater, Lee, 387
Rationalizers, 106, 159
Recession, 71, 192; *see also* Depression, economic; Employment; Inflation; Unemployment
Recreation, 62, 75, 76, 121, 261
  Budgeting for, 285
  Expenditures, 23–25, 101
Regression, 121, 133, 264
Rejection, 66, 98, 99, 107, 110, 134, 261
Remarriage, 99, 140, 170–171, 173–176; *see also* Marriage
Remedial loan societies, 342
Rent supplements, 192, 211
Repossession, 44, 191, 204, 332, 333, 350

Resentment, 131, 133, 164, 239
Resistance, 164, 201, 205, 229, 235, 236
Resources; *see also* Assets; Budget(s); Cash; Savings
  Community, 80, 261, 317, 318
  Economic, 160, 162, 169, 186, 193, 261, 356, 369
  Personal, 80, 317–320
  Tangible, 93, 289–290
Retirement, 28, 43, 121, 125, 126, 128, 131–139, 171, 310, 364, 369
Revolving credit, 334; *see also* Credit
Rich, Margaret E., xx, 386
Rivlin, Alice M., 138
Roberts, Robert W., 389
Roby, Pamela, 17, 386
Roles
  Confusion in, 159
  Of family members, 68–69, 87, 88–89, 99, 159, 163, 167, 200, 229–230, 234–236, 269–270, 358–359, 382, 384
  Female, 93, 145, 155, 216
  Male, 87, 145, 153, 163, 216, 378
  Models, 87–88
  As protector, 87, 113
  As provider, 87, 163
  Reversal of, 133
  Of social worker, 89, 115–116, 153, 154, 165, 170, 176, 186, 213, 219–221
  Of unmarried father, 152
Rubin, Theodore Isaac, 389
Rudd, Nancy, 386, 393
Ruderman, Florence A., 388
Rules, family, 87–88
Russell Sage Foundation, 345

Sales contract, 276
Saving, 62, 100–101, 111, 121, 125, 131, 142, 261, 275, 276, 277, 293–297, 355; *see also* Dissaving
Savings banks, 287, 293–297
  Accounts, 383
  Interest, 293–294, 296
  Passbook, 295
Savings and investment, 286–288, 297–298, 369, 372, 378; *see also* Budget(s)

As budget item, 286
Cash, 294
Forms of saving, 287, 293
Goals, 287, 288
Government bonds, 286, 293, 296
Interest, 294, 295
Needs, 286–287
Patterns, 286, 287
Savings and loan associations, 276, 293, 295
Scherz, Frances, xx, 86, 139, 209, 387, 388, 389
Schmiedeskamp, Jay, 387
Schorr, Alvin, 388
Schumacher, E.F., 386
Securities, 297–298
Security, 238, 239, 338; *see also* Loans
Self; *see also* Identity
 -employment, 293, 362
 -esteem, xi, 15, 123, 135, 146, 153, 156, 189, 199, 213, 226, 237, 261, 277, 356
 -fulfillment, 56, 80, 163, 193
 -help, 237
 -realization, 56, 80, 163
 -responsibility, 244
 -sufficiency, 91, 135, 189
Separation, 124, 166
Separated families; *see* Divorce; Separation; Single parents
Service charges; *see* Fees
Sex differentiation, 68, 87
Shelter, 25–26, 30, 31–34, 75–76, 90–91, 120–121, 127–129, 141–143, 150–151, 171, 201–202; *see also* Budget(s); Home ownership; Housing
Shields, Hannah, 388
Simon, Ann W., 388
Single adult, 140–143, 268, 300, 352
 And credit, 142
Single father, 152–154, 155, 252, 361
Single mother, 148–152, 155, 223–224, 239, 277, 361
Single parents, xvi, 12, 58–59, 143, 154–172, 200–201, 250, 273, 300; *see also* Living patterns; Single father; Single mother

Small businesses, 239, 292–293, 368
Small loan companies; *see* Consumer finance companies
Smuts, Robert W., 388
Social agencies, 346, 349
Social-cultural factors, 55
Social Darwinism, xii
Social expectations, 75, 164
Social factors, 63
Social functioning, xvii, xx, 3, 60, 68, 89, 143, 146, 186, 210, 213, 226, 228, 230–231, 237, 355; *see also* Family functioning
Social insurance, 75, 210, 211; *see also* Social Security
Social policy, xv, xviii, 147, 210–236; *see also* Health; Income maintenance; Public assistance; Transfer payments; and various individual programs and services
Social Security Act, xiii, xvi, 19, 125, 153, 211, 218, 221, 222, 226, 252, 299, 310, 314; *see also* AFDC, OASDHI, Supplemental Security Income (SSI)
Social Security Administration, 216
Social Security Benefits, 16, 128, 129, 131, 136, 154, 155, 192, 230, 232, 234, 260, 266–267, 286, 357, 362, 369
Social Services Amendment, xv, xvi
Social services, xv, xvi, 188, 208, 213–216, 238, 244, 248, 252, 254, 290; *see also* Public assistance; Social Security Act
Social status, 5, 63, 69, 73, 97, 109, 149, 239
Social union, 56, 72, 82–85, 356, 383; *see also* Marriage
Social values, 97, 360, 361
Social welfare
 Agency, xii, xv, 182, 186, 360
 Objectives, 210
 Programs, 216–229
 Regulations, 216–221, 222
Social worker, xvi, 28, 66–67, 73, 89, 105, 115–116, 135, 154, 156, 162, 165, 193, 215, 216–221, 226, 230–231, 235–236, 237, 239–243, 245–250, 254–256, 261–262, 264, 266,

270–272, 278, 284, 289, 292, 297, 303–304, 310, 317, 320, 322–323, 331–332, 346, 352, 359, 361–362, 366, 381, 384; *see also* Counseling; Counselor's attitudes
Socialization, 87, 114, 277
Societal attitudes, xv, 49, 63, 64, 71, 94, 137, 144, 145, 148, 155, 211–212, 237, 255, 286, 384
  Expectations, 64, 72, 75, 89, 160, 182, 229
  Values, 162, 384; *see also* Values
Sparks, Jared, 51
Spending patterns, 22, 23, 30, 75, 125–126, 143, 261, 361; *see also* Expenditures
Spending plan, 185, 356, 362
Spending units; *see* Consumer units
Spenders, 105
Standard budgets, 218, 221–226, 254, 282
Standard of living, 17, 21, 23, 51, 126, 160, 181, 191, 192, 219, 259, 262, 263, 311, 351, 360
Star, Alvin D., 385
State Benefits and Services Advisory Board (California), 149
Stepchildren; *see* Children
Stepparents; *see* Parents
Stocks, 286, 290, 298
Store credit; *see* Credit
Stress, 79, 89, 163, 166, 181, 190, 191, 215
Suicide, 16, 143, 166, 357
Supplemental Security Income (SSI), 136, 211, 216, 218, 221, 226, 230, 232, 233–234, 240, 311, 317
Support laws, 80; *see also* Child Support
Survival needs, 13, 59, 61, 93, 95, 96, 115, 172, 192, 216, 229, 230, 287
Survivor's rights; *see* Living patterns, variations in; Wills

Taittonen, Edith, 389
Taxes, 24, 27, 28, 77, 129, 143, 158, 170–171, 185, 197, 275, 276, 279–280, 285, 290, 350, 362, 368; *see also* Budget(s)

Temporary Disability Insurance (TDI), 311
Thirty-day account; *see* Charge accounts
Thrift, 77, 102, 162, 286; *see also* Money; Societal attitudes
"Thrifts"; *see* Savings and loan associations
Time deposits, 295
Tippett, Katherine S., 391
Towle, Charlotte, 95, 119, 388, 389
Transfer payments, 7, 15–16, 73, 111, 117, 132, 210, 213, 230, 233
Transportation, 25, 27, 34–35, 60, 76, 91, 93, 121, 129–130, 171, 261, 267, 272, 283; *see also* Budget(s); Motor vehicles
Troelstrup, Arch W., 391
Trust, 72, 92, 94–95, 146, 151, 153, 156, 199, 213, 221, 226, 228, 321, 356; *see also* Distrust
Truth-in-Lending Act, 34, 291, 344

Unconscious, 182, 184; *see also* Awareness; Conscious
Underemployment; *see* Unemployment
Unemployment, 7, 13, 61, 71, 117, 189, 192, 216, 233, 311
  Insurance, 233, 310–311, 369
Uniform Consumer Credit Code (UCCC), 346
Uniform Small Loan Law, 345
United Way, 317
Unions, labor, 290, 347
Unmarried father, 152–154
Unmarried mother, 148–152, 231–232
Unmarried parents, 143–146; *see also* Legal aspects
Unpaid bills; *see* Debt
Unrestricted money payment, 111, 226–232; *see also* Public assistance
Upper-income families, 97, 98, 151, 170, 192, 246, 383
Urban family budgets; *see* Annual consumption budget; Family expenditures; Spending patterns
Utilities, 23, 281; *see also* Budget(s)

Index

U.S. Congress Joint Economic Committee, 145
U.S., Department of Agriculture, 25, 26, 27, 264, 360
U.S., Department of Labor, 29, 344

Values, 72, 84, 97, 360, 361, 384
Variants in living patterns; *see* Family life cycle; Living patterns
Veblen, Thorstein, 47, 51, 386
Veterans, 16, 70, 71, 254, 280
  Benefits, 73, 154, 170, 314–315
  Loans, 32, 239, 242, 343
  Insurance, 306
Voluntary agencies, xii, 192, 210, 347; *see also* Public assistance agencies; Public welfare; Social agencies

Wage assignments; *see* Assignments; Attachment; Garnishment
Wage Earner Plan, 347, 349–350; *see also* Bankruptcy
Wages; *see* Earnings
Walshok, Mary L., 388
War on Poverty; *see* Economic Opportunity Act (EOA)
Webb, Robert L., ix
Weisberg, Miriam, 389
Welfare Planning Council, Los Angeles Region, xiv
Welfare Rights Organization, 150
Weller, Jack E., 388
White-collar workers, 11, 78, 97
Whyte, W.F., 386
Whyte, William H., Jr., 386

Wills, 135, 137–138
Winckowski, Anthony, ix
Woener, Ralph, 387
Women
  And credit, 142
  Heads of household, 5, 13, 16, 17, 33, 154
  And mortgages, 142, 315
  Working, 8, 10–12, 57, 73, 74, 75, 78, 80–82, 90, 93, 120, 123, 131, 142, 145, 163, 191, 223
Women's Movement, 80, 150, 216, 259
Widowhood, 173, 310
Work, 68, 73, 75, 93–94, 233; *see also* Mothers, working; Societal attitudes; Women, working
  Adjustments, 223
  Ethic, xi-xii, 16, 93–94, 131, 137, 212
  Incentives, 192
  Training and placement, 212
Worker's (or Workman's) Compensation, 147, 211, 311–312
Working poor, 192
Working wives; *see* Mothers, working; Women, working
Worthiness, xi, 94, 239, 261
Wright, Carrol, 263

Yancey, William L., 387
Youmans, Kenwood C., 51, 77, 86, 385

Zeegers, Machiel, 388